People and Housing in Third World Cities

People and Housing in Third World Cities

Perspectives on the problem of spontaneous settlements

D. J. DWYER
Professor of Geography
and Head of the Department of Geography,
University of Keele, England;
formerly Professor of Geography
and Head of the Department of Geography
and Geology, University of Hong Kong

LONGMAN
LONDON and NEW YORK

Longman Group Limited,
Longman House,
Burnt Mill, Harlow, Essex, U. K.

Published in the United States of America
by Longman Inc., New York

First published 1975
First paperback edition 1979
Second impression 1981

Dwyer, Denis John
People and housing in Third World cities.
1. Underdeveloped areas – Housing
I. Title
301.5'4'091724 HD7391 78-40795

ISBN 0-582-49017-0

Library of Congress Catalog Card Number: 74–84346

Printed in Singapore by
Huntsmen Offset Printing Pte Ltd.

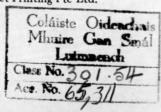

For Shirley, who went with me

Contents

Plates

Section III. Between pages 228 and 229.

Acknowledgements

We are grateful to the following for permission to reproduce copyright material:
The American Academy of Political and Social Science for extracts from the article 'The pattern of urban and economic development: social implications' by C. Bauer Wurster from *American Academy of Political and Social Science Annals*, **305**, 1956; The American Anthropological Association for an extract from 'Urbanization and ethnic identity in North Sumatra' by E. M. Bruner from *The American Anthropologist*, **63**, No. 514–15, 1961; American Geographical Society for an extract from the article 'Spatial patterns of population in Indian cities' by J. E. Brush from *Geographical Review*, **58**, 1968; an extract from the article 'The growth and functional structure of Khartoum' by G. Hamdam from *Geographical Review*, **50**, 1960; and an extract from the article 'Population growth of Karachi: the example of a large city in developing countries' by Zafar Ahmad Khan from *Geographical Review*, **24**, 1969; the editor for an extract from the editorial in *Architectural Design*, February 1956 (now entitled *Architectural Design Cost and Data*); the editor for extracts from 'Town planning in Delhi' by J. R. Ewing from *Economic and Political Weekly*, 4, 1969; the editor for an extract from the article 'Growth of the world's urban and rural population 1920–2000' by the United Nations from *Ekistics*, **29**, 1970; an extract from the article 'Circular migration and the growth of towns in East Africa' by W. Elkan from *Ekistics*, **25**, 1968; an extract from the article 'Housing in the National Development Plan: an example from Nigeria' by O. Koenigsberger from *Ekistics*, **30**, 1970; and an extract from the article 'Environmental security and housing input' by J. C. Turner and R. Goetze from *Ekistics*, 1967; Far Eastern Economic Review Ltd for an extract from 'Tsuen Wan township' by W. J. Smyly from *Far Eastern Economic Review*, **33**, 1961; Ford Foundation Ltd for extracts from 'International urbanization survey', New York, 1972; the editor for extracts from the article 'Encounters with Istanbul: urban peasants and village peasants' by P. Suzuki from *International Journal of Comparative Sociology*, No. 5, 1964; the author and Journal of the American Institute of Planners for extracts from 'Barriers and channels for housing development in modernizing countries' by J. C. Turner from *Journal of the American Institute of Planners*, **23**, 1967; and an extract from 'Housing priorities, settlement patterns and urban development in

modernizing countries' by J. C. Turner from *Journal of the American Institute of Planners,* **34**, 1968; the editor for an extract from the article 'Action planning in Calcutta: the problem of community participation' by C. Rosser from *Journal of Development Studies,* **6**, 1969–70; the editor for extracts from the article 'Trends and issues in Latin American urban research 1965–70' by R. M. Morse from *Latin American Research Review,* **6**, 1971; and extracts from the article 'Latin American squatter settlements: a problem and a solution' by W. Mangin from *Latin American Research Review,* **2**, 1967; Liverpool University Press for an extract from the article 'Mass housing in rapidly developing tropical areas' by G. A. Atkinson from *Town Planning Review,* **51**, 1960; and an extract from the article 'Ndirande: a squatter colony in Malawi' by H. C. Norwood from *Town Planning Review,* **43**, 1972; Martin Secker & Warburg Ltd and Random House Inc. for extracts from *A Death In The Sanchez Family* by Oscar Lewis; The New York Times for an extract from the article 'Kishan Babu' by J. Lelyveld from *New York Times*, 8 September 1967; the author from extracts from a dissertation 'Squatting in Salvador: an explanatory study' by Mrs Nan Pendrell; the editor for an extract from the article 'Reorganizing for housing and development' by Asteya Manalad-Santiago from *Philippine Journal of Public Administration,* **13**, 1969; Ateneo De Manila University for an extract from 'Philippine social organisation and national development' by J. J. Carroll from *Philippine Studies,* **14**, 1966; Times Newspapers Ltd for an extract from the article 'Calcutta struggles to stem inrush of Bengalis seeking to escape starvation' from *The Times*, 31 May 1971, reproduced from *The Times* with permission; United Nations Educational, Scientific and Cultural Organization for extracts from *The Social Implications of Industrialization and Urbanization*, © Unesco, 1956; and an extract from *Urbanization in Asia and the Far East* edited by P. M. Hauser, © Unesco, 1958; The United Nations for an extract from 'Housing in Africa', New York, 1965; an extract from 'Urbanization in Latin America: results of a field survey of living conditions in an urban sector' by the Economic Commission for Latin America, 1963; and an extract from Department of Economic and Social Affairs report of the Ad. Hoc. Group of Experts on Housing and Urban Development, New York, 1962; University of California Press for an extract from *India's Urban Future*, edited by Roy Turner, reprinted by permission of the Regents of the University of California; The University of Chicago Press for extracts from the article 'Migrant adjustment to city life: the Egyptian case' by Janet Abu-Lughod from *American Journal of Sociology*, **67**, 1961; and an extract from the article 'Rural-to-urban migration in Iraq' by D. G. Phillips from *Economic Development and Cultural Change*, **7**, 1957–58; and the author, author's agents, The Bodley Head Ltd and Viking Press Ltd for an extract from *The Comedians* by Graham Greene, copyright © 1965, 1966 by Graham Greene. Reprinted by permission of the publishers.

Those now in their active years were born in an economic, social, physical and cultural environment which differs enormously from the one they may live to see. They were taught by teachers who had been raised in a world whose features are now fading rapidly; and they are called upon to instruct a new generation whose future living conditions are still shrouded in mystery.

United Nations, Department of Economic and Social Affairs, 1970

1

A major urban form

Oh São Paulo!...All dressed up in velvet and silk but with cheap stockings underneath – the *favela*.

Carolina Maria de Jesus
Child of the Dark

After the decision to leave the village had been taken, the main problem of the family was funds for travelling expenses. There was little difficulty for families going to nearby towns. The bus or train fare was small. In any case, most families walked. Three-quarters of the families going further afield, however, could neither save enough nor borrow enough to meet all their travelling expenses. They travelled part of the way by train, hung around for a while and then usually decided to try their luck without tickets.

They faced innumerable difficulties. The general experience was that in the course of a 100-mile journey to Delhi by slow trains a family would be ejected from the train at least four times. Sometimes the men would be detained at one station and the women and children put off the train at another. Families were then likely to remain broken up for weeks. Most of the ticketless migrants were maltreated by the railway authorities, even to the extent of being mercilessly beaten. Families in transit sometimes starved for days. A few committed small thefts: others resorted to begging. All took a very long time to reach their destinations. The longest time taken by a migrant family to travel from Nagpur to Delhi was thirty days, whereas the Grand Trunk Express takes twenty-two hours. After arrival, even getting out of the stations presented serious difficulties. The next problem was to find a place for resting a while. The bridges, old buildings, temples, shady trees and the footpaths near the railway station became their first resorts. Then migrants who had arrived in the city earlier helped the newcomers to find sites where they could erect small huts (Deshmukh, 1956, esp. pp. 182–3).

Aspects of urban deprivation

In the early summer of 1971 India's largest city, Calcutta, was once again in crisis. By then, over 5 million refugees had crossed the border of East Pakistan, fleeing before the Pakistan army. A vast column of hungry and homeless people had begun to converge on the city, for the Indian government relief centres, hastily opened near the border, could provide shelter only for a fraction of those in need (Hazelhurst, 1971).

Local government officials were trying to prevent the entry of refugees into Calcutta at all costs. Roadblocks were established but even so refugee camps sprang up in the suburbs and by night deeper infiltration into the city was taking place. The refugees reaching Calcutta were the fortunate ones, simply by virtue of having got so far: everywhere in the countryside, outside of the government relief centres, refugees were beginning to die of starvation. 'There are no shelters and they crouch or huddle in the rain like frightened animals in the wilderness,' Hazelhurst (1971) stated in an eye-witness report. Every form of shelter – even trees, bushes and overhanging rocks – had been occupied early in the exodus. Taki, a small place on the border, had 8 000 people as against its normal population of 3 000. Eventually most of Taki's refugees would join the march to Calcutta. Cholera was already established among them and would add an extra dimension of horror to that city's troubles. And even before the influx, almost 2 million of Calcutta's population were living either in cramped and squalid huts or literally on the streets.

Though gross in degree, these glimpses of migration and the problem of urban shelter in India are by no means unique in kind in the Third World. The 'Barrio of 65' is a hillside spontaneous settlement[1] on the edge of Bogota, Colombia (Schulman, 1966). It clings to the foothills of the Andes on the eastern edge of the city. A wide dirt path, an unofficial extension of the city's Calle 65, winds through the area and gives it its name. In 1966 there was about 1 200 residents living there in 250 huts; undoubtedly there are many more today. The Barrio of 65 originated in the late 1940s through local property owners building shacks for renting to newcomers. The open spaces between the shacks and more permanent buildings nearby were gradually occupied. Finally the erstwhile tenants and many still newer arrivals began to build their own shacks on the hillside above, which was owned by the municipality. Month by month a few more shacks crept upwards, typifying a situation of expanding squatter occupation known only too well in almost every Third World city.

Urban services are practically non-existent in the Barrio of 65. Illness and mortality rates are exceptionally high. Water has to be fetched in old cans from a municipal hydrant at the base of the hill. There is no electricity, except for those few huts that illegally tap the electricity company's power line. For the most part, small wood fires have to suffice for cooking. A few privies belong to certain privileged families, their doors

[1] Though the more familiar term 'squatter settlement' is used in this book in addition to the more recent one 'spontaneous settlement' for the makeshift housing areas erected by the poor in Third World cities, the latter is preferable because the term 'squatter' carries prejudicial legal implications which are often not conducive towards the solution of the problems such settlements pose – as subsequent pages will show. The rapid development of spontaneous settlement as a ubiquitous feature of Third World cities in recent years has already given rise to a rich collection of local terms. Such settlements are known as *ranchos* in Caracas; *callampas* (and more recently *campamentos*) in Chile; *favelas* in Rio de Janeiro; *barriadas* (more recently *pueblos jovenes*) in Lima; *villas misarias* in Buenos Aires; *colonias proletarias* in Mexico City; *barong-barongs* in Manila; *kwettits* in Rangoon; *gecekondu* in Istanbul; and *bidonvilles* wherever French is spoken.

secured by padlocks. Fortunately, there are others that are not so exclusive. In either case water carrying excrement from the privies runs almost continuously in black streams alongside the paths of the *barrio*. Children are playing everywhere so, not surprisingly, infant diarrhoea and other intestinal complaints take a heavy toll. Measles outbreaks also kill large numbers; death from malnutrition is also known. Women here have many children – contraception even of the simplest kind is hardly understood – and it is a rare family in the *barrio* that does not speak of having one or more *angelitos* in heaven.

The usual foods are potatoes, rice and a hot drink made from unrefined sugar. Sometimes there may be a little soup made from scraps of meat or fish. On rare occasions a chicken raised among the children of the *barrio* will be killed. Living space is extremely limited, usually a single room with a small lean-to for cooking. The settlement consists of masses of tightly packed shacks ringing small common patios where clothes washed in a nearby stream are hung to dry, household waste accumulates, children play and chickens and perhaps even a pig are enclosed. In the houses ceilings are low, windows are rare and the floor is bare earth. One or two handmade beds will be placed against the walls, one being reserved for the parents, perhaps with the youngest child. Other children crowd as many as five to a bed or sleep on the dirt floor. The family's few possessions will be kept securely locked in a trunk at night. A chair and small table may also be squeezed into the room. Clothes hang from the walls. This can be home for a dozen people.

Two further examples must suffice here. The first is the Asima area of Baghdad (Phillips, 1958, pp. 410–19). The Asima was originally waste land to the east of the bund which surrounds Baghdad as protection from the floodwaters of the Tigris. It was a desert site covered with pits for the digging of mud and clay for building purposes. Both the municipality and private individuals used it as a dumping ground for animal and human excreta as well as for rubbish. Additionally, some of the city's drains discharged over the bund into the area just after receiving washings from the abattoirs. After the occupation of the Asima area by settlers, a sizeable stream of this foul liquid wound its way through their conglomeration of mud buildings.

There were few sanitary facilities in the new settlement. Privies consisted only of a shallow hole surrounded by a piece of reed matting or a mud wall, and in any case less than one in twelve of the families had access to a privy. The remainder of the inhabitants still further polluted the ground all around them. No house had any kind of plumbing; instead two families were profit-making proprietors of outdoor water taps. There were no bathing facilities of any description in the entire settlement of almost 40 000 people. Untreated trachoma, debilitation from intestinal parasites, tuberculosis and a variety of other illnesses were prevalent.

The typical hut was built over a light wooden frame with walls and roof of reed matting plastered with mud. A few huts were built solely of reeds, in most cases as temporary shelter for new arrivals. Nine-tenths of the families had one room only, and on average there were almost five persons to each room. Most families had some bedding, a kerosene cooking stove, a rug for sitting on and a storage chest; a few owned a table and even perhaps a transistor radio. Other household items were few and far between but the kerosene stove, and sometimes the presence of food rejected by the downtown markets, represented great wealth in the eyes of rural people visiting relatives in the Asima, for in the marshlands to the south they had to subsist almost entirely on bread and had only brush and dung for fuel.

Looc is a squatter area on the edge of Dumaguete City in the Philippines, near the cargo piers and practically at the gates of Silliman University (Chang Shub Roh, 1970). One family in Looc is composed of eight members. The husband is a stevedore on the local waterfront earning 12 pesos a week. The wife is a washerwoman and earns 10 pesos a month. This gives the couple an average monthly income of 58 pesos. They have three teenage children and three younger children. They are renting their hut for 15 pesos a month. They subsist almost entirely on maize, which costs them 28 pesos a month. After paying the rent and for the maize, they have only 15 pesos. Occasionally, they have meat and some vegetables on Sundays; at other times there is perhaps a little dried or salted fish to help the maize down. Their only immediate answer to their problems is that 'God will take care of us', though in the longer run they plan to send their children to look for work as housemaids and houseboys in the capital city, Manila.

The houses of Looc generally consist of two small rooms at the most and are made largely of bamboo with a *nipa* palm thatch. There is no electricity. A few public standpipes have been supplied by the city, but for a community of over 1 000 people water for drinking, bathing and laundry is in very short supply. The taps are all located along a main road and the water has to be carried to the huts in 5-gallon kerosene cans, the children helping sometimes with smaller containers. A few inhabitants far from the taps have dug shallow wells and risk unsafe water rather than make several treks to the public taps each day.

There are no sewers in Looc and garbage collection is almost non-existent. The nearby beach serves both as a public toilet and a convenient dumping ground. For this reason it is popular with local dogs as well as with the pigs kept by some households. Only two families in five have made any provision for a private toilet, usually a hole in the ground surrounded by bamboo or *nipa* walls. Are the residents of Looc aware of community problems? Almost two-thirds said they were, but the same proportion also indicated general satisfaction with their lives. Few would want to live in the countryside because conditions there are regarded as being even worse.

World urban growth

In order to gain a more general perspective on the problems of spontaneous settlement represented by the case studies just presented, it will be useful at this point to look first at some aspects of the overall trend of world urban growth. However, it will be as well to introduce immediately two general qualifications which apply to this book, one relating to data and the other to method. In Third World urban studies there is, as yet, a series of scattered case studies and very little more. Further, in terms of coverage such studies are heavily biased towards the largest cities and the smaller urban places have so far been grossly neglected. In large part the problem of generalization also involves the available statistics, for they are all too often demonstrably crude, incomplete and inexact. An added complication, only just beginning to be approached in research in the social sciences, is that in almost every case published national statistics in the Third World tend to be cast in the mould of census models derived originally for the industrialized countries and thus usually fail to achieve complete relevance to the reality of the Third World urban situation.

In the case of Nigeria, for example, towns were officially defined for the 1952 census as 'centres forming compact groups, each with a population of not less than 5 000', but as Eze (1970, p. 166) has pointed out, it is nowhere clear what exactly constitutes compactness or how it is measured. In any case, if compactness is equated with housing density, it is by no means a satisfactory index of urban status, that is, an indicator of rural–urban differences. The adoption of 5 000 as population cut-off point is, of course, highly arbitrary, though this kind of qualification applies equally to most censuses in both industrialized and Third World countries.

As a result of the application of this definition to the Eastern Region of Nigeria, the results of the 1952 population census showed the Nsukka Division in the north to be relatively highly urbanized and most of the central area of the Eastern Region to be almost completely rural. Even the most cursory field inspection, however, would reveal that such a distinction is highly misleading. In Owerri province in the central part of the Eastern Region, for example, important towns and smaller growth centres such as Umuahia (population 12 259), Okigwe (6 807), Uzuakoli (9 507), Nbawsi (5 607), Omoba (5 140) and Ogwe (5 358) were excluded 'for no apparent reason', states Eze (1970, pp. 167–8), while a number of indigenous market towns such as Ndizuogu (13 459), Nguru (18 398), Mbieri (20 979) and Uli (16 112), also failed to qualify, presumably because they lacked the necessary degree of 'compactness'. On a national basis, the census definition seems to have been much more liberally applied in the Western Region and this may help to account for the fact that 48 per cent of the population of the Western Region was returned as being urban compared with only 14 per cent in the Eastern Region. Sadly, more recent Nigerian census experience has also been unhappy, particularly that of the 1963 census, which was widely considered to be unreliable and thus succeeded only in adding to the statistical confusion. In Liberia the 1962 census was even suppressed by the government for a time because it indicated a lower population total than had been officially expected. More recently, the 1965 census of the Central African Republic was also discredited, again for political reasons, and a second count ordered in 1968, while the preliminary results of the 1973 Nigerian census have been greeted internationally with considerable scepticism.

One particular illustration of the quality of data that may go into the making of generalizations on Third World cities is the elementary matter of the size of the population of Kinshasa, Zaire, in the mid-1960s, though admittedly it is an extreme case (Knoop, 1966, pp. 119–20). Reliable data for the period since 1959 being completely lacking, estimates made in the mid-1960s ranged from 1.2 to 2 million, implying a threefold or even fivefold population increase over five years. Finally, after much exasperation on the part of city officials and visiting advisors because of the absence of a reliable figure, a careful survey of population trends by staff from Lovanium University resulted in a fairly reliable estimate of 800 000 for the end of 1964.

These African examples, of course, represent unique cases. In more general terms, it is worth noting that the information published by the United Nations on population living in agglomerations of 20 000 persons or more, some of which is used in the paragraphs to follow, is based on

Table 1.1 Growth of the world's urban and rural populations (millions)

Year	*Total population*	*Rural*	*Urban**
1850	1 262	1 181	81
1900	1 650	1 426	224
1950	2 520	1 796	706
1970	3 628	2 229	1 399

* Population in places of 5 000 and more.
† Projection based on data available in December 1968.
Source: Davis, 1971, p. 12.

census returns or reliable estimates from almost all of the industrialized countries, but that data of a similar quality is completely lacking for more than half the population of the Third World (Trewartha, 1969, p. 147). In these circumstances, the question of method arises. Generalization on the basis of detailed statistical manipulation of such data often proves rewarding only to those with little field knowledge, for the published statistics are only an indicative means to an end and not cohesive and valid parameters which will provide meaningful measurements of vital dimensions of the urbanization process in the Third World. All too frequently they are a dangerously deceptive crutch, likely to collapse if undue weight is placed on them. The synthesis and interpretation of case studies on the basis of wide personal field experience – the approach adopted in this book – is therefore essential, even though open to the charge of subjectivity. Marriage between published information and field interpretation becomes critical.

It is thought that between 1800 and 1970 the population of the world living in towns of 5 000 inhabitants or more increased from 81 million to 1 399 million, or by seventeen times (Table 1.1). Total world population grew much more slowly, in fact by a little less than three times over the same period. The last 150 years or so has therefore seen a revolutionary shift in the location of the world population and in the relative importance of city and countryside. Nevertheless, the earth as a whole is not yet very highly urbanized (Table 1.2). The transition to a fully urbanized world – that is one as urbanized in terms of population distribution as the United States or Britain today – is proceeding so rapidly, however, that it could be completed within less than a century, given a

Table 1.2 Historical change in world urban and city proportions (percentage of world population)

Year	*Proportion urban**	*Proportion in cities of 100 000†*
1800	3.0	1.7
1850	6.4	2.3
1900	13.6	5.5
1950	28.2	16.2
1970†	38.6	23.8

* Population in places of 5 000 or more.

† Projection based on data available in December 1968.

Source: Davis, 1971, p. 10.

continuation of present trends. This vast urban transition surely poses one of the most fundamental issues of our times.

Much of the future development towards a more fully urbanized world will concern the Third World, though historically the process has been led by the today's industrialized countries. The urban process is by no means new: there were towns over 5 000 years ago, but before the Industrial Revolution they were relatively few. The acceleration in the urbanization process which occurred during the late eighteenth and early nineteenth centuries was associated with industrialization and it affected first the countries of Western Europe and later the USA. The new industries in these countries made such demands that, as Hoselitz (1962, p. 168) has stated, '. . . in the long run the period of European industrialization and urbanization must be regarded as one characterized by shortage of labour'; but health conditions in the cities were so poor that at certain periods comparatively little of their population growth occurred through natural increase. Their expansion was at times in large measure due to their power to attract rural migrants. Concurrently, the rationalization and technical development of agriculture allowed declining rural populations to participate in raising living standards resulting from national economic growth.

Today, there are two distinct facets within the general urbanization trend. The industrialized countries are showing declining rates, but because they include only one-quarter of the world's population this has not been sufficient to retard the trend. The massive populations of the Third World, in contrast, appear still to be in the earlier stages of an urbanization more massive than any before.

Unlike the early industrial cities, contemporary cities in the Third World are not death-traps; in fact their health records are almost as good as today's cities in industrialized countries, and they are far better than those of the Third World's rural areas. The Third World city has benefited disproportionately from the conquest of death that has taken place in the tropics during the last three or four decades but at the same time the fertility of its inhabitants has remained very high both by the contemporary and by the historical standards of the cities of the industrialized countries. As Davis (1971, p. 8) reports, city-dwelling Muslim couples interviewed in Lebanon in 1957 had a fertility that would yield 6.6 children to each wife if she lived through the reproductive period; in Accra, Ghana, the figure in 1960 was six children; in Bangalore, India, the average women aged forty-five and over had borne 5.3 children.

This combination of 'pre-industrial fertility and post-industrial mortality', to quote Davis (1971), has given the contemporary Third World city the greatest rates of natural increase ever found in cities. Yet rural–urban migration is also proceeding apace. The Third World today is the scene of the greatest movements of people in history, and though the waves of political refugees from wartorn areas usually make the headlines, it is a quieter, spontaneous movement of people from the countryside to the cities which constitutes the mainstream. Paradoxically, the rate of urbanization and the current size of the major cities throughout the developing world seem to be more expressions of lack of economic development than the results of it (Dwyer, 1968*a*). Hoselitz (1962, pp. 164–5) for example, has drawn attention to the marked lack of coincidence between rates of urbanization and those of industrialization in India and his observations could well be applied more generally. Conditions in the cities, poor though they may be, nevertheless seem to be becoming increasingly preferred by the rural masses. It can only be concluded that this largely reflects the abysmal lack of development in the countryside.

The result is a swelling tide of rural–urban migration. To take the case of metropolitan Manila as an illustration, the projected 1977 population of the city based on a rate of natural increase of 3.2 per cent alone (the projected national average rate of population growth for the period 1955–77) would be 3.7 million (UN, Department of Economic and Social Affairs, 1960, pp. 14–15). But the lowest United Nations estimate of actual population for the city in 1977, based on current rate of growth, is 5.1 million, indicating the possible addition of almost 1.5 million

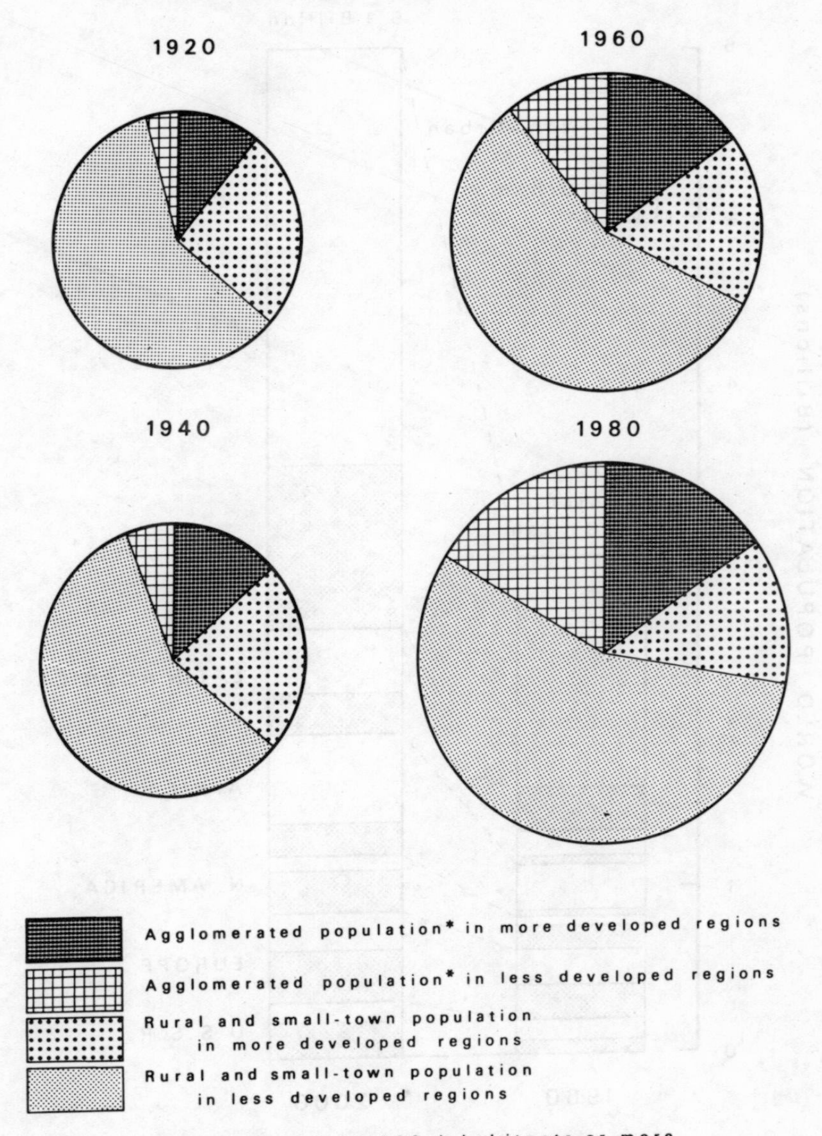

Fig. 1.1 Size and composition of world population, 1920–1980

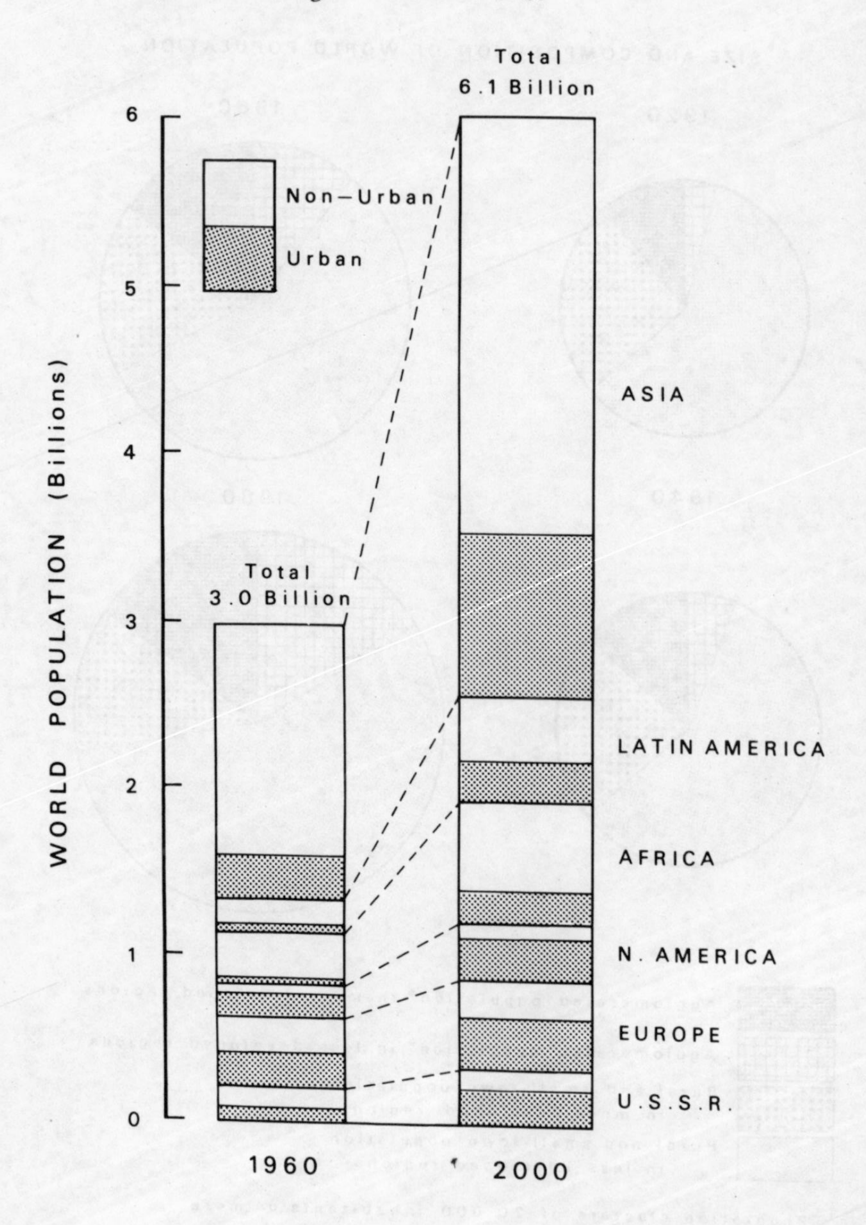

Fig. 1.2 Estimated growth of world urban and rural population, 1960–2000

in-migrants and their children during the decades of the 1960s and the 1970s. The United Nations 'high estimate' for the 1977 population of metropolitan Manila is 6.2 million. What makes such figures as these even more disturbing is that so far urban growth in the developing world, significant though it has been in recent decades, has made but little impression on the vast reservoirs of population in the countryside. Figures for Venezuela show that while the number of people living in urban areas (in this case towns and cities of 5 000 or more inhabitants) increased massively from 0.74 to 4.3 million during the period 1936–61, the nation's non-urban population also grew, from 2.6 to 3.2 million (Friedmann, 1966, p. 132). In all, probably just over half of the current growth of cities in underdeveloped countries can be attributed to in-migration (Davis, 1971, p. 4).

As a result of these trends, the balance of urban populations between the industrialized countries and the Third World is in process of most significant change. Urban populations in the developing countries are now growing twice as fast as those in the industrialized countries. They are also growing in numbers greatly exceeding those of the industrialized countries even during the periods of the latters' most rapid growth.

In consequence, whereas the number of people in settlements of 20 000 inhabitants or more in the industrialized countries grew from 198 million in 1920 to 450 million in 1960, or more than doubled, this increase was dwarfed by a quadrupling of similar populations in the Third World, from 69 to 310 million (UN, Department of Economic and Social Affairs, 1970, pp. 472–3). The growth of such populations in the industrialized countries is expected to amount to 211 million during the period 1960 to 1980 and to 240 million during the period 1980 to 2000. However, in the Third World an additional 383 and 743 million respectively is expected for each period, and by the year 2000 the Third World should account for 1 436 million of the expected world total of 2 337 million living in settlements of 20 000 or more (*ibid*., p. 473). By the end of the present century the balance of world urban population will have very definitely tipped towards the Third World (Fig. 1.1), indeed at present we are just over the point of equilibrium in urban population distribution between the industrialized and the developing countries. In all probability we have reached the end of an era of association of urbanization with Western style industrialization and socio-economic characteristics. The magnitudes alone of some of the urban increments expected in the Third World are such that it will probably become increasingly debatable to what extent this urbanization can be related to past Western urban experience.

There are, of course, significant differences both in rates of urbanization

Table 1.3 World urbanization, 1950 and 1960

Regions	*Level of urbanization (percentage of total population)**		*Percentage of increase*
	1950	1960	
World total	21	25	17
More developed regions	37	41	10
North America	43	46	6
Europe (excluding USSR)	37	40	8
Northwestern	52	54	3
Central	37	40	9
Southern	23	27	16
USSR	31	36	17
Australia and New Zealand	58	65	12
Less developed regions	14	18	28
Africa	10	13	37
North	21	26	23
South, West, and East	6	9	50
Asia	14	18	26
Excluding China (Mainland)	17	19	15
China (Mainland)	10	15	50
Latin America	25	32	28
Argentina, Chile, Uruguay	47	56	19
Remainder of Latin America	21	28	33

* In places with 20 000 or more inhabitants.

Source: Trewartha, 1969, p. 152.

and in the distribution of urban populations within the Third World itself (Fig. 1.2). Africa is the least urbanized of the major regions but also the one which is now becoming urbanized the most rapidly. There is a marked difference within Africa, however, between the countries north of the

Sahara, which already have reached a level of urbanization comparable to that of southern Europe, and those to the south which, with the exception of South Africa, as a group are the least urbanized on Earth outside of Oceania (Table 1.3).

A similar dichotomy is apparent in Latin America – which in general is by far the most highly urbanized major region of the Third World – between Venezuela, Chile, the River Plate countries and the remainder. The problems associated with urban growth in Africa and Latin America, severe as they may be, are nevertheless dwarfed by those of Asia which, largely because of the vastness of its total population, is already an urban colossus even in comparison with the industrialized countries. It has been estimated that in 1960 Asia contained between 36 and 39 per cent of the total world population in towns of 20 000 inhabitants or more, depending on how China's urban population was estimated (Trewartha, 1969, p. 156). This compares with 5 per cent for Africa and 9 to 10 per cent for Latin America, with 23 to 24 per cent for Europe (excluding the USSR) and with 12 to 13 per cent for North America. In terms of bald statistics Asia's probable urban future is indeed frightening, for it is expected that by the year 2 000 its urban population, even defined at the relatively high cut-off point of 20 000 persons, will have increased to 993 million (UN, Department of Economic and Social Analysis, 1970, p. 473). This compares with a 1960 level of 265 million when already in terms of their physical facilities many of Asia's cities were being described as in a state of crisis. Clearly, it is in Asia that the core of most Third World urbanization problems lies.

Growth of spontaneous settlements

There will be about 6 billion people on earth by the year 2000 and as many as one-half of them may be urban, if the size criteria used to define urban settlement is considered as a more realistic 5 000 persons. The staggering task for the second fifty years of the present century has been and is to provide a tolerable urban environment for an increment of people four times as large as that which was added to world urban populations in the 100 years before 1950. This is in addition to making up past deficiencies in urban facilities of massive proportions. Unfortunately, however, in terms of individual Third World cities what Carrol (1966, p. 585) wrote of Manila in 1966 all too often typifies the contemporary urban situation:

> In the past twelve months Manila has had a water shortage in which some 70 per cent of the Metropolitan area was without regular service

> . . . it has had a garbage crisis . . . there has been a school crisis, though a minor one this year . . . electric services went through a bad period some months ago . . . mail is in a continual state of crisis and in general it seems better to give up trying to use the telephone . . . police and fire protection are unreliable . . . the constantly increasing burden of traffic and the condition of the roads discourage one from venturing beyond walking distance. In other words, social organization in the Manila area has not been able to maintain these services in the face of population increase and normal wear and tear on facilities; and at times it appears we are returning to a *barrio* [village] type of existence.

Similarly, Pendrell (1968, pp. 68–9) has written of Salvador, Brazil, where she was working during May to September 1965:

> Public services, such as running water, sewage mains, garbage disposal, and lighting are in precarious and costly supply. During the field-work period both the Cathedral of São Francisco and the public library curtailed their hours of daily admission; the former because of an increase of almost 25 per cent in the cost of electricity, the latter because the city's electric service had broken down. Every newspaper in Salvador runs at least one photograph and news item each day condemning another breakdown of water or sewage main; another failure to collect garbage in still another *barrio*; another collapse of a building after heavy rainfall, etc.

Serious physical deficiencies are all too obvious in almost every city, but in no aspect of provision is the task so daunting as in housing. The towns, both large and small, are increasing in population at rates generally not less than 2.5 per cent a year and often up to 10 per cent a year (Table 1.4). Yet the numbers in spontaneous settlements, the makeshift housing areas erected by urban squatters, are growing at even greater rates. For example, such rates are now reaching 12 per cent annually in several countries, notably Mexico, Turkey, the Philippines and Peru (J. F. C. Turner, 1967, p. 168). What this means for Brazil for instance is that from a situation of near equality in numbers in 1964 within a total population of 80 million, the urban population is expected to increase to 66.6 million by 1976 compared with a rural population of no more than 43.5 million. On present trends, 25 million of Brazil's urban population of the mid-1970s will be living in *favelas*, and the rate of growth of population in such spontaneous settlements will be averaging 7 per cent annually (Juppenlatz, 1970, p. 173).

Table 1.4 Growth rates of cities in certain Third World countries, 1960–70

Country	*No. of cities**	*No. of cities, with annual percentage rate of population growth 1960–70*				
		0.1–2.5	*2.6–5.0*	*5.1–7.5*	*7.6–10.0*	*Over 10.1*
UAR	12	3	9			
Nigeria†	12	2	5	2	1	
Tanzania	1				1	
Mexico	17	4	6	5	1	1
Brazil	33	4	17	8	2	2
Chile	4	3	1			
Iraq	5		3		1	
Indonesia	21	2	16	1	2	
Philippines	8		8			
Pakistan	16	3	3	7	2	1
	129	21	68	23	10	4

* Urban agglomerations above 100 000 in population in 1960.

† Port Harcourt and Onitsha declined in population.

Note: This table is indicative only since data for some of the cities listed is available only for the administrative area of the city itself whilst for other cities data for the whole urbanized area is available. As the fastest growing suburbs are sometimes to be found outside of the administrative boundaries of cities, the above figures represent a conservative estimate of rates of urban growth.

Source: Based on data from Davis, 1969, vol. 1, Table E.

Although an increasing number of individual case studies is now appearing, there is as yet relatively little information of a comparative nature on spontaneous settlements. This is especially true of historical studies. In Peru, a report on Lima as early as 1746 was denouncing the formation of *barriadas* and urging that the inhabitants should be sent back to the mountains (Mangin, 1967*a*, p. 91). In Hong Kong, almost immediately after the foundation of the colony in 1841, the Governor had to forbid the erection of illegal, mat-shed dwellings in the new city of Victoria (Wong, 1969, p. 32). Certainly, there were both large numbers of poor people and some spontaneous settlements in Third World cities throughout the colonial period. There were also often relatively large areas indigenous in building form in which the inhabitants enjoyed legal tenure.

Thus in a Mexican city, Merida, in the common colonial pattern in Latin America the ruling elite lived in a Western-style centre, virtually monopolizing its facilities. In surrounding Indian *barrios*, however, Maya was spoken and indigenous costumes worn. The huts were of rural types and the streets impassable for wheeled vehicles. Many of the Indians worked in the city centre. Colonial growth steadily displaced the Indian *barrios* outwards, and it is an interesting reflection, as Morse (1965, p. 49) points out, that in many ways these *barrios* can be viewed as traditional communities resisting the city whereas, as the next chapter will show, today's spontaneous settlements, though similar in form, seem to be composed largely of groups seeking to gain access to the city in socio-economic terms.

Spontaneous settlement in its evolution as a major urban form is much more recent; indeed this very recency constitutes a significant facet of the overall problem, since only within the last decade has the importance of study and planning for such settlements been at all widely recognized. The first large *favela* in Rio de Janeiro is said to have originated in 1910 as a result of an influx of population from the countryside after an unsuccessful uprising against large landholders (Juppenlatz, 1970, p. 72). In Baghdad, spontaneous settlement first appeared as a major problem in the 1930s (Gulick, 1967, p. 252). The present pattern of *bidonville* development in and around Tripoli became noticeable during the Italian period, though its origins were much older. Traditionally there have always been encampments around Tripoli made by semi-nomads moving seasonally to the city, but during the late nineteenth century illegal hutted areas inhabited largely by Negroes were first noted. These later included a large number of former slaves from the Fezzan, and by 1912 Lapworth (p. 126), a British writer, was bemoaning the growth of settlements of 'poor Bedouins, Arabs and Fezzans – a heap of huts composed of sticks, palm leaves, and all the dirty rags and refuse of the city'. In Caracas *ranchos* were noted about the turn of the century but, as chapter 4 demonstrates, the first important wave of *rancho* building did not occur until the late 1920s when petroleum exploitation in Venezuela started to bring wealth to the capital (Marchand, 1966, p. 127).

Already, within the space of only three or four decades, populations in Third World spontaneous settlements have become very large both in absolute numbers and in relation to total urban populations. The 1954 census of Algeria showed that 30 per cent of the population of the three largest towns – Algiers, Oran and Annaba (Bône) – were living in *bidonvilles*. There were an estimated 180 000 persons in the *bidonvilles* of Casablanca and 110 000 in those of Tunis in 1960, while 90 000 persons were living in shantytowns in Lusaka in 1969. For Tripoli, in the early 1960s the comparable figure was 50 000 persons. One-quarter of the total population of Baghdad was living in squatter settlements in 1960; the figure for Istanbul was 21 per cent. At the same date such settlements were accommodating half of Ankara's population.

In Latin America recent estimates have included a figure of 800 000 squatters, or one-fifth of the total urban population, in Rio de Janeiro in 1965. This compares with figures of 203 000 in 1950 (8 per cent of total urban population) and 600 000 in 1964 (16 per cent) and implies that the growth rate of population in the *favelas* has reached four times that of the city as a whole. Santiago, the capital of Chile, had one-quarter of its total population in *callampas* in the early 1960s, while the figures for Lima, the capital of Peru, show 800 000 in the *barriadas* in 1970 (one-third of the total urban population) compared with 500 000 in 1965 and 100 000 in 1958. Over 40 per cent of the population of Mexico City is currently living in *colonias proletarias*. In Asia, Djakarta has about 800 000 persons living in spontaneous settlements, one-quarter of its total population; the latest estimate for Manila is 767 000 (compared with only 23 000 in 1946). Singapore, despite a massive rehousing programme, is said still to have about 350 000 and perhaps as many as 500 000 remaining in spontaneous settlements. For Kuala Lumpur, the figure is 185 000 persons or 37 per cent of the total urban population.[1]

Besides the sheer size of the problem today, and its relatively sudden onset, two further features are worth noting. First, rates of growth of spontaneous settlements are still accelerating in relation to rates of growth of urban populations as a whole. In other words, the problem, huge though it is, is not yet as serious as it will undoubtedly soon become. Second, although most of the estimates given above are for very large cities, spontaneous settlement has become a major urban form in Third World towns and cities of all size ranges. Figure 1.3, which shows the situation in Peru in 1961, illustrates this. The one-fifth of the total population of Rio de Janeiro that live in *favelas* compares with 30 per cent in similar settlements in the smaller city of Forteleza and with 40 per cent in Recife.

[1] Estimates for the various cities mentioned in the paragraphs above were obtained from the following sources: Algerian towns: UN, 1965, p. 1; Casablanca and Tunis: Hance, 1970, pp. 284–6; Tripoli: Harrison, 1967, p. 418; Baghdad: Gulick, 1967, p. 252; Istanbul and Santiago: Abrams, 1966*a*, p. 13; Ankara: Juppenlatz, 1970, p. 15; Rio de Janeiro and Lima: Juppenlatz, 1970, p. 15, and Morse, 1965, p. 50; Mexico City: J. F. C. Turner, 1968*b*, p. 354; Djakarta and Kuala Lumpur: Poethig, 1971, p. 122; Singapore: Poethig, p. 124, and Buchanan, 1972, p. 192; Manila: Philippines, National Housing Council, 1969, p. 29.

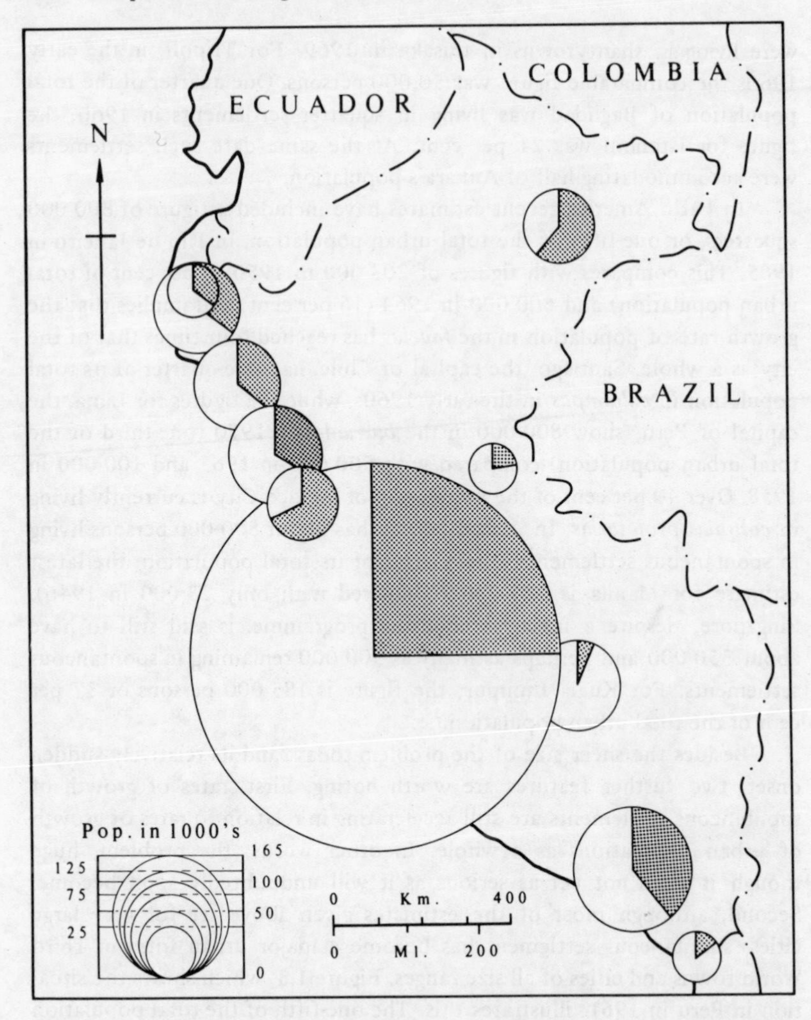

Fig. 1.3 Spontaneous settlement in Peruvian towns, 1961. Proportion of total town population in spontaneous settlements shaded

In the Philippines, 27 per cent of the population of Baguio City, 25 per cent of that of Ozamis City, 10 per cent of Cotabato City, 22 per cent of Surigao and 45 per cent of Marawi were living in *barong-barongs* in 1964.[1]

[1] Estimates from the following sources: Forteleza and Recife: Juppenlatz, 1970, p. 15; small towns in the Philippines: Laquian, 1968, p. 7.

Locational and physical characteristics

What are the major locational and physical characteristics of spontaneous settlement? A comprehensive answer is impossible at the present time, largely because of a dearth of good case studies and also because little, if any, work of a comparative nature, drawing together available evidence from Asia, Latin America and Africa, has been attempted previously. What follows is therefore little more than a review of the major current sources of information and it should be noted that African case studies in particular have been hard to find. There is, for instance, no mention of spontaneous settlement as a distinctive, modern urban phenomenon in the course of a 350-page book by Mabogunje on *Urbanization in Nigeria* (1968).

With regard to overall factors influencing the location of spontaneous settlements within cities, it is worth noting firstly that in the Third World city, in contrast to the contemporary city in the industrialized countries, it is often the rich rather than the poor who find their choice of residential locations circumscribed, both by extensive spontaneous settlements on possible building sites and by urban land values which are usually relatively high even in comparison with those in the industrialized countries. The poor, in contrast, may attempt to occupy any unused site as squatters, and only infrequently are they subsequently dispossessed. Thus patterns of availability of unused land and the nature and direction of channels of communication of such information to squatters, both as individuals and in groups, play some part in determining patterns of spontaneous settlement at any given time and in any given urban situation. Over and above this, the areal distribution of rich and poor in the Third World city has been, and is, at least as dichotomous as that in the cities of today's industrialized countries, and arguably more so because of the relative numerical weakness of the middle classes. In Manila today there are whole communities of upper-class and upper-middle-class people living behind high walls with access restricted by armed guards, a situation strongly reminiscent not only of the contemporary city in the United States but also of the walled city of colonial days in the Third World, within which lived the expatriate administrators, soldiers and merchants of the colonial power.

It was traditionally at the city centre, with easy access to the seats of governmental, commercial and ecclesiastic power, that the colonial elites lived.[1] Just as in the cities of the industrialized countries, however, elite

[1] Except where indigenous urban development was already strong before the colonial period, for example in Yorubaland. Spatially segmented colonial development then tended arise adjacent to existing city cores which displayed very mixed socio-

locations have displayed strongly centrifugal tendencies in more recent years. As Amato (1970) has demonstrated recently, for example, the desertion of the centre of the city of Bogotá by the elite has been a striking feature of its recent residential development. This movement dates from the early decades of the present century when the success of Colombian coffee on world markets brought wealth to some families and also triggered off a wave of commercial expansion in and around the capital's central business district. The upper income groups began to move immediately north of the city centre, into La Merced, Teusequilla, Armenia and Magdalena (Fig. 1.4), and by the 1930s the segregation pattern of the city by socio-economic class had changed radically. Further significant moves by the elite have also taken place subsequently, each one to the north into more peripheral areas, leapfrogging the middle-income residential groups growing up round previous elite locations.

Similar patterns have been observed in Quito, Santiago and Lima. The upper income groups have left the centre for the periphery, where they now live at low densities, well insulated from the poor of the city, generally in the areas best favoured by microclimate, urban services and transport facilities. In the case of Quito, as with Bogotá, the upper income groups lived round the principal plaza from the founding of the city in the sixteenth century until the first decades of the present century. New European-style houses then began to appear on the north-eastern edge of the built-up area on relatively flat land which contrasted favourably with the more difficult terrain characteristics of the southern portions of Quito. During the 1950s the elite moved still further out, to spacious California ranch-style residences. Again surrounding middle-income groups were bypassed, but this time the movement was to relatively high ground commanding magnificent views and receiving the warm afternoon sun, which is eagerly sought because of Quito's altitude (Amato, 1970).

In South and South-east Asia and in East and West Africa, where the colonial period is much more recent and its urban legacy perhaps even more apparent, elite locations are still often tied to closed reservations, both government and privately owned, in which senior politicians, civil servants and executives in commerce and industry reside, usually at subsidized rents. Mabogunje (1968, p. 299) has demonstrated, for example, that residences in such reservations account for a substantial proportion of those belonging to the highest residential category in presentday Lagos; in

Footnote continued from p. 21.
economic characteristics. Ibadan, Nigeria, is a good case in point, as are many Indian cities, notably Delhi.

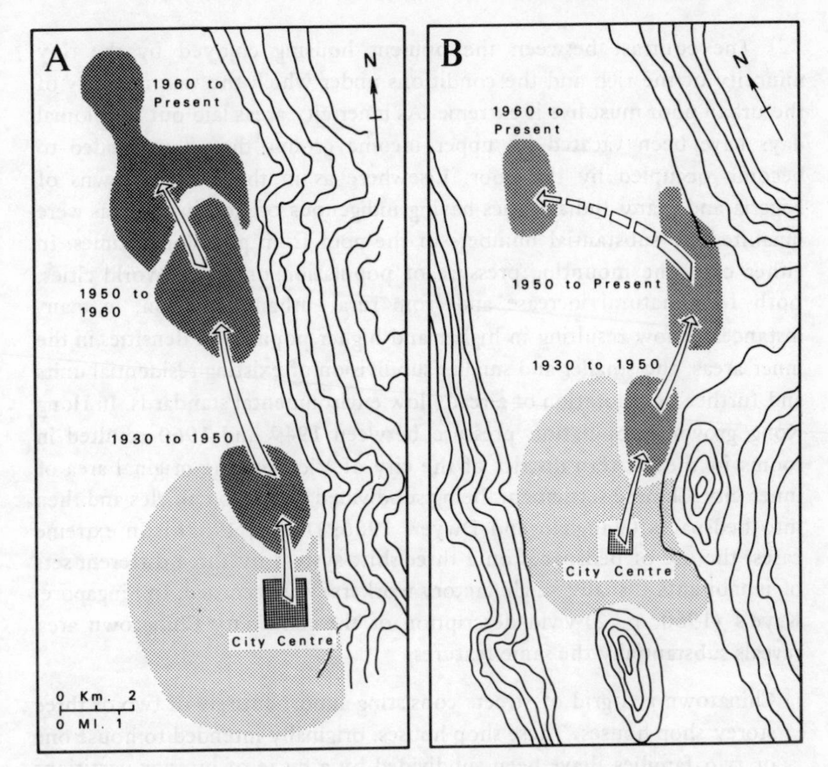

Fig. 1.4 Movement of elite residential locations in (A) Bogota and (B) Quito

fact, in his classification of residential districts in the city he places reservations alone in the high grade. The oldest of such high status districts, that of East Marina, dates from the 1850s, when Britain established a consulate there. Today the colonial officials have been replaced by a new elite, the indigenous political leaders of Nigeria. Other politicians, important but of lower rank, are found in the Ikoyi Reservation in the eastern part of Lagos Island, which was originally laid out in the 1920s for British civil servants. With the exception of the Railway Compound in the northern part of the city, the other major reservations, six in number, date from as late as the 1950s. Apart from the presence of domestic servants, they are all extremely segregated communities in terms of socio-economic status. In the older high status districts the housing tends towards colonial types, reaching even the extreme of imitation of the English country house, complete with fireplaces. The newer areas display 'a variety of delightful and elegant tropical designs', according to Mabogunje (1968, p. 301).

The contrast between the opulent housing enjoyed by the tiny minority of the rich and the conditions under which the vast majority of the urban poor must live is extreme. As inner city areas laid out in colonial days have been vacated by upper income groups they have tended to become occupied by the poor. Elsewhere as in the Yoruba towns of Nigeria and many Indian cities having indigenous origins, inner areas were inhabited by substantial numbers of the poor from precolonial times. In either case, the mounting pressure of population on Third World cities, both from natural increase and from rural–urban migration, in many instances is now resulting in higher and higher population densities in the inner areas, the smaller and smaller subdivision of existing residential units and further deterioration of already low environmental standards. In Hong Kong growing population pressure between 1949 and 1960 resulted in rooms in the western district of the city of Victoria, the original area of inner city Chinese settlement, being subdivided first into cubicles and then into bedspaces (Vaughan and Dwyer, 1966; Dwyer, 1968*b*). In extreme cases, the use of bedspaces on a three-shift system by three different sets of inhabitants (usually single factory workers) was recorded. In Singapore, Kaye's (1960, p. 2) vivid description of the inner city Chinatown area reveals substantially the same features:

> Chinatown is a grid of streets consisting almost entirely of two or three storey shop-houses. These shop-houses, originally intended to house one or two families, have been subdivided by a maze of interior partitions into cubicles, the majority of which are without windows and in permanent semi-darkness. Most of these cubicles are about the size of two double beds, placed side by side. In one such cubicle – dark, confined, insanitary, and without comfort – may live a family of seven or more persons. Many of them sleep on the floor, often under the bed. Their possessions are in boxes, placed on shelves to leave the floor free for sleeping. Their food, including the remains of their last meal, is kept in tiny cupboards, which hang from the rafters. Their clothes hang on the walls, or from racks. Those who cannot even afford to rent a cubicle may live in a narrow bunk, often under the stairs.

Much the same flavour is conveyed by the following description of a Mexico City *vecindad* by Oscar Lewis (1969, pp. xxii, xxiv–v).

> Guadalupe and Ignacio continued to live in the Panaderos *vecindad*, although the landlord divided their large room in two and rented the front part, containing the window, to a shoemaker. The remainder, still

called No. 1, was a small dark room with a tiny anteroom for a kitchen. In the nine years they lived here, they managed to furnish it with a narrow iron bedstead and spring, but no mattress, an old wardrobe, a small wooden table, a shelf for an altar, a large chair, and two small stools. All of these were bought secondhand. There was a blanket, a pillow, and sheet for the bed, a secondhand charcoal brazier for cooking, a few clay pots, jars, cups, glasses, and plates and spoons but no table knives or forks, no clock, and no radio at the time of our study. Guadalupe's collection of religious pictures, some hanging in frames, others tacked to the wall, was the largest in the *vecindad* and a source of great pride to her. Two of the pictures had been passed down from her grandmother and she considered them heirlooms . . .

. . . of the twenty-five heads of families in the *vecindad*, only nine were born in Mexico City. The other sixteen came from towns and cities in the states of Morelos, Mexico, Hidalgo, Quertaro, Guanajuato, and Aguascalientes. The average length of residence in the capital was 26.2 years; the range was from twelve to forty-nine years. Most of the original residents of the *vecindad* came in extended family groups or soon helped relatives to find apartments there. Because of the low fixed rent and other economic factors, the tenants did not move away without good reason. The average length of residence in the *vecindad* was about fifteen years.

In the old town, or *casbah*, of Algiers the overall density of population had already reached 3 750 inhabitants per hectare (1 500 per acre) by 1934. Nevertheless, in the later 1950s the situation became much worse because of the influx to the towns caused by the Algerian war. This explains

the swarming human masses in some quarters where houses are crowded one against the other, the masses of children one meets in the streets, and the presence of so many men gossiping in groups on their doorsteps or playing dominoes in such large number in the Moorish cafes (UN, 1965, p. 1).

For, as the authors (Descloitres *et al.*, 1961, p. 32) of *L'Algerie des Bidonvilles* comment,

The home is too small to allow of a decent family life and offers no more than a tiny abode to its members. . . . In general, therefore, because of its extremely small size the Muslim dwelling amounts to no more than a night shelter.

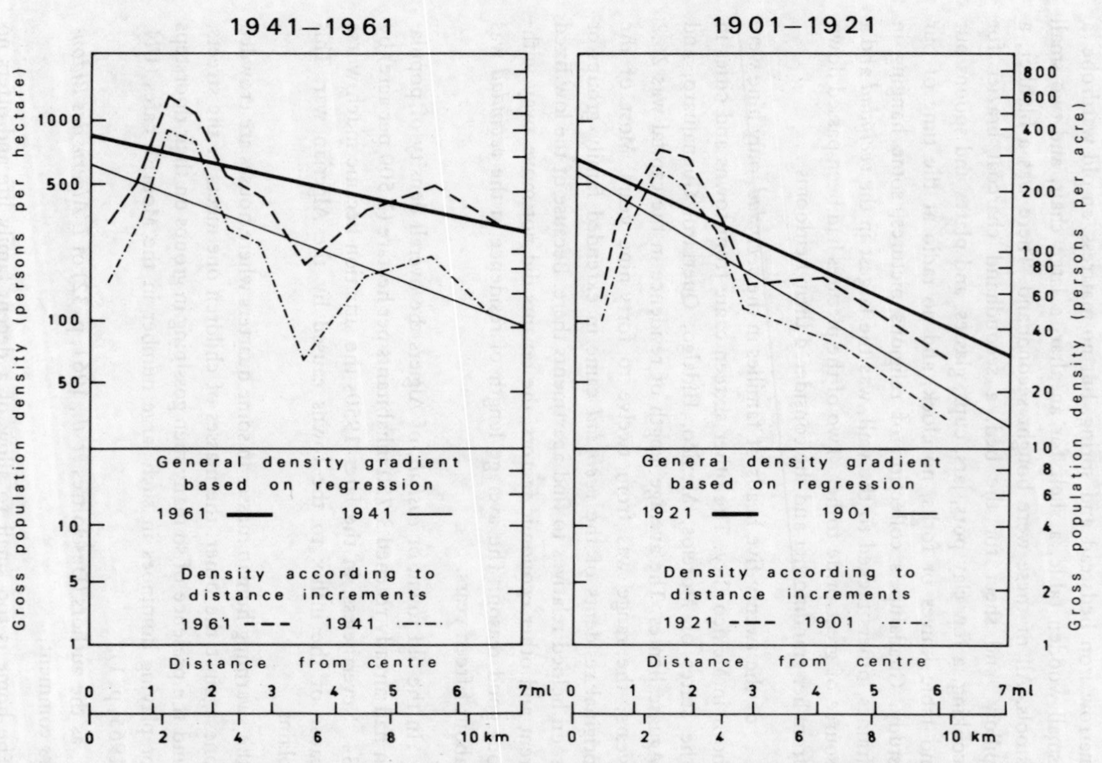

Fig. 1.5 Secular trends in population density, Bombay Island 1901–61 (adapted from Brush, 1968, p. 382)

As yet there do not seem to be any comparative studies tracing the secular movement of population densities in representative samples of Third World cities. In view of the present housing crisis this is clearly a topic of great importance. Brush (1968) has carried out an excellent analysis of density patterns in Indian cities, however, which could well serve as a model for future work. He finds that in the case of cities centred on an indigenous bazaar, such as Ahmedabad and Poona, there has been a tendency towards progressive intra-urban concentration concurrently with growth in the total number of inhabitants. In the great port cities founded during the colonial period, such as Bombay, Calcutta and Madras, concentration in the central wards is increasing, but population is also building up on the periphery. Bombay Island has unusually long and continuous population records for India and these show (Fig. 1.5) that during the forty years 1881 to 1921 the increase in the city's population from 773 000 to 1.17 million was absorbed by expansion in both the central and the northern parts of the city. Between 1921 and 1961 the population of the Island increased to 2.77 million and by the latter year population densities throughout the city had risen to new high levels, even though large areas for urban development had been opened up on nearby Salsette Island since the late 1940s. Today Bombay as a whole represents the apex of India's urban population concentration. The 1961 census recorded a gross density of 3 300 per hectare (1 320 per acre) in one of the central divisions of the city, Bhuleshwar, which covers 17 hectares. This compares with a maximum gross density of 1 875 persons per hectare (750 per acre) in Calcutta census divisions at the same date and with maximum figures of less than 1 250 persons per hectare (500 per acre) for Madras.

Only in cities characterized by very marked dualism between the indigenous centre and a later colonial centre and with relatively low overall population densities, such as Hyderabad-Secunderabad and Bangalore, and in the planned new towns, such as Jamshedpur and Chandigarh, is little increase in inner area population densities observable. 'It is clear', states Brush (1968, p. 380), 'that a large share of population growth in Indian cities has been absorbed into existing urban areas, resulting in progressive congestion in the previously occupied tracts.' In Poona the maximum gross density reaches 2 000 per hectare (800 per acre) in the old town, but immediately outside density falls to below 250 per hectare (100 per acre). These are the inner suburbs. They have not yet received much spillover from the crowded central city and they remain occupied by housing for the relatively affluent. Beyond this belt density starts to rise sharply again as newer areas of close, unplanned spontaneous settlements are reached.

The negative relationship of distance from the city centre to population density which has been observed so widely in cities in the industrialized countries clearly can by no means be taken for granted in the contemporary Third World, nor can the inverse relationship between population density and urban growth rates that has been previously postulated (Berry *et al.*, 1963; Newling, 1956). The city in the United States and other economically advanced countries may be in process of being turned inside-out through the increasing affluence of urban populations, the decay of functions at the centre, the growth of suburban commercial and shopping nodes, the residential flight to the suburbs and the development of commuting on a scale undreamt of by previous generations, but in the Third World the situation is very different in several important respects.

Because of their general poverty, comparatively few dwellers in Third World cities can afford to pay for much transport, and what accounts for the location of many peripheral spontaneous settlements such as those observed by Brush in Poona is not the emptying of the inner areas but rather the reverse: the development of residential conditions near the city centre to levels approaching absolute human saturation in terms of the possibilities of further subdividing residential living space in the given socio-economic and cultural context. In Ibadan, Nigeria, for example, during the present century the traditional and relatively spacious compounds which housed the indigenous population in extended families in the heart of the old city have become broken up into a number of separate housing lots. New buildings have been erected on every available space in and around the compounds and today the area is characterized by largely one-storey houses so closely packed together that densities of 1 500 to 2 500 persons per hectare (600 to 1 000 per acre) have been achieved.

This 'growth by fission', as Mabogunje (1968, p. 226) describes it, has obviously resulted not only from social forces making for the break up of the extended family as a social unit in Ibadan but also from the sheer pressure of people upon the inner areas, both from the natural increase of the indigenous urban population and from in-migration. The situation has now been reached in which many of the rooms of the houses, no more than 2.5 by 3 m (8 by 10 ft), are inhabited in some areas by an average of 4.6 persons (Fig. 1.6), and living conditions in the core area are indeed appalling:

> Most of the houses are built of mud and sticks and cow dung is used to wipe the surface of the floors which are anything but smooth. Most of the houses have no kitchens and cooking is done in the corridor. An observer can see beads of carbon on the walls of the corridor. Most of

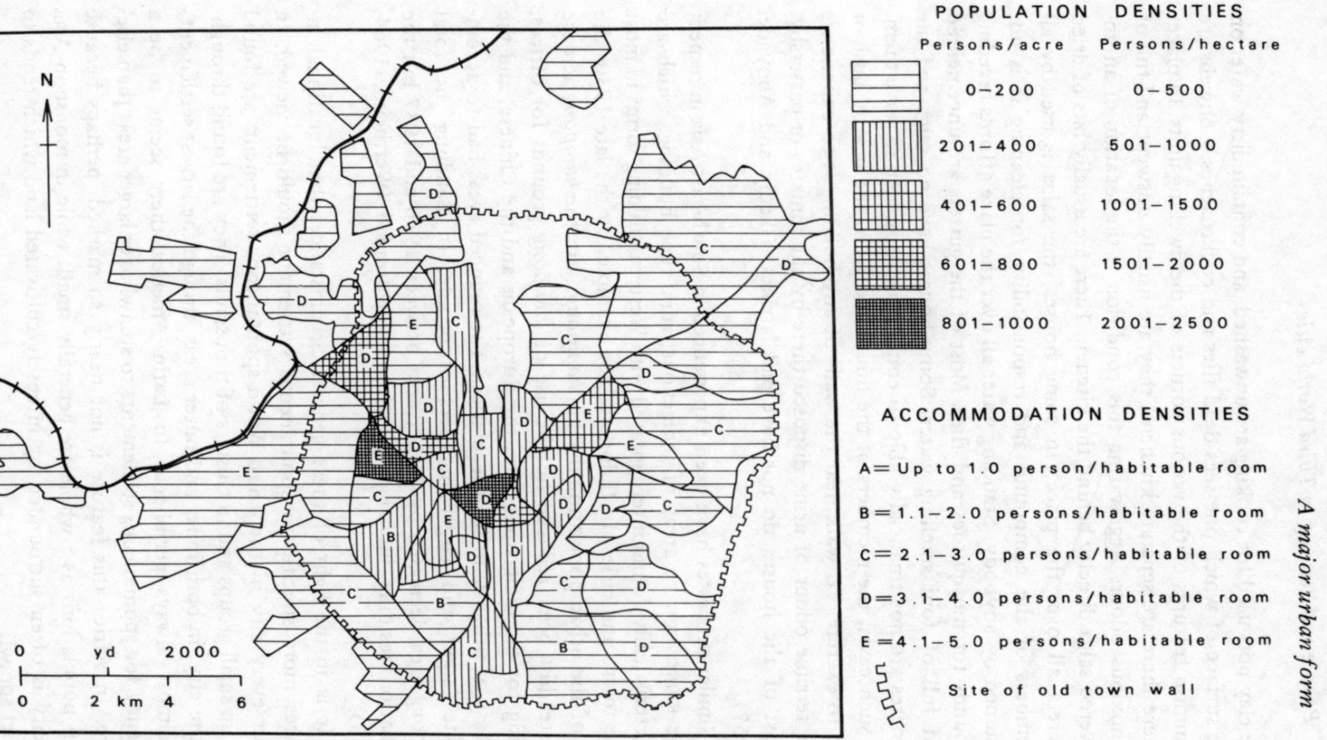

Fig. 1.6 Population and accommodation densities in Ibadan, Nigeria (Mabogunje, 1968, p. 228)

the clay pots used for cooking are unwashed, and contain dirty water on the surface of which one sees dead flies and cockroaches. Cobwebs are common features of the various corners of the dwelling units. In places where there are separate kitchens, they are usually unswept and full of obnoxious odour. Aggravating this condition is the location of an uncovered salga directly behind the kitchen. There are usually bits of dried excreta all over the place. In some houses, the salga is used by all members of the compound and responsibility for cleaning it is not assumed by anybody. Standing water all over the place affords breeding grounds for mosquitoes and flies. Most of the gutters are uncemented and full of foul smelling water. Some houses have no salga and the inmates are not financially able to employ nightsoil men to serve them. In such cases, the members of the household go to the nearby bush or pit to excrete. To walk near the walls of any building is to experience the terrible odour of urine disposed there by the inmates or passersby. Most of the houses do not have pail latrines (Okediji and Aboyade, 1967).

Similar processes have been experienced in South-east Asia in respect of the *kampongs*, or areas of indigenous, rural-type building, which are characteristically found interdigitated with Western building forms in most of the towns and cities. In Indonesia, for example, by the late 1930s the mass of the urban population lived in *kampongs*, but the *kampong* acreage had steadily been reduced by the use of *kampong* grounds for offices, housing for the indigenous elite, the Europeans and the Chinese, and the purchase of urban land for speculation. The reduced areas had to accommodate larger and larger numbers of people. In Bandung the total *kampong* area decreased by 25 per cent between 1910 and 1937 but the population residing in *kampongs* almost quadrupled (Wertheim, 1964, p. 233).

It is in the light of these general circumstances that locational influences more specific to spontaneous settlement should be viewed. In almost every city in the Third World spontaneous settlements are found both in small groups and in clusters of thousands. They are found throughout the city, in both inner and outer areas, though the largest settlements are almost always peripheral. In Latin America there seems to be a tendency for spontaneous settlements to sprawl over larger areas than elsewhere. In Africa this feature is not nearly so marked, perhaps because urban populations as a whole are generally small, while in monsoon Asia the city is often surrounded by intensely cultivated land which tends to restrict sprawl.

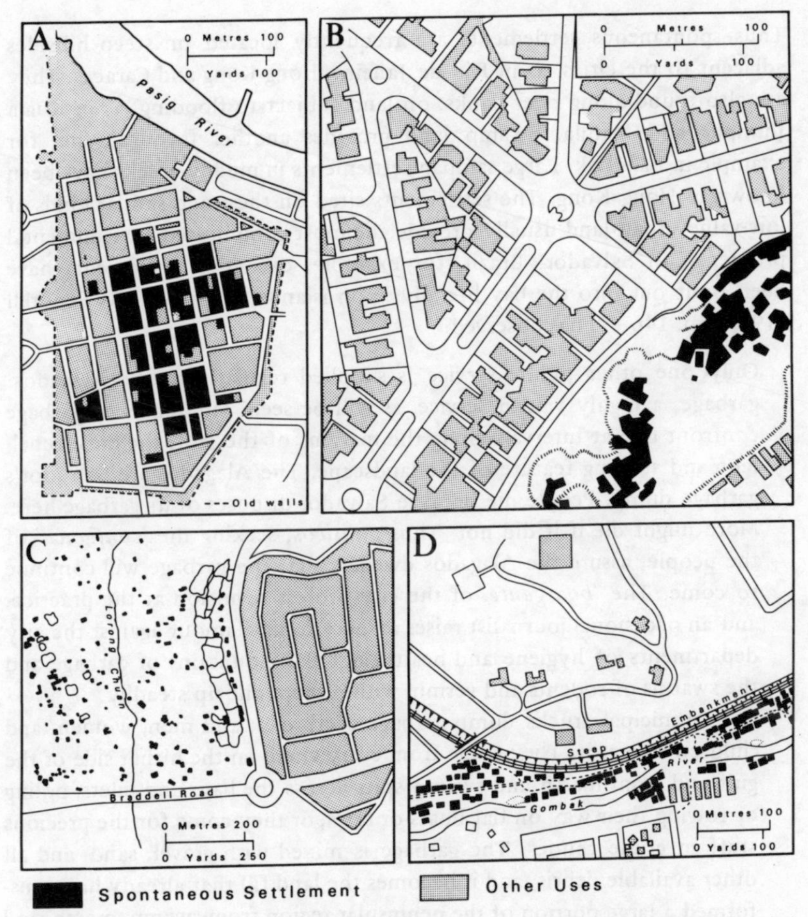

Fig. 1.7 Typical sites for spontaneous settlement. (A) Manila (Intramuros), (B) Caracas (Jones, 1964), (C) Singapore, (D) Kuala Lumpur (McGee, 1967, p. 162)

In present circumstances, while lack of control of squatter invasions is fairly general, the factor of greatest importance to poor people desperate for homes is land availability. Thus land being held vacant for speculative purposes, including individual inner city lots, is frequently at risk, though for tactical purposes state or Church land is usually preferred to private property by spontaneous settlers. Vacant sites close to factories or construction projects are especially valued because of the possibilities of casual labour there. The most significant kind of available land, however, is that which has a very low value for more regular urban uses (Fig. 1.7).

Thus spontaneous settlements are frequently located on steep hillsides adjacent to the cities, as in Rio de Janeiro, Hong Kong and Caracas. They are also found along river banks, on land subject to flooding, as in Kuala Lumpur and Manila. Swamp land provides another favoured site, for example in Bangkok. Large sampan settlements in muddy creeks have been known in Hong Kong. The settlements sited on these and similar kinds of low-value urban land usually provide the most complicated environmental problems. In Salvador, Brazil, for example, extensive settlements have been built out into the bay literally upon islands of garbage. As Pendrell (1968, pp. 146–7) has observed:

> Only one other public service is supplied regularly to the Alagados: garbage, a highly valued service, as will be seen. Mountains of garbage confront one at intervals along the margins of the gulf; the most repellent and striking feature of the landscape. The Alagados are Salvador's garbage dump. People die because Salvador disposes of its garbage here. More might die if it did not. Thus *politicos*, seeking the *'confianca'* of the people, assure the Alagados dwellers that the garbage will continue to come. The *'boa gente'* of the city profess revulsion at the practice, and an occasional journalist raises an occasional clamour against the city departments of hygiene and health, but the mountains of garbage and the swarms of rodents and vermin within them pile up steadily.
>
> Municipal trucks dump garbage every day, and men, women, and children collect it. They come from everywhere on the hither side of the gulf and from marsh and swamp spits across the bays and inlets, poling or rowing their way on flat boats or rafts; or they come for the precious stuff in crude canoes. The garbage is mixed with gravel, sand, and all other available debris, and it becomes the land fill that already has transformed a large portion of the peninsular region from swamp, marsh, and water into dry land. Garbage also helps to implant the wooden stakes that are driven into the water and on which houses and broadwalks are built continually as more people come to live in the Alagados, putting up huts farther and farther out into the gulf.

As yet there is no generally accepted theory of spontaneous settlement location. We have little more than scattered empirical observations. In Lima, for example, the 1968 census recorded 431 000 people in the inner city *tugurios*, or tenement areas, compared with 649 000 in the *barriadas*, or spontaneous settlements. This latter figure had risen to 800 000 by 1970. The largest *barriadas* were on the periphery of the city, some of the more recent ones over 25 km (15 miles) from the centre. They were strung to the north and south out along the major highways into Lima and also concentrated in the western suburbs adjacent to the international airport and the major industrial zone. There was another grouping of spontaneous settlements near to the largest city market, which was regarded both as a source of employment and as a good information centre. Most *barriadas* were on state-owned land.

As with other categories of settlement, processes of invasion and succession may affect the location of spontaneous settlements as the city expands, though again these have been but little studied so far. For the twin cities of Victoria and Kowloon in Hong Kong, Wong (1969, pp. 112–71) has suggested proximity to areas of high-intensity mixed land use (for job opportunities) as the major controlling element in spontaneous settlement location. In Hong Kong circumstances the ideal location consists of proximity to jobs, a good water supply and tolerable relief, but if necessary the two latter characteristics will be sacrificed in favour of difficult sites within convenient reach of jobs. On the edge of the urban job market, but in areas with good water supply and flat land, spontaneous settlements are found in which agricultural activities play a part in the economy. As the more regularly built-up area of the city expands, spontaneous settlements may be displaced centrifugally into areas of poorer relief and worse water supply (Fig. 1.8). There is also replacement of largely agriculturally-oriented spontaneous settlers by urban-oriented spontaneous settlers.

J. F. C. Turner (1968*b*, pp. 358–60) has carried this simple model a stage further by suggesting a distinction in terms of the location of spontaneous settlements between cities in early transition, midtransition and late transition. He sees the early transitional city – Lima early this century for example – as one in which population growth is relatively slow (2 or 3 per cent per annum) and mostly due to natural increase. There are comparatively few in-migrants and most of the poor can be housed in subdivided buildings adjacent to the city centre.

In Turner's mid-transitional city, in-migrants form an important part of the low-income population. The city tends to be large, with a population of over 1 million (like Mexico City in 1950), and the poorest are again found crowded into the more central areas. This is because the spontaneous settlements are relatively distant from sources of employment. In these circumstances spontaneous settlements owe their origins more to well-established city workers who have migrated to the fringes of the city from inner tenement areas. It is they, not the poorest, who can afford the transport costs involved in such new residential locations.

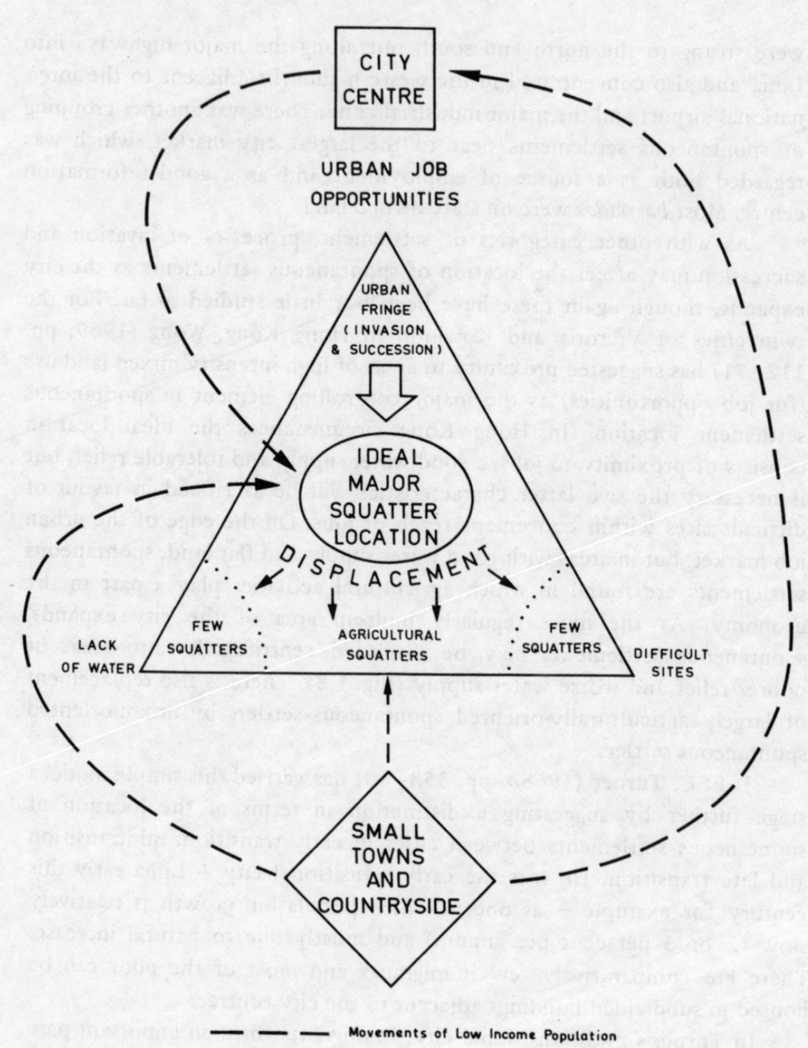

Fig. 1.8 Typical movements of low income population in Third World cities

Contemporary Mexico City differs again from this pattern and may be classed as late transitional according to the Turner model. It has a population of around 6 million and not only is its population growth beginning to level off but the proportion of migrants in the population is also falling. The poorest are perhaps no longer quite so poor as ten or twenty years ago. Further, as a result of commercial expansion, inner ring accommodation for the poor has become less in quantity and consequently more expensive. The growth of the city has passed over some formerly peripheral spontaneous settlements and many of their original inhabitants have moved further out, renting or selling what have become inner suburb dwellings to poorer newcomers either from the more central areas of the city or from the provinces.

At this stage the poorest can afford a limited amount of transport; some of the less poor are more mobile than ever before: lower-class residential locations as a whole are therefore rapidly expanding in area. At the same time, population densities near the centre remain high, though they may be stabilizing or even starting to fall. Mexico City's old tenements, the *vecinidades*, are concentrated in an arc round the historic centre of the Zocalo. In the early 1960s about 0.5 million people were living in them, largely crowded into single rooms. Virtually all the housing in this area is available for rent rather than sale. Rents are low absolutely, though not in terms of space occupied and facilities enjoyed, and the *vecinidades* form the principal reception area for migrants from other parts of Mexico. Today, largely because of migration towards more peripheral locations, some reduction of population is underway. Of five such neighbourhoods covered by a study in 1958, only one had gained substantially in population since 1950 (Frieden, 1966, p. 78). Third World cities at this stage of development, though previously characterized by compactness, are beginning to sprawl, but in large part on a rather different basis than cities in the industrialized countries. Since Lima's 1960 urban development plan was approved, for example, because of the rapid spread of spontaneous settlements nearly half of the subsequent physical development has occurred in areas not officially scheduled for development at all (J. F. C. Turner, 1968*b*, p. 354).

The local environment of spontaneous settlement

One important reason for the general movement to the cities that is now under way in the Third World is of course that conditions in the countryside are as bad if not worse than those that the migrant can expect in the cities. This certainly includes housing conditions. In a sample survey of fourteen villages in Upper and Lower Egypt, for example, it was discovered that 27 per cent of the dwellings had no roof at all (Abrams, 1966*a*, p. 7). The 1961 census of Peru showed that 39 per cent of rural dwellings consisted of one room and 29 per cent of two rooms. The occupancy rate for 44 per cent of rural dwellings was three or more persons per room. Few had windows, running water or sanitation (Cabello, 1966, pp. 113–14). In all, more than 1 billion people in Asia, Africa and Latin America are either homeless or living in conditions that have been described by the United Nations as a menace to health and an affront to human dignity (Abrams, 1966*a*, p. 7) and these include both rural and urban dwellers.

Degradation takes on a variety of physical forms in the cities. In spontaneous settlements (though not all can be described as degraded environments, nor are spontaneous settlers necessarily the worst off in every city) degradation often takes the form of high densities of population and minimal living spaces in the least desirable locations. On the steep hills which sprout from among Rio de Janeiro's luxurious apartment blocks, densities in single-storey shacks reach 1 250 persons to the hectare (500 per acre). In Manila, in huts along the muddy creeks leading into the Pasig River, on the city's north foreshore, or along the railway tracks, densities are similar. In Casablanca densities in the *bidonvilles* average about 1 000 per hectare (400 per acre), and two-thirds of the plots, which measure about 5 by 6 m (16 by 20 ft) have more than one shack on them. In Hong Kong, in a similar physical setting to Rio, densities in spontaneous settlements of up to 5 000 per hectare (2 000 per acre) have been experienced.

These and similar densities imply extremely small living spaces and almost totally congested environments in spontaneous settlements. They are aggravated in their human impact by generally chaotic building layouts and usually by an almost complete absence of rudimentary urban services. In Calcutta, two-thirds of the inhabitants of the *bustees* have less than 2.7 sq. m (30 sq. ft) of living space, while more than half of the *bustee* households have to share water taps with between 10 and 100 other households (Rose, 1967, p. 232). Less than 10 per cent of *bustee* households are lucky enough to share toilet facilities fewer than ten other households. It is not surprising in these circumstances that Calcutta has become notorious as the cholera capital of the world. Something of the same situation exists in Tripoli (Harrison, 1967, p. 420). The *bidonvilles* there are generally characterized by inadequate sanitation and unsafe water supply. Epidemics are a recurring problem. Typhus has been a serious threat; more recently there have been smallpox epidemics. Not surprisingly, the incidence of tuberculosis, a disease of overcrowded conditions, is consistently high, as it is in Hong Kong.

There are many parallels elsewhere in the Third World. In Kingston, Jamaica, nine persons occupy huts 5.5 sq. m (60 sq. ft) in area. Families of five or six have been reported as occupying dwellings of a similar size in

Plate 1 The problem: Lubumbashi, Zaire

Photo: United Nations

Plate 2 The problem: The Ndirande area of Blantyre, Malawi

Photo: H. C. Norwood

Plate 3 The problem: Santiago, Chile *Photo: United Nations*

Plate 4 The problem: Lima, Peru *Photo: United Nations*

Plate 5 The problem: Caracas, Venezuela *Photo: United Nations*

Plate 6 The problem: Djakarta, Indonesia *Photo: David G. Williams*

Plate 7 The problem: Singapore *Photo: D. J. Dwyer*

Plate 8 The problem: Hong Kong *Photo: Hong Kong Government Information Services*

Siloe area of spontaneous settlement of Cali, Colombia. One large squatter area in Beirut consists of living units of from one to three rooms with a total of 6 to 10 sq. m of living space, the average occupancy rate being nine persons per unit. The Algiers *bidonvilles* surround the city centre and consist largely of huts measuring approximately 3 by 3 m (10 by 10 ft). The average size of family in them is just over four persons and there is often a goat to be housed as well. In Hong Kong, a survey of spontaneous settlements in the Shaukiwan area of Victoria City revealed that the average gross floor space per person was 2.3 sq. m (26 sq. ft) and the net floor space (that is, the area enclosed by the walls and lockable with doors) was 1.5 sq. m (17 sq. ft). The highest net floor space per dwelling unit recorded was 7.9 sq. m (88 sq. ft) per person, and the lowest an almost incredible 0.5 sq. m (6 sq. ft).[1]

There is one further feature of the physical environment in which the poor live in spontaneous settlements which is significant, both in terms of the possible amelioration of their lot, discussed in later chapters, and in terms of general urban environmental problems. Spontaneous settlements are almost never exclusively residential. The Diamond Hill area in Hong Kong (Fig. 1.9) is a case in point. This settlement covers about 12 hectares (30 acres) on the southern slopes of Diamond Hill in the north-eastern suburbs of Kowloon. Before the expansion of the city, and the onset of Hong Kong's severe housing problems in the late 1940s, it was largely an agricultural area. By the late 1950s it had become a very large spontaneous settlement, though some agriculture still remained. There has been some regular urban development in the area also. Its population is estimated to be over 55 000 with spontaneous settlers predominating.

A survey carried out in 1968 showed that 67 per cent of the squatter buildings and 73 per cent of all buildings in Diamond Hill were residential (Table 1.5). Wooden and tin huts predominate. The area is a jungle of environmental problems, water supply being the most crucial. Apart from some old-established houses, no dwellings in the area have taps of their own. Water for cooking purposes has to be obtained largely from standpipes provided by local welfare associations. Some of the wealthier households have dug wells but the water obtained from them is not entirely safe and so is usually used only for washing. A few public standpipes have been provided by the government since 1962 but these are inadequate.

[1] *Source*: Kingston, Algiers and Tunis: Abrams, 1966*a*, pp. 6, 14; Cali: Juppenlatz, 1970, p. 68; Beirut: UN, Department of Economic and Social Affairs, 1971*a*, p. 89; Hong Kong: Golger, 1968, pp. 362, 377.

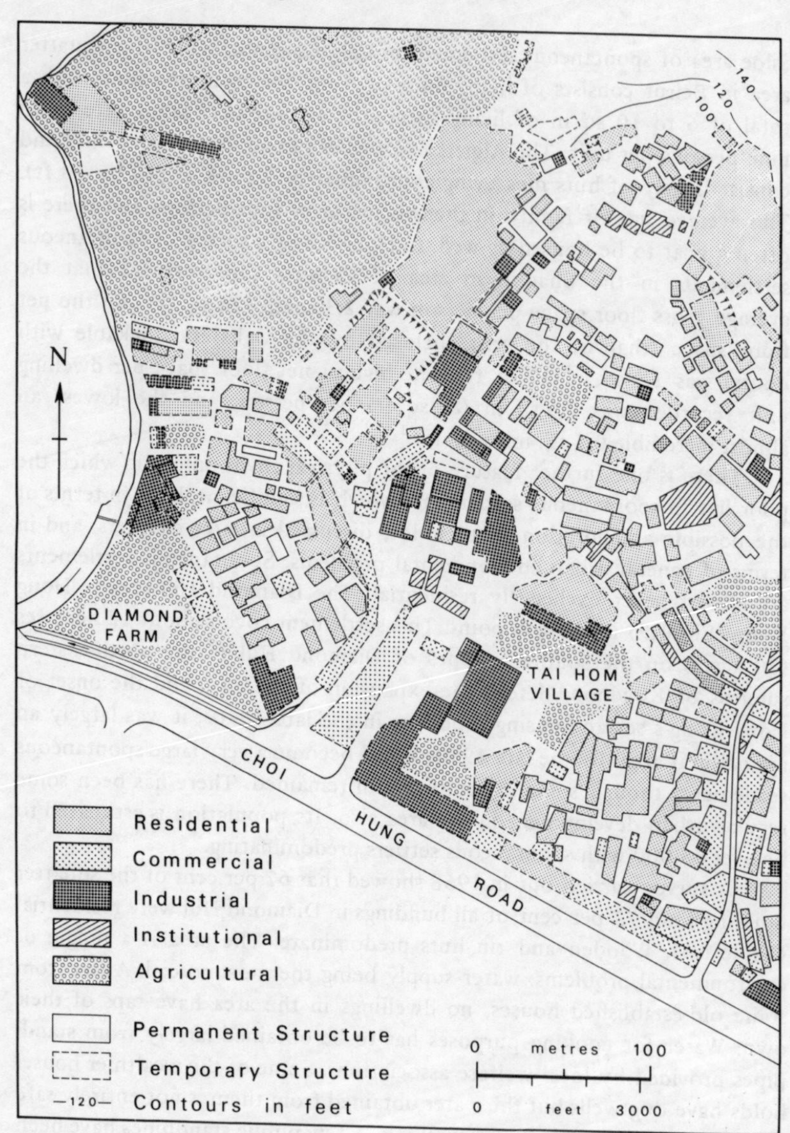

Fig. 1.9 Land use in the Diamond Hill area, Kowloon, 1968

There is a complete lack of an effective sewage system. Rubbish and human excreta are unrestrainedly thrown into the nullahs along which the small streams of the area flow and also into the smaller gutters along the

Table 1.5 Land use in the Diamond Hill area, Hong Kong, August 1968

Type of structure	*Use*	*Number of structures*	*Percentage of total*
Squatter: Temporary*	Residential	1 939	46
Squatter: Temporary*	Commercial	347	10
Squatter: Temporary*	Industrial	132	4
Squatter: Temporary*	Institutional	5	—
Subtotal		2 113	60
Squatter: Permanent†	Residential	753	21
Squatter: Permanent†	Commercial	166	5
Squatter: Permanent†	Industrial	120	3
Squatter: Permanent†	Institutional	32	1
Subtotal		1 071	30
Squatter total		3 184	90
Non-squatter: Temporary	Residential	38	1
Non-squatter: Temporary	Commercial	11	—
Non-squatter: Temporary	Industrial	49	1
Non-squatter: Temporary	Institutional	—	—
Subtotal		98	2
Non-squatter: Permanent	Residential	184	5
Non-squatter: Permanent	Commercial	28	0.8
Non-squatter: Permanent	Industrial	19	0.6
Non-squatter: Permanent	Institutional	44	1
Subtotal		275	8
Non-squatter total		373	10

* Temporary structures: substantially built of wood, tin or materials other than concrete or brick.

† Permanent structures: substantially built of concrete or brick.

Source: Fung, 1969, p. 18.

paths which run through the maze of huts. Mosquitoes and flies thrive during the summer rainy season and at this time the blocking of the nullahs by accumulated rubbish makes flooding frequent. In exceptionally rainy weather minor landslides may be expected. There are only four public latrines for the whole area. Paths are generally muddy and almost unwalkable except in the middle of the dry winter season. The winter brings its own hazard. Fire can race quickly through the tinder-dry wood of the closely packed huts should someone be careless with a kerosene cooking stove.

From the point of view of local entrepreneurs, Diamond Hill, despite its degraded appearance, is a promising area. Industrial land is very expensive in Hong Kong, usually out of the reach of the small-scale industrialist. The result has been massive infiltration into residential buildings by small-scale industries and a proliferation of small factories within areas of spontaneous settlement (Dwyer and Lai, 1967). Family labour, particularly female, is both obtainable and relatively cheap in the spontaneous settlements. In addition, the possibility of clandestine operations encourages industries there which normally would be excluded from mixed residential and commercial areas. Dyeing, camphor manufacture and the baling of metal scrap are three cases in point.

The exact number of industrial enterprises in areas such as Diamond Hill is difficult to establish but the 1968 survey previously referred to showed that 9 per cent of all structures in the area were industrial. This is probably a conservative estimate. Diamond Hill produces a wide variety of industrial products, generally from establishments with less than twenty-five workers. In textiles, the spinning, weaving and dyeing of cotton are all represented in the area (Table 1.6). A variety of small metal products is produced; there is machine building, the breaking and storage of metal waste and car repairing. Small workshops making plastic flowers and toys are often seen. Furniture making and saw milling are present. Foodstuffs are prepared for sale under the most unhygienic conditions imaginable, and there is even distilling. The making of brooms, paper, wax, pigfeed, incense, wigs and rubber shoes are also found.

Commercial activities are strongly represented too; in fact 16 per cent of all structures in Diamond Hill are commercial. Small shops selling cigarettes, sweets and soft drinks are found all over the area. The main access roads into the settlement are lined with restaurants and with stalls selling vegetables and meat. There are also some barber shops, photographers, clothing shops and even laundries.

This type of mixed land use is probably better represented in the

Table 1.6 Industrial structure of the Diamond Hill area, Hong Kong, August 1968

Industry	*Number of temporary structures*	*Number of permanent structures*	*Total*
Metals			
Metal products	18	28	46
Machine making	26	5	31
Metal waste storage	6	–	6
Other	8	–	8
Textiles			
Spinning	5	9	14
Weaving	18	6	24
Dyeing	26	2	28
Other	–	4	4
Plastics	16	30	46
Furniture	24	4	28
Saw mills and timber yards	18	4	22
Food and drink	6	10	16
Miscellaneous	10	37	47
Total	181	139	320

Source: Fung, 1969, p. 45.

Hong Kong spontaneous settlements than in most others in the Third World because of the rapidity of Hong Kong's industrial growth during the last twenty years or so. But it is common elsewhere in lesser degree. Almost 9 per cent of the rooms in the *bustees* of Calcutta are partly or wholly places of work (Bose, 1967, p. 91), while five years after the establishment of the *barriada* of Pampa de Cueva in Lima 7 per cent of the houses were being used either as shops or workshops (J. F. C. Turner, 1968*b*, p. 360).

From an amenity point of view, industrial, and even some forms of commercial development usually add to the difficulties of the majority of families of living in spontaneous settlements such as Diamond Hill. Some of the industries in Hong Kong's spontaneous settlements are fire hazards. Bean curd baking, welding and the manufacture of plastics fall into this category. With others, such as the making of hollow-ware, metal boxes and machine building, noise is a serious problem. The bleaching and dyeing industries produce unpleasant fumes, while flies and vermin abound in the vicinity of the small bakeries and noodle shops.

Against this, there are grounds for believing that because of the general poverty and consequent inability to afford much transport in Third World cities, classical Western 'garden city' principles of strict land use zoning and the segregation of the major types of urban activity are probably inappropriate to most situations. The correct solution is usually not removal of small-scale enterprises from residential areas but rather the harnessing in an acceptable manner in terms of amenity of the commercial and industrial vigour many spontaneous settlements display. As will become clear from subsequent chapters, the same kind of observation can also be made about the general housing problem in Third World cities, the most striking physical symptom of which is the squatter hut.

2

Socio-economic characteristics

Not only does the content-meaning of 'rural' and 'urban' shift from one technological era to the next and from one cultural context to another, but the universally visible contrast between hamlet and city, even of one time and place, blinds rather than illuminates.

Janet Abu-Lughod, 1969

Who are the inhabitants of the spontaneous settlements?[1] Eleanora, who lives in the Invasão Popular I settlement in Salvador, Brazil, is in her early forties. She was not born in Salvador itself but in the town of Conde. Eleanora was twenty-four when she arrived in Salvador. Soon she married a man who had come into the town from the rural interior. Her husband died shortly after their seventh child was born. The house they built is quite well made of mud and timber with a thatched roof, but it has no services. Inside it is divided into three spaces by cardboard and flattened tin cans.

There is a table but no proper chairs. Wooden platforms raised slightly above the mud floor and covered with straw are the beds. Eleanora earns her living by sewing, so there is also an old sewing machine. Her eldest son, aged fifteen, helps a little by selling sweets on the streets from a tray hung round his neck. Her eldest daughter, aged ten, is enrolled at the John F. Kennedy school nearby, but she is undernourished and often too ill to go. The five younger children play in the mud around the house. Eleanora is best at embroidering children's dresses. One will take her eight days but she will receive only a pittance for it. Her one comfort is that there is usually *farinha* (manioc meal) and *feijão* (beans) each day. Most days the children will also be able to have a small cup of milk through a United States aid programme.

Bertrand, who participated in the Invasão Popular II invasion, another spontaneous settlement in Salvador, is in a very different position. Every day he is not at work he drives from his two-storey home to the house he is building in the invasion area. The new house is to be a present for his wife on her next birthday. It will be completely equipped with electric lighting, gas cooking, piped water and sewage disposal.

Bertrand is a municipal employee with a good income. In addition to his highly prized office job he handles his retired father-in-law's business affairs for a fee and receives rents from another house he built previously in the Invasão Popular II invasion. He and his wife were born in Salvador and they both went to the university. Bertrand readily concedes that middle-class and rich people buy squatter shacks from the poor, and even that they put up shacks themselves in order to establish claims to occupancy. Their ultimate intention is to build houses to their own standards, either for renting or for living in. This, he says, is something that has to be done 'because real estate and houses cost so much in Salvador' (Pendrell, 1968, pp. 124–7, 153–6).

[1] Personal names and the names of the spontaneous settlements cited in this section are pseudonymous.

Some case studies

Perhaps the most widespread of the many erroneous generalizations about spontaneous settlements current today is that they consist of relatively homogeneous populations of very recent migrants from the countryside who are illiterate, unschooled in the ways of the city, poverty-striken even by local standards and largely unemployed. 'Suffice it to say', McGee (1967, pp. 159–60) has stated of urban squatter settlements in South-east Asia, 'in general they represent the most recent and the poorest of the city's population. . . . It is to these areas that the new migrants to the city move.' In fact, the actual situation, in South-east Asia and in the developing countries generally, is very much more complicated even to the extent that the degree of generalization attempted in this chapter is extremely hazardous because of the variety of migration histories and socio-economic characteristics such settlements display.

One case in point is the Klong Toey squatter area of Bangkok. With a population of about 25 000 people, Klong Toey is the largest of Bangkok's squatter areas. It is built on land owned by the Port Authority of Thailand, which over the years has resolutely opposed improvements in facilities in the area for fear of making the settlement seem permanent or, indeed, of encouraging still more squatters to move in. A survey carried out by the Department of Social Work of Thammasat University (1970) revealed that the population of Klong Toey is a well-balanced one in terms of the sexes, there being almost an equal number of males and females, and that it is also a predominantly young population. Persons fourteen years of age and younger constituted 48 per cent of the total, while only 1 per cent was aged sixty-five or over. Two-thirds of the total number of families were nuclear, and the settlement was characterized by families in a relatively early stage of development, that is, young parents with children.

In terms of Thailand as a whole, migration to Klong Toey was shown to be local (and thus to be conforming to one of the classic laws of migration, that the greatest proportion of migrants moves only a relatively short distance), in that 77 per cent of the household heads were born in Central Thailand and a quarter of these within Bangkok itself. Of those household heads born outside of the city 85 per cent gave their desire to find a job as the reason for their in-migration.

The number of workers in each family averaged two at the time of the survey and 95 per cent of the household heads claimed to be working. Clearly, in terms of finding a job of some kind, the migration into Bangkok represented by the very presence of a large majority of the families in the settlement has been successful. However, details of the actual jobs of household heads revealed a typical Third World urban employment situation. Only 6 per cent of those employed were engaged in manufacturing. The remainder were working within Bangkok's grossly inflated tertiary economic sector: in construction, transport and trade. One-quarter of the household heads were self-employed, a figure which probably indicates a high degree of reliance on employment in casual and petty occupations of a service nature. The general economic status of Klong Toey is indicated by the fact that 61 per cent of the families were found to be earning less than 1 500 *baht* a month at the time of the survey, a figure frequently used in Bangkok to define 'low income families', and that no less than 25 per cent of families earned only half of this sum or less. As for recency of immigration, the survey showed that half of the household heads had lived in Klong Toey for ten years or more, three-quarters for five or more years and only 6 per cent for less than one year. The median age of the houses, as estimated by the residents, was 8.5 years but 12 per cent were sixteen years old or older.

Another recently published case study, from Blantyre in Malawi (Norwood, 1972), emphasizes the individuality of spontaneous settlements for it indicates important differences from the Klong Toey pattern in certain respects. Ndirande is the most populous of the squatter colonies of Blantyre, which is the largest town in Malawi. Located only 3 km (2 miles) from the city centre, on government land, it grew because of its accessibility and also because it was outside the city boundary until 1963 and therefore not covered by planning and building controls. In 1966 the total population of Ndirande was 12 538 but there were almost twice as many males as females in this population – a marked divergence both from the Klong Toey case and from the national average for Malawi as a whole – and in addition children of school age were very much underrepresented (Table 2.1). These figures reveal an urban situation which is common in Africa south of the Sahara and also well known in certain other parts of the Third World, for example in India. There is a high proportion of single men in Ndirande who are working or seeking work in Blantyre. As Norwood, the director of the survey, points out, women and children are frequently either not brought to the city or are sent back to the villages when the children reach school age because of reduced school fees in the rural areas, the desire for a traditional education and the difficulty of securing school places in Blantyre.

Though it proved difficult to determine the precise character of employment in Ndirande, a detailed survey of heads of household carried out by Norwood (1972) in a similar squatter area in Blantyre indicated

Table 2.1 Demographic structure of Ndirande, Blantyre

	Ndirande %	*All Malawi* %
Male	58.5	47.4
Female	41.5	52.6
Children, 0–14 years	15.9	18.5
Children, 5–14 years	16.4	25.4
Males, 19 years and over	32.2	20.9
Females, 19 years and over	16.3	25.3

Source: Norwood, 1972, p.137.

that 48 per cent had regular employment in the town. However, the remainder were either 'self-employed' or unemployed and were probably in the same kind of situation in seeking petty jobs in the service sector of Blantyre's economy as has been described for Klong Toey. No survey of incomes was carried out but, as Norwood states (p. 137) it is reasonable to suppose that Ndirande as a whole is a very poor community:

> Housekeeping for a housewife in a squatter area is obviously a precarious business. Budgets can be upset by any minor variation such as a puncture of a bicycle tyre. Most people employed in Blantyre are paid monthly. There is a marked decline in the use of buses to and from Ndirande towards the end of each month. Likewise, some children are not able to attend school continuously due to lack of school fees. Every effort is made to reduce expenditure on food by growing as much maize as possible locally and every spare piece of ground is occupied by maize during the rainy season, including the steep hillsides.

In the case of Bogotá, Colombia, still other socio-economic variations within the universe of spontaneous settlement emerge, as Flinn and Converse (1970) have shown through a comparative study of three areas of recent settlement on the periphery of the city. All three areas studied can be categorized as spontaneous settlements, though two of them are subdivisions occupied after illegal sale for urban residential use rather than squatter invasion areas. In the Flinn and Converse study El Carmen and El Gavilán (the latter a pseudonym) comprise the *barrios clandestinos*, or illegal subdivisions, while Las Colinas is typical of Bogotá's *invasiones*, or squatter areas.

The study was designed specifically to test some of the common assumptions about spontaneous settlements referred to earlier in this chapter. Attention was first directed to the assumption that peripheral shantytowns consist of homogeneous populations of the illiterate and unemployed; that they are in fact a 'septic fringe', as they have been characterized by Breese (1966, p. 118). Flinn and Converse point out that their surveys of El Carmen, El Gavilán and Las Colinas show that relatively low proportions (between 21 and 37 per cent) of the heads of household had received no formal education and that almost one-fifth of household heads in El Carmen had completed primary education. (In the invasion area of Las Colinas, however, only 6 per cent of household heads had attained this latter educational level.) Few families in the three areas do not have at least one member engaged in a job, the highest rate of unemployment, 6 per cent, again occurring in Las Colinas, the squatter invasion area.

It is reasonable to assume, of course, that a significant proportion of those who reported themselves as working were in fact engaged in marginal service occupations, as in the cases of Klong Toey and Ndirande previously outlined. This is borne out by the fact that the survey indicated that few of the residents of the invasion *barrio* could afford to pay the rents necessary for more regular accommodation of a similar space standard in the city. Only 11 per cent of the families of this area were earning 750 pesos a month or more, but as might be expected the situation was much better in both El Carmen and El Gavilán, 40 per cent and 31 per cent of the families respectively being above this figure.

As with the Klong Toey and Ndirande studies, the Flinn and Converse survey indicates clearly the dangers of generalizing about the socio-economic character of spontaneous settlements, but in this case even within a single city, for Bogotá's *barrios clandestinos* evidently contain families at a higher level of socio-economic attainment than the *invasiones*, as might be expected from the fact that the inhabitants of the former have had to pay for their lots. The migration histories involved also reveal some important differences, for example a much lower percentage of the inhabitants of Las Colinas were found to have moved directly to Bogotá than the inhabitants of either El Carmen ro El Gavilán.

Further, as was emphasized in the previous chapter, it can by no means be assumed that it is always the most recent and poorest migrants to the city who build spontaneous settlements on its periphery. Large sections of the inner areas of Bogotá are inhabited by recent migrants sharing rooms, kitchens and other services. The Flinn and Converse study showed (p. 464) that 15 per cent of the inhabitants of El Gavilán, 18 per cent of Las Colinas and no less than 27 per cent of those of El Carmen settled first in the central city before moving to their present locations, and it is estimated that perhaps 40 per cent of all migrants to Bogotá proceed first to the city's inner zones. In addition, 27 per cent, 43 per cent and 39 per cent of the populations of El Carmen, El Gavilán and Las Colinas respectively were shown to have lived in the city for five years or longer.

Origins

The case studies outlined above, from Bangkok, Blantyre and Bogotá, illustrate the complexity of rural–urban migration processes in the Third World, particularly in the relationship of rural–urban migration to the creation of spontaneous settlements. In seeking to generalize about the origins of the inhabitants of spontaneous settlements it is exceedingly difficult to evaluate at secondhand the evidence available in published case studies, including those quoted above, without knowing precisely whether adequate precautions were taken during the field surveys reported to eliminate the known tendency of respondents born in rural areas to give their place of birth as the nearest town.

This factor undoubtedly accounts to some degree for a reduction in the proportions of true rural dwellers recorded in surveys both of in-migration generally and of the populations of individual spontaneous settlements; though when it was fully taken into account in a survey of in-migration to Santiago, Chile, carried out in the early 1960s the results nevertheless confirmed earlier findings that a high proportion of the adult migrants had been born in smaller towns (Herrick, 1965, pp. 51–2). Two-thirds of the economically active migrants in Santiago had been born in towns recorded as having more than 10 000 inhabitants in the 1960 census, and only one-seventh claimed birth in places with fewer than 1 000 inhabitants which could clearly be classed as rural. From this and other studies there appears to be little doubt that the Chilean case is a classic example of another migration phenomenon which has direct bearing on the problem of spontaneous settlement: step migration from small town to larger town and ultimately towards the metropolis. In addition to the Chilean case, migrations of this type have also been reported in respect of Buenos Aires, Recife, Guatemala City and Mexico City, and it has been estimated that, in all, perhaps one-quarter to one-third of all migration to the large cities of Latin America occurs as step migration (Morse, 1971*a*,

p. 23). There can be little doubt that step migration is widespread in the developing countries generally.

Within Santiago itself, the proportion of migrants in the *callampas*, or spontaneous settlements, approximates to their proportion in the city as a whole; in other words, migrants, and especially recent migrants, are not disproportionately concentrated in the peripheral shantytowns. These findings are paralleled, though in varying degree, by studies from other parts of the Third World. In a survey of the Kinsengo squatter area of Kinshasa, Zaire, reported by Knoop (1966, pp. 125–6), for example, it was observed that the original wave of settlers in the area consisted of families from the city centre who had taken the opportunity to seize land in order to escape from the overcrowded inner areas when law and order broke down immediately after the Belgian withdrawal. Only later did the character of Kisengo change somewhat, for after the settlement had become established it began to form a reception area for single male migrants from the interior.

Despite the difficulties of estimation, it is almost certainly true for Latin America that a substantial proportion of migrants to the larger urban areas characteristically proceeds first to inner-city areas. This has been amply confirmed by both Mangin (1967, p. 68) and Morse 1971*a*, p. 23) with reference to a large variety of case studies. The same tendency undoubtedly exists in both Asia and Africa, though whether the proportions of migrants currently successful in finding inner-city accommodation are as high as in Latin America is perhaps more doubtful. It would seem that in most African cities the opportunities for residence in inner-city areas would probably be proportionately fewer than those in South America because of a lesser development of multistoreyed tenement areas, while in south and eastern Asia such inner areas have for long been very much more densely peopled than those in Latin America and already they may well have approached their limits in terms of human carrying capacity. Nevertheless, it can fairly be said for the Third World as a whole that spontaneous settlements are seldom, if ever, formed exclusively by in-migrants coming directly into the city.

In respect of migration from outside the city two major patterns may be distinguished, and each has its implications both for the spontaneous development of housing and for general living conditions within squatter settlements. The first, step migration, has already been mentioned, particularly in relation to the Chilean case. Here it may be added that where patterns of step migration are concerned the most fundamental move made by the rural migrant in his first, that is, the move from the farm to a neighbouring small market town. It is as a result of this move that the migrant becomes personally involved with urban ways, as an urban dweller, for the first time, although as Anthony and Elizabeth Leeds (1970, esp. p. 233) have demonstrated this is not to say that town ways would necessarily be totally unknown to him before his move.

At each later migrational stage, even though he may eventually reach the metropolis itself after several additional moves, the migrant remains within an urban setting, and though the host towns may become progressively larger the same degree of fundamental adjustment and adaptation that was involved in his first move is not called for. To take the case of Chile again as an illustration, four-fifths of the migrants to Santiago come from the adjacent central provinces, and even within this core area the effect of distance from the capital as a discouragement to migration is remarkably linear, as Herrick (1965, p. 26) has shown. Approximately two-thirds of these migrants have been born in towns of 5 000 or more people; they are not rural migrants. Rather, it seems, a decanting process is taking place in which townsfolk are moving towards the capital and their places in the smallest towns are being taken by rural dwellers. This is, of course, simply a variation within the general pattern of step migration: it may even represent an intragenerational series in which subsequent generations of the original migrants make the later moves. There is virtually no return movement down the urban hierarchy.

The second major pattern of migration is that of direct migration from the countryside to the larger city, without intervening steps. Here the available evidence is very scattered and most of the case studies are ambiguous because of their failure to make clear not only whether the origins of the migrants studied were truly rural but also the degree, if any, to which step migration is involved in the in-migration process. (For a typical example see Beaujeu-Garnier, 1962.)

In general, by far the clearest evidence comes from Africa, particularly with regard to what has been termed target migration. It is well known that in Africa there are considerable numbers of people moving from the countryside directly to the larger towns, and also that such people often contribute significantly to the growth of spontaneous settlements (see, e.g., Nairobi University Housing Research Unit, 1971). In other case studies, Gallin (1965, pp. 121–5) has described the migration of families or parts of families from Hsin Hsing village in Taiwan directly into the capital city, Taipeh; Bogue and Zachariah (1962) have emphasized the important contribution made by migration from India's villages in swelling populations of towns and cities of all sizes; and McNicoll (1968,

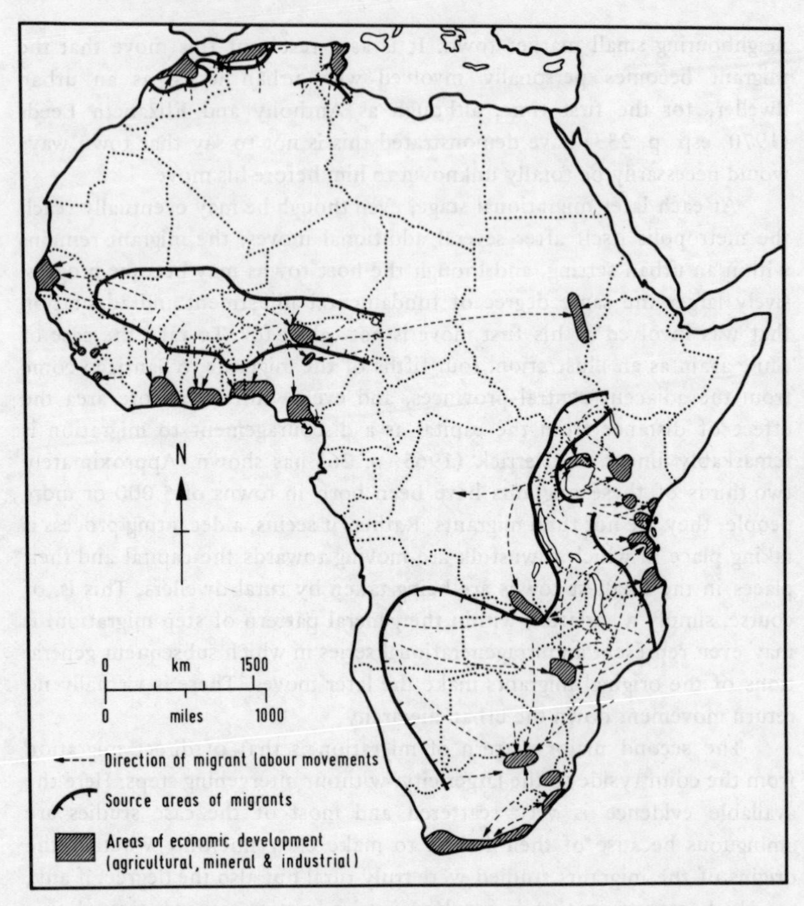

Fig. 2.1 Major migrational movements in Africa (Steel and Prothero, 1964, p. 205).

p. 75) while emphasizing the difficulties of assessing the available evidence, has illustrated the importance of migrants from the countryside of West Java in the composition of Djakarta's population.

With regard to Africa, Prothero (1964) has described in general terms the growth of significant streams of labour migration from the countryside, largely as the result of the development of natural resources, the founding of towns and the introduction of taxation during the colonial period. 'On a conservative estimate,' he states (p. 203), 'at least 5 million people are involved each year in migrant labour movements in Africa south of the Sahara.' Some of this labour is required in areas of cash crop production, particularly at harvest time, but there is also a good deal which flows into towns associated with mines, factories, inland commerce and sea trade. Certainly, economic factors are dominant in these migrations. The major lines of movement are shown in Fig. 2.1. In West Africa they generally follow a north to south line, with migrants from the poor farming areas of the interior seeking work in towns or on cash crop farms on or near the coast. Some West African migrants may travel as much as 1 000 km (620 miles), though there is little detailed information on such journeys. Seasonal changes of climate have an important influence upon migration patterns, for the usual cycle is for the migrant to leave home between late September and November, when work on the harvest has been finished, and to return home in the following April and May to cultivate his farm at the onset of the wet season.

In eastern Africa labour migration tends to involve workers in much longer absences from home, generally between one and two years, though there are also some seasonal migrations on the West African pattern, for example to the islands of Pemba and Zanzibar for the clove harvest. The main areas of attraction are the farms of the Kenya Highlands, sisal estates in Tanzania and areas of cotton and coffee cultivation in Buganda, but also the copperbelt towns of the Congo and Zambia, the mines of the Witwatersrand in South Africa, and the towns and cities of the region generally.

Typical of the West African migrational situation are the Toucouleur migrants, young men who work in Dakar for less than a year before returning to their villages, and their case has been particularly well analysed by Diop (1960). Most of the adult migrant labourers in West Africa are males who move into the towns without their families, states Prothero (1964, p. 207). They are often unmarried; in fact one of the common motives for leaving the village is to earn sufficient to make a marriage possible. Such migrants are frequently reluctant to make their move to the town permanent, however, presumably because their close attachment to their home areas and the high status they enjoy in the villages as annual migrants are more important to them than additional economic gain.

Parallels to this situation can be found in eastern Africa, though within the longer time cycle previously mentioned. As Mitchell (1961, pp. 232–3) has pointed out, here too, as in West Africa, to a high degree the circulation of labour between countryside and town rather than its permanent migration into the towns became a characteristic feature of the urbanization process during the colonial period, one which has begun to weaken somewhat only in very recent years. In this pattern the African worker is constantly migrating back and forth between the industrial and the tribal areas, the overall pattern of distribution masking the movement of individuals.

> His participation in the cash economy of the towns (or on the farms), however, leaves his obligations and duties to his rural kinsmen and his general involvement in the tribal social system unchanged. He sees his ultimate security to lie amongst his tribesmen from whom he is able to claim support and succour in terms of his kinship relationship to many of them. He sees his position in the community ensured by his holding cultivation rights with them in a relationship which links him to his headman and his chief. The cash he needs to satisfy fringe wants and not his basic subsistence needs . . . he has no need to stay in the town once his needs are met (Mitchell, 1961, p. 233).

In other words he is a target migrant: the sooner he achieves his goal, the sooner he will return to his village, at least for a time.

There is plentiful evidence of this general situation in African case studies though, as previously stated, the stability of town life seems to be increasing. Some Indian experience confirms it also, and at least one published case study of target migration has been made in South-east Asia. Whether this kind of migration is at all representative of the situation in Latin America is more doubtful. With regard to Africa, Southall (1969, pp. 474–5) has claimed of Nairobi, that '. . . the mass of the Kikuyu, Luyia, Luo and Kamba . . . do not regard it as their city to the extent of being able to commit themselves and their families to it and that, correspondingly, their interests, goals, and identifications are but partially urban'; while from a rural viewpoint Van Velsen (1960) has stressed the fact that, far from breaking down traditional social forms, labour migration is an extremely significant factor in ensuring the continuation of the tribal society of the Tonga of Malawi because the absent villagers generally maintain an active role in the social and political structure of Tongaland and 'those who manage to settle in the towns permanently and have given up the intention to return to the village are the exception rather than the rule' (p. 267).

For India, Eames (1967) has claimed generally that investigations have revealed that many of the seemingly independent and nuclear urban families (not to mention the large proportions of single male migrants found in many Indian towns and cities) are in reality primarily appendages of village extended families. This assessment is strikingly confirmed by Ames (1968) in his study of the company town of Jamshedpur, which indicated that many workers consider their stay in the town only 'temporary', even after having lived there twenty or thirty years. They see themselves as but one segment of a larger family, the locus of which is the countryside:

> Typically the household where the elders live, for example the ancestral home at the native place, serves as the headquarters for the property group and the custodian of the property. The other households are like satellites, located around the country at places of work or study. Members 'orbit' from one household to the other. The parents and unmarried children will live in the native village, for example, while the sons and their wives and children will move to the cities for jobs. The wives of the sons will take turns returning to the native place for three months a year to care for their parents-in-law or to produce their own children. The composition of the household therefore constantly fluctuates: it may be conjugal in structure one month, sub-conjugal the next, and joint during the third month when brother's or father's family visits for a 'temporary' stay of three to six months (p. 60).

Additional evidence comes from Bombay where one of the unexpected results of a demographic study of the city reported by Zachariah (1966; esp. pp. 362–3) was evidence of appreciable reverse migration, out-migration of former in-migrants being particularly noticeable during the first few years of their stay in the city and especially among those who were above thirty-five years of age. Of those persons enumerated in Bombay in 1951, the rate of out-migration during the decade 1951–61 was 18 per cent for males and 13 per cent for females. Within these fractions, about 30 per cent of male migrants and 20 per cent of female migrants moved out of Greater Bombay during the first three or four years of their stay. Additionally, among migrants who moved into the city at ages above thirty-four years, more than 60 per cent left within three to four years of their arrival. Some of the persons classified in this manner would be visitors to the city, others would be government servants and executives on transfer, but Zachariah suggests that the figures also comprise not only those who came to the city looking for work and were unable to find any, but also workers returning after ten to fifteen years of service in the city to take up their ancestral land, retired workers going 'home' and the wives and children of unskilled workers returning to villages where life was cheaper.

The supporting South-east Asian case study mentioned earlier was made in the mid-1950s in Thailand by Textor (1956), among the Bangkok *samlor* (pedicab) drivers. In 1933, when the *samlor* first made its appearance on the streets of Bangkok, *samlor* driving was made a restricted occupation, open only to Thai nationals and closed to the city's considerable Chinese community. Since then, *samlor* driving has become very much an in-migrant occupation. In October 1954 there were 11 784 men legally authorized to drive *samlors* in Bangkok, more than four-fifths of whom had been born up-country, the vast majority of them in the north eastern provinces. Further, Textor found that,

> The Northeasterner tends to be a back-and-forth migrant rather than a settling migrant. . . . The factors determining a Northeastern drivers length of stay in Bangkok are economic and psychological. If it is a bad farming year and the driver's wife, parents and relatives are capable of harvesting the meagre crop, the driver is likely to remain in Bangkok during the harvest time. If the harvest is heavy, he is more likely to return to give a hand. He is also likely to help during planting time. However, if his *samlor* income during harvest or planting time is particularly high, then he is somewhat less likely to return home. On the psychological side, the most frequently mentioned factor is that of loneliness. Among the great majority of Northeasterners who leave their wives and families behind, most men before long find themselves yearning for the familiar surroundings of home, village and temple (pp. 16–17).

Of a group of *samlor* drivers from the northeastern provinces who had come to the capital between 1946 and 1953, the median man had spent an aggregate of only twelve to eighteen months in the city, reported Textor, whereas during that time he had perhaps gone back to the north-east five to ten times.

Although circumstances of this kind are known in South America, the general migrational situation there seems to be radically different from that of Africa and India. As Morse (1971*b*) has observed, the widespread networks of rural social organization of considerable historical continuity found in the latter areas have little parallel in Latin America. This is because:

> In southern South America, Brazil, and the Caribbean, Amerindian settlement patterns disintegrated under the impact of European economic institutions. In Meso- and Andean America this was less true. . . But even in highland America the trauma of conquest was so severe, the Amerindian population decline so precipitous, and the reconcentration of rural workers so widespread that extended indigenous social systems such as one finds in India and Africa had no chance for survival (pp. 32–3).

In consequence, frequently the only effective social unit is the household, large agricultural villages functioning as communities are not typical, and present trends seem to be towards even greater dispersal. Although urban migrants frequently visit their communities of origin, little permanent return migration has been reported.

The operational implications of the above discussion of the origins of the inhabitants of spontaneous settlements may now be outlined in terms of the primary distinction made earlier between step migration and migration from the countryside directly to the larger towns and cities.

Where circumstances involving step migration prevail, it can be expected that the effect of cultural differences upon the in-migrant and the degree of psychological and sociological adjustment called for will be least within the setting of the metropolis and greatest within the smallest market towns. This has implications both for housing policies and for the general process of modernization which will be explored later in this chapter. Further, inasmuch as there may conceivably be correlations between improved economic status and the later stages of migration history where a step sequence is involved (given that almost all current Third World studies show a desire to improve economic status as the major migrational motivating force), and inasmuch as selectivity in migration will presumably continue to be operative, it could be hypothesized that within a pattern of step migration the worst problems of poverty and urban adjustment in spontaneous settlements may be expected within the smaller towns to which rural dwellers make their first moves rather than within the metropolis. Unfortunately, however, almost all case studies of spontaneous settlement published to date have concentrated on the cities and larger towns and none so far, it seems, have compared housing conditions at different points along the urban hierarchy of a single country.

With regard to migration directly from the countryside to the larger towns and cities, it has been demonstrated that an important distinction exists between permanent migration and target migration, the latter still being a prevalent form of migration in some parts of the Third World. In a setting of permanent migration and ultimate family formation, most of the generally recognized housing desires, especially those concerning long-term improvement in the family housing situation, may be expected to operate, but within a setting of target migration the urban housing response will probably be very different. On a basis of a large number of employment histories, Houghton (1960) has constructed a typical migrant profile for South Africa, one of a worker who has spent 64 per cent of his working life between the ages of sixteen to forty-seven away from home, taking on thirty-four different jobs during that period and remaining an average of forty-seven weeks in each job. What, it may be asked, would be the urban housing response of such a person? Incentives to improve the dwelling would be minimal, and unless the various employers provided shelter, living conditions would probably remain permanently not very much different from those of the Bangkok *samlor* drivers described by Textor (1956, p. 397):

> Migrant housing is marked by extreme simplicity. (Some drivers, in fact, sleep sitting in their vehicles, though the police discourage this practice and it seems to be on the wane.) Often the migrant has only a flat hard surface on which to stretch out his body at night, frequently without even a mosquito net to protect him. I have sometimes visited one relatively well-managed lodging house at 6.00 a.m., in time to see hosts of just-arisen drivers emerging from small crannies and sleeping platforms in *samlor* storage garages, from lofts, from porch floors, and from one-room family stalls all characterized by a virtually complete lack of furniture and other appointments. Articles of personal comfort and convenience are in many cases almost non-existent.

As Rosser (1972*a*, pp. 40–1) has observed with reference to Calcutta, the basic problem with target migrants is that as far as assimilation into the city is concerned they remain outsiders:

> They camp out in the city (a most significant aspect of the problem of building effective demand for urban housing), sleeping on the pavements or grouped in male 'messing families' in ramshackle *bustees* or jute lines in conditions of appalling sanitation. They live and sleep inside the shops and offices, back stairways of hotels, docks, factories or construction sites where they work. They create demands on urban services, contribute powerfully to the dramatic deterioration of the urban environment, but have little stake in the city as such, little concern for civic progress or civic pride, and little interest in the quality of the urban infrastructure or social services.

As an added element of irony concerning the improvement of urban living conditions, there are recorded cases in Africa of target migrants living in these, and worse, conditions in the towns while at the same time subscribing money to improvement unions, the objective of which is the development of modern public amenities in their home community in the countryside. Money collected at the branch unions of such organizations –

such as that of Ogbomosho, which reaches not only throughout Nigeria's towns but also into other West African countries – is sent back to the countryside to build roads, wells, schools, churches, clinics and other facilities (Plotnicov, 1970, pp. 76–7).

Selectivity

Migration, both step and direct, is well known to be selective in many of its aspects and most of these also have significant bearing on urban housing problems. Sex selectivity in migration has already been touched on in the previous section of this chapter, particularly in the discussion of target migration. Here discussion of this and certain other aspects of the in-migration process will be expanded with additional examples, for as has already been indicated above there is abundant evidence that to a significant degree housing policies in Third World cities must be concerned not only with provision for families who may be considered to be relatively stable within the urban setting but also with the more intractable problem of providing suitable accommodation for large numbers of single in-migrants who may differ markedly from the general pattern of their host communities, not only in marital status but also in age and mobility.

In order to indicate some of the major aspects of migration processes within the Third World setting the case of Colombia may be outlined. The rate of population growth in Colombia accelerated from 2.2 per cent during the period 1938–51 to 3.2 per cent in the period 1961–64. At the same time, urbanization proceeded apace, the number of towns with populations of over 20 000 increasing from sixteen in 1938 to forty-seven in 1964 and the proportion of the population living in them rising from 13 to 36 per cent over the same period. The annual net outflow of people from rural to urban areas almost doubled; in addition there was also some inter-rural movement into new areas of agricultural colonization.

In a study of these major migrational changes carried out during the period 1963–65, Adams (1969) collected field data from seven representative areas organized into three groups based on the distance of each area from its nearest industrial centre in terms of travelling times of one hour, four hours and eight hours or more (Table 2.2). It was found that five of the seven areas had 37 to 45 per cent of the people enumerated living outside their general area of birth. This was a much higher degree of mobility than Adams expected, especially in the remote areas. As might be expected from the classic laws of migration, further breakdown of the data showed that the proportion of migrants to the larger towns and cities

Table 2.2 Characteristics of out-migration in Colombia by travel time to nearest industrial centre

Areas by travel time to nearest industrial centre	*Proportion of people enumerated not living in area of birth**	*Average number of years of formal education achieved†*
One hour		
Sopó	0.37	3.7
Barbosa	0.45	3.2
Four hours		
Guamo	0.16	2.2
Tamesis	0.40	4.0
San Gil	0.25	2.1
Eight hours plus		
Urrao	0.45	3.8
Contadero	0.43	3.4

* People who did not live in *municipio* of birth or in an adjacent *municipio*.

† Refers to all of the people enumerated in the area.

Note: Based on farm family interviews carried out by Adams in Colombia 1964–65.

Source: Adams, 1969, p. 530.

decreased as travel time increased; but in the more remote areas a higher proportion of migrants was moving into nearby villages and towns, possibly to begin a chain of step migration.

As regards the age and sex of the in-migrants, almost four-fifths had left the area of their birth before the age of twenty-five and almost nine-tenths had left before the age of thirty. A large majority of those who migrated were single, and females were well represented, possibly because of marriage movements or the demand for relatively low-paid domestic servants in the urban areas. Whole family migration was not common. These findings have been confirmed by other Colombian studies, principally of migration into Bogotá. Converse (1965, p. 534) reported, for example, that 95 per cent of the people he interviewed came to Bogotá before they were married and that 90 per cent were less than thirty years of age.

The educational status of the migrants, as revealed by the survey carried out by Adams, was very much as has been reported in migrational studies elsewhere, for his findings confirm that formal education plays a positive role in rural migration, the two areas with the lowest levels of education also having the lowest rates of out-migration. The average level of education for non-migrants was also significantly lower than that for migrants. Further, a general tendency could be detected for those who moved only to a neighbouring *municipo* rather than further afield (a rural-to-rural or a rural-to-village move) to have educational levels as low or lower than the non-migrants. From this it is clear that in Colombia, as in many other developing countries, it is those who receive most education in the rural areas who tend to move into the urban areas, though it may also be the case that the nearby villages and smallest market centres benefit least from this mobility in terms of receiving relatively well educated migrants.

Once again it must be emphasized that so far very little is known about the characteristics of migration to, and housing conditions in, the smaller towns of the Third World. As Morse (1971*a*, p. 34, f.n., 16) has aptly put it, 'small towns fall between the stools of the bushwacking anthropologists and macrocosmic social scientists who appreciate metropolitan amenities and the chance to consort with national elites'. It is not possible from the published information to enlarge on the study by Adams in this respect, but useful supplementary insights into the general Colombian migrational situation as it affects the capital, Bogotá, have been provided by Flinn from his study of the *barrio clandestino* of El Carmen.

Flinn (1968, p. 79) observed that 62 per cent of the household heads of El Carmen came either from Cundinamarca, the state in which Bogotá is situated, or from the adjacent state of Boyaca (in addition to 12 per cent born in Bogatá itself); that 68 per cent of the in-migrant household heads were born within 100 miles of Bogotá, and that fewer than 5 per cent were born 200 miles or more from the city. There was some evidence of step migration, inasmuch as one-third of the inhabitants of El Carmen changed their place or residence at least once before migrating to Bogotá and that 42 per cent were born in places of over 2 000 in population.

Of greater importance in the present context is Flinn's analysis of migrational histories of the heads of household of El Carmen within Bogotá itself. In common with most other Latin American cities, Bogotá has developed a grossly overcrowded *zona negra* immediately around its central business district which contains migrants from almost every part of Colombia. Flinn shows that 26 per cent of the in-migrant respondents in the El Carmen survey lived in the *zona negra* before moving to the shanty-town fringe, and also that an additional 16 per cent settled first in inner

Table 2.3 Median amount of pesos brought to Bogotá by in-migrant household heads, 1965

Pesos	*In-migrants to shantytown fringe*		*In-migrants to central city*	
	Frequency	*Percentage*	*Frequency*	*Percentage*
I. 0 to 499	38	62.3	40	88.9
II. 500 plus	23	37.7	5	11.1
(*a*) 500 to 999	8	13.1	0	0.0
(*b*) 1 000 to 4 999	8	13.1	3	6.7
(*c*) 5 000 to 9 999	5	8.2	2	4.4
(*d*) 10 000 to 15 000	2	3.3	0	0.0
Total	61	100.0	45	100.0
Median	425 pesos		210 pesos	

$X^2 = 9.42, P - 0.01.$

Source: Flinn, 1968, p. 85.

city areas just beyond the *zona negra*. Generally, those who migrated directly to the central city areas had fewer cash resources compared with those who settled on the city's fringe (Table 2.3), a median of 210 pesos against 425 pesos at the time of the survey, and they were similarly disadvantaged with regard to the possession both of skills and of personal possessions such as household goods and tools of a trade. Thus, in general, the more affluent settled immediately in the peripheral shantytown. To some extent, however, this relationship was modified by kinship ties, since two-thirds of those initial settlers in the shantytown who on income criteria might have been expected to proceed first into the inner city areas were influenced in their choice of a peripheral location by relatives who were already living in the same shantytown neighbourhood.

Seventy per cent of those who moved subsequently from the inner city to El Carmen stated that they were motivated by the desire to own a home site and improve their living conditions, and this group as a whole had experienced considerable upward occupational mobility during their stay in Bogotá. These latter are crucial points which will be developed further in chapter 6, for in such cases the spontaneous settlements in question, far from forming a refuge for poverty stricken rural migrants, are simply suburbs developing in a Third World setting, and moreover suburbs which, like others of a more regular kind in a Western city, function on a higher socio-economic level than do the city's most crowded inner residential areas. They can hardly be classified as slums, at least as that term has been conventionally understood so far, and certainly it cannot be said of them, as the United Nations Economic Commission for Latin America (1963, p. 15) said of Santiago's *callampas* in general, that they 'represent a rejection by the city of elements already living in it, whether born there or not, and differing from the rest of the urban population more in degree of poverty than in origin'.

Attention may now be turned from the Colombian case study just outlined to comparisons of the migrational selectivity described with situations of urban in-migration in other parts of the Third World. For Bombay, Zachariah (1966; esp. pp. 364–5) has stated that though it is not possible to give a precise estimate, there is no doubt that in the early 1960s at least four out of ten of the married migrant males were not living in the city with their wives, and that the proportion might even have been as high as six out of ten. Overall, the migrant population was a youthful one, the age of maximum in-migration being close to twenty years. The sex composition of the migrants greatly favoured males, with an excess of males exceeding 800 for every 1 000 females. In each age and sex group the proportion of single migrants was found to be greater than in their places of origin. The situation was obviously one of high rates of in-migration of single males, coupled with significant in-migration of married males unaccompanied by wives and families.

In general, it may be said that something of the same situation obtains in South-east Asia, though not to such a marked degree as in India, with the exception that Manila does not conform to the usual South-east Asian pattern in regard to the sex composition of the migrant stream. Most South-east Asian towns and cities have sex ratios which are weighted in favour of males when compared with corresponding national sex ratio figures, and the urban populations tend to become more masculine as the size of the locality increases, a situation which has been reported as reflecting 'primarily the sex composition of migrants from rural areas and villages' (UN Bureau of Social Affairs, 1957*b*, p. 108). The excess of urban males is particularly marked in the age groups between fifteen and forty-four. Manila is a major exception, for female dominant in-migration patterns have become characteristic since the late 1940s, possibly reflecting the great concentration of higher educational facilities in the capital and a demand for female labour, principally in domestic service.

The female dominant pattern of migration to Manila is very commonly reproduced in Latin America, with the important exception of the migra-

Table 2.4 Sex ratios of in-migrants in Santiago, 1962

Age of arrival	*Masculinity index*
Less than 15	85
15–29	62
30–49	75
50 and over	57

Source: Elizaga, 1969, p. 334.

tion of Andean Indians (Breese, 1966, p. 83). This pattern forms another basis for some differentiation of this region from the other major parts of the Third World in terms of the assessment of housing problems. To return to Santiago as an example, a sample survey of in-migration into the city in 1962 reported by Elizaga (1969, pp. 333–4) revealed a masculinity index of only 72, a low figure even after allowing for masculine overmortality. It appears that the differential by sex has increased in recent years, for the index was 67 for the five-year period immediately preceding the survey compared with 76 for those migrants who arrived in the city before 1942. A further important feature was that the masculinity index was very low in the young adult ages (Table 2.4) – that is, during the family formation period – when at least half the migrants arrived in the city; in fact for those who had arrived during the 1950s, the most recent group at the time of the survey, it was still lower than that shown in Table 2.4. This picture is broadly confirmed by Herrick (1965, p. 73), who emphasizes both the youth of Santiago's recent migrants and the preponderance of females within the migrant stream.

Finally in this review of migrant selectivity, attention may be returned to Africa. Here, as previously noted, the urban situation is one of marked male dominance, not only in respect of in-migration but also in the general population composition of the towns and cities. An indication of the Rhodesian situation in 1961 is given in Fig. 2.2. As Mitchell (1969, p. 478) has remarked, it is characteristic of a migrational situation in which young males migrate to the towns, spend the early years of their adult life there and finally returned to their rural homes when they have reached their mid-forties in age, and of young couples who send at least some of their children back to the rural areas when they have reached puberty. Mitchell has classified the inhabitants of the Zambian line-of-rail into three broad categories, and his classification could well be applied

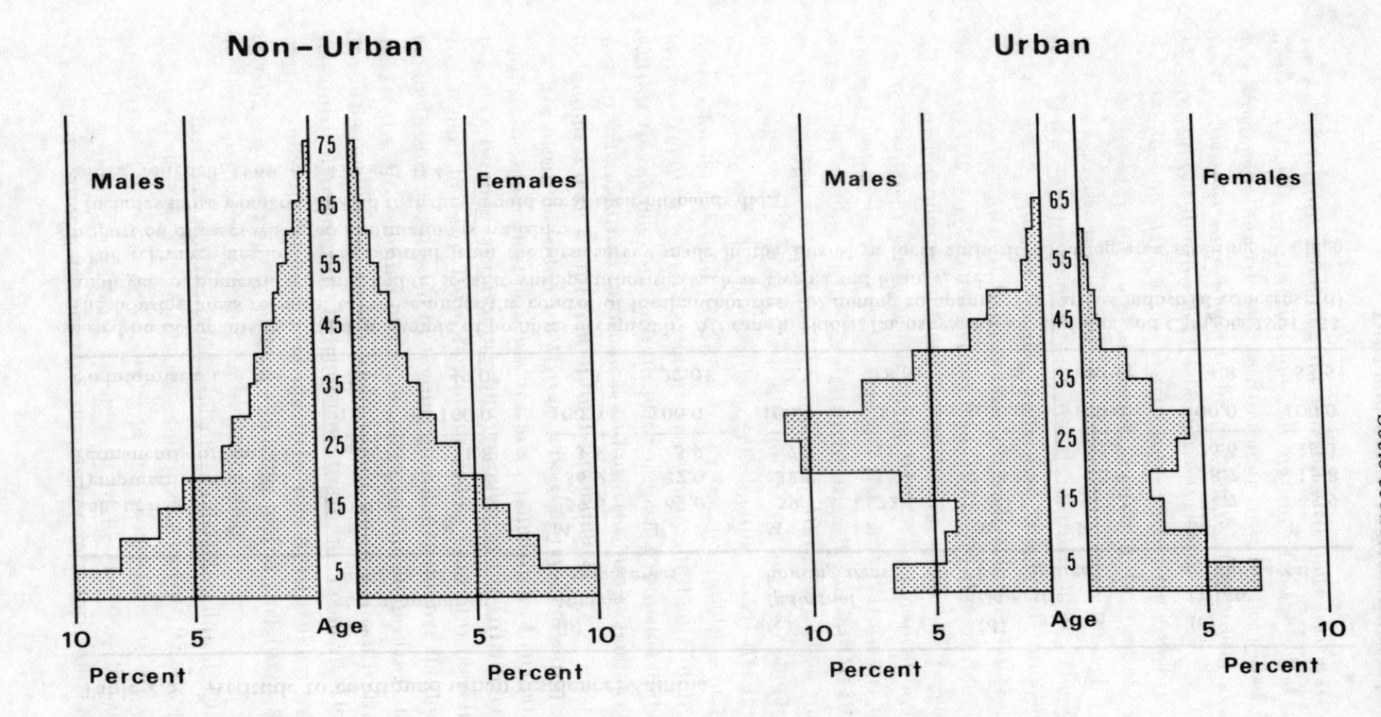

Fig. 2.2 Age and sex structure, urban and non-urban African population, Rhodesia, 1961 (Mitchell, 1969, p. 477)

Table 2.5 Attitude to continued urban residence, Zambia

	(a) *Local authority housing areas*		(b) *Mining housing areas*		(c) *Industrial housing areas*		(d) *Domestic housing areas*		(e) *Private housing areas*	
	M	F	M	F	M	F	M	F	M	F
Labour migrant	51.4	64.7	59.6	67.0	59.5	72.5	60.7	69.2	34.7	45.9
Temporarily urbanized	37.8	23.5	36.9	27.0	32.7	15.6	34.0	16.9	38.7	15.8
Permanently urbanized	10.7	11.8	3.5	5.9	7.8	11.7	5.2	13.9	26.6	38.3
	100.0	100.0	100.0	100.0	100.0	100.0	100.0	100.0	100.0	100.0
No information	16.8	49.0*	2.3	27.0†	2.3	18.6†	1.5	10.1†	4.8	33.5†

Based on occupants of a random sample of premises occupied by Africans in Ndola, Luanshya, Kitwe, Mufulira and Chingola 1951–53. The housing areas refer to: (a) those under the control of local authorities; (b) mining companies; (c) various industrial concerns; (d) employers of domestic servants; and (e) local township authorities such as Twapia and Fisinge, etc.

* The relevant questions were omitted from the first survey made in the Luanshya local authority housing area resulting in a high proportion of cases where no information is available.

† Includes those women who said that they would do as their husbands did.

Source: Mitchell, 1969, pp. 479 and 484.

more widely in Africa south of the Sahara. The first category is that of the labour migrants, those in towns for a specific purpose who have no intention of staying longer than necessary; the second is that of the temporarily stabilized, those who intend to return to their rural homes some day, but not in the immediate future; thirdly, there are the permanently urbanized, who have no wish to abandon town life. Reworking data from a sample survey of the inhabitants of line-of-rail towns which was carried out by the Rhodes–Livingstone Institute in 1951–53, Mitchell demonstrates the very small proportions that can be considered to be permanently urbanized (Table 2.5). Though recent investigations have tended to suggest that periods spent by African migrants in the towns are getting longer, Elkan (1968, p. 238) has claimed that 'there is nothing to indicate that there has been any basic change in the pattern of circular migration'. In these circumstances, he points out, the possibility of the persistence of important currents of circular migration well into the future must be taken into account in planning for urban development. This latter is an aspect of the overall Third World housing problem which will be discussed further in chapter 6.

Spatial grouping

So far in this chapter the major points made are as follows. First, it is extremely unsafe to generalize about the socio-economic characteristics of spontaneous settlements, not only within nations or within regions, but even within single cities. A great deal more field work is necessary in the spontaneous settlements themselves not only to form a body of empirical information from which valid theories may be drawn but also as an indispensable basis for individual action programmes concerned with housing or general environmental improvement. Secondly, it can by no means always be assumed that spontaneous settlements are composed of rural migrants. Intra-urban movements from overcrowded inner areas are of importance. In addition, within the general flow of migration there are two distinct components of significance: direct movement from the countryside to the towns and the cities, and step migration from town to town up the urban hierarchy. Each of the latter has its own particular implications for housing policies, the most obvious (and intractable) ones occurring where migration is largely of a target or circular character, heavily dominated by males and producing large proportions of what Mitchell terms labour migrants and the temporarily stabilized.

Within the host towns, significant variations in housing demand will result from variations in the age, sex and marital status of in-migrant streams. Unfortunately, there is very little published information available on migration patterns of those already married before leaving the rural areas, apart from certain Indian case studies such as the one by Zachariah outlined above, yet this is clearly an aspect of in-migration which is of major importance in considering housing strategies for the urban areas. In general, it appears that individual migration predominates on the Third World scale, though individual migration is not necessarily single person migration in the sense of marital status, for wives and families are often left behind. The other important aspects of the migration process which have been stressed here in relation to housing strategies are age selectivity and sex selectivity: a high proportion of migrants is young and unbalanced sex structures are common. Married couples in the early stages of family formation are therefore by no means the only component of the housing problem. Nor, as Flinn's study of Bogotá demonstrated, is the problem of the growth of spontaneous settlements solely linked to the growth of migration, for it is safe to say that almost all spontaneous settlements contain a proportion of inhabitants with origins within the host town.

The final topic which remains to be discussed in the present chapter is the spatial grouping of in-migrant populations within Third World cities and the implications this phenomenon holds in respect both of the growth of spontaneous settlements and of the formulation of realistic housing policies in the Third World context. This is a highly important issue, for in a situation in which the volume of in-migration to the cities of the developing countries has accelerated markedly over the last four or five decades – and one in which a good proportion of the migrants is undoubtedly from rural areas – vital questions must arise as to the psychological and sociological quality of the migrants in terms of their integration into the life of their host cities and their contribution to the role of the cities as innovating organizations and major growth points in national economic development (Dwyer, 1972*d*, pp. vii–xvi). As Abu-Lughod (1961, p. 23) has pointed out, 'numbers alone should alert us to the probability that migrants are shaping the culture of the city as much as they are adjusting to it'.

The classic sociological view of the city, advanced by Louis Wirth (1938), as an agglomeration of large numbers of heterogeneous people in a dense, permanent settlement implies not only anonymity and dependence on impersonal relations but also tolerance, indeed encouragement, of change. It seems, therefore, that one of the most vital questions that can currently be asked in social research on the Third World city is whether (and if so, to what extent and in what manner) current in-migration of what, albeit crudely, may be termed rural-type people is affecting the role of the city as a centre of socio-economic change as that role has been understood in the West, at least since the Industrial Revolution. There do seem to be growing indications that it is unsafe to continue to embrace the rural–urban continuum as a conceptual framework in so far as it implies complete locational dichotomy of social characteristics between city and countryside.

In elaboration, several examples may be cited. A case in West Africa is the Zabrama migrant to the urban areas of Ghana from Niger (Rouch, 1954, pp. 54–60). He is a single man, or if he is married his wife remains in his home territory. In the urban areas he is organized into village communities according to his origin which do not allow him to leave the social milieu of his native home. He recognizes a system of urban chieftainship which is a transplant of the traditional. His room, shared with perhaps five others, all from his home district, has been described by Rouch as 'a little regional cell'. He takes little, if any, part in social interaction with Ghanaians, to the extent that a stand at the race course in Accra is called the 'Zabrama stand' and one of the local cinemas is known as the 'Zabrama cinema'. A further indication from Africa concerns Xhosa migrants in East London, South Africa. Of these Mayer (1962, p. 4) has stated: '. . . They attach themselves to their own particular cultural minority, and recreate as far as possible the moral and cultural atmosphere of their own (pre-urban) homes'; and that they '. . . mean to stay in Rome but will not do as the Romans do'. 'We are entitled to call urbanized', claims Mayer in summarizing the East London situation, 'only those who have moved in some profounder sense than mere physical change of abode'.

These examples may be extended by parallel case studies from other parts of the Third World. Hamdan (1960, p. 38) has studied a Khartoum spontaneous settlement and reports that 'within the village racial segregation is absolute. Each tribe has its separate quarters'. Similarly, in a perceptive study of the movement of a group of migrants from a remote Anatolian village to an Istanbul spontaneous settlement, Suzuki (1964, p. 210) has illustrated how they '. . . kept only to themselves and sought moral and social succour within their own group. By following this path of adjustment to city life, they embellished several of the features characteristic of the way of life in an Anatolian village, in the new urban environment.'

This band of migrants consisted of twenty-five families and they came from a village which was relatively isolated until 1950. The village is given the pseudonym Ortaköy by Suzuki. Its inhabitants were all farmers, cultivating small plots largely for their own subsistence, using primitive tools and sources of energy and living by a code emphasizing cooperation and close kinship. In the initial moves in 1952 three leaders were financed from funds pooled by the families. After they found jobs they constructed shelters in a squatter area and summoned their families. When these initial families were settled, the remaining families in the group were advised to move from the village. By 1960, twenty families had moved: one had found a job which included a house, ten had built huts in the same squatter settlement, four more were tenants of huts nearby, and the remaining five families had settled in other *gecekondu* (squatter) complexes within Istanbul.

In January 1959, Suzuki relates, a mutual fund was established through voluntary association by the Ortaköy villagers in Istanbul. Every family from Ortaköy living in the capital joined the club, the primary purpose of which was to provide a ready source of capital to meet emergencies among Ortaköyans. The money collected up to March 1960 was put to uses which are significant in terms of the present discussion. According to Suzuki (p. 211), these were:

1. A bolt of green cloth – green being one of the traditional colours of Islam – was purchased for TL90 [Turkish lira] in March of 1959. This bolt was sent to the *hoca* or religious teacher in Ortaköy for him to dispense as coffin coverings for funeral ceremonies.
2. After having been discharged from the hospital for an operation of the stomach during which time the patient was under full government care, a fellow Ortaköyan received TL200 from the *sandik* [mutual fund: lit. 'strong box']. This amount, donated in February 1960, was given to the patient to help cover his fare back to Ortaköy where he was to convalesce.
3. A second *hemseri* [fellow villager] was striken with tuberculosis and hospitalized for nine months. Although he received a small stipend in accordance with Turkey's workmen's compensation laws and was under government medical care during the nine-month period, the patient's wife and child would have been in dire financial straits had not the *sandik* provided them with TL600. And when the disease was fully arrested, the patient and his family were given an additional TL400 in March 1960 to return to Ortaköy for rehabilitation.
4. In the fall of 1959, an old woman in Ortaköy was brought to

Istanbul, operated on for an internal disorder, and sent back to Ortaköy all on *sandik* money. Close to TL1 000 of the *sandik* treasury was used for this purpose.

5. In March 1960, the *sandik* members purchased a Colemantype lamp for TL200. This lamp was sent to Ortaköy for the mosque there.
6. Ever since its inception *sandik* money collected among its members has been used to help Ortaköy migrants during their first months in Istanbul. Basic necessities and in some cases, one month's rent, have been provided for the newcomers.

Thus, in only three of the six cases were funds expended for Ortaköyans living in Istanbul. Clearly, links with the village had remained extremely strong, as did village patterns of life within the city itself. To quote Suzuki once more (pp. 211–12):

> With respect to cooperation, the patterns carried out in the Anatolian village appear to have been transplanted in the new milieu. Thus, whether the activity was constructing a shack, gardening, hauling water and fuel, or child care, mutual aid and reciprocal labor practises were the means by which these migrants accomplished domestic work. Additionally, social outlets were organized among themselves to the exclusion of non-Ortaköyans. This was true whether the event in question was a picnic, funeral, sight seeing tour or party. Indeed they were almost totally oblivious to non-Ortaköy people even in situations when the latter group were their neighbours in the shack settlement.

Turning to eastern Asia, Hauser (1957, p. 79), a leading authority on urbanization in the area, was claiming in 1957 that already by then the cities had become '. . . in large measure an agglomeration of folk societies'. Gallin (1966, p. 123) has indicated that most migrant families from the vicinity of Hsin Hsing village, Taiwan, live together in the capital Taipeh 'as a group to perform some of the same religious ceremonials as they did in the village itself'. In respect of Indonesia, Versluys (1964, p. 50) has pointed out that various *kampongs* in Djakarta are populated by individual groups from the countryside of western and central Java who keep to their own tradition and laws, while Bruner (1961, pp. 514–15) has summarized the effects on the Toba Batak of their migration into Medan thus:

> The city Batak do not assimilate to urban culture in Medan but they do maintain close ties with their rural relatives in the villages. Examined from a structural point of view, the Toba Batak communities in village and city are part of one social and ceremonial system. The Indonesian

village is often presented as an isolated world in itself, a closed self-contained entity, relatively static, while the city is a true dynamic centre, the seat of art, culture, and political authority and exciting, active and sometimes wicked place in which the residents become westernized and emancipated. . . . But this conception does not apply to North Sumatra. The rural and urban Batak are linked through a complex communication network in which Western ideas and goods do flow from city to village, but the flow of people and of moral support and vitality of the *adat* (customary law) is primarily in the other direction. The cultural premises and roots of urban Batak life are to be found in village society. . . . Most urban Batak have more meaningful associations with their rural relatives in the highlands than with their non-Batak neighbours in Medan.

Further evidence which could be cited in more detail if space permitted included Butterworth's (1962, p. 262) observation that twenty-seven of his thirty-one informant families of Mixtec Indian migrant settlers from the *municipio* of Tilantongo in the State of Oaxaca lived in adjacent *colonias* in Mexico City near the airport. There is Caplow's (1952) assertion for Latin American cities that:

. . . the relatively high rate of increase of the urban population has had the effect of slowing down the acculturation of in-migrants, by reducing the need for demographic circulation. The slow rate of acculturation, in turn, helps to account for the survival of indigenous culture patterns in close proximity to the metropolis, and the failure of many urban culture traits to diffuse through the economically dependent hinterland.

In addition, there is Harrison's (1967) excellent study of the grouping of migrants in the city of Tripoli in Libya (Fig. 2.3) while, finally, the work of Phillips on the Asima squatter area of Baghdad may be cited. Phillips (1957–58, p. 4l3) found that no less than 78 per cent of the in-migrants in the Asima sample she investigated had originated from the Amara district, a predominantly rural area of poor tenant farming in the south-east of Iraq.

The major issue common to all these case studies (but not explored in them) is whether the traditional and rural characteristics so widely commented on can be expected to fade fairly quickly as migrants become more accultured to city ways. In other words, given the present demographic and migrational circumstances concerning Third World cities, is it still possible to envisage an automatic, oneway adaptation of rural

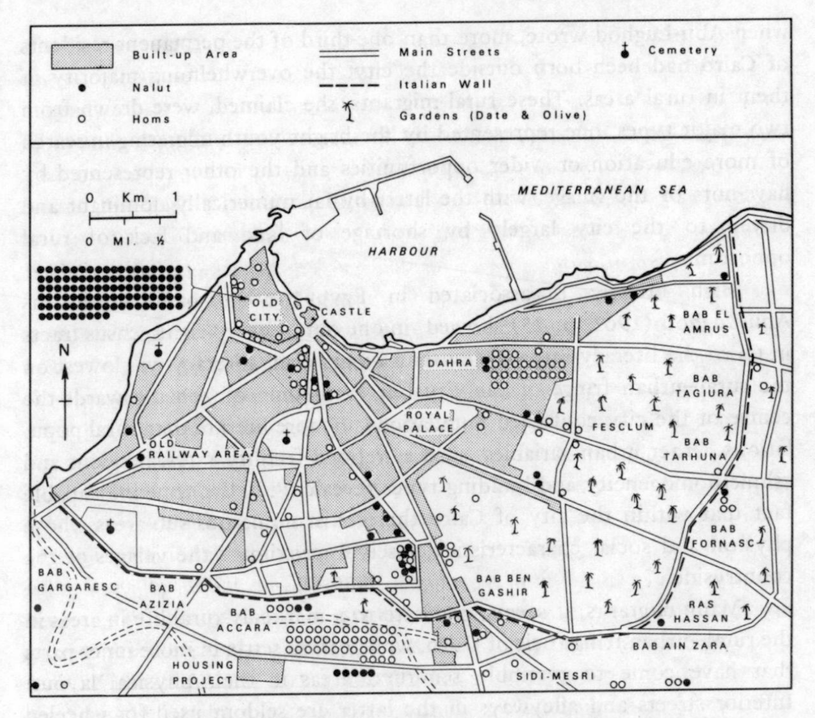

Fig. 2.3 Grouping of migrants in Tripoli, Libya. Each symbol equals one migrant on a sample survey basis, 1963–64 (see Harrison, 1967, for details)

migrants to an absorptive urban culture and to ignore the possibility of feedback and mutual assimilation? Is today's rapid urbanization as perfectly correlated with change, other than the obvious demographic change, as it was at earlier periods when the urbanization process was very much more associated with the presently industrialized countries? Might not Third World cities rather be in process of becoming more rural and traditional in many of their psychological and sociological characteristics, especially within residential zones characterized by heavy in-migration from the countryside, which are often areas of spontaneous settlement?

Unfortunately, very little research has been conceived in these terms so far and therefore evaluation of such issues is not possible here. However, Abu-Lughod (1961) in a perceptive review of migrant adjustment to city life in Cairo has been quite explicit in suggesting that because of the high rate of rural in-migration the culture of Cairo as a whole is not now characterized chiefly by the anonymity, secondary contacts and other classic features of urban life specified by Wirth (1938). In the early 1960s, when Abu-Lughod wrote, more than one-third of the permanent residents of Cairo had been born outside the city, the overwhelming majority of them in rural areas. These rural migrants, she claimed, were drawn from two major types, one represented by the bright youth migrating in search of more education or wider opportunities and the other represented by have-nots of the village, with the latter by far numerically dominant and driven to the city largely by shortage of land and lack of rural opportunity.

High literacy is associated in Egypt with urbanism; yet, as Abu-Lughod (1961, p. 25) showed, in one out of every eight census tracts in Cairo the literacy rate was less than 25 per cent. Literacy was lowest on the rural–urban fringe of the city but even some of zones towards the centre of the city contained populations no more literate than rural populations. Other urban variables, such as refined fertility rates, religious and ethnic homogeneity and building types revealed '. . . the same inescapable fact that within the city of Cairo there exist numerous sub-areas whose physical and social characteristics closely approximate the villages of the countryside'.

Many migrants, it seems, gravitate to a markedly rural life in areas in the rural–urban fringe belt of Cairo, while others settle in more inner parts that have come to resemble semirural areas in their physical layout. Interior streets and alleyways in the latter are seldom used for wheeled traffic; they function not only as pathways but also as meeting places, playgrounds and tethering areas for animals. Often the top floor of a tenement dwelling will be most highly prized because it will be possible to construct there the massive oven which fills one room and characterizes the Egyptian rural house, thus not only making it possible to bake bread daily but also providing a warm bed for the winter for the family on top of the oven.

In employment, while in large-scale factories the mixing of diverse people undoubtedly occurs, the overwhelming majority of industrial and commercial enterprises in Cairo are very small, employing only a few persons, often within the family. Moreover, it is common for new migrants to be guided into urban jobs in the same concerns as those from their villages who have migrated earlier. All in all, '. . . migrants to Cairo are active creators of a variety of social institutions whose major function is to protect migrants from the shock of *anomie*', and '. . . while there may be a wide gap between the least-sophisticated villager and the most-sophisticated urbanite, there is certainly no indication that migrants necessarily pass from one pole to the other' (*ibid.*, pp. 31–2). There is, in fact, a third type, that of the 'traditional urbanite', Abu-Lughod (1969) asserts, existing as a separate social dimension and not as an intermediate point along a rural–urban continuum, which must be taken into account in research into the urbanization process in the developing countries if the consequences of contemporary changes are to be predicted as part of a scientific approach towards the physical planning of urban areas. In Cairo today, this third type probably accounts for more than half the city's population.

These findings raise important issues of an ecological nature which are directly relevant to the planning of housing provision. If what might be called social engineering is to be a goal of physical planning for the future Third World city, and if it is suspected that the volume of rural–urban migration might be fundamentally altering the psychological and socio-economic character of such cities, the question arises as to whether planned residential dispersion may be required in order to stimulate the absorption of in-migrants into the 'urban' and 'modern' sector of the socio-economic system of the city. If the normal Western-oriented sociological approach towards urban absorption is followed – that residential dispersion is a vital aspect of the incorporation of recent migrants into the dominant social system of the city – then spatial planning to achieve social goals in the housing of rural migrants in the cities must assume a more important role in programmes of national economic development than is now the rule. Among other considerations, this has implications for sites-and-services schemes of housing provision where these are conceived as *in situ* improvements for existing spontaneous settlements which will be further discussed in chapter 6.

In conclusion, in this general context it is worth emphasizing that housing provision in Third World cities in general, and the problems posed by the growth of spontaneous settlements in particular, should not be seen solely within the traditional town-planning framework of the benefits stemming from ease of circulation, the achievement of assemblages of land uses most closely approaching the optimum, and of such considerations as the health, moral, political and other possible hazards of overcrowded conditions. It is a matter rather of the appreciation of a whole range of possible benefits of improved housing provision which do not at first sight appear to be directly economic or of direct relevance to national economic planning. In this context, it is worth reiterating Catherine Bauer Wurster's (1956, p. 60) injunction, which aptly summarizes much of the argument advanced in the latter part of this chapter, that 'extremely bad housing conditions may have a harmful effect not only on welfare and working efficiency *per se* but also in the failure to provide adequate incentives for constructive social adaptation or satisfactory new values to replace traditional goals'.

3

Confusion, apathy and symbolic schemes

'And what do the vegetarians propose to do here?'
'Apart from the distribution of free literature – translated of course into French – we plan to open a centre of vegetarian cooking in the heart of the capital.'
'The heart of the capital is a shanty town.'

Graham Greene
The Comedians

'Demolition Starts 9 a.m.', to quote a headline from the *Philippine Herald* of 3 May 1968. In too many Third World cities this seems to be the only answer to the problems posed by the rapid growth of spontaneous settlements in recent years. In this particular case, the newspaper was reporting official plans to deal with squatter huts in the Memorial Park of Quezon City, an urban area contiguous with Manila. Demolition teams from the City Engineering Office, the Parks and Wildlife Office, the city's Department of Public Services and the Police Department were to meet at the Quezon City Hall before proceeding to the target area. Mayor Amoranto told the *Philippine Herald* that only a restraining order from higher authorities could prevent the demolition operation. He himself had ordered the teams not to entertain requests from squatters to spare their homes; to be fair to the squatters, however, he had also urgently asked President Marcos for a relocation site.

A few days later the newspaper was carrying a report that a group of squatters was seeking a court injunction to prevent the demolition work. The squatters were claiming that the Mayor had no right to order the operation since the Quezon Memorial Park was not city property; they said its ownership was disputed by three leading Filipino families, and that one family had already enclosed with barbed wire what it considered to be its private property and was allowing the building of huts within this area for monthly fees. It was also reported that the squatters were planning to come out with full-page advertisements in all the metropolitan dailies calling the attention of the President to the consequences that would result from the demolition. In another move, the President of the Federation of Barrios and Civic Organizations ('to which all civic organizations at the Park are affiliated', stated the *Philippine Herald* of 8 May 1968) sent a telegram to President Marcos asking for postponement of the demolition at least until an alternative site could be developed.

Later the same day, President Marcos set aside 50 hectares of the San Pedro Tunasan estate in Laguna province for the resettlement of squatter families evicted from the Quezon Memorial Park. The President also directed his Defence Secretary to send a construction battalion to complete road access to the new site within one week; the Budget Commissioner to release the necessary funds immediately; the General Manager of the Water Authority to install artesian wells within 48 hours; and the army to provide military vehicles to carry the squatters to their new site.

Confusion

This kind of confused approach toward the growth of spontaneous settlements is unfortunately all too typical. One of the most notorious examples, again from the Philippines, concerns the eviction of squatters from the Intramuros area of Manila in 1963. Intramuros was the original fortress core of the colonial city which the Spaniards founded in the late sixteenth century. An area of churches, convents, large Spanish-style municipal buildings and narrow cobblestone streets, it stood virtually unchanged behind massive walls until the Second World War, but during the American reoccupation of Manila, because of its fortress characteristics, almost the whole of Intramuros had to be razed to the ground in order to expel the Japanese. The Manila urban area in general was also devastated, four-fifths of its buildings being either destroyed or damaged.

Immediately after the war, an influx of people into Manila of previously unknown proportions began, one which has, if anything, accelerated in more recent years. The result has been a massive development of spontaneous settlements, in the initial phase on central sites levelled in the fighting (Fig. 3.1). The biggest concentration of all grew up in Tondo, to the north of the Pasig River, because of job opportunities for labourers in the North Harbour and also because of the existence of the Divisoria and other markets in the area which provided work for vendors. In Tondo, not only were the cleared sites quickly taken up but substantial settlements also developed along the foreshore. Most of Intramuros, which is just across the Pasig River from the central business district, was also occupied very rapidly. In 1963 it was estimated that there were 22 100 persons in the area (Juppenlatz, 1970, p. 100). At that date Manila had an estimated 282 730 squatters compared with 23 000 in 1946 and 98 000 in 1956. This grim picture has since deteriorated even further, as Fig. 3.2 indicates. An official survey carried out in March 1968 revealed that there were 767 112 persons living as squatters (*ibid.*, p. 99), while a later report (Poethig, 1971, p. 122) has it that by 1971 the number of squatters had reached almost 30 per cent of Manila's total population of about 3.7 million.

In August 1963 the Manila Court of First Instance handed down a decision that in order to effect an abatement of public nuisance, squatters in the city could be required to vacate their premises (Dwyer, 1964, pp. 145–6). This decision, based on a provision in the city charter, circumvented a previous court injunction against the eviction of squatters which had prevented action by the city authorities. In December, following the failure of the squatters to vacate their premises voluntarily, the city authorities undertook a large-scale eviction operation within the walls of

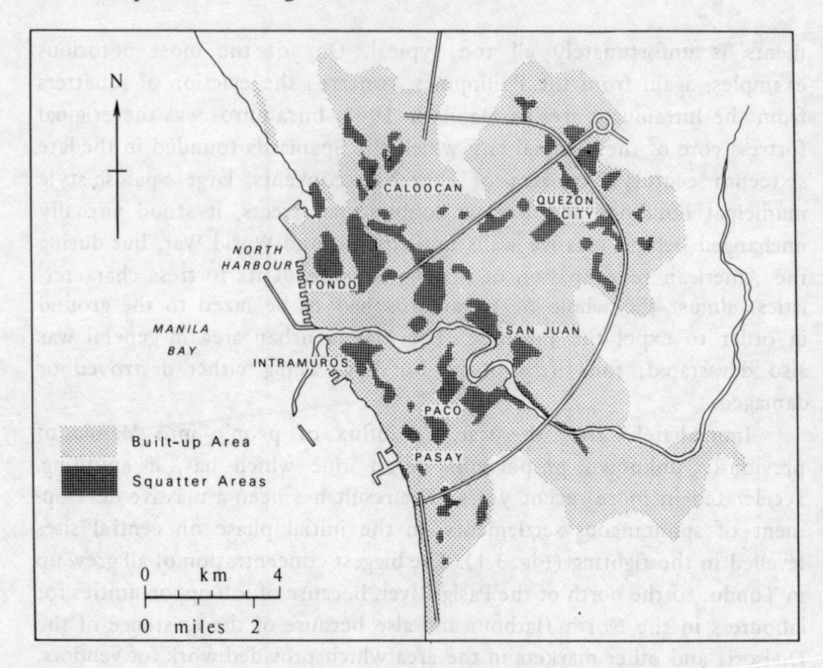

Fig. 3.1 Location of spontaneous settlements in Manila (Juppenlatz, 1970, p. 98)

Intramuros and also in the Tondo and North Harbour areas. Within two weeks, 2 877 shacks were demolished in Intramuros and some 11 000 squatters moved to Sapang Palay, a small municipality of about 600 persons in Bulacan Province, some 27 km (17 miles) from Manila. The squatter areas were completely razed by fire in accordance with previously announced plans for the restoration of the ancient Spanish walls, the repaving of the streets and the transformation of Intramuros into a national cultural centre through the construction of a museum, a city university, an open amphitheatre, an art gallery, an auditorium and a convention hall.

Trucks carrying the squatters from Manila to Sapang Palay at first were turned back at the boundaries of several neighbouring local government units, including the municipalities of Makati, Mandaluyong and Caloocan in Rizal Province and Quezon City, on the grounds that some of the squatters might escape and try to settle in those areas. At Sapang Palay, the *Manila Chronicle* (9 December 1963) commented: 'There seemed to be no planning at all in the allocation of sites for squatters' new

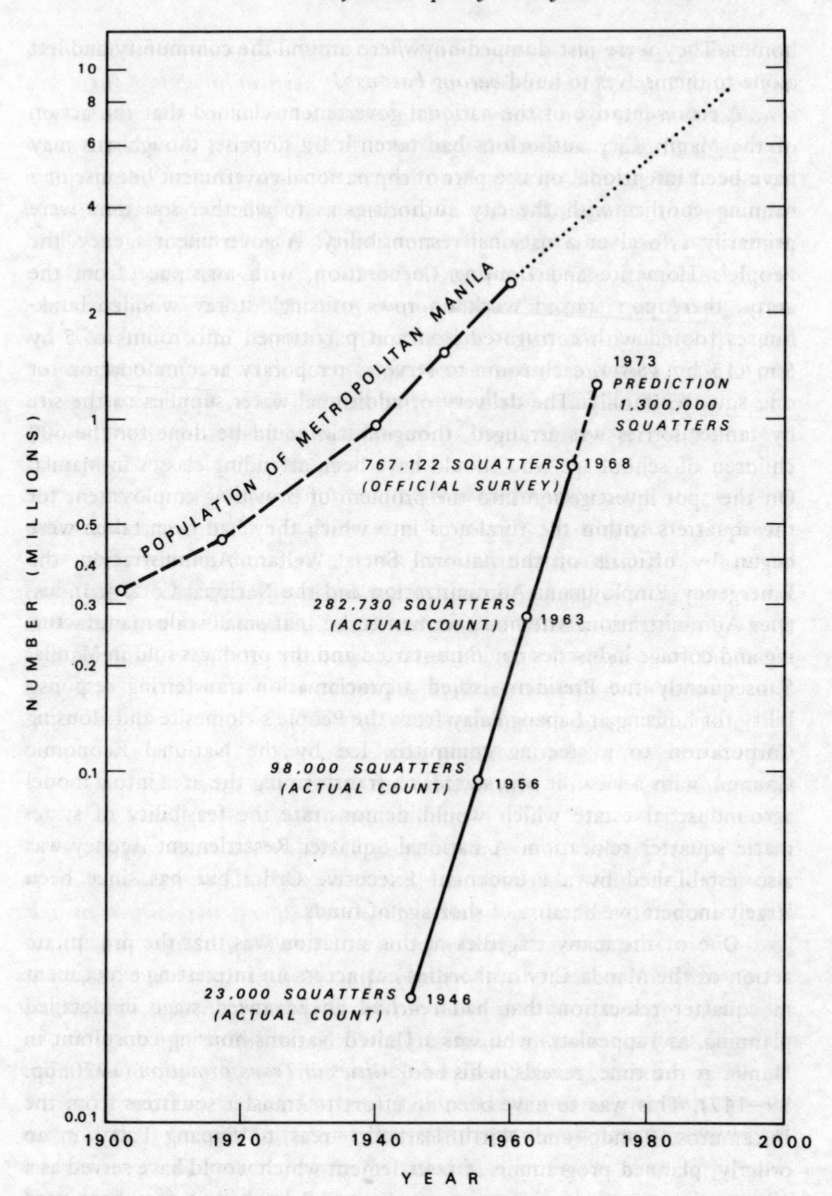

Fig. 3.2 Total population and number of persons in spontaneous settlements in metropolitan Manila (Juppenlatz, 1970, p. 101)

homes. They were just dumped anywhere around the community and left alone to themselves to build *barong-barongs*.'

A representative of the national government claimed that the action of the Manila City authorities had taken it by surprise, though this may have been intentional on the part of the national government because of a running conflict with the city authorities as to whether squatters were primarily a local or a national responsibility. A government agency, the People's Homesite and Housing Corporation, with assistance from the army, thereupon started work on rows of single-storey wooden bunk-houses roofed with corrugated iron and partitioned into rooms of 5 by 5 m (15 by 15 ft), each room to serve as temporary accommodation for one squatter family. The delivery of additional water supplies to the site by tanker lorries was arranged, though little could be done for the 600 children of school age who should have been attending classes in Manila. On the spot investigation into the problem of providing employment for the squatters within the rural area into which they had been taken were begun by officials of the national Social Welfare Administration, the Emergency Employment Administration and the National Cottage Industries Administration. The hope seemed to be that small-scale manufacturing and cottage industries could be started and the products sold in Manila. Subsequently the President issued a proclamation transferring responsibility for housing at Sapang Palay from the People's Homesite and Housing Corporation to a steering committee led by the National Economic Council, with a view, it was stated, to transforming the area into a model agro-industrial estate which would demonstrate the feasibility of systematic squatter relocation. A national Squatter Resettlement Agency was also established by a Presidential Executive Order but has since been largely inoperative because of shortage of funds.

One of the many tragedies of this situation was that the precipitate action of the Manila City authorities cut across an interesting experiment in squatter relocation that had reached an advanced stage in detailed planning, as Juppenlatz, who was a United Nations housing consultant in Manila at the time, reveals in his book *Cities in Transformation* (1970, pp. 89–147). This was to have been an effort to transfer squatters from the Intramuros, Tondo and North Harbour areas to Sapang Palay in an orderly, planned programme of resettlement which would have served as a pilot project for evaluation purposes. Sapang Palay had, in fact, been used once before for squatter relocation without much success. Flash-floods in 1959 had made homeless many squatters in the Manila area who had built their homes in dry stream beds, and as an emergency operation official funds had been made available to the People's Homesite and Housing Corporation, the principal public housing body in the Philippines, for the purchase of 625 hectares (1 500 acres) at Sapang Palay for relocation purposes. The government made no additional funds available for the proper physical development of the site, however, and this proved to be well outside the limited financial means of the People's Homesite and Housing Corporation. Further, not only was there practically no work available in the predominantly rural area in which Sapang Palay is located but local soil conditions made small-scale subsistence agriculture difficult. The result, predictably, was a general exodus of the relocated squatters from the site after a few months, and by the end of 1962 fewer than 600 families remained.

The new plan was the brainchild of a Presidential Slum Clearance Committee which had been established in 1950 to find sites suitable for relocating squatters moved from the more central areas of Manila. As a result of the deliberations of this Committee, a technical working group was established early in 1963 with the aim of planning another attempt at removing squatters to Sapang Palay. As Juppenlatz (1970, p. 117) points out, one of the most severe problems was finance, for although at the time of its formation in 1947 the People's Homesite and Housing Corporation had been officially charged with dealing with urban slums and providing low-cost housing, only token financial appropriations had ever been provided by the government. For its part, the Presidential Slum Clearance Committee had been given funds only for the purchase of land and not for the physical development of the sites it acquired. The solution arrived at was an attempt to distribute the relocation costs involved through all relevant government departments, but this was inevitably a clumsy compromise involving laborious consultation with thirteen departments and official agencies and, in the eventual plan, provision for the presence of their representatives on the relocation site, each with a field office and responsibility for part of the overall action programme.

The project as a whole involved first the identification of those areas of spontaneous settlement in Manila where action was most urgent, a careful survey of the number of families involved and their income levels and the preparation of educational programmes to be carried out among the families prior to their relocation. Meanwhile, the sites for housing were to be marked out at Sapang Palay, water and electric power supplied, schools, markets, health centres and administrative offices built and preparations made for the establishment of a small industrial estate. The residential sites were to be planned on the basis of core housing, that is, the erection of simple wooden frame housing, with *sawali* (woven bamboo) walls, a bamboo slatted floor and aluminium sheet roofing, which could later be extended by the residents themselves. It was hoped that the new residents would be able to repay the People's Homesite and Housing Corporation by instalments for the land and the value of the construction materials as their local economy developed.

The planned basis of the economy was to be cooperative agriculture and cottage industries. Eighty hectares (200 acres) of the site were to be set aside for irrigated ricefields on a cooperative basis; encouragement was also to be given to families to engage in fruit and vegetable gardening and poultry and pig raising. 'The income which each family could derive from the programme would be directly proportional to the personal efforts of the family members involved, and to the extent to which the marketing facilities were involved', states Juppenlatz (1970, p. 121).

> It was proposed that the families themselves should constitute the labour force required to build the new community, with the greater part of the pay for their labour taking the form of a ration of food from the United Nations World Food Programme donations. This, with a small cash payment, would continue until their own home-subsistence programme became effective.

In the longer run it was expected that small-scale industries, largely of the cottage type, could be established, including shoemaking, tailoring, the hand-weaving of abaca fibre grown locally and coconut matting, and furniture making. In all, it was an ambitious scheme but one which it is very doubtful could have succeeded, if only because of the uncertainties surrounding its initial financing, the multiplicity of departments and agencies called on to participate, the somewhat doubtful economic base which it was proposed to create for the settlers, and the complicated cooperative structure which underpinned the whole project. Practically overnight, however, through the City of Manila's clearances the Sapang Palay scheme, which for all its faults was arguably the best prepared approach to date to the problem of spontaneous settlement in Manila, was transformed, as Juppenlatz (1970, p. 126) puts it, into 'a local Mayor-made emergency, involving 25 000 near-destitute people'.

Although a great deal of emergency reception work was accomplished by various government departments, individual officials and voluntary agencies at Sapang Palay both during and immediately after the forced mass relocations (and, indeed, as Juppenlatz (1970, p. 135) states, 'it is much to the credit of the emergency team that none of the members of the relocated families died from illness, epidemics, or exposure, as was the case in the former transfer of squatters in 1960'), it has not subsequently proved possible either to carry out the ambitious agricultural projects originally planned or to attract anything like a sufficient amount of industry to the area. The result has been that well over half the families relocated have since moved out of Sapang Palay, presumably back into Manila, and that, to quote a Special Committee of the National Housing Council, 'those who remain are trying to eke out a miserable life, with able-bodied males working in Metropolitan Manila and going home on weekends. Others have built ghost houses for speculative purposes, with no real intentions of ever occupying them' (Philippines: Nat. Housing Council, 1969, p. 34). And all this, not surprisingly, has occurred despite the symbolic establishment in 1966 of a national Central Institute for the Training and Relocation of Urban Squatters based at Sapang Palay and charged with divizing solutions to the problem of spontaneous settlement and providing for training, rehabilitation and relocation.

Apathy

In general, the best that can be said for most official policies towards problems of spontaneous settlement in the developing countries is that they are characterized by a neglect that is usually benign but exceptionally may not be, according to local circumstances at any particular time. The Sapang Palay episode is only one of several examples of irrational outbursts of official activity which have resulted in disaster for a substantial number of poor families. Others are not hard to find. Local government officials in Rio de Janeiro have repeatedly descended on individual *favelas* in order to eradicate them and remove their occupants to the edge of the city. In October 1970 the author saw the *Favela do Catacumbas* being removed from one of the more central areas while a new *favela* was openly in process of formation only a few hundred yards away. This was only one of the latest of a long line of similar illogical actions, perhaps the best known being the mass removal of 30 000 *favelados* to the Vila Kennedy relocation site in the early 1960s, a housing project financed in large part with United States aid funds. Vila Kennedy was later rightly characterized as a 'foreign aid flop' by the *Wall Street Journal* (20 March 1967), which speculated that 'it's a safe bet that President Johnson won't be taken here when he visits South America'. Located 33 km (21 miles) west of Rio de Janeiro, there were no industrial jobs for miles around, and it cost one-third of the daily income of the poorest *favelados* even to purchase a round-trip bus ticket into the city.

Another case which may be cited is that of Baghdad where, after the overthrow of Premier Qasim in 1963, a concerted effort was made to round up squatters and relocate them at Madinat al-Thawra on the north-east edge of the city (Gulick, 1967, p. 252). Nine years earlier in the same city, when floods drove squatters from peripheral camps to seek protection inside the bund, they had been forcibly moved back after the flood waters receded.

In Salvador, as elsewhere in Latin America, battles with the police have regularly occurred during squatter invasions, while in the *bairro* of Maralhina invaders of private land were repelled by a private army of 200 men organized by the landowner. Several people were killed in the latter incident. As Pendrell (1968, p. 164) has reported, once installed in spontaneous settlements, an overwhelming proportion of Salvador's squatters reject the idea of relocation to official projects. One reason for this is the widely publicized dissatisfaction of those squatters in Rio de Janeiro who have previously been relocated to 'low cost' *vilas* such as Vila Kennedy.

Several governments have gone even further than the local use of police and have sought to return spontaneous settlers from the urban areas to the countryside, exercises which in the reality of economic opportunities in the Third World's rural areas seem particularly futile. In Niger, for example, all unemployed urban youths were required by law in 1962 either to perform some service or to return to the countryside. As might be expected, this law has since proved singularly ineffectual (Hance, 1970, p. 278). Similar measures have been promulgated in Zaire, Kenya and Tanzania in recent years; Tanzania has even tried imposing travel restrictions to Dar es Salaam. In Djakarta, officials faced with dealing with a population in spontaneous settlements which now exceeds 0.75 million, have started to round up those without any regular shelter and to send them to special rehabilitation camps on the outskirts of the city (Poethig, 1971, p. 122). At these *banti-sozial*, as the camps are called, families found suitable for training are sent to rural resettlement areas in Sumatra and Borneo. So far, as with previous Indonesian schemes of transmigration to the outer islands, the number of migrants has not been large; in fact, by one means or another many of those officially scheduled for resettlement never reach their destination and are soon back on Djakarta's streets.

Generally, however, energetic approaches to the problem such as these, misconceived though they may be, are not characteristic of governments and urban authorities in the Third World. Most are largely apathetic, and there are several reasons for this. In the first place, many authorities, it seems, regard themselves as politically powerless to affect the course of events once spontaneous settlements have become established. In many cities spontaneous settlers are not only acknowledged to be effectively organized, if only for the purposes of seizing land and subsequently preserving and improving their position, but are also feared for their revolutionary potential. Recent official moves to relocate squatters from the Tondo area of Manila, for example, have met with tightly organized local opposition. The squatters have united to press their interest in the land and a Council of Tondo Foreshoreland Community Organization has been formed to represent about seventy individual squatter groups in their confrontation with the authorities (Poethig, 1971, p. 123).

Squatter organizations in Latin America are perhaps more widely known. Mangin (1967*a*) has remarked that the degree of organization by *favela* associations in Rio de Janeiro is striking: 'They have organized everything from private water systems, markets, labour division, and groups to raise money to buy the land on which they live, to Carnival dance groups essential to the famous Rio festival' (p. 70). In Lima and Rio de Janeiro, he comments, the national political parties figure somewhat in squatter settlement politics, while in a few cases trade unions have been involved, for example in the development of a squatter area in Arequipa for members of a graphic arts union and one in Chimbote for steel workers.

Generally, however, the fear of squatter organizations which is frequently displayed by governments and urban administrations is misplaced, for the vast majority of such organizations have strictly local objectives related to their own settlements rather than ambitions towards revolution or even influencing the course of politics at a national level. Laquian's (1964) work on the Isla de Kokomo squatter settlement in Manila has provided a detailed case study which confirms this assessment. The Isla de Kokomo settlement grew up on the edge of Manila shortly after the Second World War as a cramped community of 132 families living in fifty-eight huts packed together on less than 1 hectare (2 acres) of tidal land. A rich widow owned the land, which had always been largely unproductive. She was only too pleased to encourage huts and collect monthly fees for each through an intermediary. As more and more families crowded in, the rents were progressively raised, but even so sharing a wooden hut in the settlement was much cheaper than occupying a room or cubicle in the tenements of the central part of the city.

In the Laquian survey one head of household from each house was interviewed. Typically, only fourteen of the respondents considered themselves skilled. These might be jeepney* drivers, electricians, plumbers or similar workpeople. The remainder did 'odd jobs' or worked as 'extra hands'; eight of them admitted to being jobless, while fourteen did not say what their incomes were because 'I have no fixed source of income'. In all, the families of the heads of household interviewed contained 151 adults, but only fifty-eight, or just over one-third, were employed.

Clearly, Isla de Kokomo is a poor, crowded community; it is also deficient in every public amenity. Its main behavioural characteristics, states Laquian, are a tight unity in face of the outside world and a surprising degree of ignorance of city, let alone national, politics. In part this introspection may be due to the attitude of more fortunate people living nearby: to them Isla de Kokomo is a tough and troublesome place which should be avoided. However, it may also be theorized, as Laquian claims, that rural dwellers like the residents of the Isla de Kokomo moving to an urban setting carry with them values of community solidarity. Some are bound by kinship ties; in addition, most of the Isla de Kokomo community are from the Visayas and share common provincial origins.

The survey was carried out at a time of some political activity. The 1963 elections were then only eleven months away and campaigning starts early in the Philippines. Most of the issues and the personalities involved had already been given ample attention by the mass media, yet twenty out of the fifty-eight respondents could not name even one of the sixteen candidates running for senator in the national elections. Perhaps even more significantly, thirty-six of the respondents were unable to name one candidate running for local councillor. The inhabitants of Isla de Kokomo were, nevertheless, sharply aware of political matters directly concerning themselves. Many of the young men were honorary policemen or confidential agents of the incumbent mayor; community benefits had also been obtained from him, such as the building of catwalks across the tidal land. Forty of the fifty-eight respondents were therefore solid in their support for the mayor, despite the fact that the national party to which he belonged had lately disowned his candidacy.

Further evidence which may be cited comes from a survey carried out in the *favelas* of Rio de Janeiro in 1961 (Bonilla, 1970, pp. 78–81), which showed that less than one-fifth of the inhabitants had discussed politics heatedly with a friend over the previous six months and that only 17 per

* Jeeps converted for public transport.

cent had attended a party meeting: this despite the fact that more than half of those interviewed stated that general living conditions had become worse during the past five years. The ambitions of the members of squatter organizations, far from being revolutionary, are, as Mangin (1967*a*, pp. 84–5) puts it:

> '. . . very similar to the beliefs of the operator of a small business in nineteenth-century England or the United States. These can be summed up in the familiar and accepted maxims: Work hard, save your money, trust only family members (and them not too much), outwit the state, vote conservatively if possible, but always in your own economic self-interest; educate your children for their future and as old age insurance for yourself.

Though squatter associations may be characterized as generally politically introspective, there are, nevertheless, usually well-formed links of mutual benefit with local politicians, as the Isla de Kokomo example shows; there may, exceptionally, even be a national association to protect the interests of squatters, as in Peru. The political interest group factor thus plays a large part in most urban planning calculations affecting spontaneous settlements. But even where this is minimal, prospects of action may be remote for a variety of other reasons. For instance, it is difficult to formulate coherent development strategies of any kind for many Third World metropolitan areas because of their subdivision into local government and other administrative units usually characterized by jealous guardianship of their own particular sectional interests. This is not a problem peculiar to the Third World. It has not yet been solved even in the cities of the economically advanced nations but, in general, the Third World is at a much more primitive stage in grappling with it. The Philippine Bureau of Census and Statistics defines metropolitan Manila as being composed of four cities and four towns (the chartered cities of Manila, Caloocan, Quezon and Pasay and the towns of San Juan, Manduyong, Makati and Paranaque), but today even these eight administrative units by no means cover the urban area as a whole. The National Planning Commission therefore includes no less than eleven more towns in its definition, while the National Waterworks and Sewage Authority omits two of the Planning Commission's towns but includes two others (Viloria, 1971, p. 137).

In all, therefore, no less than twenty-one local government units have been recognized by one section of the national administration or another as belonging to contempory metropolitan Manila; and many of these units, it should be added, are characterized by an almost continuous display of antagonistic attitudes towards their neighbours. It is indeed a remarkable experience on driving into central Manila to encounter a large warning sign stating 'You Are Now Leaving Pasay City', exactly as if one was crossing the Iron Curtain.

In India, the Calcutta Metropolitan Planning Organization has no mandate for areas outside West Bengal, yet in regional terms, especially in respect of in-migration, it has been clear for many years that Calcutta's problems hinge upon developments in the four-state area of eastern India comprised by West Bengal, Bihar, Assam and Orissa. Caracas, to take an example from South America, has spread from its original site in what is now the Department of Liberatador in the Federal District eastwards along its valley into the Sucre District of Miranda State. Though one general plan does now exist for the whole urban area, its implementation has been almost paralysed through these administrative divisions. Further confusion arises from the fact that because Caracas is the capital the national ministries also conduct operations within the city. To the two areal divisions are therefore added three governmental levels of administration: national, departmental or state, and municipal (Franco, 1971, p. 35). Very rarely, then, are pressing problems such as the spread of spontaneous settlements able to be considered in their totality.

Furthermore, even within the limitations of planning in this respect, it is true to say that few cities have organized local financial arrangements in such a way as to maximize housing development. A feature of most Third World cities is the existence of relatively large tracts of unoccupied or under-utilized urban land obviously being held for speculative purposes. In the inflationary conditions that have characterized many Third World countries urban land has proved one of the best investments, and often high rates of return have been possible for speculators through failure to levy and collect realistic property taxes in such a manner as to penalize the holding of idle land. High rates of tax delinquency are also common: 50 to 60 per cent in Naga City in the Philippines, for example (Romani and Thomas, 1954, p. 105). Where landowning interests predominate in both national and local politics there are few grounds for expecting such situations to be fundamentally reversed. It is often said that rural land reform is a necessity for many parts of the Third World but what is at least as urgently needed is urban land reform.

In addition, physical planning has too often become simply one of the many playthings of politics in the Third World. This is true in at least two important senses. One is that in many cases physical planning organizations form part of the general system of dispensation of patronage by successful politicians so common in developing countries. This largely accounts for the rapidity with which planning organizations are closed down and new ones founded or, where this does not happen, the regularity with which senior staff are replaced in many agencies. In the Philippines, for example, an Urban Planning Commission was created in 1946 to prepare general plans for the zoning and subdivision of urban areas. With the inauguration of a new national administration, the Commission was supplemented in 1947 with a Real Property Board to deal with problems involving real estate in connection with the planning of Manila. Neither body had any practical effect. A Capital City Planning Commission was created in 1948 and charged with the preparation and execution of a master plan for a new national capital at Quezon City. The plan was completed in 1949 but has not yet been translated into reality.

With a change of government in 1949, the Capital City Planning Commission, the Real Property Board and the Urban Planning Commission were abolished and their powers transferred to an agency within the Office of the President known as the National Planning Commission. A master plan for Manila was completed by this Commission in 1954. The Municipal Board of Manila conducted public hearings on the plan but as late as 1963 had failed to enact new zoning ordinances for the city. Meanwhile the Local Autonomy Law of 1959 empowered local authority boards and city councils to adopt their own zoning regulations and, though the National Planning Commission might be consulted, it reserved the final decision for the local authorities to make (Dwyer, 1964, pp. 168–9). Such a case history could be multiplied at least twentyfold from cities elsewhere in the Third World, as could the following assessment by Manalad-Santiago (1969, pp. 223–4) of the multiplicity of agencies currently involved in housing provision in the Philippines:

> One visiting housing expert to the Philippines remarked that there is a tendency in developing countries generally to create new agencies to solve old problems. The Philippines is no exception to this. In fact the Philippines is one country whose governmental machinery is characterized by the presence of a number of agencies usually performing the same or overlapping functions. In other cases, there are numerous organizations discharging related functions which if concentrated in one or a lesser number of agencies could be performed much more effectively.
>
> At present the administrative bodies in operation performing housing and other related activities can be placed conveniently into four major

groups. To the first group belongs those which help formulate housing policies and programs namely, the National Economic Council (NEC) the top economic planning body in the country which prepares economic and social development programs; the Presidential Economic Staff (PES) which insures consistency between policy formulation and policy implementation; the National Planning Commission (NPC) which is the central physical planning body in the Philippines in charge of the preparation of general plans, zoning, subdivision and building regulations; and the Presidential Assistant on Housing and Resettlement Agency (PAHRA) which acts as a coordinating body among the various agencies concerned with housing, and also makes proposals in regard to policy. Another major group consists of those agencies which provide housing or housing lots or both. These agencies are the People's Homesite and Housing Corporation (PHHC) whose primary objective is to provide decent housing for those who are unable to do so, homes at low cost to replace those which should be eliminated for hygienic or other reasons, and community and institutional houses for destitute individuals and families; the local government units which can resell to their residents home-sites acquired by them in their respective jurisdictions; the Land Authority which provides housing and other accommodations for settlers in rural areas upon their arrival in new settlements; and the Bureau of Lands which is engaged in subdividing and allocating public lands in or near urban areas for sale as residential lots. A third group is composed of agencies which finance home-building to which belong the Government Service Insurance System (GSIS), which grants loans to its members for home construction and to private parties for subdivision development and construction of low cost houses thereon; the Social Security System (SSS) which gives housing loans to its members for home construction and also undertakes its own housing projects; and the Development Bank of the Philippines (DBP) which grants loans to private homebuilders and local governments for the purchase of landed estates and their resale after subdivision. Also included are the Home Financing Commission (HFC) which operates a mortgage insurance program for individual and developmental loans and the Philippine National Cooperative Bank which is the organization authorized to issue cooperative housing loans. Finally, there is a fourth group which consists of those engaged in activities affecting housing among which are the Central Institute for the Training and Relocation of Urban Squatters (CITRUS) responsible for the promotion of economic sufficiency and social stability of former urban squatters, the National Waterworks and

Sewerage Authority (NAWASA) charged with the maintenance and operation of the waterworks system of the country, the National Power Corporation which provides electricity and electrical services to homes and industries, and the local government units which provide the necessary municipal services indispensable to safe and comfortable living.

It would appear from the above organizational description that housing and its various aspects are well taken care of, and that whatever housing problems exist at present can be easily solved with the combined efforts of the abovementioned administrative bodies. This is not the case, however, as shown by the housing shortage which worsens with the increasing backlog in actual construction as compared to estimated needs, and the unabated formation of slums and squatter areas. Many attribute these to the inefficiency of the various organizations to perform their functions effectively. A visiting housing expert stated that the important elements or agencies for the administration and operation of any kind of Housing and Urban Development Program in the Philippines are already existing but they are, however, working independently instead of together, have made no policy declarations, and have insufficient funds to carry out the functions with which they are charged under the various laws. In a recent document submitted to President Ferdinand Marcos on January 7, 1969, one of the basic problems of the housing program which was recognized was the fact that the government institutions charged with housing functions are in confusion, overlapping in jurisdiction, and do not perform many vital aspects of their functions and powers. The said document also called attention to the absence of any cabinet department responsible for coordinated national housing and urban development program and policies of the government, and to the absence of any central financing agency for housing and urban development.

In the second sense in which physical planning has become the plaything of politics in many developing countries lies much of the explanation of its almost total dedication to what might be called 'paper planning'. Many Third World cities now have their master plans, but these are largely static land use exercises, influenced to an undue degree by the planning experience of the more developed nations of the West, and especially by British practice; indeed it has by no means been uncommon for the preparation of such plans to be contracted out to consultants from Western nations and even completed in part in the West by persons who possess but the briefest acquaintanceship with the communities whose futures the plans concern. As Kindleberger (1952) has stated of World Bank reports in general, all too often 'the missions bring to the underdeveloped country a notion of what a developed country is like. They observe the underdeveloped country. They subtract the latter from the former. The difference is a programme.' In these circumstances it is doubly unfortunate that, largely because of their own elitist origins, as well as because of the location in the West rather than in the developing countries of all the town planning training institutions of high prestige, local planners do tend very much to conform to the following stereotype by a (characteristically unnamed) United Nations 'expert' for one Asian country (quoted in Atkinson, 1960, pp. 101–2):

> The majority of town planners and builders I met have been trained in England or America and had come back home filled with the security attached to the acquisition of occidental science. Now, they were about to be faced with paradoxical problems: where the countries of Europe and America backed up by a great number of architects and engineers have elaborately evolved their own techniques, the local town engineers on returning home must meet human problems of a much wider scope, and that with scanty technical means.
>
> Their being utterly at a loss is understandable. They would in fact have all needed at once an extremely wide outlook to cope with the mass of problems and a remarkable liberty of technical conception to make up for the deficiency of means. Such attainments are but rarely achieved in the West where the selection is nevertheless more involved.
>
> And so what could be expected happened: except for some rare exceptions – corresponding to the average percentage of superior beings in any country – the majority of town planners or engineers merely carried out the teaching acquired in the West without either discrimination or adaptation to the new economic and social conditions. . . . The faculties of town planners who had to deal with one of the world's densest populations were beclouded by the density standards of Stevenage New Town.

As a result, master plans for Third World cities are often excessively rigid and antiseptic in concept. Most fail to give due weight to the growing significance of spontaneous settlement within the urban form or, where they do, tend to look forward to a millennium where all squatter huts will be eliminated and replaced by regularly laid out housing in the image of the Western city, without specifying the immediate rungs on this particular ladder to urban heaven. In particular, analysis of the financial aspects of such strategies is usually conspicuous by its absence. To make this criticism is not to allocate total responsibility to the planners involved. Because of the patronage relationship of urban planning to politics in many developing countries, and particularly because of the dominance of landowning interests in politics, the political prospects of decisive action in favour of the community as a whole on any significant scale are generally bleak. Yet, paradoxically, there is a political need to delineate an image, the blueprint for the rosy urban future which is, it seems, always just about to be born: hence 'paper planning', which is idealistic in concept and merely symbolic in execution, and a public image of physical planning as an exercise which is quite unrelated to the realities of everyday life as Asok Mitra (1968, pp. 31–2) has perceptively pointed out in respect of India:

> In the popular mind, town planning has come to be strangely associated with *bhavans*, show-pieces, expensive plate glass, steel, concrete, aluminium, decorative dust-gathering useless louvres and frills . . . streets too wide as in Chandigarh for any earthly use, and parks which cannot be enjoyed, it being too dangerous to cross over to them. Town planning thus grows into a mystique too deep for the citizen who in his turn loses interest. The gulf between planner and beneficiary widens, favouring the former's alliance with the source of power and money.

In these circumstances, spontaneous settlement, being unplanned, unpretentious and apparently chaotic, is usually either totally neglected in the delineation of the image of the future or else condemned.

One example of such ineffectual 'master planning' is that for Delhi, which has been roundly criticized by Ewing (1969) in an important review. In the first place the Plan, as amended in 1967, is almost impossible to implement in a coherent manner because it involves an urbanized area which covers not only Delhi Union Territory but also parts of the adjacent States of Haryana and Uttar Pradesh, which are not subject to any common planning authority. Further it is not clear who is responsible for implementing the Plan. The proposals are not linked to specific agencies, though the Delhi Development Authority has general responsibility for administering the area.

Specific objectives of the Plan are also open to criticism. Ewing (1969) seriously questions the stated policy towards Old Delhi, which is to remove 'noxious industries and village-like trades' and to induce higher-income people to move out through providing middle- and upper-class housing elsewhere. 'That is, the community will be gutted of its jobs and potential community leaders and organizers', he claims (p. 1595). He contrasts the official planning view of Old Delhi, which terms it a 'slum', with that of Fonseca (1969), an architect well known for an analysis of the area which stresses its positive attributes:

> Although the city is not systematized according to hexagons, triangles and axial routes in the image of New Delhi, it is nonetheless well-ordered. It is a pedestrian city suited to the harsh climate; the tight-knit character necessitated by the insecure times when it was established.

If Old Delhi is a slum, states Ewing, it is as the result of years of neglect and not, as the Plan suggests, because of processes inevitable in low-income communities.

One major theme of the Delhi Plan is limitation of growth, despite the fact that even in the United States and Britain, where urban government is fairly strong, the record of development controls is not impressive and that in India urban authorities are widely recognized as one of the weakest elements in public affairs (Ewing, 1969, p. 1593). To deflect incoming migrants and also to limit population growth through relocating some government employment from Delhi, the Plan proposed six 'ring towns' around Delhi in classic British New Town fashion. To date, however, little if any of the growth of these towns has originated from Delhi, nor has Delhi's population growth been significantly checked. Ewing asserts that as the 'ring towns' grow, Delhi will only grow at still faster pace – 'to the magnetism of Delhi itself, subsidiary magnets will have been created' (p. 1596) – especially as the furthest such town is only 25 km (15 miles) from the edge of Delhi, by no means an impossible commuting distance. Despite a proposed 1 mile wide Green Belt, again *à la* Britain, an added danger is, of course, that development will be attracted not so much into the 'ring towns' as to vacant land between the towns and Delhi, taking advantage of proximity to both and adding significantly to the urban sprawl. Ewing additionally points out that relative to the other million-plus Indian cities industrial development is very much underrepresented in Delhi, and there are good reasons for thinking that its industrial base could be expanded. Yet the Master Plan states quite arbitrarily that '20 per cent of working population in industries . . . would not spoil the pleasantness and dignity of a National Capital'. Why, with sensible planning and effective administration, should not 'pleasantness and dignity' be compatible with a much more vigorous programme of industrial development, he asks. 'Can India, at this critical stage in her development, with a much lower economic resource base than most Western nations, *afford* the garden city biases of Ebenezer Howard and Le Corbusier?' (p. 1597).

As for housing, the Plan calls for the construction of 25 000 units per year. Yet the output of the building industry is only 6 000 houses. It is simply not possible to quadruple the capacity of the local building industry virtually overnight or to absorb in a conventional manner the share of investment which the Plan, in theory at least, proposes to allocate toward the solution of Delhi's housing problem. Inevitably, it seems, a high proportion of what little housing is eventually constructed will be for government servants, and it will be built to a standard quite outside the wildest dreams of the mass of Delhi's poor.

Symbolic schemes

In developing countries, Wheaton and Wheaton (1972, p. 146) have asserted, it will probably be typical that approximately three-quarters of the total investment and constructional resources devoted to housing are used for high income families, perhaps one-fifth will be devoted to middle-income families and only token amounts to low-income families. As there are few data on the distribution of housing supply by social class, the Wheatons' assessment cannot be definitely confirmed, but this generalized pattern would appear to be realistic. This contrasts significantly with patterns of provision in the economically advanced countries. With the major exception of the United States, where the proportion of housing resources devoted to the low-income groups remains relatively small, housing resources in the latter countries tend to be assigned much more in proportion to the distribution of income between the three classes, say in a 20 : 50 : 30 ratio, thus reflecting a compromise between the market power of the high- and middle-income families and the social and political power of the low-income families. As part of their distorted pattern of provision, most Third World countries build only a little public housing in their cities, often in symbolic schemes which are claimed to be low-cost housing projects but are usually quite outside the means of the very poor. The fortunate few who live in such schemes typically are heavily subsidized.

Malaysia is a very good current case in point in this respect. Kuala Lumpur, the capital, has experienced extremely rapid growth in recent years and over the period 1947 to 1970 its population has risen from 291 000 to 783 000 persons. Perhaps as much as half of this increase can be attributed to in-migration (Ali Bin Esa, 1971, p. 98). Housing problems

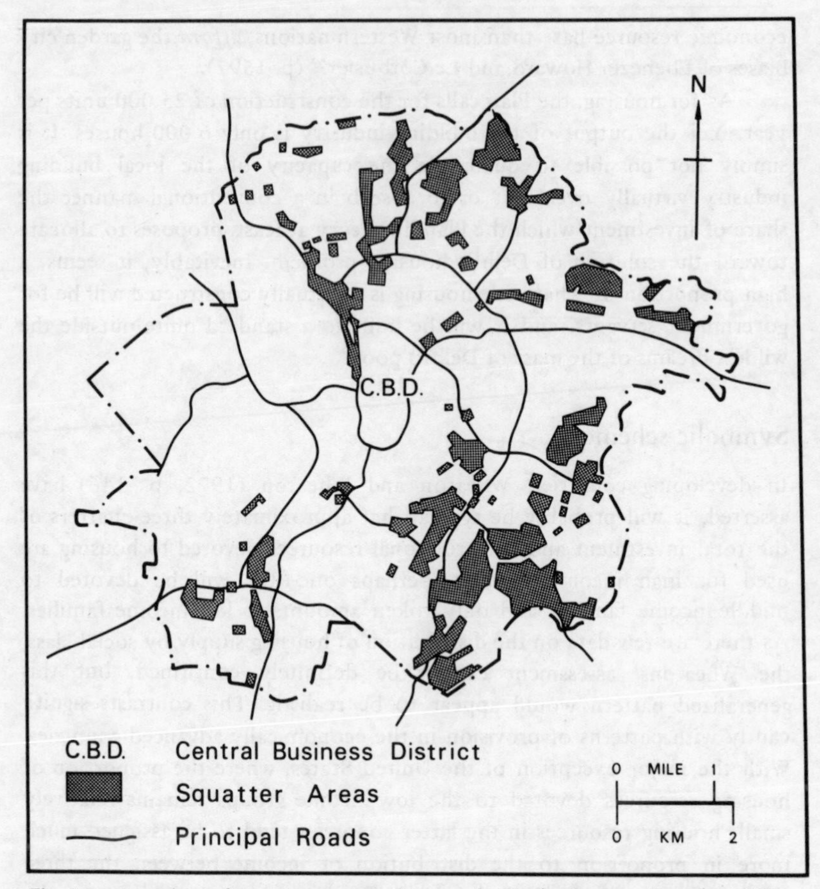

Fig. 3.3 Location of spontaneous settlements in Kuala Lumpur (Laquian, 1971, p. 99)

in the city have become extremely serious, with the result that about 37 per cent of the population now lives in spontaneous settlements (Fig. 3.3) and these occupy as much as 13 per cent of the total Federal Capital area, mostly on state land.

The First Malaysia Plan (1966–70) estimated that between 30 000 and 35 000 low-cost houses would have to be constructed in Malaysia between 1966 and 1970, with the programme mainly centred on the Federal Capital because of the extent of the squatter problem there. An industrialized housing system developed in Denmark was initially adopted and provided 3 000 dwelling units in four and seventeen-storey blocks, but very few squatters were able to move in because of the relatively high rents. The factory producing the prefabricated units was never able to achieve full efficiency because not only was the size of the local construction programme limited, but also transport costs for the panels to other parts of Malaysia were found to be prohibitive. The project as a whole therefore proved abortive and the factory was closed.

Housing in Malaysia is a state government responsibility, though Federal assistance for low-cost housing is given in the form of loans and technical expertise is provided on a federal basis largely through a housing trust. There can, therefore, be no national construction programme. In the event, 22 522 low-cost housing units were completed throughout the country during the First Malaysia Plan, a considerable shortfall even on the Plan's modest target. In the Second Plan (1971–75) M$89.6 million are to be allocated to housing for lower-income groups, a sum which even if fully used will represent a reduction from the M$99.7 million spent on low-cost housing during the First Plan (Tan Soo Hai, 1972). However, favoured groups will continue to receive relatively large allocations: M$30 million for the housing of government employees, M$177.8 million for police housing and M$43 million for armed forces' housing for example. In all, planned bugetary allocations for public housing total M$545 million during the Plan period. Attention to the housing problems of the low-income groups is obviously small even within the limits of the funds available for housing; so too is the place of housing provision in the framework of developmental provision as a whole. The M$545 million allocated for housing is only 7.5 per cent of total expenditures.

The urban showpiece of Malaysia is Petaling Jaya, a new town adjacent to Kuala Lumpur which has now reached a population of 70 000 persons (Fig. 3.4). Petaling Jaya was originally conceived as a squatter resettlement area during the early 1950s but in succeeding years this objective very rapidly became superseded by housing provision in the area for the middle classes. The site consisted mainly of rubber and tin-mining land, the larger area being undulating country under rubber which was easily cleared for residential development. Development began in February 1952 and initially 1 000 timber houses for squatters from Kuala Lumpur were completed, each family being assigned a building plot at a relatively low price and being assisted with finance for house building.

At that time squatter problems had considerable political significance because of the Communist rebellion, but by the end of 1957 the political situation had become easier and with the completion of the two-lane federal highway from Kuala Lumpur to Klang and Port Swettenham, which passes through Petaling Jaya, the possible dormitory function of the

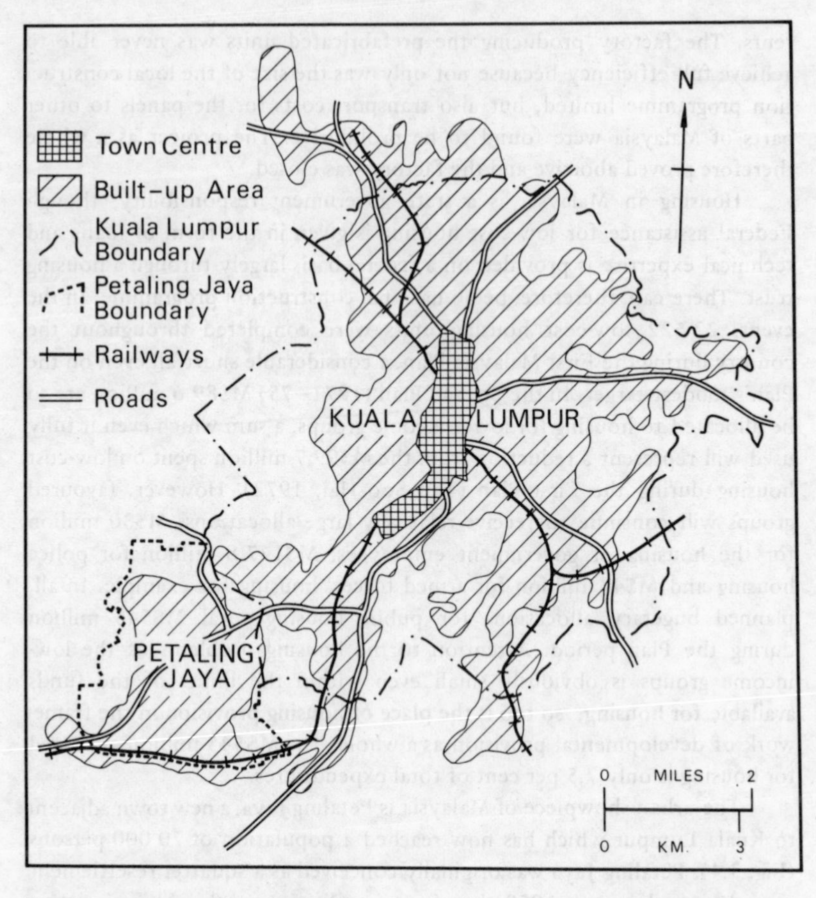

Fig. 3.4 Location of Petaling Jaya

latter had become widely appreciated. Though a Petaling Jaya Authority was established in 1954 to develop the site in a comprehensive manner, little further was done for Kuala Lumpur's squatters within the new town. Most of the residential lots were sold off for bungalow development, to individuals, contractors and such institutions as the Malaya–Borneo Building Society, usually at prices well below what the market would have stood (McGee and McTaggart, 1967, p. 6). At the same time, Malaya's largest industrial areas were laid out in Petaling Jaya and, because of the restriction of competing imports and the location of the new industrial sites adjacent to the capital city, they were very quickly occupied. A situation thus arose which was the very antithesis of rational planning: workers moving each day from Kuala Lumpur to the factory jobs in Petaling Jaya and executives and civil servants travelling in the opposite direction, from their residences in Petaling Jaya to offices in Kuala Lumpur. Meanwhile, problems of spontaneous settlement in Kuala Lumpur have continued to grow in seriousness.

Almost every developing country has indulged in this kind of housing symbolism, though usually to lesser degree, and sometimes the results have been even more bizarre. Abrams (1966*a*, p. 179) has related how in Quezon City in the Philippines the Agency for International Development financed a model core housing project which consisted of four toilets built back to back. The Agency wished only to rent out the land and the core and expected each tenant to build a house around his toilet. Without prospects of ownership, there was insufficient inducement for Manila's squatter families. The project, which came to be known as 'Flushing Heights', foundered and extinguished AID's interest in Philippine housing. A similar case may be quoted from Thailand, where an Urban Renewal Committee was created in 1958 to deal with the squatter problem in Bangkok. Up to 1969 this and other agencies had built only a token 7 000 housing units, and the Urban Renewal Committee's major achievement had been to expell 10 000 squatters from land upon which the SEATO headquarters was built without providing them with any alternative accommodation (Poethig, 1971, p. 121).

In India, according to Van Huyck (1967, p. 1025), the central government in granting housing subsidies to the various states in the late 1960s, stipulated an upper limit for construction costs of 6 600 rupees per family in units of 21.5 sq. m (232 sq. ft). The maximum family income for qualification for such housing was set at 250 rupees per month and the maximum rent at 21 rupees per month. In relation to demand, very little of this kind of housing has ever actually been built. Further, one calculation has shown that the actual cost of housing a family in such accommodation would be 938 rupees a year, not counting the cost of city services (*ibid.*, p. 1026). Subtracting rents (and assuming that all rents were paid, a theoretical situation which is usually far from actual in India) the net cost would be 680 rupees per family. Because of the incidence of indirect taxation in India, that group of families within the nation earning between 100 and 150 rupees per month would contribute 226 rupees annually to this subsidy, while that group of families earning less than 100 rupees per month would contribute a further 68 rupees. Clearly, India's poorest families bear a very substantial proportion of the cost of such schemes. Yet if it is assumed that 15 per cent is the maximum proportion that a lower-class Indian family can devote to rent, only those families earning over 173 rupees a month could afford to live in them. In other words, in symbolic low-cost housing projects it is often the poorest who very largely subsidize the not so poor.

A good deal of what is wrong with these and other 'low-cost' housing schemes lies in faulty conceptualization of realistic housing standards. In a few words, most 'low cost' houses are too expensive for the people for whom, at least in theory, they are designed. Instead of seeking marginal but widespread improvements in the present position, the major objective of most housing and planning policies in recent years has, it seems, been the avoidance of building what is described as 'substandard housing' and represented as the first step towards 'urban slums', even though the relevance of the housing designs adopted in this spirit to the actual standards of the mass of the urban population they are supposed to serve is usually minimal. Thus in India, the dominant school of thought has been expressed by the journal of the Indian Institute of Town Planners (1955) as follows:

> The basic standards in housing and planning are arrived at not only from considerations of cost but also from considerations of creating the desirable sociological and physical environment necessary for the healthy growth of the individuals and the community. Such standards have been established by various committees and technical missions . . . recommending the two-roomed house with adequate sanitary and other facilities as the barest minimum if the normal aspiration of healthy living is to be achieved. . . . These standards cannot be lowered, whatever the community, whatever be the location and whatever the economic situation in the country. Substandard housing is but a step towards slums. Deliberate substandard housing will defeat the very purpose of housing as it will lead towards the creation of future slums. The basic standards must be adhered to all costs.

As chapter 6 will emphasize, such ideals, far from being constructive reflect only a blind unwillingness to face up to the reality of the housing situation in the developing countries. They inhibit the development of standards meaningful in the local situation. In Nigeria, the Western Nigeria Housing Corporation developed the Bodija housing estate in Ibadan in recent years, again a symbolic scheme which involved only 322 houses (Adedeji, 1971, pp. 65–6). As elsewhere, this estate has benefited only the middle and even some of the upper classes. The cheapest house on the estate in 1971 was £N1 000, a sum which was relatively high even for the class of housing being built, in part because of the refusal of the Corporation to use local building materials. In Fort Lamy, Chad, seven-tenths of all households receive less than the equivalent of US$40 a month, but an officially built 'low-cost' dwelling cost $48 a month in rent in the early 1960s (Nerfin, 1965, p. 547). Rhodesia's cheapest form of public housing rented at the equivalent of US$11 a month in 1965, yet 67 per cent of the wage earners in Salisbury, 72 per cent in Bulawayo, 80 per cent in Gwelo and 85 per cent in Umtali earned less than $34 a month (*ibid*.). Clearly, in all too many countries official thinking on standards of provision for the poor is far out of line with their actual economic situation.

Housing needs

Over and above these important political, organizational and conceptual efficiencies, the very size of existing urban housing deficits and the probable extent of future needs has now reached such staggering proportions in most developing countries as almost to induce a general state of mind among responsible officials that no practical solution of any kind is possible, and this is another reason for the symbolic housing schemes. As Rosser (1972*a*, pp. 93–4) has put it:

> Few mental activities in India are likely to translate an Indian administrator, planner or academic in Delhi instantly into a state of transcendental immobility as is any contemplation of the all-India scale. And one is often tempted to believe that in the face of this overwhelming scale, there is a distinct intellectual preference for inaction rather than micro-action, no matter how effective and relevant the latter is to the contemporary development scene.

To take some specific examples of the current massive dimensions of need, partly as a result of the Korean War, during which about a quarter of the total housing stock was destroyed, but more recently because of the extremely high rate of growth of its population, Seoul had only 453 000 houses in 1970 to meet the needs of 789 000 households (Ro, 1971, p. 159). Natural increase in the city is running at 2.3 per cent per year, whilst in some years recently in-migration has raised Seoul's overall rate of annual population growth to 7 per cent. South Korea's housing situation is shown in Table 3.1. In the towns, as well as the additional housing needed because of rapid population growth, there is also, as elsewhere in the Third World, a considerable problem of deterioration of the existing housing

Table 3.1 The housing situation in South Korea, 1968

	Nation	*Cities*	*Rural areas*
Population	29 752 791	10 152 899	19 599 892
Households	5 210 420	1 866 187	3 324 233
Housing units	3 885 996	982 507	2 903 489
Shortage of housing units	1 324 424	903 680	420 744
Percentage of housing shortage	25.41	47.91	12.66
Percentage of annual household increase	2.84	6.61	1.14
Space per household (sq. ft)	270	256	277
Space per person (sq. ft)	47	43	47
Number of persons per household	5.7	5.5	5.8

Source: Ministry of Construction, 1968; quoted in Ro, 1971, p. 160.

stock, especially as many of the urban houses are made of wood and other non-permanent materials which deteriorate rapidly in Korea's harsh climate. In total, Korea needs some 205 000 houses every year if a major impact is to be made on the housing problem both urban and rural, but on average only some 73 000 new units are built, and these mostly by private enterprise. In its First Five Year Economic Development Plan (1962–66) the government planned to build 60 000 units of housing, but in the event only 40 000 units were completed and less than four-fifths of the budgeted housing funds were spent. The private sector completed an additional 280 000 housing units during the Plan period but total housing construction, government and private, was only one-third of that required.

Korea's Second Five Year Development Plan (1967–71) envisaged massive participation in housing provision by the private sector; 500 000 housing units were planned, only 30 000 of which were to be built by the government, a total less than that achieved in the First Plan. As yet there are no signs that private enterprise can meet this challenge. 'With foreign exchange and other financial difficulties, it is now becoming apparent that this anticipation may not be fulfilled and that the government must take a more active role in the housing field if it is to solve the problem', stated one observer in 1969 (Ro, 1971, p. 161). South Korea's recent housing experience mirrors very closely the all too obvious gap which exists in most Third World countries between paper planning and physical performance as well as the paradox that even in the better-off Third World countries the housing situation is deteriorating rapidly. Even though South Korea achieved very satisfactory rates of economic growth during the 1960s, its housing situation became worse rather than better.

India is another, and of course quantitatively much more important, case in point (Tangri, 1968). In the four biggest cities – Calcutta, Bombay, Delhi and Madras – approximately 65 per cent of all households live in one room or less and the average number of persons per room for each city varies from 2.9 to 3.7. India's biggest cities generally have the lowest vacancy rates for housing, which is another way of suggesting the pressure of crowding, and urban water supplies, latrines, sewerage systems, lighting and other amenities are everywhere grossly inadequate. Tangri (1968, pp. 521–2) has claimed that, in general, urban housing kept pace with urban growth up to the beginning of the Second World War, though this seems doubtful. What is more certain is that wartime conditions produced rates of urban growth never previously experienced; that the partition of the Indian subcontinent immediately after the war caused an inflow of some

Table 3.2 Urban population and housing in India

Year	*Urban population (millions)*	*Index of population*	*Houses: net stock (millions)*	*Index of net housing stock*	*Index of space* per capita	*Space* per capita *(sq. ft)*
1921	28.09	100.00	5.70	100.00	100.00	113.00
1931	33.46	119.12	6.80	119.30	100.15	113.17
1941	44.15	157.12	8.60	150.88	95.99	108.47
1951	62.44	222.29	10.30	180.70	81.29	91.86
1956	73.43	261.40	10.68	187.30	71.65	81.00
1961	83.67	297.86	11.45	200.88	67.44	76.21
	(78.94)	(281.03)	(10.80)	(189.47)	(67.40)	(76.16)
1966	97.00	345.31	12.30	215.78	62.49	70.61
	(91.52)	(325.80)	(11.65)	(204.38)	(62.73)	(70.88)

Note: Figures in parentheses refer to the population according to the new classification of urban areas in the 1961 census. Population figures for 1966 are estimated by assuming a 3 per cent compound annual rate of growth of population between 1961–66, the same rate as for 1951–61.

Source: Tangri, 1968, p. 524.

millions of refugees from the areas allocated to Pakistan and many of these converged on the cities; and that in succeeding years one important index of India's continuing economic problems has been a vast migration of people from the countryside to the urban areas. By 1951 there were perhaps 10.3 million houses for an urban population of 62.4 million. About one-third of the urban housing stock was in excess of fifty years old and it was estimated that over 1 million new houses per decade would be needed in the urban areas just to keep the existing stock intact.

Table 3.2 shows the position in more recent years. India's urban population grew by 20 million between 1951 and 1961. If an average household of five persons is assumed, population growth therefore created an additional need for about 4 million housing units. A further million units were required because of obsolescence, making the total 5 million, but at best only half this target was met. By 1966, taking into account further urban population growth, rates of construction of new housing units, and housing stock lost through obsolescence and 'slum clearance' (though fortunately the latter has not yet been very significant), the total urban housing deficit had probably reached 6 million units. The future is not entirely clear because of possible variations in the compound rate of growth of India's urban population (recent official planning has apparently used projected annual urban growth rates of between 4.5 and 6.5 per cent), but in terms of the number of additional housing units required for the urban areas up to 1981 (Table 3.3), the only realistic immediate prospect for India, at least in terms of conventional thinking on housing provision, seems to be a steady worsening of already desperate housing conditions.

As with India, it is difficult to predict future urban population figures for other large areas of the Third World with any certainty. For Africa, the United Nations Department of Economic and Social Affairs (1965, p. 9) considers it reasonable to assume that urban populations will increase twice as fast as total populations during the period 1960 to 1975, that is the 1960 population of 37 million in urban areas of 20 000 or more inhabitants will more than double to 76 million by 1975, implying an annual rate of increase of 4.9 per cent. As chapter 2 indicated, of all parts of the Third World Africa exhibits perhaps the greatest degree of flux in contemporary family and household patterns, and this is another complicating factor in assessment. Data is also relatively more scanty. However, if an average urban household size of five persons is taken, it appears that during the period 1960 to 1975 some 8 million new housing units would be required in the urban areas simply to cater for population increase;

Table 3.3 India: Urban population growth (millions) and housing needs (million units)

	Percentage annual compound rate of growth								
	2.0	2.5	3.0	3.5	4.0	4.5	5.0	5.5	6.0
Increase in population, 1961–81	38	50	64	78	94	112	131	152	174
Additional need for housing for population growth	7.6	10.0	12.8	15.6	18.8	22.4	26.2	30.4	34.8
Obsolescence requirements	2.0	2.0	2.0	2.0	2.0	2.0	2.0	2.0	2.0
Slum clearance	1.1	1.1	1.1	1.1	1.1	1.1	1.1	1.1	1.1
Total housing needs	10.7	13.1	15.9	18.7	21.1	25.5	29.3	33.5	37.9

Source: Tangri, 1968, p. 526.

additional construction would also be needed to alleviate existing housing shortages and to allow for obsolescence.

Details of the position in individual towns and cities are equally depressing for any other part of the Third World (UN, Department of Economic and Social Affairs, 1965, pp. 10–12). In Dakar, Senegal, 45 per cent of the population lives three or more to a room and 64 per cent is served neither by electricity nor by water supplies. In Accra, Ghana, the number of persons per house increased from 14.2 to 18.4 between 1948 and 1960. The capital of Chad, Fort Lamy, is built almost entirely of traditional materials. As chapter 6 will show, this need not in itself be objectionable but in Fort Lamy, as in the 'traditional' parts of most African cities, there is an almost complete absence of proper layout, virtually no sanitation or refuse collection, and only 1.5 per cent of the total dwelling stock is equipped with electricity and water. In all, perhaps less than one-half of the urban population of Africa lives in what can be considered adequate housing, even using minimal construction, occupancy and environmental standards.

The position in Latin America, in brief, is that in 1950 25 per cent of the population lived in urban areas of 20 000 or more inhabitants; a decade later this proportion had risen to about 32 per cent, and the urban population had increased to 69 million (UN, Department of Economic and Social Affairs, 1965, pp. 26–34). The projected annual rate of urban population growth between 1960 and 1975 is 5.6 per cent, which will mean an urban population of 157 million in the latter year. The United Nations assumes an average household size of 4.7 persons. Thus population increase alone would require an additional 18.7 million housing units in the urban areas to meet needs arising between 1960 and 1975, to say nothing of provision for the reduction of existing crowding and replacement of deteriorated housing units.

Overall housing requirements for the Third World are summarized in Table 3.4. Though there are significant gaps in population information about Asia – for example, there is no census later than that of 1953 for China's huge population and information relating to the housing position in that country is extremely fragmentary – it is clear even from the grossest of estimates that Asia's housing problems completely dwarf those of any other part of the world. Not only are Asia's needs for new housing by far greater than those of Africa or Latin America but crowding in Asia's large cities is much more excessive. Of the total of 67.5 million new dwelling units necessary to meet population increase alone in Third World cities during the period 1960 to 1975, no less than 41 million units are needed in Asia, 22.4 million additional units are required in the Third World for

Table 3.4 Estimated housing needs of Africa, Asia and Latin America 1960–75 (in millions of dwelling units)

Housing required to provide for:	*Average annual requirements*						*Total requirements*	
	1960–1965		*1965–1970*		*1970–1975*		*1960–1975*	
	Urban	*Rural*	*Urban*	*Rural*	*Urban*	*Rural*	*Urban*	*Rural*
Population increase								
Africa	0.4	0.9	0.5	1.0	0.7	1.1	7.8	14.7
Asia	2.2	4.0	2.7	4.2	3.2	4.3	41.0	62.1
Latin America	0.9	0.4	1.3	0.3	1.5	0.3	18.7	4.8
Subtotal	3.5	5.3	4.5	5.5	5.4	5.7	67.5	81.6
Replacement of obsolescent stock								
Africa	0.1	1.1	0.1	1.1	0.1	1.1	1.8	16.1
Asia	1.1	6.3	1.1	6.3	1.1	6.3	16.5	94.0
Latin America	0.3	0.7	0.3	0.7	0.3	0.7	4.1	10.3
Subtotal	1.5	8.1	1.5	8.1	1.5	8.1	22.4	120.4
Elimination of existing shortages								
Africa	0.1	0.7	0.1	0.7	0.1	0.7	1.8	10.7
Asia	0.7	4.2	0.7	4.2	0.7	4.2	14.6	62.6
Latin America	0.2	0.5	0.2	0.5	0.2	0.5	3.4	6.9
Subtotal	1.0	5.4	1.0	5.4	1.0	5.4	19.8	80.2
Totals	6.0	18.8	7.0	18.0	7.9	19.2	109.7	282.2

Source: UN, Department of Economic and Social Analysis, 1965, p. 4.

the replacement of deteriorated stock and 19.8 million units in order to eliminate existing shortages, and again Asia's needs bulk very large in these staggering totals.

Housing and national planning

Another way of looking at Third World housing needs is to consider the annual output of new dwelling units necessary per 1 000 of the population. In general, an output of between nine and eleven new dwellings per 1 000 population is called for during the period 1960 to 1975, with urban needs falling between eleven and sixteen per 1 000 (Table 3.5). The extremely formidable nature of this task becomes clear when it is realized that very few even of the most economically advanced countries produces more than eight new dwellings annually per 1 000 of their population (UN, Department of Economic and Social Affairs, 1965, p. 3). The United States, for example, despite a great deal of national concern with urban problems, manages only between seven and eight per 1 000; France produces seven per 1 000, West Germany ten, and Sweden nine. In the ECAFE region generally, current rates of construction of new dwelling units are only one or two per 1 000 of population, except in Hong Kong, Singapore and Japan. Hong Kong, which is discussed in chapter 5, is very exceptional indeed, having achieved a rate of dwelling construction of thirteen units per 1 000 population, which compares with those of New Zealand and the USSR as being among the highest in the world.

Much of the interpretation of bald figures of this kind depends, of course, upon two factors: accommodation standards, which have already been referred to in this chapter, and the place housing provision occupies in official priorities. In most Third World countries investment in housing occupies a very minor place indeed in national development plans. Thus in the Nigerian six-year development plan of 1962–68 housing appeared under the general heading of Town Planning, together with planning surveys, physical planning, land acquisition, land development, the provision of utilities and the construction of industrial estates; and the development expenditure allocated to this group of activities as a whole was only 6.2 per cent of the total (Koenigsberger, 1970, p. 393). As is usual in such plans, Town Planning was classified as a social overhead. The Nigerian plan contains no precise estimates of the dimensions of the housing problem but Koenigsberger has calculated the minimum needs for the towns to be 47 000 new units a year, with perhaps 61 000 being a more realistic figure if modest improvements in the housing situation are to be sought. This

Table 3.5 Dwelling output per 1 000 population required to meet housing needs of Africa, Asia and Latin America for specified years 1960–75

	1960			*1965*			*1970*			*1975*		
	Urban	*Rural*	*Total*	*Urban*	*Rural*	*Total*	*Urban*	*Rural*	*Total*	*Urban*	*Rural*	*Total*
New dwellings required per 1 000 population	15.8	10.7	11.6	15.0	9.5	10.6	13.7	9.4	10.3	11.1	8.7	9.3

Source: UN, Department of Economic and Social Affairs, 1965, p. 5.

order of output has never been remotely approached in Nigeria; in fact, during the first three years of the plan period (before the plan was overtaken by the civil war) the public sector produced less than 500 new units a year and only two-fifths of these were for low-income groups.

In explaining why so few houses were built by the public sector the first answer would have to be lack of investment. But the official allocations, though meagre, were not completely unworkable. A realistic sites-and-services programme for low income groups could have been instituted with the available funds, allowing the distribution of perhaps 48 000 plots annually to people wanting to build their own houses (for a discussion of sites-and-services programmes see chapter 6); in addition about 5 000 houses yearly could have been constructed for the lowest income groups (*ibid*., p. 395). Quite simply, the money, was not spent in the most effective way.

Another fundamental fault lay in the structure of the development plan. No preferred strategies, firm targets or action programmes for housing provision were laid down. This led to inaction by the public sector and the wrong kind of action by the private sector, claims Koenigsberger (1970, p. 393):

> Nigerian investors were not told how, when and where to invest in housing. They were left to their own devices, and lacking guidance through the national plan, decided upon what appeared the most profitable course. Houses were built for foreign firms, embassies and other wealthy clients. The middle and lower income groups were left to help themselves as well they could by building illegally on the outskirts of cities or by squatting on public land.

The fundamental fallacy, as with so many development plans in the Third World, was a blind belief that social benefits would flow from a development programme drawn up on an exclusively economic basis. Hence no attempt was made to state the social objectives which should have been the basis for planning or to explore possible linkages between inputs for social advancement and those for economic development.

The Nigerian situation is typical of that of most developing countries, for as Wheaton and Wheaton (1972) and many other writers on housing have pointed out, current economic development theory gives a very low priority to housing provision as a factor involved in economic growth and regards it as a social overhead, a consumer rather than a producer good, resource absorbing rather than resource producing. This is doubly unfortunate since in developing countries private investment is usually low and therefore total investment in housing is small, perhaps 1 or 2 per cent of the gross national product compared with approximately 5 per cent in Western Europe and 4 per cent in the United States (the latter of course being not only markedly higher percentages but also proportions of much larger *per capita* national products).

Perhaps the major reason why investment in housing forms such a minor part of most national plans in the developing countries is that as yet no clear evaluation of such investment has emerged in terms quantifiable within a cost-benefit framework. Various writers have insisted on the benefits to the development process to be derived from improved housing, but almost always they have been expressing intuitive suppositions rather than quantifiable facts concerning the rate of return from housing inputs, and usually the possible alternative uses of such capital as might go into housing have been ignored. As a report of a United Nations group of experts (UN, Department of Economic and Social Affairs, 1962*c*, p. 14) on housing and economic development states in a typical argument:

> Good modern residential communities provided in place of dilapidated unfit housing can, by the very environmental change they create, release new energies and ambitions of value for economic development. . . . Inadequate housing and decayed neighbourhoods in themselves can actively inhibit belief in the possibility of economic development and social progress. New housing is a tangible proof of progress and, therefore, likely to be an incentive to further advances.

In this situation, as Abrams (1966*a*, p. 106) has pointed out, the approach of development economists to the problem of housing provision has been a 'modified devil take housing' one at best. Some have adhered to the extreme view that, as one writer on the Colombo Plan countries (quoted by Abrams, p. 106) put it: 'There are too many urgent things to attend to . . . the problem of house building in this part of the world is one about which we don't want to be too urgent. The most important thing is to help people obtain the facilities to increase production.' Others have conceded that there may be cases where some housing expenditure can be justified in the national plan, but because of the pressing need for capital for directly productive investment, allocations for such needs cannot be very much: that is, 'The problem is not a choice between housing and other investment; the problem is how much housing you must have in order to make other investment pay off' (M. F. Millikan, quoted by Abrams, p. 107). There are, nevertheless, difficulties even with this latter approach. As Abrams (1966*a*, p. 109) has observed, the economists' 'exceptions' for permissible housing often tend to multiply, even to the point of rendering the main argument suspect. More of the resources and capital than the economists wish to allow for housing improvement may be consumed anyway, particularly if privileged groups (special workers, executives, government employees, officers in the armed forces and the like) are successful in demanding new housing. In Baghdad, for example, significant areas have been reserved for housing development by cooperative societies. These societies largely consist of professional people who are government employees and the tracts, called in Arabic *mudun* ('cities'), are named after the societies. Thus there is the Officers' City, the Police City, the Engineers' City and even a Housing Department Employees' City. Most have received state land at extremely low prices (Gulick, 1967, p. 252). The relatively privileged thus continue to build relatively costly houses. Only the rank-and-file suffer.

In these somewhat confused theoretical circumstances, the work of Burns and Khing Tjioe (1968) may well prove to be of great importance. In a research note published in 1968, they outline the results of a rigorous study of a Korean housing project which goes further than any other previous work in attempting to quantify the benefits as well as the costs of housing provision. The traditional criterion for allocating development capital, they point out, is profitability but, particularly with housing, this concept fails to apply if precise measurement of outputs in monetary terms is not possible. Their objective, therefore, was to devise a method for evaluating in monetary units the total returns, not only economic but also social, that accrue from housing inputs.

Broadly, there are two investment sectors that compete for development capital, the productive sector and the social overhead sector. Housing may be considered to fall within the latter, together with education and health, the supposition being that improvement in the quality of housing, education and health leads to improvement in the quality of labour, thus making the directly productive sector more efficient. Seen in this light, claim Burns and Khing Tjioe, social overhead capital is not only directly complementary to productive capital but may also be substituted for it. This is because it is possible to regard its development contribution as a share of the increased output of the productive sector. The possibility of substitution also applies among the subsectors of housing, education and health, as well as between the two major sectors, production and social overhead. So long as output is homogeneously measured for a series of social overhead projects, then the same target level can be arrived at in various ways through permuting the possible inputs.

Housing outputs, Burns and Khing Tjioe postulate, may be transmitted to the productive sector through two channels, the physiological–biological and the psychosocial. The former could be measured in terms such as reductions in absenteeism through illness, where these are attributable to housing quality; the latter in such terms as better motivation or posture towards work, as reflected by productivity, in so far as this could be shown to be attributable to better housing. In addition, the benefits of improved housing accruing not only to the worker but also to his family have to be considered. If, for instance, better child health, improved study facilities and greater capacity to pay for education (the latter due to the worker's increased productivity) resulted, and in total led to higher income for the children after entering the labour force, these benefits should also be calculated and monetized as higher deferred income. Likewise, investment in education facilities becomes more effective if school absenteeism falls as a result of better housing. All these, and other linkages, have to be assessed and monetized before the return on housing investment can be calculated and compared with the returns from other forms of development input.

The field research was carried out at a remote site at Hambaeck, South Korea, where a coal mine had been started in 1955 and a new housing project built by the mining corporation for its employees eight years later. The survey extended from September 1962, one year before the new housing was occupied, to two years afterwards. The new housing, 500 units, was substantially better than the old. It had running water, sanitary facilities and electricity, which had not been available in the old houses, and the amount of habitable space per person was double that available previously.

With regard to changes in personal incomes, the survey compared changes in labour productivity of a sample of fifty rehoused miners with a control group of fifty non-rehoused miners. During the year preceding rehousing the average productivity and earnings of both groups was the same. After rehousing, the average weekly earnings per rehoused worker increased from US$13 to US$17.40 within ten months, or by 28 per cent, and this was both a true increase in productivity, since the production process was labour intensive and incentive wages were paid, and also one which could not be accounted for by changes in the local environment or working conditions external to housing. Another facet of the investigation involved the collection of medical histories from sample groups. Again, holding the non-housing environment constant, it could be shown that an annual health benefit from housing measured as a saving of fifty clinical visits per hundred of the rehoused population had resulted, plus a saving on hospital services.

In summary, Burns and Khing Tjioe point out that in this particular case, since the site was remote and the mining corporation provided work, health and housing facilities, an unusually large share of the total benefits from rehousing accrued directly to it as a result of its housing investment. More normally, a high proportion of the benefits would 'escape' from the housing investor into the national economy at large. The mining corporation's investment in the housing project was US$691 300. Burns and Khing Tjioe calculate that the total benefits accruing to it could be monetized at an annual rate of US$184 360 before operating expenses of US$71 840. The net return, US$112 530, therefore yielded 16.3 per cent on the investment, which compares very favourably with most returns on possible alternative investments in South Korea during the same period (these averaged 10 per cent for all industries). Rents received by the corporation by themselves would have resulted in a substantial loss on the investment. The principal contribution to the favourable earnings rate from the investment came from the possibility of scale economies in mining production, that is, from the more efficient use of existing plant and equipment at higher levels of output. This, in turn, was attributable to the improved quality of the labour force resulting from better housing.

It is possible that if this pilot project could be repeated more widely with similar results a significant revaluation of the relationship between housing investment and economic development might take place, resulting in greater proportions of the national resources of Third World countries being directed towards housing provision. As the examples quoted earlier in this chapter emphasize, however, even in such circumstances major problems of organization and housing strategy would still need to be solved. The fact remains that most developing countries have not yet faced up to these basic issues and, as a result, do not spend the funds they already have available for housing in the most effective way.

4

High-rise responses: Caracas

In Caracas the expansion has been explosive and architects, blessed with money and luxurious materials, have transformed a colonial town into a sophisticated capital.

Editorial note, *Architectural Design* February 1956

Pérez Jiménez, dictator of Venezuela from 1952 to 1958, left vast monuments to his rule scattered around Caracas. There was the most luxurious and costliest officers' club in the world. There was the Centro Bolivar, something of a replica of the Rockefeller Centre in New York. There was an ostentatious hotel on the top of Mount Avila complete with an ice rink and direct connection to the city by funicular railway. And there were the superblocks. The superblocks were his authoritarian answer to Venezuela's increasingly pressing problem of urban shelter. They were, in a sense, gigantic political symbols of his faith in a future for Venezuela's urban poor of his own dictatorial fashioning. In all, Pérez Jiménez poured half the total public expenditures of his regime into the capital. During his dictatorship Venezuela made a greater investment in public housing than any other country of Latin America with the exception of Puerto Rico. The superblock programme collapsed ignominiously in 1958 and today Venezuela is still searching for realistic national housing policies.

Caracas

Caracas is built in a narrow intermontane valley about 25 km long by 5 km wide (15 by 3 miles). Its expansion to the north is effectively restrained by the formidable barrier of the coast range which separates it from the Caribbean. To the east, south and west a series of lower and more irregular hills allows fingers of building to be pushed into minor tributary valleys of the Guaire. The Guaire River, which traverses the main valley from west to east, has been displaced towards the south by the growth of alluvial cones along the foot of the northern hill barrier, and it was on part of this relatively higher ground near the western end of the valley that the original urban nucleus of Caracas was laid out by Diego de Losada in 1567. Caracas was successively a provincial capital and the seat of the Spanish captain–general of Venezuela before becoming the capital of the independent republic in 1821, but until very recently its growth was extremely slow. Venezuela had remained a poor, sparsely populated agricultural country. As a result, as late as 1920 the population of Caracas was only 92 000 and the city occupied little more ground than its original grid-iron layout of the late sixteenth century (Fig. 4.1).

It was the discovery and development of Venezuela's oil resources during the late 1920s which triggered explosive urban growth. By 1948 Caracas had reached 600 000 in population, and by 1962 2 million, figures indicative of a rate of metropolitan growth since the early 1930s four times that of national population growth. As it fed excessively on the

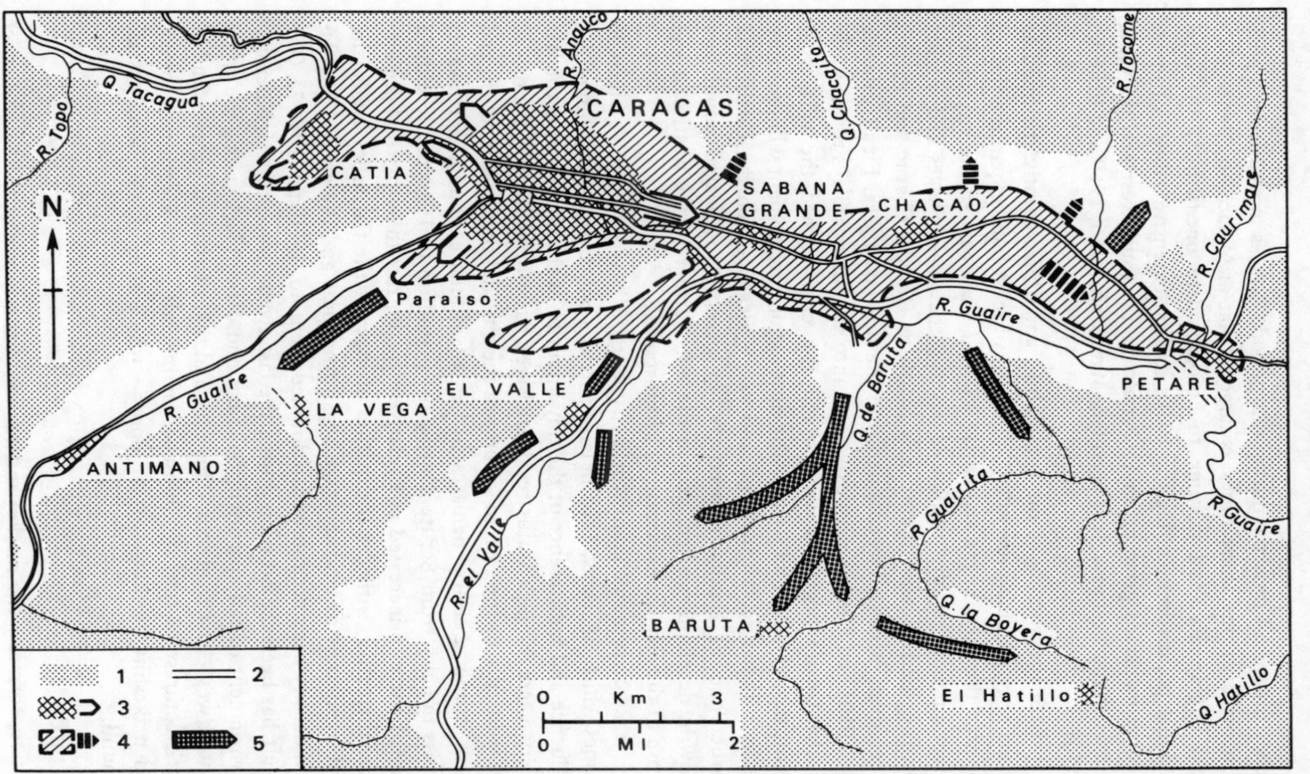

Fig. 4.1 The expansion of Caracas. Key: 1. High ground; 2. Principal roads; 3. Old Caracas and isolated villages, with growth axes between the two wars; 4. Extent of Caracas and growth axes during the 1950s; 5. Present growth axes (Marchand, 1969)

riches of the oil industry during this period, Caracas moved from a position twice to one three times as large as that of Maracaibo, Venezuela's next largest city, and it came to accommodate one-fifth of the total national population. During the 1930s its first extensive suburb of upper income mansions grew up in El Paraiso to the south-west and the Catia district in the west also developed (see Marchand, 1966, 1969 and Penfold, 1970).

With the coming of the automobile, and more recently the building of major roads along the valley, the focus of most rapid expansion shifted towards the east. Sugar and coffee *haciendas* adjacent to the city in this direction were rapidly swallowed up and the small villages and market towns associated with them, such as Sabana Grande, Chacao and Petare, successively became incorporated into the urbanized area. Finally, during the 1950s and 1960s urban expansion into the minor valleys to the south of the Guaire began in earnest and the city reached the villages of Antimano, El Valle and Baruta. The next major development will probably be in a broad rectangular hill and valley area between the Guaire and Baruta and El Hatillo respectively. In view of anticipated population growth, development here and in the hills further to the west, east and south of the city seems certain to be substantial.

Like every other Third World city, Caracas has its elegant high income homes which, it seems, exist in large part as a public demonstration of the affluence and indifference of the tiny minority of the elite. During the last thirty years the high status residential area has moved from El Paraiso in the west first to the eastern suburbs of the city and then to the south, and there is now a clearly demarcated belt of affluence running northwards across the city from Baruta. During the period up to 1950 the developed area of the city increased at a relatively greater rate than the total population; thereafter, with the occupation of most of the flat valley lands, the first symptoms of land shortage began to appear and the general population density has since more than doubled (Penfold, 1970, pp. 105–7). One result has been the creation during the last twenty years of a high density environment of tall apartment buildings and office blocks along the city's central west–east road axis. This zone and that of affluent homes stand in stark contrast to tens of thousands of *ranchos* – the illegal, unplanned, and makeshift dwellings of the poor – which cling to the hillslopes all around.

Petare

Petare, formerly the market and administrative centre of the Sucre district of Miranda state, was one of the principal settlements overtaken by the extension of Caracas into the eastern part of the Guaire valley. Its population had increased only from 1 400 to 4 000 during the 200 years prior to 1936; in the next thirty-five years it rose in startling fashion to 78 000 (Brisseau, 1963, p. 10). Petare originally occupied a restricted level area between the relatively steepsided valleys of two of Guaire's minor tributaries from the north. Hills surrounded it to south-west, south and east. It was largely on the hills, but also to the west on flat land in the Guaire valley itself, that the new inhabitants found shelter, in *ranchos* (Fig. 4.2). The proximity of Caracas alone explained the sudden transformation of Petare, for the *ranchos* grew both through the attraction of people to the wealth of the capital from the countryside and smaller towns and also through what was largely speculative building displacing people from older parts of the urban area.

The first *ranchos* were constructed in the area during the Second World War (Brisseau, 1963). They were essentially a response to the redevelopment of the Silencio district of west-central Caracas. The redevelopment displaced the urban poor of Silencio. Some went into the already large *rancho* areas to the west and south of the city but probably the larger number moved out to Petare, then 6 km (4 miles) away from the eastern edge of the urban area but connected to it by both road and railway. They settled at Las Brisas to the south-west of the old town on low hills which then overlooked sugar *haciendas*.

Towards the end of the Second World War two new *rancho* areas, San Miguel and Campo Rico, had begun to develop to the north of the suburb of El Dorado. They were matched about the same time by the beginnings of the present extensive *rancho* growth to the east of Petare, in the Buenos Aires and El Carmen areas. Significantly, the further colonization of this area, in the early 1950s, received a major impetus from the superblock housing programme. As the government razed *rancho* areas elsewhere in the city, a proportion of those displaced moved to Petare. Barrio Union, for example, was formed in this way.

Every state in Venezuela is represented in the *ranchos* of Petare, for the rural–urban migration characteristic of all developing countries has probably been reflected more fully there than in any other of the major *rancho* areas of Caracas. A survey carried out in the El Carmen area in 1961 showed that of sixty-one heads of families investigated only eleven had been born within the Caracas urban area. In contrast, thirty-nine had come from parts of Miranda state outside of the urban area, while the states of Trujillo, Lara, Yaracuy, Aragua, Carabobo, Guárico and

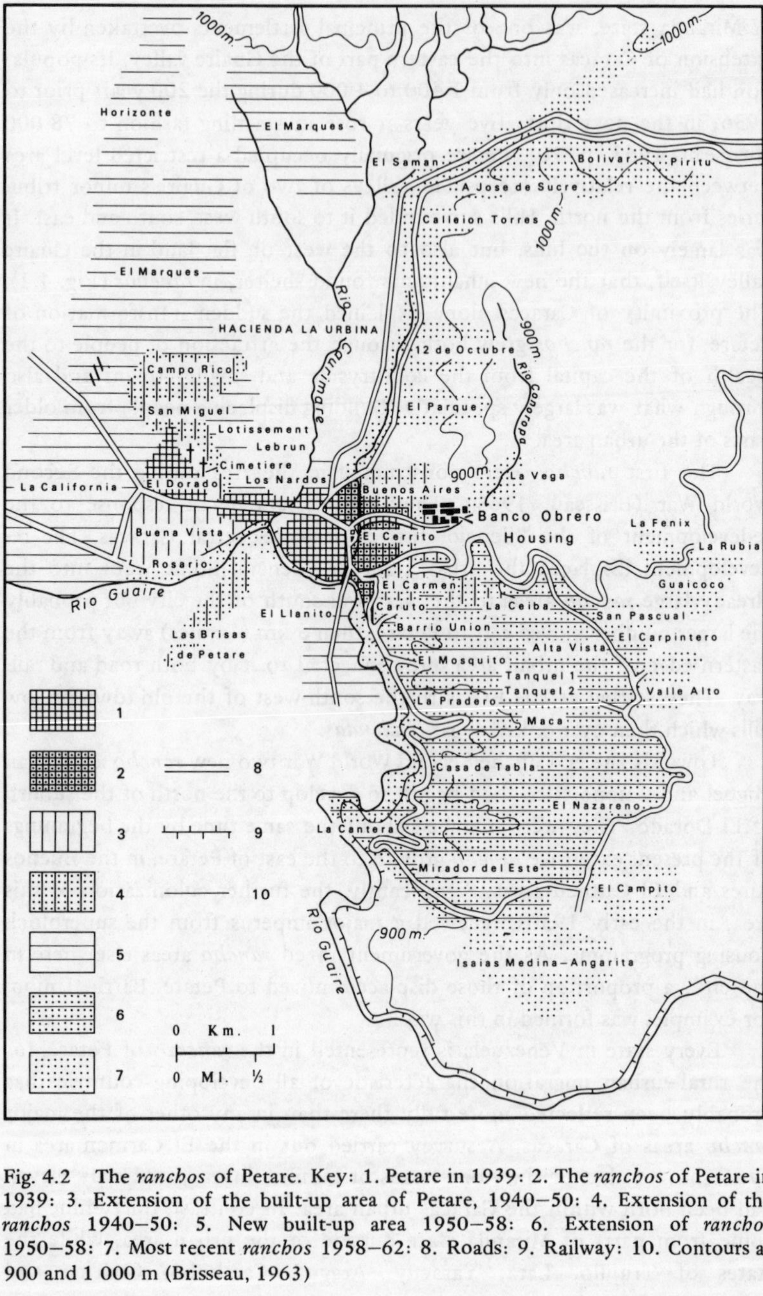

Fig. 4.2 The *ranchos* of Petare. Key: 1. Petare in 1939: 2. The *ranchos* of Petare in 1939: 3. Extension of the built-up area of Petare, 1940–50: 4. Extension of the *ranchos* 1940–50: 5. New built-up area 1950–58: 6. Extension of *ranchos* 1950–58: 7. Most recent *ranchos* 1958–62: 8. Roads: 9. Railway: 10. Contours at 900 and 1 000 m (Brisseau, 1963)

Anzóategui were also represented (Brisseau, 1963, p. 30). The displacement of people by speculative building was reflected in the fact that one-third of the families had lived in other parts of Caracas before settling in Petare.

By the early 1960s the *ranchos* around Petare were expanding even more rapidly than ever before. The overthrow of Pérez Jiménez in January 1958 had led to a popularly elected government after a short period of rule by *junta*. A policy of ameliorating conditions in the *ranchos* through wage labour by the *rancheros* themselves was embarked upon. Its chief result was to cause an unprecedented influx from the countryside. To quote Brisseau's succinct assessment (p. 18): 'Les populations rurales qui avaient voté en majorité pour le parti accédent au pouvoir venaient réclamer, a Caracas même, le prix de leur appui électoral.' A new major road built north from Petare towards Guarenas in 1959–60 quickly attracted a series of *ranchos* to the slopes of minor ravines nearby, while the great series of *ranchos* to the east of Petare was further extended through the completion of a ring road in that area which enabled such outlying communities as El Campito, El Nazareno and Valle Alto to be set up. With these developments, *ranchos* around Petare came to occupy 246 hectares (590 acres), or eighteen times the area of the original market town.

The superblocks[1]

In Venezuela's largest effort to solve the *rancho* problem to date, ninety-seven high-rise apartment buildings, known as superblocks, were constructed between 1954 and 1958 by the Banco Obrero, the principal official housing agency, at the instigation of Pérez Jiménez. Eighty-five were located on twelve sites in Caracas (Fig. 4.3); the remaining twelve were built in the nearby port of La Guaira. The superblocks cost roughly US$200 million and housed about 180 000 people, 159 000 of them in Caracas, or 13 per cent of the capital's 1.2 million population of that time. The avowed aim was to eliminate the *ranchos*. Often *ranchos* were bulldozed out of existence with only a few hours notice. The whole scheme proceeded at headlong pace. Little thought was given to the design of the blocks after the first had left the drawing board; in fact some of the earliest designs subsequently proved more viable than later modifications.

In all 16 069 apartments were provided in the Caracas superblocks.

[1] This section is largely based on Carlson (1960–61, 1968).

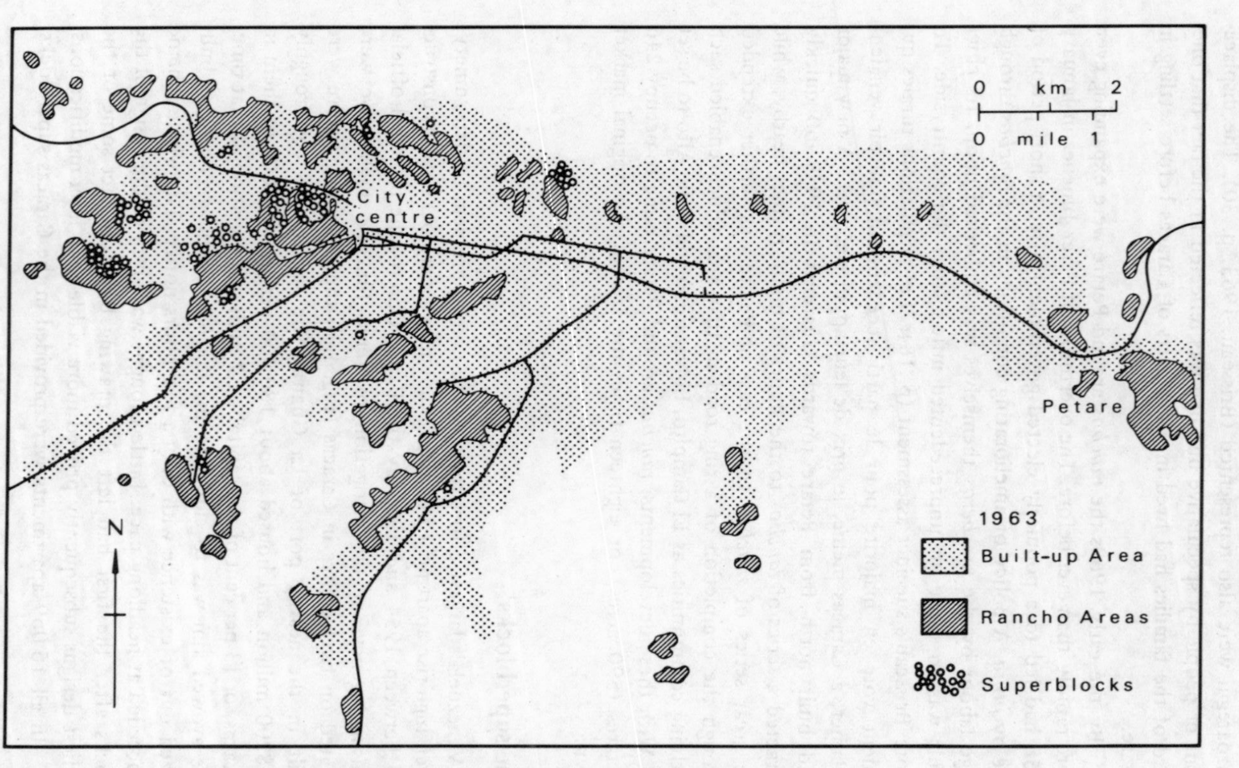

Fig. 4.3 Location of superblocks and *rancho* areas in Caracas, 1963 (Jones, 1964)

According to type, there were 150, 300 or 450 apartments in each block. All had fifteen storeys, access being through lift towers and staircases. Though their sizes varied from two to four bedrooms, all the apartments were relatively large in floor area and luxurious in facilities compared with the *ranchos* (Fig. 4.4). Some of the sites also included four-storey walk-up blocks containing twenty-four units. The total area covered by the superblock estates was 330 hectares (750 acres) and the net density was about 575 persons to the hectare (250 to the acre). The average construction cost per apartment worked out at US$10 000.

Government-owned sites were, of course, in short supply throughout the capital and in these circumstances most of the superblock developments tended to be located towards the edges of what was then the urban area, mainly on its northern and western sides, singly, or in pairs or threes (thirteen blocks in all) or in larger groups of eight to thirteen (thirty-two blocks). But almost adjacent to the business district, immediately to the east, was placed the largest group of superblocks of all: thirty-eight fifteen-storey and forty-two four-storey buildings accommodating 103 000 people. This was *Urbanizacion 23 de Enero* which was to become notorious as symbolizing all that was wrong with the programme.

By the beginning of 1958 the superblocks were in chaos. Four thousand families had invaded vacant apartments. Squatter shacks were lapping their walls and filling all the planned 'green' spaces. (It was later shown that the construction of the superblocks had aggravated the general housing problem through attracting still more migrants to Caracas from rural areas.) Rent delinquency had reached staggering proportions (over US$5 million was owed). Because there was little or no maintenance, the physical fabric of the schemes was rapidly deteriorating. *Urbanizacion 23 de Enero* was in the hands of violent political extremists and the superblocks generally had an unsavoury reputation for crime of all kinds. Overcrowding and illegal subletting were characteristic. On the administrative side the general picture was one of incompetence and disorganization. Most of the planned social facilities had not been constructed, for example there were schools for only 24 000 children out of school-age population in the superblocks of 40 000 to 50 000. Community centres and recreation facilities were scarce. Only one or two of the planned nursery schools and a few of the medical posts were operating, whilst most of the police posts were untenable.

One immediate consequence of the overthrow of the Pérez Jiménez regime in January 1958 was the suspension of the superblock building programme. The new government initiated a review of the situation under

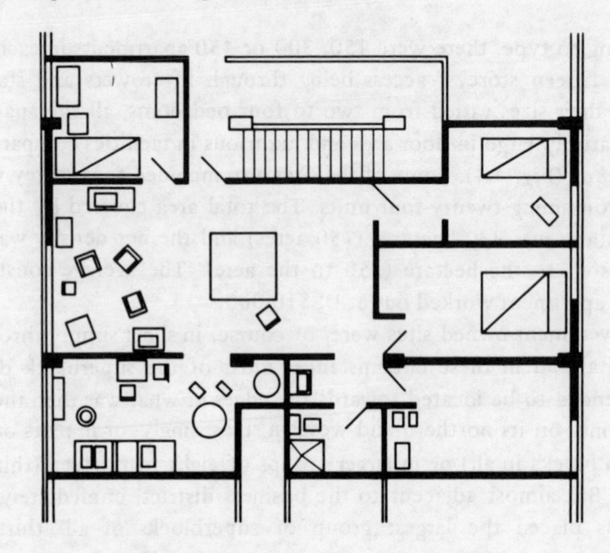

(A) Area: 840 sq. ft. ($76m^2$)

(B)

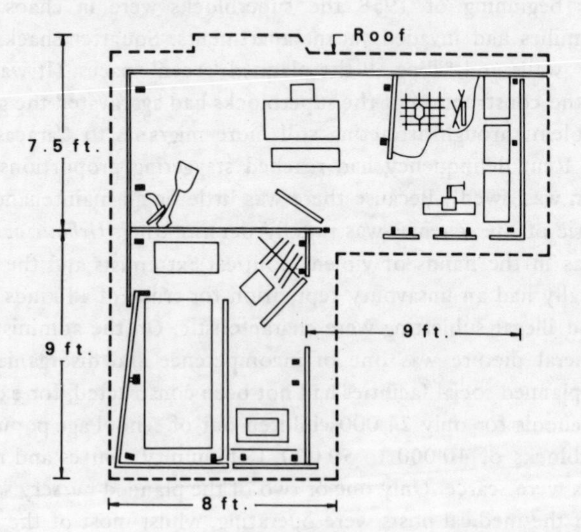

Area: 200 sq. ft. ($18m^2$)

Fig. 4.4 A typical apartment in a superblock (A) (Turner, 1963) and a typical Caracas *rancho* (B) (Carlson, 1961)

the direction of the Inter-American Housing and Planning Center of the Pan-American Union which on publication became a classic of its kind (Banco Obrero, 1959). The investigation showed by means of evaluation surveys of the kind which should have been carried out in the early stages of the programme that two-thirds of the heads of households in *23 de Enero* and as many as four-fifths of those in another project, *Urbanizacion Simon Rodriguez*, were in-migrants from the provinces. Their level of education and that of their families as a whole was relatively low (a fact reflected in the condition of many of the apartments), while levels of unemployment and semi-employment were serious. In *Simon Rodriguez* 25 per cent of the heads of families were unemployed and a further 30 per cent in only casual occupations (Mendoza, 1969, pp. 141, 143).

The socio-economic patterns revealed were on the whole much more typical of the *ranchos* than of any other part of the city and this was hardly surprising since four-fifths of the families in the superblocks had been forcibly moved from *ranchos*, often with only a few hours' notice. The sense of grievance against these moves still rankled, and it was usually directed against the Banco Obrero. Because of the low economic status of many families, inability to pay the relatively high rents and maintenance charges in the superblocks had become a major problem, for it had led the financing of the programme as a whole into serious difficulties and also to inescapable pressures on families to sublet and thus seriously to overcrowd the apartments. The plain fact was that the majority were occupying property worth two or three times the amount of rent they could reasonably afford to pay.

Perhaps potentially more explosive were the social aspects of the superblocks. The tenants were largely an unselected group, uneducated in and unaccustomed to relatively high density urban living and hetrogeneous in the extreme. Social work and educational programmes conceived in terms of their transition from *ranchos* to superblocks were virtually non-existent. Many of the basic community facilities had not even been built. Destruction of facilities and other overt signs of social disorganization were commonplace. The most pressing need, therefore, was to organize an approach to the problems posed by the superblocks through social organization and estate management. In fact, the evaluation survey showed that, calculated over a sixty-year period which was taken to be the useful life of the superblocks, administrative and management costs could in the circumstances reasonably be expected to more than duplicate initial investments for land, construction and services. In a nutshell, the architectural and technical deficiences of the programme were far less than those in administration and management. This is a lesson which, it seems, has yet to be learned widely elsewhere in the Third World in relation to high-rise public housing schemes.

The remedies proposed were comprehensive, but they could only be long-term. (*Urbanizacion 23 de Enero* remained the main centre of political violence in the metropolitan area until 1963 and even in the later 1960s the superblocks as a whole were still in process of becoming a normal part of the city structure in social terms.) They were aimed primarily at creating a spirit of collective responsibility and an awareness both of the existing problems and of the role which the inhabitants themselves would have to play in seeking solutions. How had the problems arisen? The evaluation project identified interrelated deficiences in many areas. A lack of careful programming was one of the principal causes, as well as a lack of clear principles both in social and in physical standards. Clearly, the whole superblock exercise had been carried out in extreme haste. It was a massive crash programme undertaken with minimal economic and social planning. There was no progressive improvement in standards nor, it seems, any learning from experience.

On the design side some significant points were made. The interior location of the staircases was identified as the most serious design defect: for many years the general condition of the staircases and common corridors remained unimaginable. In the majority of the buildings a further design problem was that balconies had been eliminated, thus frustrating needs formerly met by an interior patio in rural housing. The evaluation project suggested that as an educational exercise every superblock should include model apartments to demonstrate the best use of space, facilities and simple economical furniture. Outside the blocks it was obvious that much greater attention would have to be given to the control of use of the 'green' spaces for eventual landscaping and the planting of large trees, and to more effective planning of each site as a whole, including children's playgrounds, sporting facilities and outdoor seating provision.

In community services by far the most serious deficiencies were found in direct government social programmes and facilities, including health services, assistance in general welfare, cultural development and recreation. The task of providing and administering an adequate range of social facilities had proved beyond the capabilities of the Banco Obrero and it was therefore recommended that responsibility for the social aspects of the superblocks should be handed over to the national and metropolitan agencies and institutions normally responsible for such work. The creation of democratically elected tenant associations was urged as a means of building up interest in community development. Special guidance and orientation for families in need through strengthened social work facilities were suggested. Additionally, a policy of legalization of existing tenancies and selling apartments to tenants on favourable terms was advocated as it was considered that ownership status would tend to produce greater social and community sense.

Urbanizacion 23 de Enero and the other superblocks have since gradually been returned to something approaching normal. Large-scale social work was begun in a section of *23 de Enero* in 1961 on an emergency basis through a team of fourteen workers, the objective being the formation of groups and concurrently an educational effort to develop a leadership to enable the groups to express their aspirations in a conscious, responsible and organized manner. Sporting abilities, vocational training courses, artistic festivals, group environmental improvement and civic education have been emphasized. A series of active social committees has also been formed representing various buildings or sections in order to identify common problems and seek solutions. All rehabilitation work has been placed under official coordinating committees. Clearly, much has been accomplished by the Banco Obrero and other official Venezuelan agencies in *23 de Enero* and the other superblock areas since the initial fiasco. The time is now ripe for a second evaluation project; this time an investigation into the efficacy of the social programmes operating in the superblocks in order to provide pointers in this vital aspect of high density urban living for other developing countries.

The *ranchos*

Caracas continues to grow excessively. By 1990 a population of at least 4.5 million is expected. At 3.1 per cent Venezuela's annual rate of natural population increase is high even by Third World standards, and that of the Caracas area itself is probably of the same order. In addition, rural–urban migration is adding 80 000 people a year to the population of the capital (Bor and Smulian, 1970, p. 15). Its *rancho* areas are growing symbiotically (Table 4.1). Today, 30 per cent of the 2 million population live in *ranchos* (A. Turner and Smulian, 1971, p. 5).

The most frightening aspect of possible future urban development is that despite the fact that a greater proportion of Venezuela's population is now living in agglomerated settlements than ever before (76 per cent in 1970 compared with 35 per cent in 1936), there is also a larger number of people in the rural reservoir of the countryside than previously: 2.5

Table 4.1 Caracas: area occupied by *ranchos*

Year	*Total urbanized area (hectares)*	*Area occupied by ranchos (hectares)*	*Percentage*
1938	1 936	104	5.3
1941	3 483	98	2.8
1951	5 636	769	13.6
1954	6 411	642	10.0
1959	8 426	1 242	14.7
1966	12 054	2 375	19.7

Source: based on Franco, 1971, p. 41.

million in 1970 compared with 2.2 million in 1936 (Table 4.2). The capacity for the intensification of present problems of urban shelter is immense, and it is conceivable that half the metropolitan population will be living in *ranchos* by 1990.

As in other Third World cities, perhaps the most basic difficulty (at least as far as conventional housing solutions are concerned) is the income level of the urban poor; this despite the fact that Caracas is a relatively rich city, producing a quarter of the nation's gross domestic product and with a median family income 70 per cent higher than that for the nation as a whole. On a national scale, Venezuela's income distribution is highly skewed between the rural and the urban sectors, between the larger and the smaller urban places and between rich and poor in individual towns and cities, but overall it has been estimated that the normal method of building housing for sale or rent has no meaning at all for 44 per cent of all families, that is those earning less than 500 bolivars a month (Turner and Smulian, 1971, pp. 4–5). As Table 4.3 indicates, approximately 28 per cent of urban families and no less than 67 per cent of rural families fall below this level.[1] The *ranchos* are thus by no means all confined to Caracas. Even as early as 1950 one-quarter of households in Venezuela's various state capitals were living in *ranchos*, including 61 per cent of the households of Guanare, 44 per cent of those of Barinas, 42 per cent of those of San Carlo and 40 per cent of those of Cumana and Tucupita

[1] As it is impossible to secure temporally coincident information on housing deficits and levels of family income this aspect of the discussion must be taken as approximate only.

Table 4.2 Venezuela: Actual and projected urban and rural population, 1936–81

Year	*Population Venezuela*	*Urban population*	*%*	*Rural population*	*%*
1936	3 364 347	1 168 039	34.70	2 196 308	65.30
1941	3 850 771	1 516 444	39.40	2 334 327	60.60
1950	5 034 838	2 709 344	53.80	2 325 494	46.20
1961	7 612 327	5 164 125	67.84	2 448 202	32.16
1964	8 426 799	5 953 540	70.65	2 473 259	29.35
1970	10 398 907	7 874 763	75.73	2 524 144	24.27
1975	12 433 970	9 866 623	79.35	2 567 347	20.65
1981	15 202 623	12 582 459	82.77	2 620 167	17.23

N.B. Urban population is defined as that in places having more than 1 000 inhabitants.

Source: Bor and Smulian, 1970, p. 6.

Table 4.3 Venezuela: family income, 1962

Income	*Families*					
Bolivars/month	*Urban*		*Rural*		*Total*	
	No.	*Percentage*	*No.*	*Percentage*	*No.*	*Percentage*
More than 3 000	45 552	5.5	6 037	1.1	51 589	3.7
1 500–3 000	122 997	14.9	18 268	3.2	141 265	10.1
1 000–1 500	137 341	16.6	37 114	6.5	174 455	12.5
500–1 000	283 742	34.5	125 324	22.0	409 066	29.4
300–500	127 553	15.4	111 103	19.5	238 656	17.1
Less than 300	107 441	13.1	171 242	47.7	378 683	27.1
Total	824 566	100	569 088	100	1 393 654	100

Source: First National Survey of Family Income and Expenditure, quoted by Torrealba, 1968, Table 3.

(Jones, 1964, p. 422). There is every indication that the position has since worsened. With regard to Caracas itself, information on the income of households in four *rancho* areas given by Jones (p. 423) indicates that in the early 1960s approximately one-third to half of *rancho* families were outside of the normal housing market in purely economic terms. In terms of the actual exercise of choice (taking into account probably reluctance to move to subsidized housing in more peripheral locations for example), this proportion would have to be increased substantially.

On the basis of the 1961 census, there is a deficit of at least 694 000 homes in both the urban and the rural areas of Venezuela (Table 4.4). To meet this deficit as well as to provide for future needs it would be necessary to build a minimum of 70 000 units a year, possibly 15 per cent by the private sector (Bor and Smulian, 1970, p. 8). Unfortunately recent official responses to this desperate situation have by and large been classically predictable in terms of current attitudes towards housing in the Third World (Torrealba, 1968).

There are at present three national housing agencies: the Banco Obrero, which was set up as long ago as 1928, the Fundación para el Desarollo de la Communidad y Formento Municipal (or FUNDACOMUN), established in 1962, and the Programma de Vivienda Rural for the rural areas. The Banco Obrero concentrates upon towns and cities over 25 000 in population and FUNDACOMUN those between 10 000 and 25 000. As Table 4.5 shows, the combined performance of these agencies has been

Table 4.4 Venezuela: housing units needed and estimated deficit on the basis of the 1961 census

	Urban areas	*Rural areas*	*Total*
Housing units necessary	1 085 064	467 483	1 522 547
Housing units occupied	−899 049	−444 377	−1 343 426
(*a*) Deficit on basis of structure	187 015	23 106	209 121
Housing units occupied	899 049	444 377	1 343 426
Housing units acceptable	679 192	−154 718	−833 910
(*b*) Deficit on basis of standards	219 857	289 659	509 516
Total gross deficit (a + b)	405 872	312 765	718 637
Acceptable units not occupied	−20 927	−3 367	−24 294
Net total deficit	384 945	309 398	694 343

Source: Banco Obrero estimates quoted by Bor and Smulian, 1970, p. 9.

Table 4.5 Venezuela: dwellings constructed by the public sector

Year	*Dwellings in urban areas*	*Dwellings in rural areas*
1961	7 498	1 187
1962	5 347	3 164
1963	6 899	4 575
1964	8 968	6 067
1965	15 726	7 079
1966	17 378	10 815
1967	22 770	10 819
1968	21 236	13 907

Source: Banco Obrero and FUNDACOMUN statistics quoted by Bor and Smulian, 1970, p. 9.

very small compared with national needs, though to be fair it has improved considerably since 1964. Further, the housing being provided in no sense reaches down to the lowest socio-economic levels in the urban areas. The Banco Obrero, for example, is building apartments largely for sale on mortgage (with a cash advance from the mortgagee equivalent to 10 per cent of the value of the apartment), and caters for the 500 to 1 500 bolivar monthly family income group (Banco Obrero, 1967, p. 11). Its recent Caricuao housing project, well on the edge of the urban area in the south-west suburbs, is typical of its work in the capital. The project consists of well-appointed apartments covering floor areas two to five times (50 to 86 sq. m: 560 to 960 sq. ft) those built by the *rancheros* for themselves and, of course, sold at a price few of them can afford (see plans in *ibid.*, Appendix, pp. 1–5).

The search for housing policies

There are, however, certain aspects of the current search for realistic national housing policies in Venezuela which give some hope for its urban future – a future which, if only because of the numbers involved, must be controlled by the urban poor – and which also are significant in the more general Third World context. Some hope undoubtedly lies, for example, in possibilities of *rancho* improvement *in situ*. In Caracas, which contains by far the largest concentration of substandard housing, the *rancho* problem

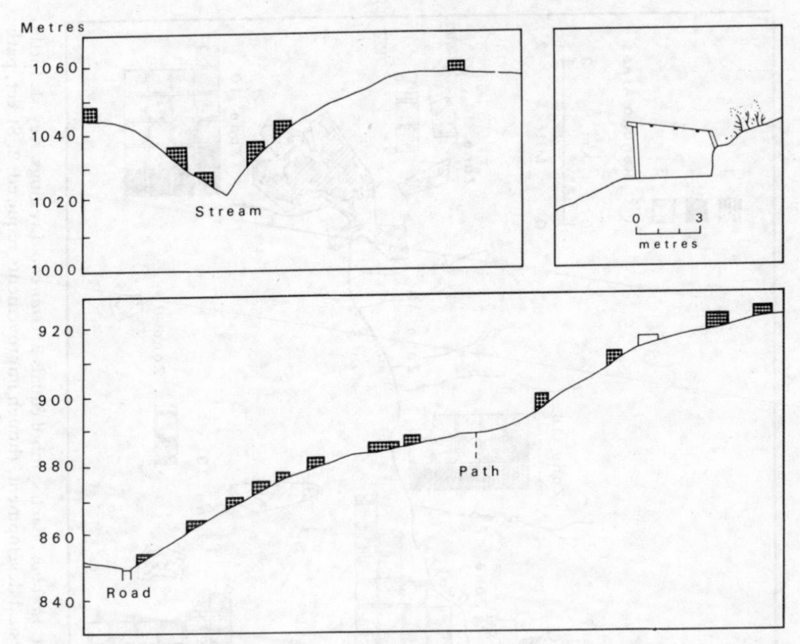

Fig. 4.5 Typical *rancho* locations in Caracas (no vertical exaggeration) (Jones, 1964)

is greatly aggravated by the physical setting of the city and the location of the *ranchos* on land considered unsuitable for better quality housing. As chapter 1 showed, this is a quite typical situation in many other Third World cities. The Caracas *ranchos* occupy two types of terrain posing physical difficulties: steep hillslopes and the sides and floors of ravines (Fig. 4.5). To the north, west and south of the old core of the city, they cling precariously to the hillsides, sometimes, as the south-west, coming quite near to the centre on spurs of higher ground. Precise locations are usually determined by access to roads. This pattern of occupance appears again in the extreme east of the urbanized area on the hillsides around Petare. Minor *rancho* areas are set deep in ravines wherever there is broken ground. This is especially the case where the Guaire basin meets the steep mountains to the north. In general, most of these commercially negative areas are municipal, state or church land.

A further significant feature of the *ranchos*, as elsewhere in the Third World, is gross deficiencies in urban services. Electricity is usually obtainable, either officially or unofficially, but the *ranchos* suffer from poor water supply, relatively little waterborne sanitation and the almost

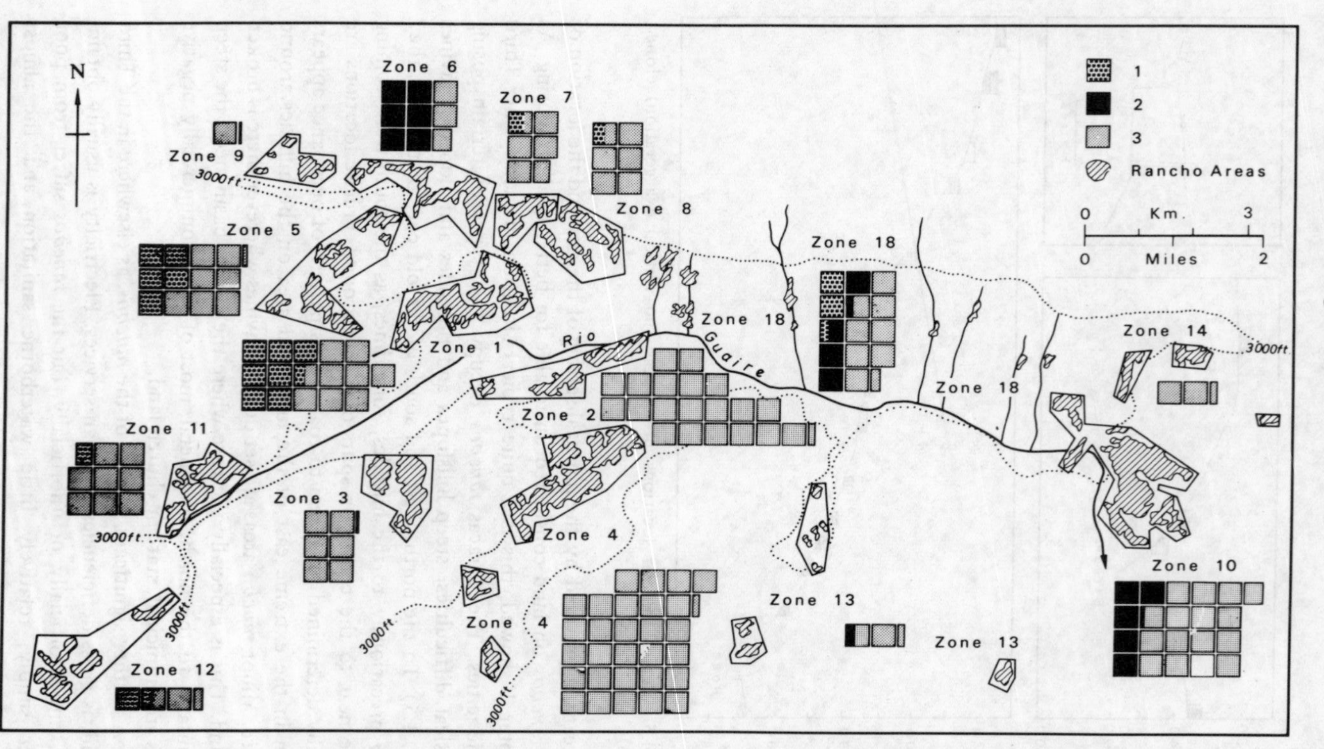

Fig. 4.6 Environmental improvement possibilities *in situ* in the Caracas *ranchos*. Each symbol equals 250 *rancho* dwellings. Key: 1. Little danger in the topographic situation: broadly acceptable pattern of physical development, though improvements required; 2. Street, path and house alignment so irregular as to require extensive remodelling; 3. Complete relocation necessary

complete absence of refuse collection, street paving and lighting. The 1961 census showed that 58 per cent of the *rancho* families obtained water by carrying it home in cans from public standpipes (Mendoza, 1969, p. 113). A further 22 per cent had to purchase their water from tanker trucks, usually at extortionate prices, while 16 per cent were reduced to obtaining water from rivers and streams, a practice that carries grave health risks. In 1961 there were only 1 675 water closets for over 50 000 ranchos (Jones, 1964, p. 422), the best facility for the vast majority of *rancheros* being a simple hole in the ground.

Nevertheless, though *rancho* houses are generally flimsy – only 13 per cent had brick or cement walls in 1961, the majority being of wood, though almost all have zinc sheet roofs (Mendoza, 1969, p. 113) – in themselves and in terms of the prevailing climatic conditions they are acceptable though minimal shelter. Moreover there is a tendency for the individual dwelling to be improved over time. Wood may gradually be replaced by brick, stone or cement; the earthen floor covered with concrete; interior partitions in the houses transformed into internal walls; and ultimately extra rooms, and even sometimes a second floor, added. If one characteristic of a slum is that it is never inhabited by those it was originally built for, the *ranchos* on this count alone cannot fall into such a category. In reality, of course, they are expressions of hope rather than despair.

An official environmental study carried out in Caracas by the Comite de Remodelacion de Barrios in 1963 divided the *ranchos* into three categories with respect to improvement possibilities (Fig. 4.6). In the first group were those *ranchos* in zones in which there was little danger in the topographic situation and when some alignment of streets and paths was evident (*ibid.*, pp. 117–32). In general these zones had an acceptable pattern of physical development, though they required the paving of streets, some improvement of lot alignment and the provision of services. Perhaps one-third of the families would need to be relocated in any general rehabilitation scheme. The second group comprised *ranchos* located in areas within which on the whole the topography was suitable and renovation possible but which suffered from street, path and house alignment so irregular as to require extensive remodelling. Besides services and the paving of streets, construction of temporary dwellings on a large scale nearby would be necessary because about one-half of the existing houses would have to be demolished. The third group comprised those *ranchos* officially designated as being 'without hope'. They were the ones on unstable, steep terrain liable to landslips, or located in ravines and subject to flood hazard. The only solution would be complete relocation. Unfortunately by far the largest number of *ranchos* fell into the third group: 33 700 houses covering an area of 1 000 hectares (2 470 acres) compared with a combined total of 16 000 houses covering 520 hectares (1 285 acres) in the first and second groups.

Though relatively limited, there would obviously be some scope for rehabilitation *in situ* in the *ranchos* of Caracas and other Venezuelan urban areas and to this end a small section within the Banco Obrero, the Departmento Urbanización y Equipamiento de Barrios, has recently been organized to carry out basic planning studies. One early result has been the planning on a pilot basis of low-cost, self-help housing projects designed by means of terracing for hillslopes of up to 60 per cent, that is for the types of terrain presently occupied by the Caracas *ranchos* (Banco Obrero, n.d.). It is hoped that with technical assistance from the Banco Obrero and loans for materials, the inhabitants of such projects will themselves to be able to construct the housing, starting first with a core consisting of living–sleeping space, toilet, washroom and a private patio for drying clothes, and later extending this through the installation of an internal staircase and the building successively of up to three bedrooms above. Water, sewerage, public lighting and paved paths will be provided, as will schools and other social facilities.

While it is hoped that in order to conserve building land relatively close to the city's inner areas, gross densities of 750 to the hectare (300 to the acre) can be achieved, a higher figure than those usual in the *rancho* areas, if there can be a criticism of this more imaginative departure in Banco thinking at such an early stage, it is perhaps that the space standards envisaged remain generous in terms of Venezuela's massive problems both of housing and of the consequences of the physical spread of the major towns and cities in terms of intra-urban linkages. The planned core of each house covers 37 sq. m (410 sq. ft) and on full development the housing unit will be 74 sq. m (820 sq. ft) in floor area. This may prove a more generous allocation than is strictly necessary. It would perhaps be significant, in terms of Venezuela's urban problems and even perhaps of those of the Third World more generally, to test during the early stages of the project whether, with appropriate design modifications both to the houses themselves and to the provision of services and facilities in the schemes in general, two families could occupy the space now allocated for each individual living unit, that is, one family to each floor. It may well prove, as it seems in Hong Kong (see chapter 5), that actual living space is not the major concern of the urban poor in comparison with expenditure on rent and location in inner areas in order to facilitate proximity to employment for the main wage earner and the maintenance of subsidiary sources of income for other members of the family.

The new towns

A further encouraging aspect of present urban policies lies in the beginnings of realistic treatment of housing problems in the development of Venezuela's new towns. Venezuela has no 'new towns policy' or legislation as such. It is further worth noting that the country as a whole is grossly deficient in trained urban planning staff; that no agreed framework for the distribution of population at national, regional or local level exists; that there is no legal obligation for the central government to prepare physical plans; that there is no overall fiscal programme relating to the towns; that no national urban planning laws exist for the control of land in the public interest; and that each local council has complete control of the use and development of land within its own boundaries (Bor and Smulian, 1970, pp. 9–10). Nevertheless, there are three new towns of international significance planned or in course of construction (Fig. 4.7). The most developed one to date, Ciudad Guayana, was conceived in 1960 to regularize and further promote the development of an area on the lower Orinoco River in which major resource concessions for iron mining and steel manufacture had been made some years previously. A new city in the Tuy Medio, 48 km (30 miles) south of Caracas, was first mooted in 1957 as one of a number of satellites designed to check population influx into the capital and accommodate overflow population and industry from it. (This new town has not yet been given a name.) The third new town is El Tablazo, which is located opposite Maracaibo across the Lake. It was proposed in 1967 as a reception centre for population inflow expected from the development of a major petrochemical complex in the area.

As Rodwin (1970, p. 33) has observed, at first glance the lower Orinoco valley hardly appears an inviting place to build a city. In Venezuela as in other developing countries virtually all roads lead to the capital, yet Ciudad Guayana is 480 km (300 miles) away from Caracas and, moreover, located in an area long considered a backwater by almost all Venezuelans. The key to its foundation lies in the potential of the Guayana region. After the overthrow of the Pérez Jiménez regime, the new government produced a three-year plan which for the first time designated developmental regions and established regional development corporations to work in cooperation with a new national economic planning authority.

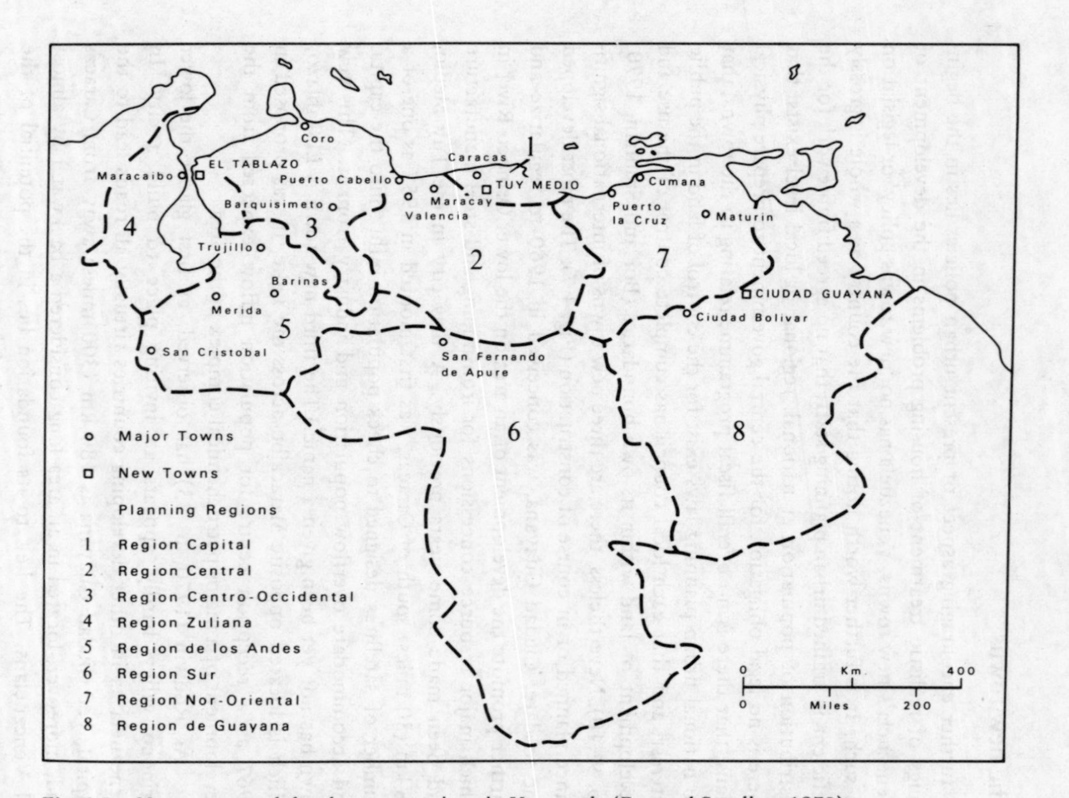

Fig. 4.7 New towns and development regions in Venezuela (Bor and Smulian, 1970)

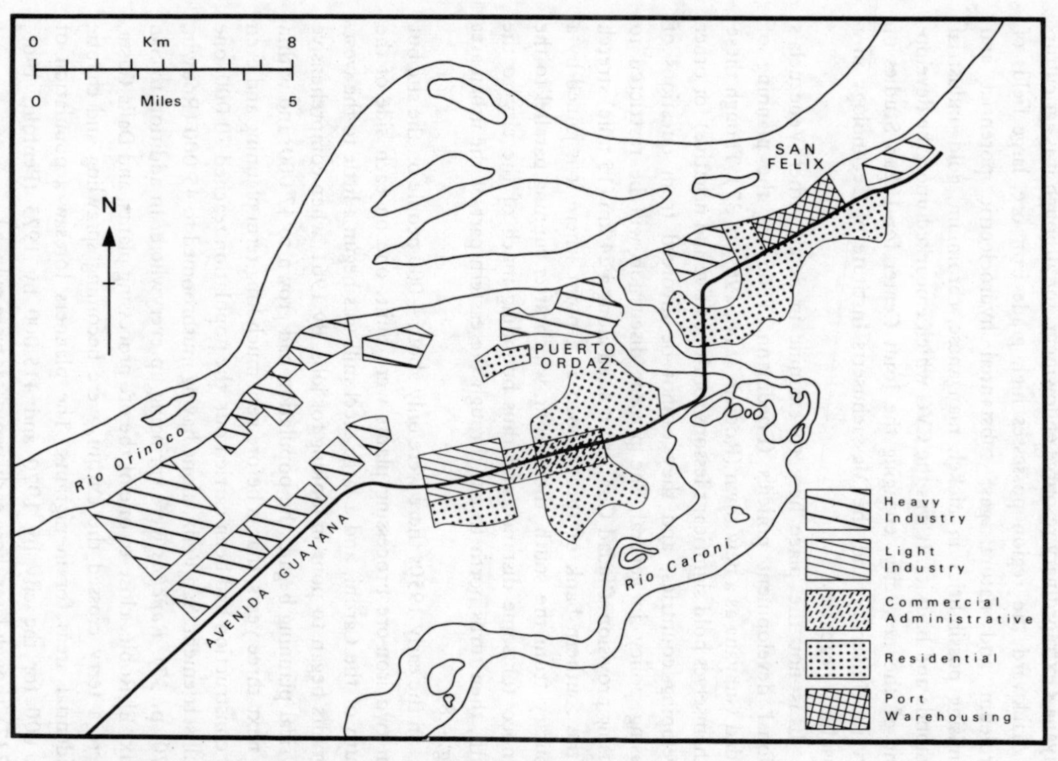

Fig. 4.8 Ciudad Guayana: planned land uses, 1970 (Rodwin, 1970)

The first such corporation was the Corporacion Venezolana de Guayana (or CVG), which was established in 1960 as an autonomous authority reporting directly to the President of the Republic. This was recognition of Guayana's extraordinary resource endowment, for although it is agriculturally backward the region possesses high grade iron ore, large fields of petroleum and natural gas, substantial hydroelectric potential and promising possibilities in nickel, manganese, chromium, gold, industrial diamonds and bauxite. It was the CVG which embarked upon the development of the new city, engaging the Joint Center for Urban Studies of Harvard University and the Massachusetts Institute of Technology in a consultative capacity.

It is not the place here to examine in detail either Venezuela's regional development policies (Friedmann, 1966) or the planning of Ciudad Guayana as a new town (Rodwin *et al*., 1969, p. 37). Though these in themselves hold significant lessons (both positive and negative) for other developing countries, and they cannot be divorced from questions of housing policy in general, the present discussion will be restricted to housing provision. Ciudad Guayana is sited along a 24 km (15 mile) stretch of the southern bank of the Orinoco at a point where it is joined by a tributary from the south, the Caroni, which after running parallel to the Orinoco for some distance and thus bounding much of the city to the south, then turns north to cut through the eastern part of the urban area (Fig. 4.8).

In the early 1950s there were only about 4 000 people on the site but then two iron-ore processing plants were built, one on each side of the mouth of the Caroni, and a large steel mill was begun a little to the west. Migrants began to pour in looking for jobs. By 1961, when comprehensive physical planning began, the population had grown to 42 000; and within the next three years, that is before very much long-term planning and even less construction had been carried out, the population reached 70 000, one small settlement, San Felix, alone having mushroomed to 45 000 (Rodwin, 1970, p. 37). *Ranchos* were springing up everywhere. In addition to San Felix, El Roble, close to one of the ore processing plants, and Dalla Costa, where a ferry crossed the Caroni, were becoming sprawling and chaotic residential areas for in-migrants. The planners foresaw a population of 250 000 for the city by 1970 and 415 000 by 1975 (Penfold, 1966, p. 237), though later these early estimates were reduced.

Ciudad Guayana reflects the central dilemma which must be faced in the development of new towns throughout the Third World: how to build a city for a population which by and large cannot afford much housing.

Fortunately, the CVG was able to acquire most of the land within the city area by purchase from private owners and the transfer of public land from other government agencies. On the other hand, its activities were restricted by the jurisdiction of other agencies, particularly in housing; and it was of course housing that was quickly identified as the most intractable of all the planning problems.

The CVG is not a housing agency and initially it was reluctant to become involved with housing (Rodwin, 1970, p. 53). It was felt that the provision of housing should be the responsibility of the Banco Obrero and private developers but at the same time it was realized that comprehensive action on the required scale was unlikely to be forthcoming on such a basis. Finally, the housing crisis reached such dimensions that the CVG was forced to intervene in 1962. An overall strategy of maximizing the contribution of the private sector was then embarked upon, with the objective of producing half of the planned investment in housing from this source, and at the same time both using public funds for the benefit of the low income groups generally and generating a substantial contribution to the housing programme as a whole through self-help construction schemes for the poorest people, who otherwise would be expected to settle in unregulated squatter areas (Table 4.6).

Table 4.6 Ciudad Guayana: investment requirements for housing, 1963–75 (millions of US dollars)

Period	*Private savings**	*CVG*	*Other government agencies*	*Private capital*	*Total*
1963–65	1.5	8.4	7.2	3.9	21.0
1966–70	19.2	11.2	41.6	41.7	113.7
1971–75	21.2	9.7	35.2	53.3	119.4
Total, 1963–75	41.9	29.3	84.0	98.9	254.1

* Includes imputed value of squatters' labour for low-cost housing.

Source: Corrada, 1969, p. 237.

As with every other major urban development scheme in the Third World, large-scale spontaneous settlement is of course unavoidable in Ciudad Guayana. The aim (as should usually be, but often is not, the case elsewhere) had to be to prevent it taking place at random and in internal patterns which made future improvement and the installation of public services impossible without substantial relocation of *ranchos* (Corrada, 1969, p. 239). This indicated a major effort within the settlement strategy for the poorest sector of the population in controlling lot sizes and the actual alignment of shacks. It also indicated that settlement or reception areas for squatters should be delineated within the city and security of tenure given in order to encourage squatters to invest both their labour and whatever money they could save in improving or replacing their dwellings. In such areas lots are now leased until the settler replaces his shack with an adequate house, at which point he can buy the land. Later studies have justified this approach by showing that in fact the average costs of expropriating *ranchos* for removal (that is, the compensation for squatters' improvements that is payable under Venezuelan law regardless of the tenure position once the initial shelter has been established) would be much higher than the costs of providing lots and installing water supply, paved streets and electricity in a programme of controlled settlement for the lowest income groups (*ibid.*).

On the assumption that if hard-core slums developed in any of the shack areas, they could be dealt with as specific problems, the CVG has experimented with ways of stimulating such settlements in acceptable areas and accelerating shack replacement. A construction manual has been issued to help improve the design and quality of new self-built homes. Partial prefabrication has also been tried with the objective of producing shell houses (columns, roof and a plumbing wall) for completion on a self-help basis, but generally even such minimal shells have proved too expensive for the lowest income groups. Some initial mistakes have been eliminated through the running of a pilot project at El Roble. These included processes of screening families both for 'antisocial' tendencies and to ensure that the poorest and most 'deserving' were given lots first, which served only to delay the allocation procedure to such a point that the policy of guiding spontaneous settlement into acceptable locations became endangered, and the imposition of unrealistic credit requirements in granting loans for the purchase of construction materials.

On the basis of experience, a general operational policy towards spontaneous settlement has now become established (Corrada, 1969, p. 297). Lots in the reception areas are granted on a 'first come, first served' basis. Families are not screened for income, though land speculation is controlled by lease arrangements that grant title to the settler only after he builds an adequate house. Shack replacement is encouraged and to this end income requirements for the granting of construction loans have been eliminated. The settler signs a self-help contract with the CVG which offers him four options: to receive payment for his labour if he builds a house and turns it over to the agency; to continue building other houses and to receive one free of charge for every three built for the agency (the ratio being determined by the relative value of the lots, construction materials and labour); to buy construction materials and the lot by means of a long-term loan; or to lease the house he is building from the agency and pay for the lease with his labour input. In the latter case the labour input in the construction of a house would lease it for three years, during which period it is hoped that the settler would be able to find regular employment and become financially able to arrange to purchase the house and lot.

Though the CVG has by no means eliminated the haphazard construction of *ranchos* – during the period 1962–65 their total number increased by about 2 500 and of these 1 500 were located at random (Corrada, 1969, p. 24) (Table 4.7) – these arrangements seem to be proving realistic as the basis for an overall policy towards the urban poor in the local circumstances. They deserve to be studied closely by other developing countries faced with the necessity for building new towns.

Table 4.7 Ciudad Guayana: housing stock, 1962 and 1965

	September 1962		*February 1965*	
	Number	*Percentage*	*Number*	*Percentage*
Shacks*	2 816	32.6	5 280	44.5
Low- and middle-cost houses†	5 745	66.4	5 965	50.3
Low- and middle-cost apartments	29	0.3	288	2.4
High-cost houses	60	0.7	332	2.8
Total	8 650	100.0	11 865	100.0

* All considered substandard and in need of replacement.
† Approximately one-quarter partially substandard.
Source: Corrada, 1969, p. 238.

Though they are at much earlier stages of development, similar approaches are being followed in the planning of the new towns in the Tuy Medio and at El Tablazo. In a sense these projected new urban centres are complementary – that in the Tuy Medio should ease pressure within the central region, particularly on Caracas, while El Tablazo is designed to help stabilize population in the west of the country, where employment in oil is falling steadily as the industry becomes more automated – and in relation

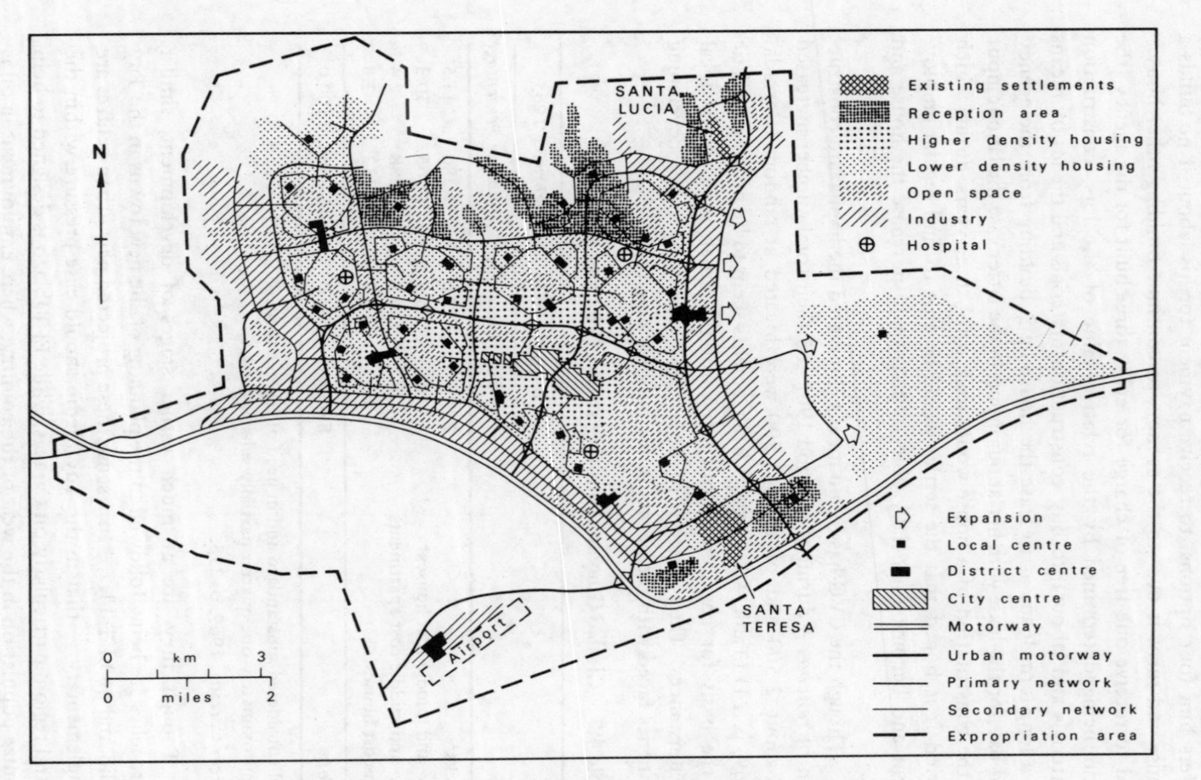

Fig. 4.9 Reception areas in the new city in the Tuy Medio (Turner and Smulian, 1971)

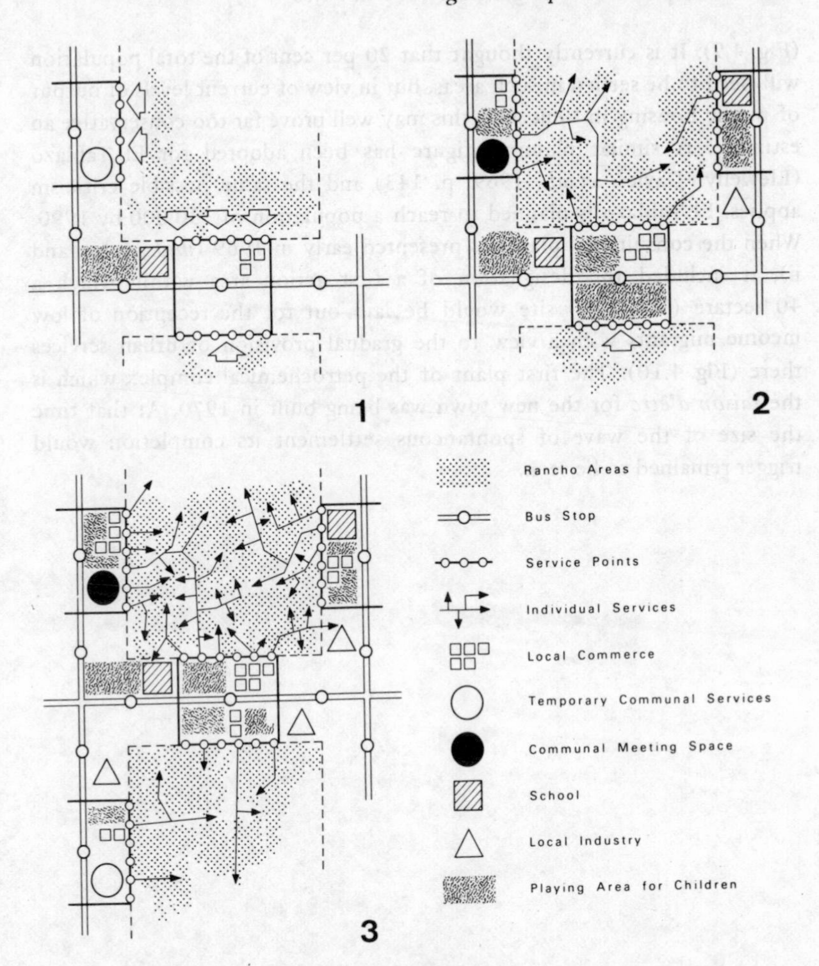

Fig. 4.10 El Tablazo: development of reception areas

to such a population strategy their success will obviously hinge largely on the ability of their planners and administrators to meet the housing needs of the poorest elements.

The new city in the Tuy Medio is expected to have a population in excess of 400 000 by 1990, mainly through in-migration. Only 20 per cent of the population will be able to afford housing built by the private sector (Turner and Smulian, 1971, p. 15). Four-fifths of the inhabitants will therefore have to be served either by the national public housing agencies or through guiding spontaneous settlement to planned reception areas

(Fig. 4.9). It is currently thought that 20 per cent of the total population will need to be settled in such areas, but in view of current levels of output of public housing in Venezuela this may well prove far too conservative an estimate. A similar planning figure has been adopted for El Tablazo (Llewellyn-Davies, *et al.*, 1969, p. 143) and the same possible criticism applies. El Tablazo is planned to reach a population of 330 000 by 1990. When the consultants' plan was presented early in 1969 (*ibid.*, vols. i and ii), it included the designation of a first action area within which a 40 hectare (100 acre) site would be laid out for the reception of low income migrants with a view to the gradual provision of urban services there (Fig. 4.10). The first plant of the petrochemical complex which is the *raison d'être* for the new town was being built in 1970. At that time the size of the wave of spontaneous settlement its completion would trigger remained to be seen.

5

High-rise responses: Hong Kong

Hong Kong is a cruel society in which very little assistance is given to the poor.

Keith Hopkins, 1971

In Hong Kong the experience with high-rise housing for the urban poor has been strikingly different from that of Caracas, and almost everywhere else in the Third World. The colonial government has now reached the stage of being landlord to 40 per cent of the total population of just over 4 million. Almost all its schemes are urban, high-rise and ultra high density. Significantly in terms of most high-rise housing programmes elsewhere in the Third World (and especially the Singapore schemes, with which they are often compared) they are directed almost wholly towards the inhabitants of spontaneous settlements and the poorest sectors of the urban community that are more regularly housed. As Prescott (1971, p. 11) has commented, Hong Kong is regarded by visiting planners with not a little astonishment: to most, the densities at which official housing schemes have been built, and private developers allowed to build, seem both incredible and unforgivable. There is almost disbelief when general densities over extensive urban areas of over 75 000 persons to the sq. km (200 000 persons to the sq. mile) are mentioned, and certain specific net site densities in excess of 12 000 persons per hectare (5 000 per acre) are received with an air of some bemusement. Nevertheless, as an urban system Hong Kong works. Moreover it can clearly be seen to work, even by the visitor, and at a level far above general Third World urban standards. Both in terms of its urban form and its rapid rate of economic growth, Hong Kong is a developmental paradox which defies easy explanation.

Urban population growth

As elsewhere in the Third World, Hong Kong's problems of spontaneous settlement have become conspicuous through rapid rates of growth of the urban population during the last two decades. At the end of the Pacific War its population stood at about 600 000: by early 1974 it had risen to 4.2 million, nine-tenths of which was within the Victoria–Kowloon urban area and two new towns, Tsuen Wan and Kwun Tong (Fig. 5.1). This population growth has had a dual basis. In the first place, rates of natural increase have been high. As far as can be ascertained from the official statistics, which are incomplete, the rate of natural increase averaged 2.6 per cent per annum over the twenty years following 1947, though in recent years the birth rate has fallen markedly: from thirty-nine per 1 000 in 1958 to twenty per 1 000 in 1972. Of greater importance than rates of general increase *per se*, however, has been the cumulative effect on population levels of refugee immigration from China.

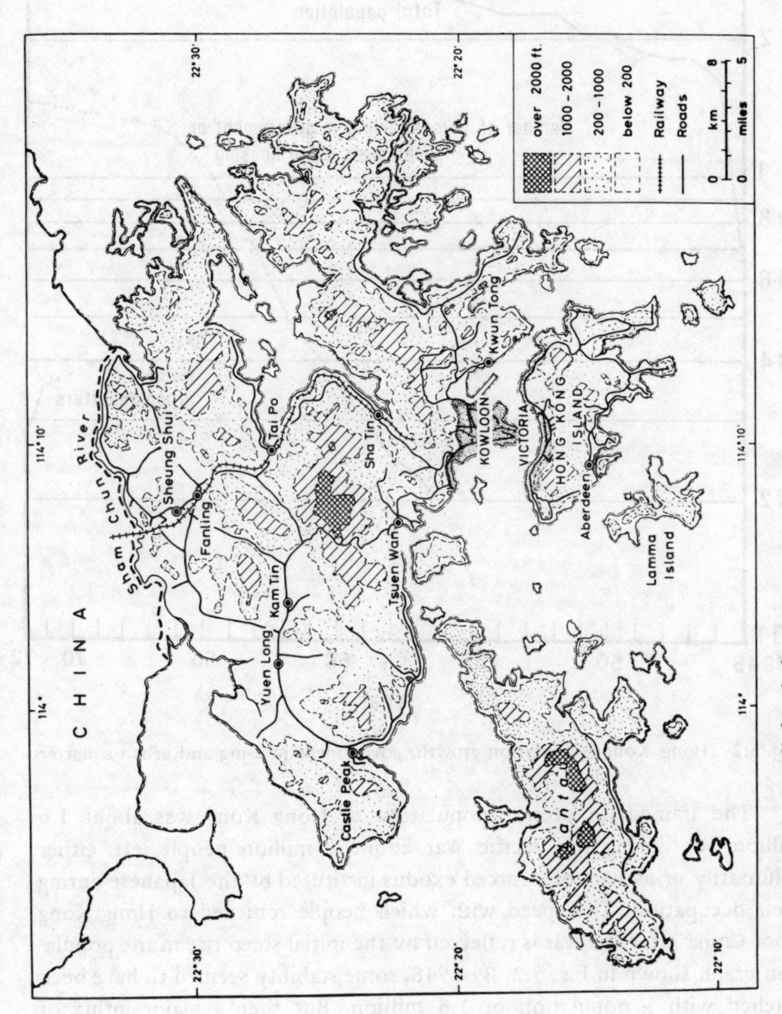

Fig. 5.1 Hong Kong: relief and place names

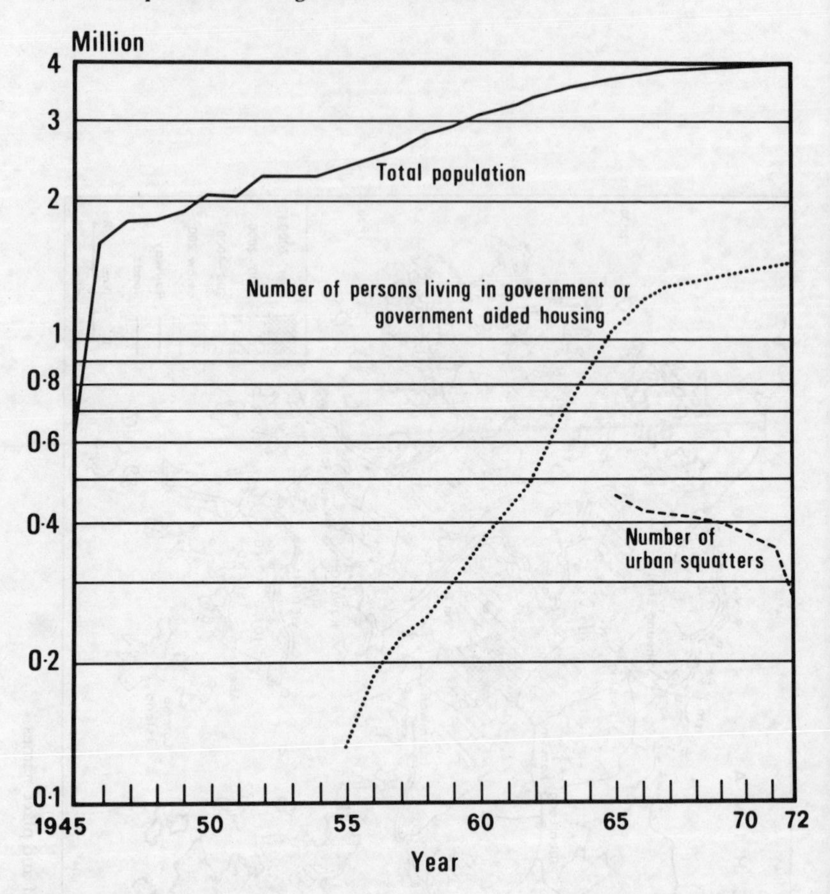

Fig. 5.2 Hong Kong: population growth, government housing and urban squatters

The immediate prewar population of Hong Kong was about 1.6 million but during the Pacific War about 1 million people left, either voluntarily or as part of a forced exodus instituted by the Japanese during their occupation. The speed with which people returned to Hong Kong from China after the war is reflected by the initial steep rise in the population graph shown in Fig. 5.2. By 1948, some stability seemed to have been reached with a population of 1.8 million. But then a major influx of refugees began because of the civil war in China (Vaughan and Dwyer, 1966). The following year brought a torrent of refugees as Kwantung peasants fled before the advance of Communist arms. In August 1949, when the fall of Canton seemed imminent, the inrush reached 10 000 persons a week, and by May 1950 the population had risen to an estimated 2.4 million. Faced with a rapidly deteriorating internal situation, the Hong Kong government imposed in-migration controls for the first time in the history of the colony. Since then illegal in-migration has operated at volumes fluctuating with changing conditions in southern China. Two incidents illustrate the extent and continuity of the human pressure against the borders of Hong Kong. First, in February 1956 the position was thought to be sufficiently stable for in-migration controls to be relaxed, and during the next seven months 56 000 in-migrants arrived, making it necessary to re-impose the controls. Again, in May 1962 the Chinese government, for reasons unknown, relaxed control over its side of the land border for one week. This resulted in a wholesale invasion of Hong Kong by Kwantung peasants which could not be completely stemmed even by combined operations by the police and the armed forces. Local estimates of the number of refugees who managed to evade arrest and deportation during this short period have varied between 40 000 and 60 000.

The total number of refugees in Hong Kong is uncertain and illegal entry is still occurring. In 1954 it was estimated that there were 667 000 persons belonging to refugee families living in the colony – almost 30 per cent of the total population of that time – and that they were mainly concentrated in the urban areas, where work or the prospect of work existed (Hambro, 1955, p. 27). The number of persons in families of refugee origin today must be well over 1.5 million. In terms of the provision of shelter Hong Kong's refugees can be considered as the equivalent of rural–urban migrants in other Third World cities. Hong Kong has swallowed them in several large gulps but by and large they have been digested, if somewhat painfully.

Housing conditions

If existing population trends continue, it is expected that by 1986 Hong Kong's present population of 4.2 million will have increased to 5.8 million. By 1986, the proportion living in the major urban areas (the cities of Victoria and Kowloon and the new urban areas of Kwun Tong and Tsuen Wan) will have risen to 94 per cent, involving an increase of 2 million persons over present numbers in these areas. The crux of the housing problem, as elsewhere in the Third World, is the present and anticipated future poverty of this population. It was officially estimated in 1968 that

HK$200 a month was the minimum economic rent at which the private developer could build self-contained residential units in Hong Kong (Dwyer, 1968*b*, p. 171). If it is assumed that a poor family can afford to devote only about one-fifth of family income to rent, then a minimum income of HK$1 000 monthly would have been required for such accommodation at that date. Approximately three-quarters of the families in Hong Kong were below this level in 1968, and it was not officially anticipated that this proportion could be reduced much below two-thirds over the next twenty years despite Hong Kong's growing prosperity.

Both for its total population and in terms of its actual and anticipated urban populations, Hong Kong is an extremely small physical entity. The colony consists of Hong Kong Island itself and the tip of the Kowloon peninsula (now the southern half of the present Kowloon urban area), which were ceded to Britain in 1841 and 1860 respectively, plus the New Territories. The latter were leased from China in 1898 for ninety-nine years and stretch from Boundary Street – in the heart of the present day city of Kowloon – north to the Sham Chun River, including numerous adjacent islands. The land area in all is only 1 030 sq. km (400 sq. miles). The 1971 population census (Hong Kong Government, 1972) showed that the overall population density of Hong Kong was 3 700 persons per sq. km (9 700 persons per sq. mile), excluding the now relatively small number of people living afloat on sampans and junks. Concentration of population in the urban areas is intense and the census showed that some of the highest urban population densities in the world prevail in certain areas. The Wanchai, Sheung Wan and West census districts in Victoria, for example, recorded gross densities of 113 000, 98 000 and 96 000 persons per sq. km (293 000, 255 000 and 249 000 per sq. mile) respectively, while those of the Mongkok and Yaumatei districts in Kowloon were 155 000 and 130 000 per sq. km (401 000 and 336 000 per sq. mile).

Such almost incredible urban population densities have arisen in part from the restricted site of the Victoria–Kowloon urban area. The city of Victoria faces its offspring, Kowloon, across one of the world's best natural harbours; indeed the existence of the harbour has been responsible historically for the growth of the twin cities (Dwyer, 1965). Both cities, and especially Victoria, are closely backed by ridges rising sharply to over 500 m (1 640 ft). Victoria extends in a narrow strip along the north coast of Hong Kong Island between the harbour and a hilly interior that culminates in the Peak. The Kowloon peninsula provides more space than the Island for urban growth adjacent to the harbour. Spreading from its southern tip, urban development has covered the central and northern

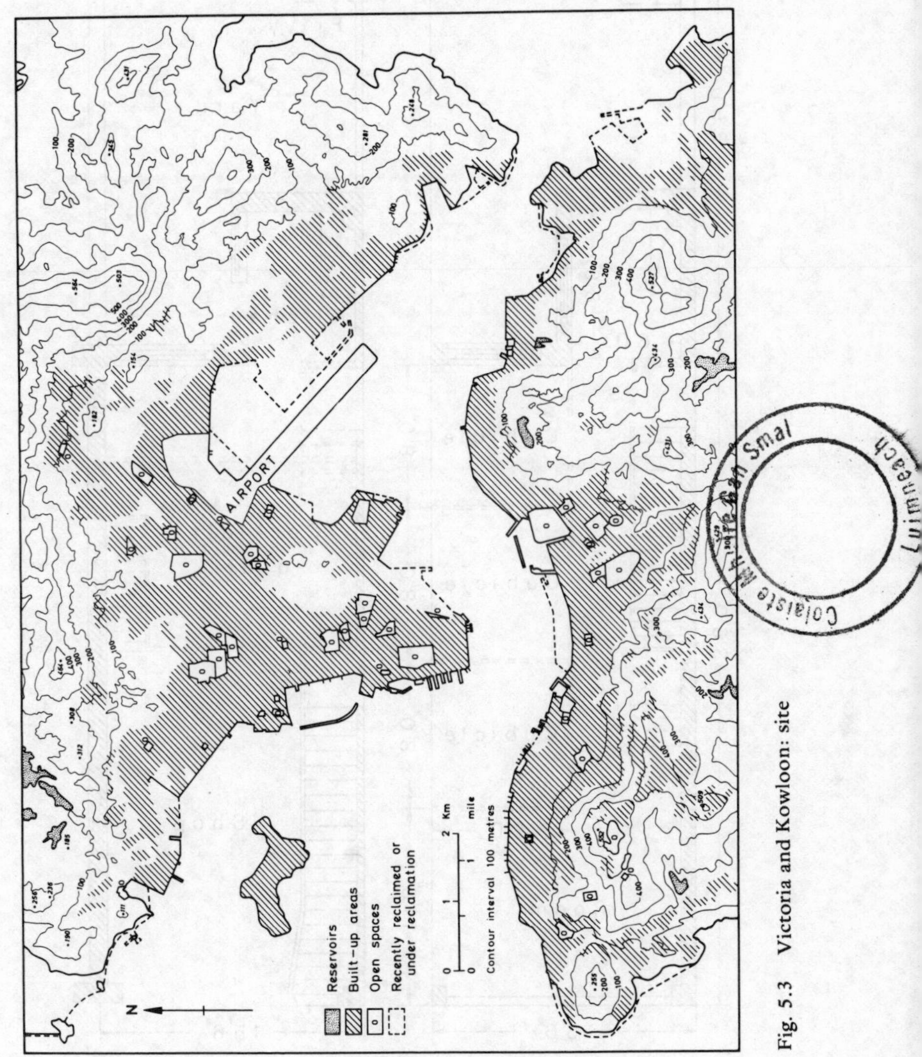

Fig. 5.3 Victoria and Kowloon: site

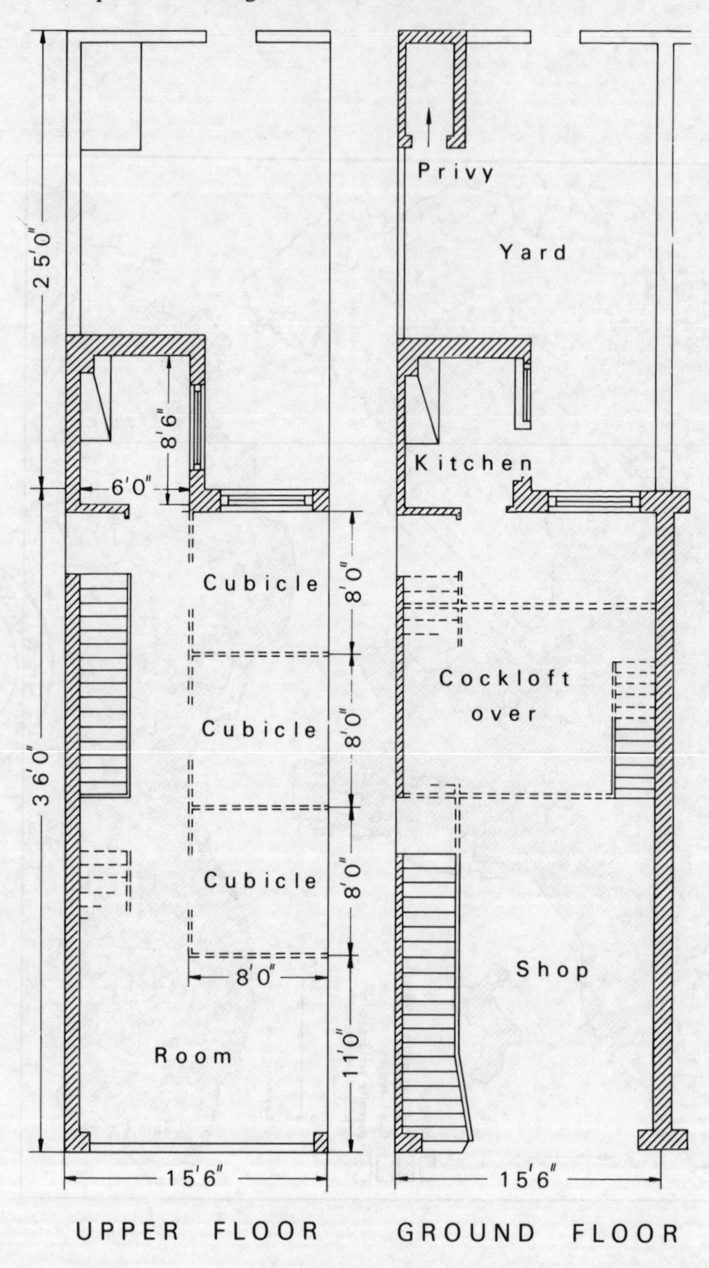

Fig. 5.4 A typical pre-1939 Hong Kong shophouse

parts of the peninsula during the postwar period, and most of it is now built over as Fig. 5.3 shows.

Nevertheless, high urban population densities have by no means resulted solely from physical restrictions on the spread of the cities. One of the classic Third World responses in terms of shelter to the problem of mass urban poverty – the smaller and smaller subdivision of accommodation in tenement buildings – has been fully experienced in Hong Kong. From their earliest days as cities, the site unit for lower income housing in Victoria and Kowloon has been small, usually 5 by 16 m (15 by *c.* 50 ft), the former dimension having been determined by the length of the China Fir pole for building purposes.

Before the Pacific War, large parts of the cities had developed as tenement housing areas characterized by standardized shophouse construction consisting of rows of open-fronted shops at ground floor level and two- or three-storeys of residential space above (Wong, 1969, pp. 31–8). Overcrowding had been a continuing problem. The ground floor consisted of one long room with a small kitchen at the rear (Fig. 5.4). Sometimes there was a small courtyard behind the kitchen, but in the nineteenth century tenements were frequently built back to back. A narrow staircase led to upper floors which were of similar pattern except that all the floor space was residential and usually divided into cubicles, one to a family. The shopkeeper on the ground floor typically housed his family in a mezzanine floor (or cockloft as it is called in Hong Kong) built over the rear part of the shop. Window space was inadequate; the small kitchens, one on each floor, had to be shared by numerous families; at most there were only three or four privies, or else (in the earlier tenements) they were not provided at all. In face of such conditions, and of the recurring public health problems resulting from them, the avariciousness of landlords and speculative builders, both Chinese and expatriate, was matched only by the strenuous efforts of various interested non-government members of the Hong Kong Legislative Council over the years to block the introduction and implementation of legislation designed to effect minimal improvement in sanitary and other facilities (Pryor, 1971, pp. 45–75).

Though this legacy still remains in parts of certain areas, particularly in the Western District of Victoria where there are now formidable urban renewal problems, what is not often realized is that the twin cities of Victoria and Kowloon are today products almost entirely of the period since the end of the Pacific War (Dwyer, 1971*a*, pp. 33–47). As a result of the war, 10 per cent of the total domestic housing accommodation in the urban areas was damaged and 10 per cent destroyed. Since the war much of the older property has been demolished to make way for new development, with the result that by the end of March 1968 only 11 per cent of the total stock of domestic accommodation constructed in the urban areas by the private sector had been built before the war (Hong Kong Government, Housing Board, 1969, pp. 3–4). In addition, the massive contributions by the public housing programmes to be outlined below have been made entirely during the postwar period. Perhaps most startling of all is the fact that new construction during the last ten years alone accounts for nearly half the permanent domestic living units in urban Hong Kong.

A feature of much of the private sector accommodation continues to be its subdivision into cubicles and bed spaces after completion, for, although housing for the high income groups is completely in private hands, in terms of total volume building by private developers in recent years has largely been directed towards the construction of multistorey tenement floors for the lower income groups, as Table 5.1 indicates. Such activity was stimulated in 1956 by a revision of the Buildings Ordinance which permitted a very much higher intensity of land use. Though new amendments were introduced in 1962 to reduce the intensity of development, a period of grace under the then-existing regulations was allowed up to 1966. The ten-year period from 1956 to 1966 saw the wholesale transformation of the older, inner urban areas. Through the combined efforts of private developers, and the public housing programmes which were introduced at roughly the same time, Victoria and Kowloon almost over-

Table 5.1 Hong Kong: residential building by private developers, 1958–66 (inclusive)

	Number (a)	*Average size (b) (sq. m)*	*Notional area (a x b)*	*Per cent of total notional area (excluding houses)*
Tenement floors	100 237	34.7	3 478 224	63.5
Small flats	25 018	43.7	1 093 287	19.9
Medium flats	6 833	72.9	498 126	9.1
Large flats	3 809	107.1	407 944	7.5
Houses	131	–	–	–

Source: Hong Kong Government, Crown Lands and Survey Office, unpublished data.

night became very largely cities of tall residential buildings up to twenty-storeys in height, whereas before they had been typified by three- or four-storey shophouses.

Growth of spontaneous settlements

After the Pacific War the floors of the tenement houses began to be subdivided into living units more minute than ever before because of the rapidly growing pressure of population. In addition to floors being partitioned off and sublet by principal tenants, the cubicles themselves were subdivided into bedspaces, and in extreme cases bed spaces were occupied on a shift system by three different sets of inhabitants. Roofs, cellars and lofts were let – the code plan for the classification of accommodation in the 1961 census included in its designations staircases, passages, hawker stalls, caves, tunnels and even sewers – and before strict official control was instituted still the population spilled out onto the pavements and the hillsides (Fig. 5.5).

As elsewhere in the Third World, the growth of spontaneous settlements within and on the edges of the cities became a parallel problem to that of the overcrowding of more regular accommodation, for the rising population could not be contained within the existing urban residential space, even through its extreme subdivision. In two years, between 1947 and 1949, the population in spontaneous settlements rose from 30 000 to 300 000 largely because of the refugee influx and by 1964 it had increased to a peak of 550 000. The squatter camps were not composed solely of refugees, however: surveys in 1949 showed many Hong Kong residents of long standing in them who had either sold their rights to occupy their previous accommodation to newcomers or else had been illegally evicted by rackrenting landlords (Dwyer, 1968*b*, p. 173). The squatter camps that developed were huge, for example that at Shek Kip Mei on the northern outskirts of Kowloon held 80 000 people at its peak, and densities in such single-storeyed hutted areas of up to 6 000 persons per hectare (2 500 persons per acre) were known.

Though there were problems of central area invasion during the late 1940s and early 1950s, spontaneous settlement became concentrated in northern Kowloon because more relatively flat space was available there for urban development than on Hong Kong Island. At its peak in 1953 a belt of spontaneous settlements each containing up to 50 000 people and comprising in all a population of over 300 000 enveloped northern Kowloon (Fig. 5.6). The planned expansion of the city was brought almost

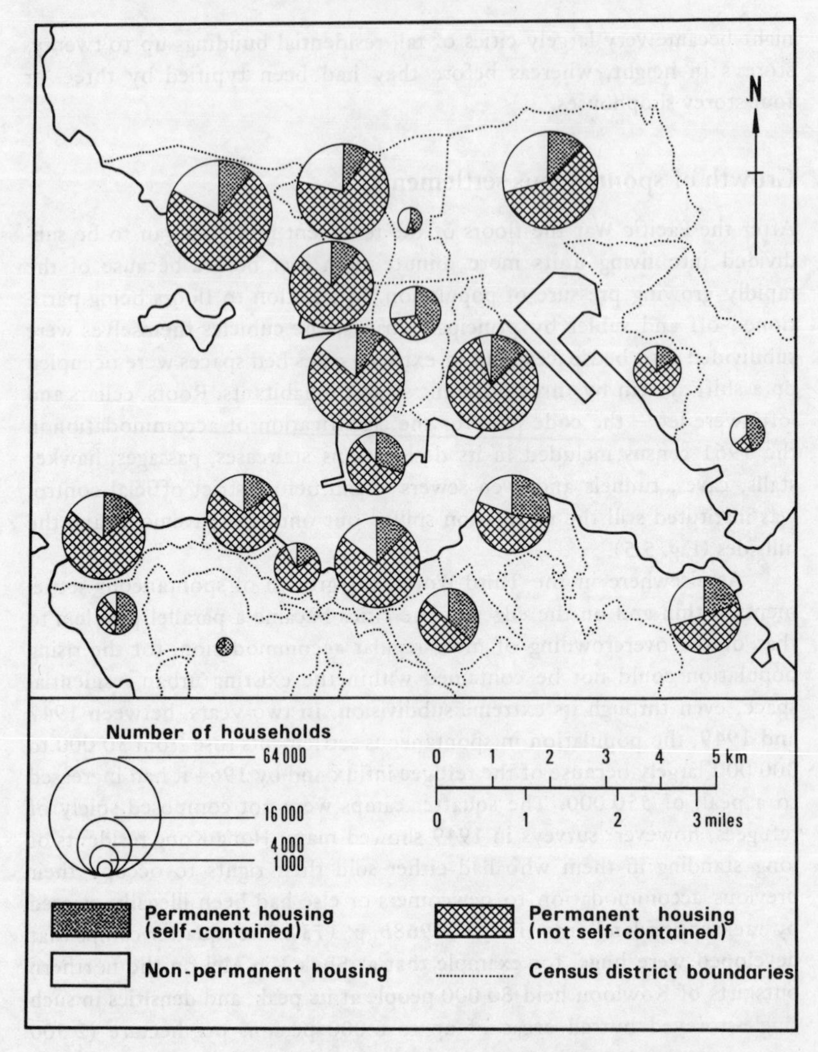

Fig. 5.5 Victoria and Kowloon: types of accommodation (1961 census)

to a halt, for the squatter camps not only covered valuable building land but also obstructed access to sites further away which were themselves empty. Within the close, almost impenetrable density of these huge settlements flourished shops, schools, restaurants, small industrial units and many enterprises that would have been illegal even in lawful accommodation (Dwyer and Chuen-Yan Lai, 1967).

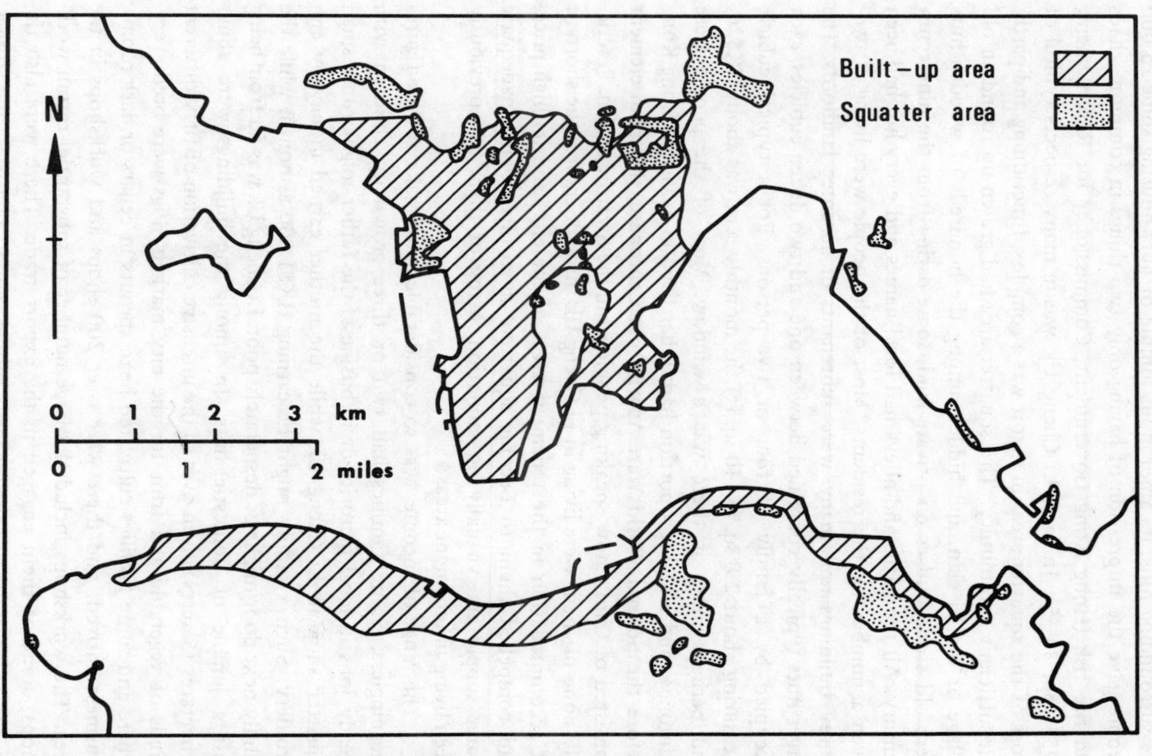

Fig. 5.6 Victoria and Kowloon: location of major spontaneous settlements, 1955

The Li Cheng Uk area in northern Kowloon was a case in point. From the surrounding hills, its amorphous jumble of huts housing some 25 000 people gave the impression of having only two things in common: chaos and fire risk (Hong Kong Government, Commissioner for Resettlement, 1955, pp. 34–5). In fact, Li Cheng Uk was in many respects typical of most of the squatter areas in that it was a complex, functioning and partly self-sufficient community. The squatter area had grown up round an old village of the Li clan, and hidden among the hundreds of wooden huts were old stone houses on private land, some dating from the nineteenth century. All the paths and alleys had local names and every hut had been given a number by the residents. Most of the people were living in two-storey buildings and many were subtenants of absentee landlords. The larger huts typically contained between one and two dozen cubicles, each occupied by a family of four or five persons. For a typical cubicle measuring about 2.8 sq. m (40 sq. ft) the monthly rent was about HK$20, and perhaps more if there was a window. Most of the people were Cantonese and a high proportion had either lived in or visited Hong Kong before the Second World War. Apart from Cantonese, the main element consisted of Chiu Chow speaking people from the Swatow region. Practically none of them were living in Li Cheng Uk through choice; the shortage of accommodation in the tenement areas of the city, and its high price, had compelled them to become squatters in a village with inadequate water supply and virtually no sanitation. Many of them had previously been living in tenement areas.

The range of incomes was so considerable as to make average figures meaningless. Some families had two or three grown up children with steady jobs in local factories or in business: the father might run a small squatter shop in Li Cheng Uk while the mother earned money by embroidery. Such a family might be earning HK$1 000 a month, while the family next door might be desperately poor. Li Cheng Uk was far from being just a jumble of domestic huts. In among the buildings were about 2 hectares (5 acres) given over to the intensive cultivation of fifty different kinds of vegetable and fruit for the city markets. Pigs were bred everywhere and some families cultivated bean sprouts in cellars or dark rooms. Business thrived, and there were over 200 shops and workshops in the area. The workshops included a large number of substantial rattan workshops, some of them engaged in the export trade. There were also tinsmiths, blacksmiths, shoe-makers, rubber goods factories and forges, mostly operating on a small scale. On the fringe of the area were a number of squatter factories using power-driven machinery for the manufacture,

Photo: United Nations

Plate 9 High-rise solutions: Barrio Sarria, Caracas

Photo: D. J. Dwyer

Plate 10 High-rise solutions: Toa Payoh, Singapore

Photo: Hong Kong Government Information Services

Plate 11 High-rise solutions: Government resettlement and low-cost housing, Hong Kong

Photo: Hong Kong Government Information Services

Plate 12 High-rise solutions: Inside a resettlement estate, Hong Kong. A somewhat idealized view

Photo: D. J. Dwyer

Plate 13 Chandigarh: Children of Chandigarh, Le Corbusier's planned city

Photo: D. J. Dwyer

Plate 14 Chandigarh: Their makeshift homes abut magnificent highways and stately public buildings

Photo: D. J. Dwyer

Plate 15 Chandigarh: But they are slowly being improved by the families themselves

Photo: D. J. Dwyer

Plate 16 Chandigarh: And all around the white monuments to 'planning', a spontaneous city of the poor is arising

among other things, of torch cases and metal castings. Besides eating houses and a market, there were three squatter schools, an unregistered Chiu Chow temple and a village fire brigade station. Apart from the original village houses, almost every structure was technically illegal. In such settlements as Li Cheng Uk, there was a continual risk of epidemics and fire. The first fortunately did not materialize, but serious fires in the spontaneous settlements became usual during Hong Kong's dry winters.

The housing programmes

Following a specially disastrous fire in the Shek Kip Mei settlement on Christmas Day 1953, in which 53 000 people lost their homes, the government began a new resettlement scheme which rapidly developed into a major programme. It is said that the outline of the scheme was worked out in a few days at meetings held to consider the Shik Kip Mei crisis, but whatever the truth of this, the official response did fall into an established Hong Kong governmental pattern of *ad hoc* responses to particular problems. An initial low density cottage resettlement project for squatters which had been started in 1951 had proved patently inadequate by the end of 1953. The new programme was based on multistorey buildings and two initial principles formulated under emergency conditions have since guided policy in this field: that resettlement should be at high density with standards such as to ensure relatively low rents, and that the land used should in general be less than that occupied by the same number of people under conditions of spontaneous settlement. The 1 million or so inhabitants of spontaneous settlements rehoused so far have been relocated in areas equivalent to only two-fifths of the land they previously occupied (Hopkins, 1971, p. 294).

The earliest type of accommodation provided by the official Resettlement Department which was established early in 1954 to rehouse spontaneous settlers consisted of seven-storey 'H'-shaped blocks, with communal washing and toilet facilities, divided into back-to-back single room accommodation units accessible by communal balconies (Fig. 5.7). The rooms varied in size from 7.7 sq. m (86 sq. ft) to 13.7 sq. m (152 sq. ft), but the vast majority were simple concrete cells of 10.8 sq. m (120 sq. ft) designed to house a family of five adults at an individual space standard of 2.2 sq. m (24 sq. ft), children under ten years of age being counted as half an adult. No separate kitchens were provided. A small number of larger self-contained flats with private balconies were provided in later blocks. In all, 240 blocks of this basic type (called Marks I and II) were built before the

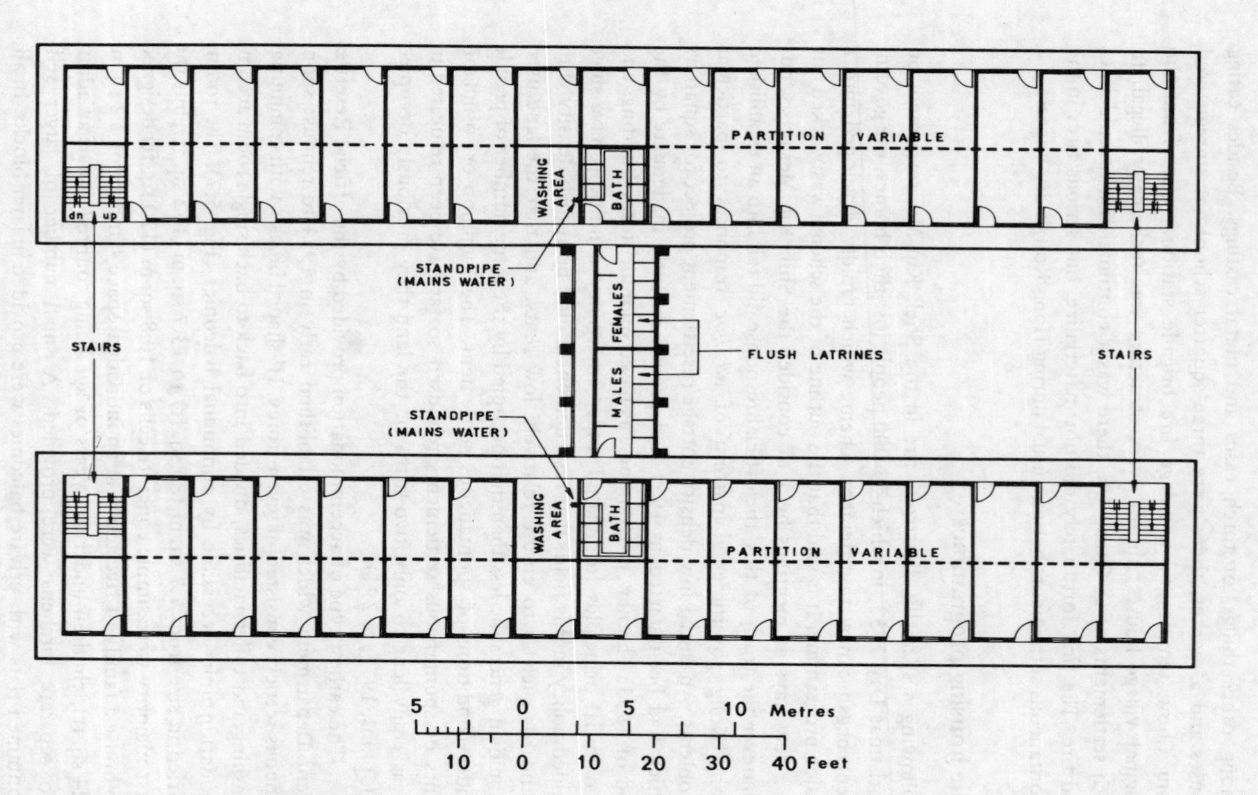

Fig. 5.7 Early resettlement blocks

design was superseded in 1964, usually at estate densities of over 4 800 to the hectare (2 000 persons to the acre).

Mark III blocks followed, of eight-storeys, then Marks IV and V, of sixteen. The design from Mark III onwards has incorporated access from a central corridor on each floor instead of from external common balconies. Thus each accommodation unit was given its own balcony. Refuse chutes and lifts were installed in these blocks and electrical points and toilets provided in the rooms. Private water taps were introduced into the design of the later Mark IV and the Mark V blocks and their installation into the earlier Mark IV and Mark III blocks was then carried out, as was the official provision of electrical points in the rooms of the Mark I and Mark II blocks. By the end of 1972 a total of 142 Mark III, 65 Mark IV and 48 Mark V blocks had been built, and the number of all blocks was 506. A scheme had also been started for converting blocks in the old Mark I and Mark II estates into self-contained flats each with toilet and water supply and some with private balconies, while from 1970 Mark VI blocks were built to an improved space standard of 3.2 sq. m (35 sq. ft) per person (Fig. 5.8). Rents vary according to the design of the block and size of room and are fixed to recover capital costs over forty years at 3.5 per cent, excluding a large subsidy element to the notional price of the land. The monthly rent of a standard room of 10.8 sq. m (120 sq. ft) in a Mark I or II block at the end of 1972 was HK$18; it had been raised from HK$14 in 1965, the first such increase to have taken place. In the newer Mark V blocks the rent of a room of 12.1 sq. m (135 sq. ft) was HK$34. These rent figures were the same in 1968 and may be compared both with Hopkins' (1969, p. 6) finding that in that year the average monthly family income of Hong Kong's spontaneous settlers was HK$496 and that of those households in the resettlement estates HK$552 and with the 1971 census figures for the distribution of household income in Hong Kong (Table 5.2).

Before the announcement of a unified administration for all official housing programmes in 1973 (a reconstituted Housing Authority) in addition to the resettlement programme three other types of public housing programme had developed in Hong Kong during the last twenty years (*see*, e.g., Hong Kong Housing Society, 1971, and Hong Kong Government Housing Authority, 1972) and had contributed to a massive change in the urban landscape (Fig. 5.9). The Hong Kong Housing Society, an independent voluntary agency, was actually first in the field of low-cost housing provision in the colony. It was incorporated in 1951 on the basis of a loan from the government at a relatively low rate of interest and the

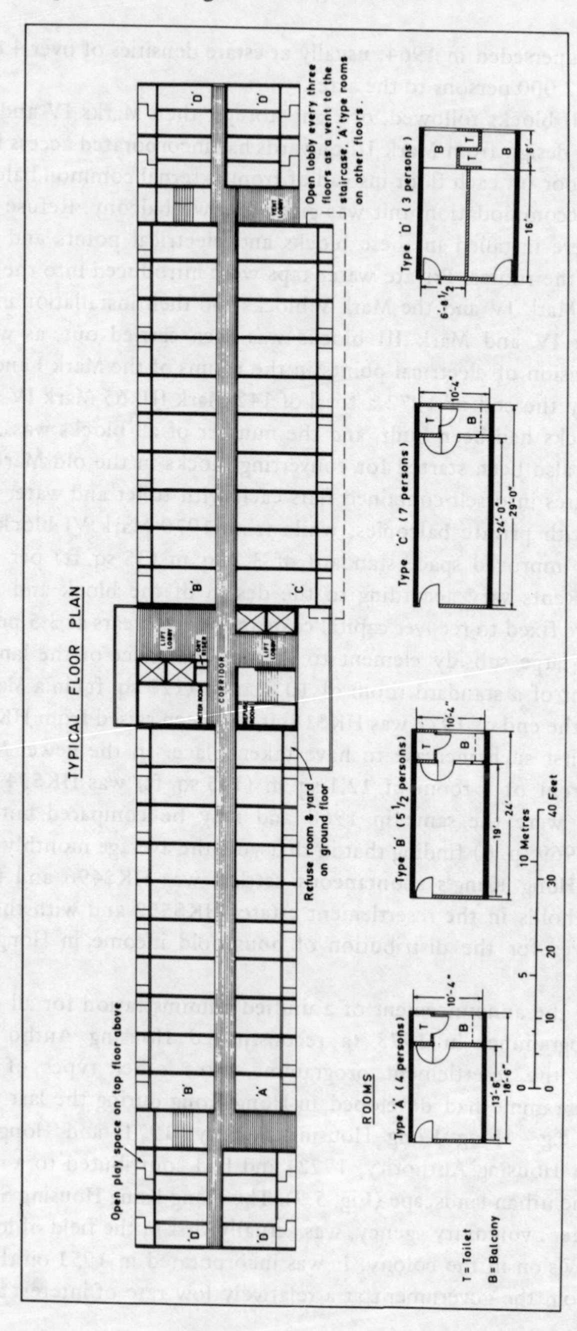

Fig. 5.8 The Mark VI resettlement block

Table 5.2 Hong Kong: distribution of household income, 1971

Income group (HK$ monthly)	*Households*	
	Number	*Percentage*
Less than 200	41 457	4.8
200–399	90 113	10.5
400–599	205 511	24.1
600–799	169 023	19.8
800–999	96 973	11.4
1 000–1 199	81 302	9.5
1 200–1 499	62 249	7.3
1 500–1 999	40 384	4.7
2 000 and over	69 996	7.9
Total	857 008	100

Source: Hong Kong Government, Census and Statistics Department, 1972, pp. 204–5.

allocation of public land for its housing schemes at one-third of the estimated market price, and its first estate, at Sheung Li Uk in north-east Kowloon, was built the following year. As Table 5.3 shows, the Society has since greatly expanded its operations. A further agency, the Hong Kong Housing Authority, was constituted in 1954 as an official body, with full autonomy to manage and operate the housing it constructed. Government finance was provided in the form of a revolving fund on which a low rate of interest was charged and, like the Housing Society, the Housing Authority received land at a cost of one-third its notional market value. Both agencies existed largely to provide housing for what might broadly be called the lower echelons of Hong Kong's white-collar class, that is families earning between HK$500 and HK$1 000 a month. Both built to a standard of 3.1 sq. m (35 sq. ft) per person, excluding kitchens, toilets and balconies. An example of such building, the So Uk estate of the Housing Authority, is shown in Fig. 5.10.

A fourth kind of public housing consisted of the Government Low-Cost Housing programme. This was launched in 1961 and aimed at providing accommodation for people with family incomes of less than HK$500 a month who were living in insanitary or overcrowded conditions, largely as tenement dwellers. The estates were built by the Public Works Department and managed by the Hong Kong Housing Authority, they

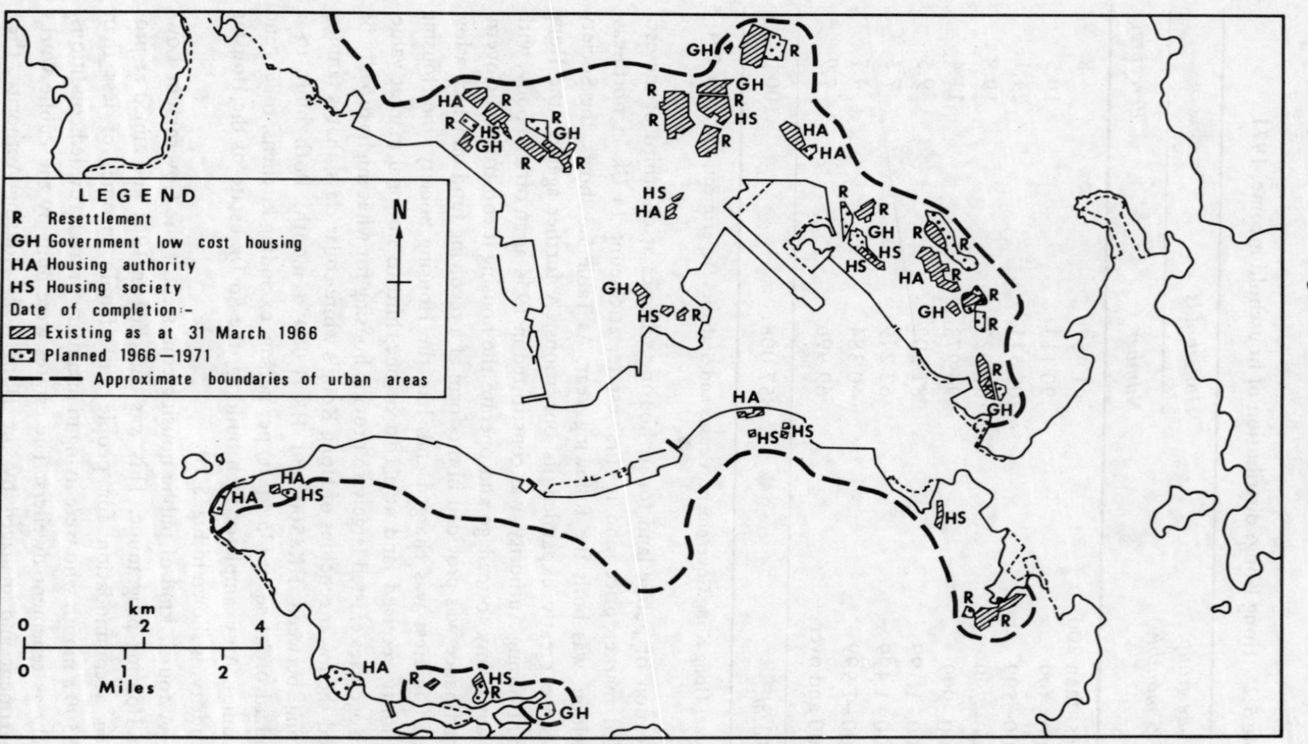

Fig. 5.9 Victoria and Kowloon: location of government and government-subsidized housing schemes

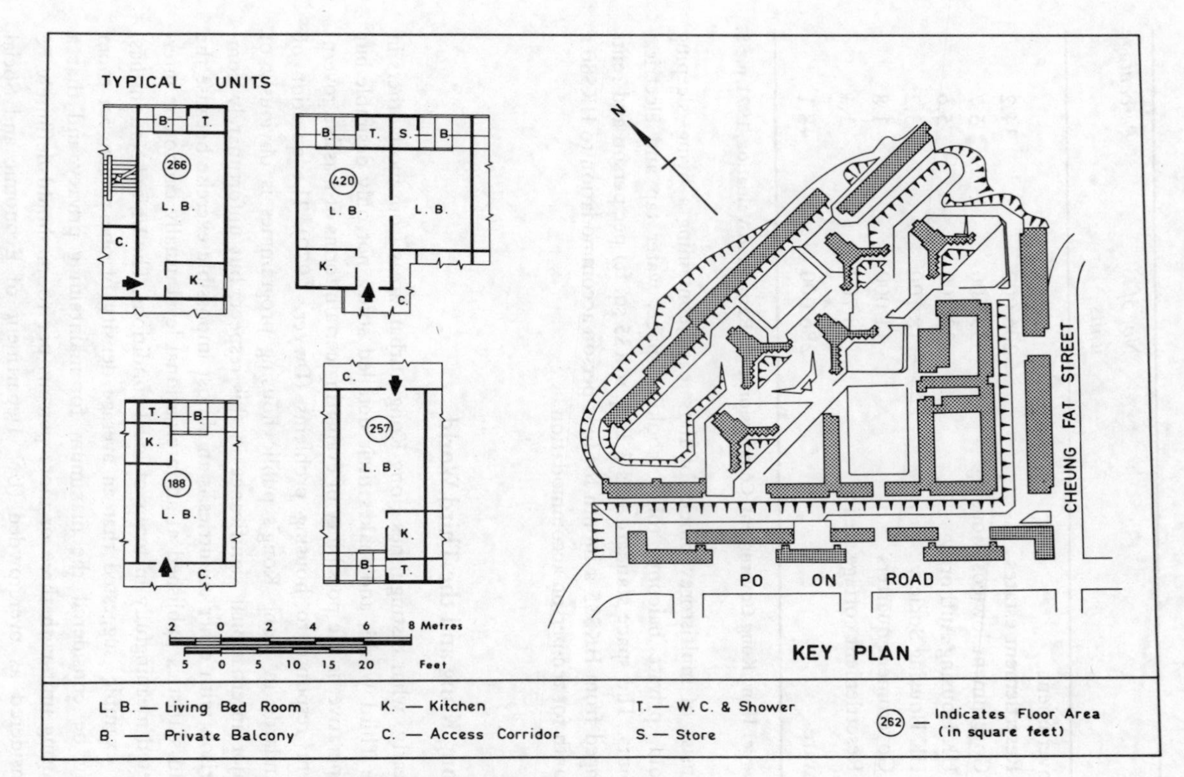

Fig. 5.10 The So Uk estate of the Hong Kong Housing Authority

Table 5.3 Supply of permanent domestic accommodation in the urban areas of Hong Kong, December 1970

	No. of units	*Percentage*
Government		
Resettlement estates	206 000	34.2
Government low-cost housing	33 600	5.7
HK Housing Authority	33 100	5.6
HK Housing Society	18 100	3.2
Government quarters	11 000	1.8
Resettlement cottage areas	8 700	1.4
Private	286 000	48.1

Source: Hong Kong Government, Commissioner for Rating and Valuation, 1971, p. 55.

consist of multistorey blocks of flats, each containing a living–sleeping room, private balcony, toilet, cooking space, water tap and electrical points. The space standard was 3.1 sq. m (35 sq. ft) per person and rents ranged from HK$35 a month for four-person accommodation to HK$80 a month for ten-person accommodation.

Hong Kong and the Third World

Clearly, what distinguishes Hong Kong's urban areas from most others in the Third World, and makes their detailed study not only desirable but imperative, is the possibility of evaluating certain forms of massive government response to housing problems (Dwyer, 1970). The question of standards in Hong Kong's public housing programmes is obviously of major international significance in this respect, but unfortunately comparison with other countries is an almost impossible exercise because the bald statistics published at an international level usually cannot be interpreted meaningfully in terms of local conditions. The United Nations has, for example, suggested that an average density of one person per room may be considered the maximum for maintaining privacy and that a housing unit with three or more persons per room should definitely be considered as overcrowded (UN, Department of Economic and Social Affairs, 1962*b*, pp. 3–4). It is plain that the whole of the Hong Kong public housing programme must be considered substandard by this definition. But is such a definition realistic in Hong Kong conditions or indeed in Third World conditions generally? The point of best comparison internationally would perhaps be with Singapore. Such a study, which would be of great importance regionally, remains to be written. A paper by Yeh and Lee (1968) sets out some statistical indicators of housing conditions in Singapore but, again, detailed comparison with Hong Kong is impossible because the Singapore data on housing standards is given in terms of 'rooms' with no indication as to room size or mean amount of space per person in each class of accommodation.

Nevertheless, some meaningful comparison can be made within Hong Kong itself, between housing standards in the public and private sectors. These are significant inasmuch as they reflect the realities of the housing position of the urban poor in the more regularly built-up areas of Third World cities, and as such they are by no means unfavourable to Hong Kong's public sector provision. It has already been pointed out that although the private sector has a monopoly in supplying dwellings for the upper income groups, such building activity is small, in terms of persons accommodated and units built, in comparison with the provision of tenement floors for lower income groups. Though the Hong Kong Building Ordinance lays down standards of provision (for example for windows, kitchens and toilets) for such tenement floors, the standards are minimal and, with subsequent subdivision of such floors into cubicles and bed-spaces, the facilities usually become quite inadequate.

It is for this reason that housing standards in the public sector, spartan as they appear, bear comparison with those in the private sector, even in recently completed tenement buildings. A survey of private sector housing on Hong Kong Island carried out by Maunder in 1963, is of interest in this respect, especially as those households able to pay more than HK$500 rent per month were excluded from it (Maunder, 1969). It will be seen from Table 5.4 that in both prewar and postwar buildings the average area occupied per adult equivalent in cubicles and bed spaces ranged from 1.1 to 2.3 sq. m (12.2 to 25.9 sq. ft). Maunder (1969, p. 66) points out with regard to these figures that the standard deviations from the means are very large but he comments that it appears that few, if any, bed space dwellers reach the Housing Authority standard of 3.1 sq. m (35 sq. ft) per person and that perhaps only 10–15 per cent of the cubicle dwellers are above it. As regards space standards, therefore, it seems that large sections of the urban population housed by the private sector fall well below the 3.1 sq. m standard and a substantial proportion is probably

Table 5.4 Habitable area in urban housing on Hong Kong Island, 1963

Accommodation type	*Habitable area (sq. m)*		*Household size (persons)*	*Adult equivalent size*†	*Unit area (sq. m)*	
	Mean	*Standard deviation*			*per person*	*per adult equivalent*
Prewar buildings						
Bed-space	2.9	2.5	3.1	2.7	1.0	1.1
Cubicle	8.6	3.9	4.8	4.1	1.8	2.1
Floor	39.8	4.7	8.1	7.1	4.9	5.6
Room	8.9	5.6	4.4	3.8	2.0	2.3
Combination*	16.5	7.8	7.2	6.4	2.3	2.6
Postwar buildings						
Bed-space	2.6	2.2	2.4	2.0	1.1	1.3
Cubicle	8.4	3.3	4.2	3.6	2.0	2.3
Floor	29.1	7.8	7.6	6.9	3.8	4.2
Room	12.4	7.9	3.4	3.2	3.6	3.9
Combination*	14.2	7.6	4.5	4.1	3.2	3.5

* Any combination of bed space(s), cockloft(s), room(s), and verandah(s).

† Adult equivalent, i.e. children under ten years counted as half.

Note: Households paying over HK$500 in rent excluded.

Source: Based on Maunder, 1969, p. 64.

Table 5.5 Amenities in urban housing on Hong Kong Island, 1963 (percentages of households)

Accommodation type	Kitchen		Water closet			Bathroom		
	Shared	Exclusive	None	Shared	Exclusive	None	Shared	Exclusive
Prewar buildings								
Bed-space	100	–	92	8	–	93	7	–
Cubicle	100	–	80	20	–	90	10	–
Flat	12	88	18	2	80	12	2	86
Floor	6	94	53	–	47	46	2	52
Room	100	–	76	24	–	86	14	–
Combination*	100	–	76	24	–	89	11	–
All types	90	10	79	16	5	85	9	6
Postwar buildings								
Bed-space	100	–	8	92	–	14	86	–
Cubicle	100	–	9	91	–	29	71	–
Flat	–	100	11	–	89	–	–	100
Floor	4	96	16	2	82	19	–	81
Room	98	2	16	84	–	29	69	2
Combination	100	–	11	89	–	11	89	–
All types	89	11	12	79	9	25	65	10

* Any combination of bed space(s), cockloft(s), cubicle(s), room(s), and verandah(s).

Source: Maunder, 1969, p. 78.

also below the former squatter resettlement standard of 2.2 sq. m (24 sq. ft), for 61 per cent of those households covered by survey were found to be living in cubicles and bed spaces (though this proportion is undoubtedly less today).

With regard to amenities, it appears from the Maunder survey that all households investigated had access to a kitchen of some kind but this may have been due to the broad definition used in the survey. Nine-tenths of the households surveyed were sharing a kitchen, and there was little difference in this proportion between prewar and postwar buildings (Table 5.5). Only 5 per cent of households in prewar and 9 per cent in postwar buildings had exclusive use of a water closet; indeed 79 per cent of those in prewar buildings had no access at all to such an amenity. In postwar buildings, in contrast, 79 per cent had shared access. A broadly similar pattern prevailed in respect of bathrooms.

It is clear from these figures that availability of amenities is at best on a shared basis. Private development of tenement floors during the postwar period may therefore be compared with resettlement blocks in provision of amenities (although there are, unfortunately, no figures indicative of the average number of people per amenity unit), and conditions in resettlement blocks appear to be markedly superior to those in prewar tenements in this respect. Provision made in Government Low-Cost Housing, Housing Authority and Housing Society estates appears in general to be superior in terms of exclusive use of amenities to all types of private accommodation except that in houses and whole flats of postwar construction. As for rents, according to Maunder (1969, p. 71) the mean monthly inclusive rent (that is, rent, rates, electricity, water and housing charges) for bed spaces in postwar buildings was HK$15.9 per sq. m (HK$1.45 per sq. ft) in 1963 and that for cubicles HK$11.40 per sq. m (HK$1.04 per sq. ft). The rent of a standard room of 10.8 sq. m (120 sq. ft) in a resettlement estate was HK$14 in that year. This gives a figure of HK$1.30 per sq. m (HK$0.12 per sq. ft), though in this case electricity charges are not included. For the Housing Society, the rent of the smallest size self-contained flat, for four persons (i.e., 12.6 sq. m (140 sq. ft), excluding kitchen, toilet and also balcony where provided) in 1963 varied from HK$52 to HK$72, or HK$4.10 to 5.60 per sq. m (HK$0.37 to 0.51 per sq. ft), again excluding electricity.

It would thus appear that, in terms of the housing the vast majority of the urban population is able to pay for, the Hong Kong official programmes are realistic if minimal. The Third World is littered with low-cost housing schemes which have proved too expensive for the urban poor for whom they were originally designed, some examples of which are given in this book. Though it is possible to take the attitude that the basic individual space allocation in the original Mark I resettlement blocks represented 'twice the area of a grave' (Hopkins, 1971, p. 297), it is perhaps a more valid, if less severe, criticism that the Hong Kong government failed to realize quickly enough that once the emergency problem of establishing control over the location and extension of spontaneous settlements had been solved, the major issue would become one of improving housing standards in both the public and the private sectors. In the public sector, too many Mark I resettlement blocks were built, and the biggest single improvement, to the individual space standard, was left as late as the 1970s, with the Mark VI design, when already well over 1 million spontaneous settlers had been rehoused. As a result, there are now problems of extreme congestion in some of the older estates because of the growth of families, and a programme of transferring families to newer estates in order to halve densities has had to be started. This is proving difficult because some of the newer estates occupy more peripheral sites, better facilities mean dearer rents, and relocation, while not necessarily breaking the work link of the main wage earner, often involves abandonment of important subsidiary sources of family income.

A further point of comparative significance concerns official attitudes towards spontaneous settlements adopted in Hong Kong, since there can be no doubt that one of the most significant effects of the indiscriminate spread of spontaneous settlements in the Third World is the negation of many attempts at comprehensive urban planning. The Hong Kong resettlement programme has been motivated much less by individual welfare than by considerations of optimum land use and of law and order; in fact in 1955, very early in the programme, the view was officially expressed (Hong Kong Government Commissioner for Resettlement, 1955, p. 30) that:

> What was required was not primarily to improve the living conditions of that section of the community which happened to be breaking the law relating to the occupation of Crown land: the task was to devise a rapid and practical method, at a cost less than prohibitive, of removing, in the interests of the whole community, the fire risk and the threat to public health and public order presented by the worst squatter areas.

Since then, the clearance of areas of spontaneous settlement has been almost wholly contingent on the demand for sites for more regular urban purposes. Squatters cannot request resettlement. There has been no attempt to seek out the poorest sections of the squatter community:

rather all families in any clearance area have been offered resettlement regardless of income (and on average only 3 or 4 per cent of clearance cases refuse resettlement). The largest clearances have been for the construction of resettlement estates and other forms of low-cost public housing to provide residential units at much higher densities than the squatter areas they replace; general urban engineering works have also been a significant user of land occupied by spontaneous settlements; and in more recent years many areas have been cleared to make way for private development.

By the same token, the massive rehousing policies have been complemented both by minimal attention to spontaneous settlements *in situ*, in terms of the provision of amenities, and by vigorous efforts in squatter control. The general tenor of policy has been to discourage squatting by making conditions in the spontaneous settlements as spartan as possible, and Hong Kong has been able to do this at least in part because, unlike their counterparts elsewhere in the Third World, the spontaneous settlers do not have votes. The replacement of wood by brick and cement is forbidden and a largely successful attempt has been made to freeze all settlements in their dimensions of 1964 by prohibiting the extension of buildings and demolishing new ones. During the 1960s the rate of such demolitions ran at over 15 000 a year. Despite the fact that it is obvious that spontaneous settlement will never be completely eliminated as an urban form in Hong Kong, and that some settlements established on steep hillsides for twenty years or more are likely to remain there in the foreseeable future, such areas remain characterized by gross deficiences in water supply, sanitation, roads and paths, public lighting, schools, health centres and other urban facilities. Yet in its own terms as a shelter, the individual squatter hut is often minimally acceptable. In this aspect of its housing policies, as chapter 6 will show, Hong Hong has lessons to learn from other parts of the Third World.

Hong Kong is strikingly deficient in research into its housing problems and policies. Perhaps the most important research question in terms of the Third World generally that could be asked at present is to what extent mass housing has influenced Hong Kong's exceptionally high rates of industrialization and general economic growth. Has rehousing led, for example, to changes in jobs, to the decline of 'traditional' occupations and attitudes, to the reorganization of families to produce increased incomes, to upward mobility, to changed motivations, to reorientation of attitudes towards education? These remain moot points in the present state of knowledge, as do definitive answers to the classic sociological questions regarding the influence of high population densities on family breakdown, crime, suicide and the like.

The new towns

Much of Hong Kong's postwar economic success has been associated with an almost entirely *laissez-faire* official attitude towards the stimulation of industrial growth. Something of this attitude still permeates urban planning but in general it has proved impossible not to plan for urban development, though in part minimally and in something of what has been characterized elsewhere as a 'firefighting' manner (Rodwin *et al.*, 1969, pp. 483–4), that is through the formulation of practical solutions on an *ad hoc* basis in response to crisis situations. Perhaps this in itself may hold lessons for other developing countries: certainly very few countries, advanced or developing, can point to elaborately contrived and long gestated master plans that have even been half realized on the ground.

The evolution of new towns in Hong Kong (and public housing programmes with them) which are large by any standards is a case in point. Within the last twenty years two major new urban areas have been created, Tsuen Wan and Kwun Tong, each of which has already exceeded 300 000 in population. The whole character of the formerly largely rural New Territories is in process of change through rapid urbanization, and these towns are part of a planned urban network in which Castle Peak and Shatin are at present in the early stages of development as the next areas for major urban growth (Fig. 5.1). The urbanization of the New Territories on such a scale must be regarded as inevitable if only for reasons of overall land availability (Dwyer, 1971*c*). Given existing trends in population growth and economic development, land for urban development on the scale necessary can only be found in the New Territories as there is very little suitable building land left in Kowloon or on Hong Kong Island.

During the early 1950s, the then small market town of Tsuen Wan became the first major focus of industrial development outside of the Victoria–Kowloon urban area (Lai and Dwyer, 1964). Industries were established there because by the time Hong Kong's postwar industrial boom got fully under way there was relatively little space for factory building within the cities. In addition, not all of the refugees who had flooded into Hong Kong had squeezed into Victoria and Kowloon. Some managed to establish themselves as farmers, causing major changes in land use and landholding patterns in the New Territories. Others settled in, or established small spontaneous settlements around, the New Territories market towns: Yuen Long, Tai Po, Fanling, Sheung Shui and Tsuen Wan. The last of them was especially favoured because of its proximity to and good communications with the cities, and because it already had some small factories. Industrial capital quickly sought out the available labour supply there, and after 1950 rapid industrial expansion began.

Much of the early physical development of Tsuen Wan was unplanned and uncontrolled. It was typical of industrial development in Hong Kong outside of the cities during the immediate postwar period that the government delayed for several years, until piecemeal urban growth at Tsuen Wan had created an urgent need for more roads, better drainage and other urban services, before it set about providing them on a planned basis. The result was that the official Hong Kong government *Annual Report for the Year 1955* (1956, p. 96) could state that 'The development of industry in the New Territories, particularly at Tsuen Wan, demands constant vigilance to maintain even minimum standards of public health', and the District Commissioner for the New Territories (1956, p. 18) could point out the same year that at Tsuen Wan 'unfortunately the development of industrial sites has far outrun what should be the parallel development of housing sites, and for lack of proper accommodation, the increasing population has had to find room for itself in squatter huts'. Even as late as May 1959 the District Commissioner was calling attention in an unpublished report to the lack of planning at Tsuen Wan and commenting that 'The old doctorine of waiting for private development before constructing public services as "works contingent upon development" has had a particularly damaging effect' (quoted in Smyly, 1961, p. 404). It was not until 1961 that the first long-term development plan for the Tsuen Wan area was published by the Hong Kong Town Planning Board, though in fact overall development control had begun in the late 1950s.

Tsuen Wan is now in process of development on a planned basis, but its earlier history may still be recognized in its urban landscape; in some parts there is still an often confused mixture of planned and unplanned elements. The core of the town is located on a narrow coastal strip between a large but shallow bay and a series of steep hills. The bay is separated from another, Lap Sap Wan, to the east, which has now largely been reclaimed, by a hilly peninsula rising to 120 m (400 ft). The two bays are almost enclosed by Tsing I Island. Small streams flow into the bays and their restricted alluvial valleys are the chief naturally flat areas in the district. Elsewhere, steep hills slope down to the sea.

Because of the severe physical restrictions of the site, much of the growth of the town has been on reclaimed land and platforms cut from the hills. The site is a difficult one, as are the others chosen for urban growth in the New Territories, and it may be asked why flat land in the farming areas has not been taken over for urban development as has happened so frequently in other countries. Much of the answer probably lies in the extreme sensitivity of the government to problems of Chinese custom and land tenure rights that has marked the administration of the New Territories since the earliest days. Although in the last analysis the Crown can resume land in the New Territories as it wishes, such action has never been officially popular. The reclamation of shallow bays and the terracing of barren hills for urban development undoubtedly minimizes such problems as well as preserving agricultural land. Whether this velvet glove policy can be maintained as the New Territories evolve into a much more complete urban system remains to be seen.

During the last ten years Tsuen Wan has become a major industrial focus, though as yet factories have been built upon less than half of the total industrial land to be provided there. The town is particularly important in the textile industries, especially in the spinning of cotton and wool, in enamelware, in chemicals and in rubber goods. Most of the factories are built on reclaimed land or on sites levelled from the hills. Given the general shortage of industrial land in Hong Kong in recent years, there is little that is remarkable in Tsuen Wan's success in attracting industrial development, especially as many of the sites have water frontage and in addition the town is close to Kowloon, and the harbour, by road. What is significant is the massive commitment of the government to low-cost housing in the area (Fig. 5.11), for this is by no means typical of other new towns in the Third World. In 1970, when the population of Tsuen Wan was 290 000 persons, squatter resettlement estates were providing accommodation for 145 000 persons and other government or government subsidized low-cost housing for a further 55 000 persons (Table 5.6). By 1976 some 100 000 families, or about 0.5 million people, may well be accommodated in government subsidized housing in Tsuen Wan (Wigglesworth, 1971, pp. 56–7).

The urban landscape of Kwun Tong, Hong Kong's other major new urban area to date, differs from that of Tsuen Wan in several important respects (Lai and Dwyer, 1965). In 1954, when the government decided to start reclamation in the Kwung Tong area for industrial purposes, part of the coast of the area was in use as a dump for urban refuse. A continuous ribbon of urban development today stretches from Kowloon to Kwun Tong, but at that time the Kwun Tong area was relatively remote. Agricultural land was extremely restricted and such villages as there were

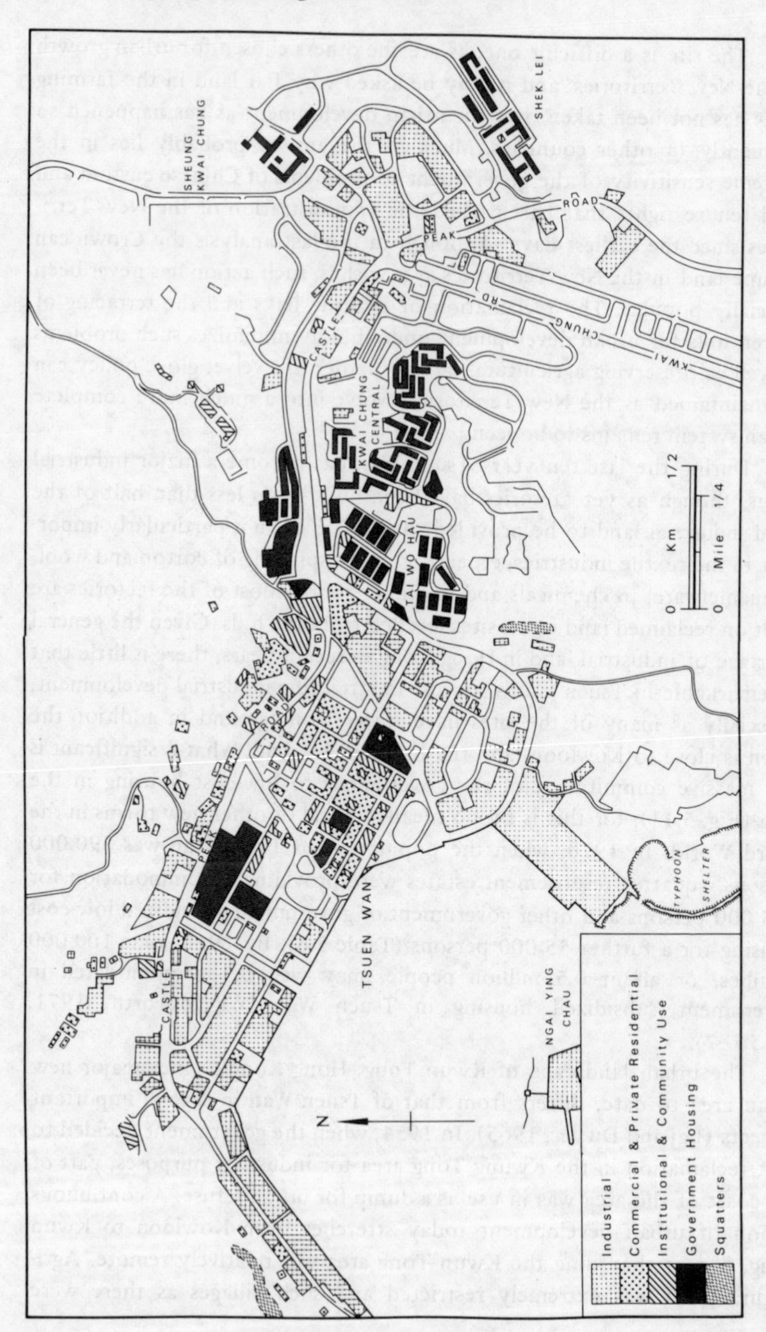

Fig. 5.11 Tsuen Wan: major land uses

Table 5.6 Housing provision in Tsuen Wan, 1970

Housing type	*Population*	*Percentage*
Government and government subsidized	200 019	68.9
Resettlement	145 157	50.0
Government low-cost housing	21 839	7.5
Housing Authority	19 830	6.8
Housing Society	13 193	4.5
Private	67 100	23.1
Private tenement and flats	58 100	20.0
Village-type housing	9 000	3.1
Squatters	23 150	7.9
Total population	290 269	

Source: Hong Kong Government, Public Works Department, Planning Division, unpublished.

around Kwun Tong Bay were very small. This in itself made comprehensive development much easier. Kwun Tong Bay was the outlet of several small streams draining a series of low hills composed of deeply weathered and highly dissected granite. The bay was sheltered by the hills from the prevailing easterly winds and much of it was less than 6 m (20 ft) deep. These factors, and the relative ease of obtaining fill from the badly decomposed granite of the hills, made large-scale reclamation possible. It was a physical setting remarkably similar to that of Tsuen Wan. The position of Kwun Tong within the harbour limits and its proximity to Kowloon were other points in its favour as the site for a town and although it is now linked by ribbon development to Kowloon it was planned on a fairly integrated basis.

When development started in 1954, the only modern installation in the area was an oil storage depot which had been built during the late 1940s. The government's scheme involved reclaiming a broad strip of the seabed running north-west from the oil installation for industrial purposes. This area is now almost completely occupied by factories and forms the biggest single industrial concentration in Hong Kong. Immediately opposite the industrial zone, a commercial centre was built, incorporating housing on upper floors, and stretching in an arc around the commercial centre, to the north, the east and the south, residential zones were developed, with an emphasis on government housing, as in Tsuen Wan.

The plan is thus a simple one and because of the comparative absence of private land ownership in the area it has been possible to implement it almost completely, with the result that the various land use zones are much more easily recognizable than at Tsuen Wan. The division between the industrial zone and the commercial and housing zones can be clearly distinguished. With regard to the latter, it is worth noting that the official commitment to housing provision has become just as great in Kwun Tong as at Tsuen Wan. In March 1967, 151 000 persons out of a total population of 275 000 were living in squatter resettlement estates and a further 50 000 in government or government subsidized low-cost housing.

As with Tsuen Wan and Kwun Tong, the development plans for Castle Peak and Shatin, which are now in the early stages of implementation, are based on large-scale reclamation from the sea and site formation in adjacent hills. At Castle Peak a town of about 0.5 million persons is to be created but, because of its distance from Kowloon (32 km (20 miles) by road), sufficient industrial and service development will have to be attracted to make the community self-sufficient to a much higher degree even than at Tsuen Wan. It is proposed to build half the town on about 166 hectares (400 acres) of reclaimed land; nevertheless, as the existing population in the area is in the order of 30 000 persons, substantial problems of redeveloping existing properties may be encountered. The basic concept of the plan is to establish groups of environmental areas devoted to a variety of land uses and served largely by internal pedestrian circulation. Each area will be accessible through systems of distributory roads which, in turn, will be linked to main roads and thence to through routes. The town centre is to be developed on the basis of buildings with commercial uses at ground level and residential uses above. At present the development of one of the areas zoned for residential purposes is going ahead. A small resettlement estate of 11 500 persons is being built there in order to complement anticipated industrial development in adjacent zones.

Few people are likely to take up residence in Castle Peak ahead of jobs, social services and community facilities. The major problem is likely to be attracting a sufficient number of factories. Industry in Hong Kong is closely tied to the harbour because most raw materials are imported and a very high proportion of the finished products are exported. To many industrialists, Castle Peak must seem remote, especially as the existing road connection to Kowloon is poor. A new arterial road is to be built to connect Castle Peak with Tsuen Wan, and possibly the Kowloon–Canton railway will be extended to enter the town from the north. Until the road improvement is completed, industrial land sales may be slack. Shatin is much closer to Kowloon and, with a new road tunnel and its existing railway connection, it enjoys excellent communications with the harbour. As with Castle Peak, a possible population of about 0.5 million persons has been envisaged, mostly in government housing, though there may be some adjustment in populations between the two towns. Because of the lack of a tidal stream in the Shatin inlet, a major problem is likely to be sewage disposal. Full or partial sewage treatment will be required, and this will be expensive. Apart from the sewage problem the site is remarkably similar to that of Castle Peak, even to the size of the existing settlements in the area.

Conclusion

Hong Kong's public housing programmes have now reached such dimensions that it would be politically impossible for the government to abandon or even substantially reduce them. There is no evidence of any such intent; indeed in 1972 a new ten-year official housing programme was announced, to start in April 1973, with a target of accommodating a further 1.5 million people. During the last two decades public housing has been provided in Hong Kong at a scale proportionate to the total population which probably exceeds that in any other part of the Third World, and a housing situation which in the 1950s had been characterised by the necessity for crisis decision-making had been transformed into one in which questions of improved official housing standards and environmental quality had become paramount. The programmes have not been without controversy. It has been claimed that the density of development has been far too high and space allocation per individual too low (Hopkins, 1971; Goodstadt, 1969). Within Hong Kong, however, the comparison between the public and the comparable sector or private housing is by no means unfavourable to public housing. Further, for a large segment of the urban population, public housing must be regarded as the sole hope of obtaining self-contained permanent accommodation. Paradoxically, the major part of the public housing programme, resettlement housing, has not been based primarily on the need to assist low income families to obtain decent housing. It has been rather a means of controlling spontaneous settlement, devised in order to free land needed for permanent development and to reduce the risk of fires in squatter camps. In carrying out this policy, both rich and poor squatter families have been rehoused, and this has led to repeated assertions that resettled squatters to this extent form a privileged section of the community, enjoying low, subsidized rents (Hopkins, 1969, 1971; Goodstadt, 1969). Against this, the argument has been that resettlement is, in essence, compulsory rehousing; that Hong Kong's remarkable economic progress has been built in part on comparatively stable internal price levels; and that the raising of rents by any large amount would be politically impossible.

Whatever their deficiencies, Hong Kong's massive public housing schemes had become by the 1970s one important element in an overall economic and social complex which had given rise to the highest rate of economic growth based on industrialization in the whole of the developing world. Their detailed evaluation in relation to the Third World generally has become long overdue for, after all, even if it could only be shown that no element of Hong Kong's accumulated housing experience was applicable elsewhere, this would be a finding in itself of significance, as well as one of some surprise.

6

Self-help housing possibilities

In an economy of scarcity, the mass of the common people, though poor, possess the bulk of the nation's human and material resources for housing. Their collective entrepreneurial and managerial skills (and spare time) far surpass the financial and administrative capacity of even the most highly planned and centralized institutional system – whether dominated by the state or by private capitalist corporations.

J. F. C. Turner, 1971

The invasion of Cuevas took place during the night of 17 September 1960 and was carried out by about 500 people. They came to Cuevas, a desert valley situated about 6 km (3.7 miles) north of the city centre, largely from the inner tenement areas of Lima, having formed themselves into the Associacion de Padres de Familia Pro Vivienda for the purpose of securing better housing a few months before. The initial reaction of the authorities was typical. Police forced the invaders off the land and the several hundred men, women and children were reduced to camping along a nearby railway embankment for some weeks while their leaders negotiated further. Eventually, because it was near Christmas, the families were allowed to occupy part of the site. At first, cane and matting shacks were set up by the settlers in haphazard fashion. But at the same time marking out of regular house lots by technicians hired by the leaders of the invasion was taking place. Some land was set aside for schools and shops. The association paid a substantial sum for the work, which took two months. As soon as the layout was completed, each family transferred its temporary shack to the plot allocated by the organizers. Meanwhile a primary school was being established and shops were appearing. A major road with public transport into the city was within easy walking distance. Soon improvements to the individual dwellings began to appear. Despite the general lack of urban services, within a few months most families had become very much better off environmentally than they had been in the inner-city slums (J. F. C. Turner, 1967, esp. pp. 170–2).

The *barriada* movement

Lima was founded in 1535 by Pizarro, and as the capital of the Viceroyalty of Peru and the obligatory centre of trade for the whole of the Spanish empire in South America, it prospered during its early years on the vast wealth extracted from Andean mines. The original gridiron nucleus of the city around the Plaza de Armas was laid out near the south bank of the Rimac River at a point which commanded its alluvial plain, one of the larger irrigable areas of the coastal region. On the nearby coast, where Lima's outport, Callao, was established, a promontory and an offshore island gave protection from ocean waves brought in by the prevailing south-westerly winds and provided the calm water anchorage necessary for overseas trade. Lima occupies a relatively flat desert site (there is almost no rainfall apart from some slight drizzle in the winter months) backed on its landward side by hills which are outliers of the Andes. The edge of the built-up area contrasts markedly with areas of rich, irrigated agriculture or,

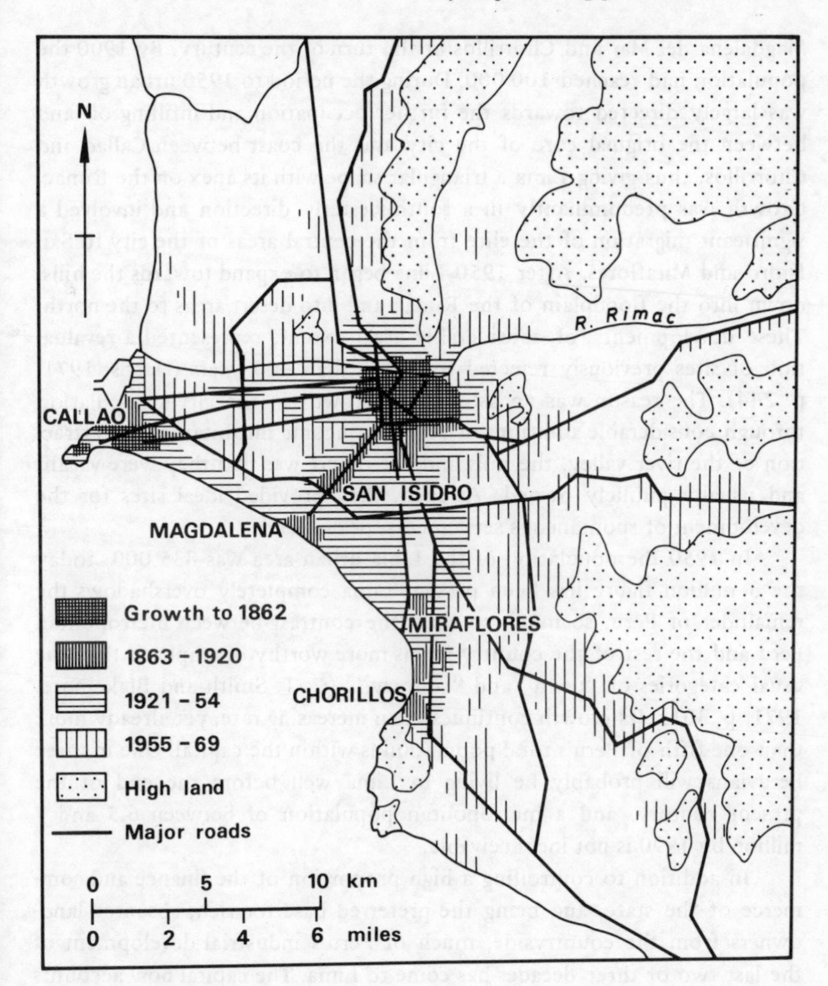

Fig. 6.1 The expansion of Lima (Deler, 1970)

where water is absent, with bare hills and the flat, dusty desert.

After its earlier magnificence, the growth of Lima, like that of Caracas, was relatively unspectacular until recent decades. Towards the end of the seventeenth century the city was fortified with walls against attack by pirates and the walls remained, constricting growth, until 1870. Only during the second half of the nineteenth century did the city expand significantly beyond its walls, into agricultural land to the south (Fig. 6.1), a movement stimulated by the opening of tramcar services to Callao,

Magdalena del Mar and Chorrillos at the turn of the century. By 1900 the population had reached 100 000. During the period to 1950 urban growth was largely directed towards the further occupation and infilling of land between the original core of the city and the coast between Callao and Chorrillos, thus giving Lima a triangular shape with its apex on the Rimac. Growth was predominantly in a south-westerly direction and involved a significant migration of the elite from the central areas of the city to San Isidro and Miraflores. After 1950 Lima began to expand towards the hills, down into the floodplain of the Rimac and into desert areas to the north. These developments, of considerable areal extent, represented a revaluation of sites previously rejected for more than 400 years (Harris, 1971, p. 244). The reason was an astonishing growth in the city's population through considerable additions of very low income inhabitants. The attraction of the river valley, the hills and the desert was that they were vacant and usually publicly owned. As such, they provided ideal sites for the development of spontaneous settlements, or *barriadas*.

In 1950 the population of the Lima urban area was 835 000: today the 3 million figure has been passed. Lima completely overshadows the remainder of Peru, so much so that 'the contrast between metropolitan Peru and the rest of the country seems more worthy of emphasis than the usual categories of "town" and "country"' (C. T. Smith and Blakemore, 1971, p. 301). Its growth continues at an increasing rate, yet already more than one-fifth of Peru's total population is within the capital. One in three Peruvians will probably be living in Lima well before the end of the present century, and a metropolitan population of between 6.5 and 7 million by 1990 is not inconceivable.

In addition to controlling a high proportion of the finance and commerce of the state, and being the preferred base for rich, absentee landowners from the countryside, much of Peru's industrial development of the last two or three decades has come to Lima. The capital now accounts for at least two-thirds of the industrial output of Peru and over nine-tenths of the financial activities (Trujillo, 1968, p. 70). As a result, its inhabitants receive two-fifths of the total national income and the city contains over half the Peruvian population with incomes above subsistence level (Smith and Blakemore, 1971, p. 302). For most entrepreneurs and executives Lima is the only attractive location in Peru: in recent years this view has come to be shared by increasing numbers of Peru's poor.

During the twenty-year period from 1945 to 1965, the number of migrants coming to Lima from Peru's small towns and impoverished rural areas increased from 25 000 to 80 000 annually, and over this period

Table 6.1 Size of original place of residence of migrants to Lima (1961 census)

Community size (population)	*Percentage*
100 000 or over	7.2
20 000 to 99 999	26.0
5 000 to 19 999	17.4
1 000 to 4 999	43.3
999 or less	6.1

Source: Cotler and Laquian, 1971, p. 113.

in-migration accounted for slightly more than half of the total population growth of the city. In-migrants now represent about 60 per cent of those aged fifteen years or more and, of course, a high proportion of Lima's children and adolescents also comes from families formed by recently arrived in-migrants (Deler, 1970, pp. 77–9). At least two-thirds of the migrants come from smaller provincial towns rather than directly from the countryside, indicating a pattern of step migration (Table 6.1) possibly similar to that of Chile outlined in chapter 2. Peru's coastal regions formerly predominated as source areas but in more recent years large-scale movements of Andean Indians from the Sierra have also become significant (Fig. 6.2).

As in most Third World cities, signs of stress on the urban fabric have become apparent in many parts of Lima during the last two decades. Water supplies had become inadequate even by 1956 (Smith and Blakemore, 1971, p. 304), and most areas of the city (apart from those occupied by the elite) which have developed since then are without piped water, services and electricity. Population growth is steadily outstripping employment expansion in manufacturing industry, and petty service occupations which represent little more than a sharing of urban poverty have become responsible for much of the recorded growth in employment. Though Lima's areal expansion has been dramatic, the construction of regular housing has fallen very far below needs. During the decade 1950–60, for example, an average of 6 847 housing units was completed annually, mostly by the private sector, but the population at this time was growing by 80 000 or even 100 000 a year, and at an occupancy rate of five persons per unit Lima required 16 000 to 20 000 new housing units a year, not counting replacements for deteriorated dwellings (Harris *et al.*, 1963,

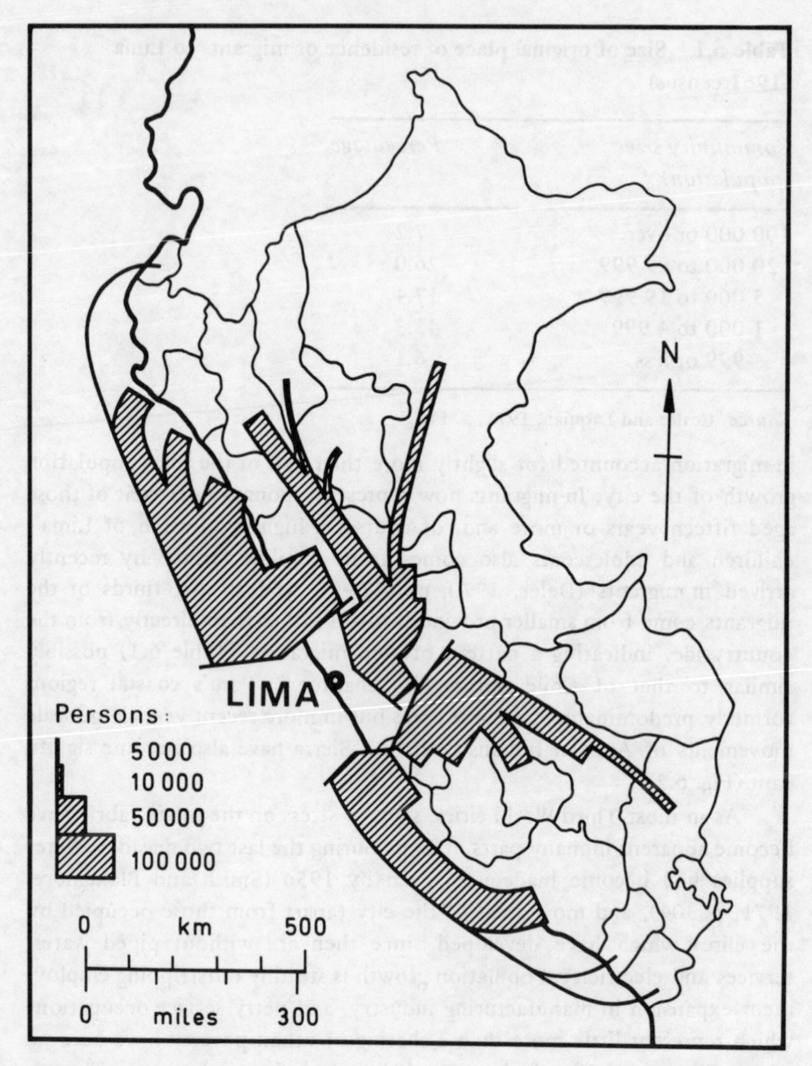

Fig. 6.2 Net migration to Lima: historical totals, 1961 census

p. 439). In fact, much of the housing deficit was met unofficially, in the *barriadas*.

The initial groups of squatter families had already begun to settle in the capital during the first decade of the present century, but their numbers were few and they were hardly noticed. More arrived after the 1940 earthquake but even as late as 1956 squatters represented less than

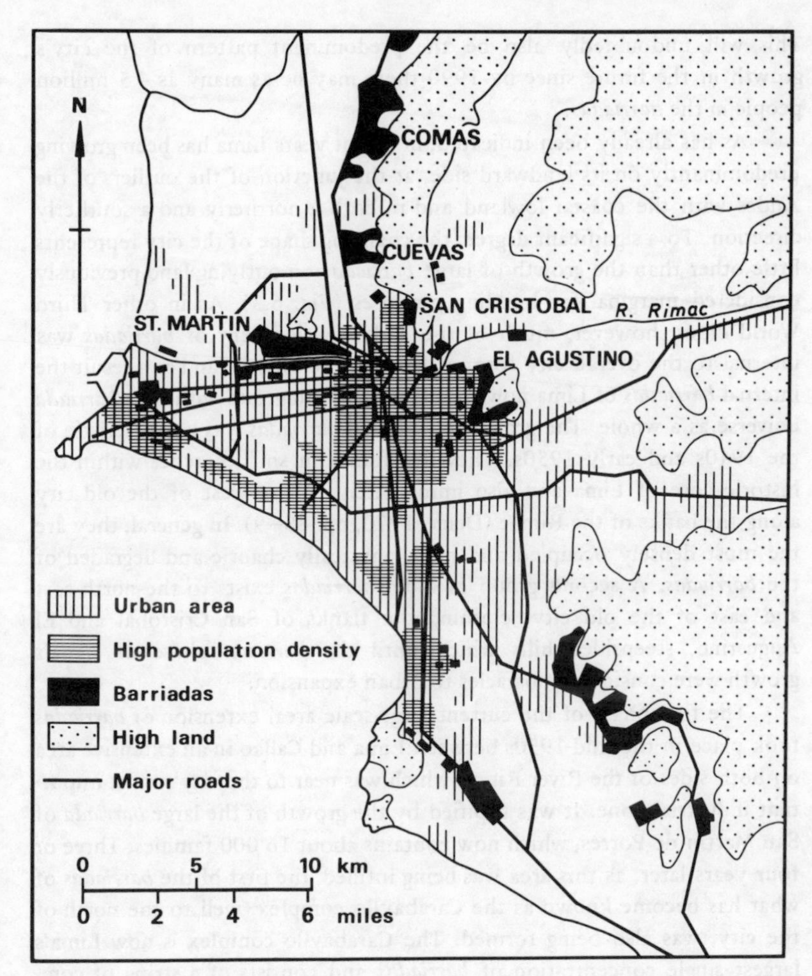

Fig. 6.3 Distribution of *barriadas* in Lima (Deler, 1970)

10 per cent of the total population of the metropolitan area (Deler, 1970, p. 87). The mushrooming of spontaneous settlements in and around the city is a phenomenon only of the later 1950s and the decade of the 1960s, for during this period the number of squatters increased from 120 000 (in 1956) to approximately 800 000, and today squatters constitute almost 40 per cent of the total population. In all, the construction of spontaneous settlements probably accounted for more than four-fifths of the physical growth of metropolitan Lima during the last decade (Harris, 1971, p. 225).

This will undoubtedly also be the predominant pattern of the city's growth in the future since by 1990 there may be as many as 4.5 million people in the *barriadas*.

As has already been indicated, in recent years Lima has been growing predominantly on its landward side, at the junction of the outliers of the Andes with the coastal lowland and in both a northerly and a southerly direction. To a significant degree, the changing shape of the city represents little other than the growth of large *barriadas* on outlying land previously considered marginal for building purposes (Fig. 6.3). As in other Third World cities, however, much of the early development of *barriadas* was internal to the overall city form rather than peripheral, and as a result the internal *barriadas* of Lima now form a distinct subgroup within its *barriada* universe as a whole. The growth of internal *barriadas* was characteristic of the 1940s and early 1950s. They are found in small patches within the historic core of Lima and also immediately to the west of the old city along the banks of the Rimac (Deler, 1970, pp. 88–9). In general, they are the most densely occupied and most physically chaotic and degraded of the *barriadas*. A second group of older *barriadas* exists to the north-east and east of the old city, clothing the flanks of San Cristobal and El Augustino, steepsided hills which until the *barriada* phase of Lima's growth were considered obstacles to urban expansion.

The first phase of the current large-scale areal extension of *barriadas* took place in the mid-1950s between Lima and Callao in an extensive area on both sides of the River Rimac which was near to the city's most important industrial zone. It was typified by the growth of the large *barriada* of San Martin de Porres, which now contains about 16 000 families. Three or four years later, as this area was being infilled, the first of the *barriadas* of what has become known as the Carabayllo complex, well to the north of the city, was also being formed. The Carabayllo complex is now Lima's largest single concentration of *barriadas* and consists of a string of communities occupying a series of west–east re-entrant valleys in the hills and stretching as far as 15 km (10 miles) from the city centre. These valleys had always been unirrigated and therefore largely unoccupied. The first invasion of this area took place in 1958 with the formation of the Pampa de Comas *barriada* and was quickly followed by the establishment of the *barriadas* of Santo Rosa y Uchumayo and Senor de los Milagros the following year. In 1960 the Cuevas settlement was begun, as has already been described, to be followed by the major *barriadas* of El Carmen and El Ermitano in 1961 and 1962 respectively. Subsequent to the formation of the Carabayllo complex, the major *barriada* developments have taken place to the south of the city in essentially the same pattern, particularly in a series of valleys adjacent to the main road into Lima from Atocongo and also along the Panamerican highway in the Chorillos area.

Bridgeheaders and consolidators

The *barriadas* of the Carabayllo complex of Lima have received a good deal of academic attention in recent years largely through the work of Turner and Mangin (see Bibliography), who have been influential in focusing the attention of planners and administrators concerned with urban housing problems in the developing countries upon possibilities of improving spontaneous settlements *in situ*. As a case in point, Turner (1967, p. 170) has outlined the development of the Cuevas *barriada*, which he describes as 'perhaps the nearest thing to a model *barriada* of its type'. Cuevas now contains about 12 000 people, almost all of them from Lima's inner city slums where, on average, the adults lived for about ten years before moving out. The Cuevas area, Turner points out, is an unsatisfactory location for down-and-outs or for very poor migrants however ambitious they might be because it is relatively far from Lima's industrial areas and from the opportunities for casual, petty employment that exist in and around the business districts. Rather, it is an ideal location for young families with more or less steady incomes who have experienced some upward mobility in economic terms. Cuevas, is, therefore, much more a self-improving suburb than a slum and, Turner (1967, p. 170) claims, so are at least two-thirds of the *barriadas* of Peru and a high proportion of spontaneous settlements in other Third World countries such as Mexico and Turkey.

The great majority of the Cuevas settlers were motivated by the desire to improve their living conditions through investing their meagre capital and, more important, their own labour in housing improvement rather than continuing to pay exorbitant rents for minimal, subdivided accommodation in the inner tenement areas. Even with a temporary shack on their own plot in the invasion area their major housing needs were satisfied, and the succeeding years could be devoted to improvement of the house, provided their tenure of the land could be retained. In the event, about eighteen months after the invasion a permanent primary school, a medical post, a police post and a chapel had been built in Cuevas, and in the following year a secondary school was established (Turner, 1967, p. 174). In 1964, the government installed a provisional water supply and during 1964 and 1965 it built several additional schools. By the latter date there were over 200 shops in the area and also a sprinkling of small-scale industries. The same year Cuevas became the centre of a new municipality, Independencia, incorporating two adjacent *barriada* areas. Perhaps most important of all, as early as 1961 Cuevas had been officially recognized as an *urbanizacion popular* by the government, a move which gave its inhabitants considerable security of tenure; and in the same year Peru enacted an historic law for the remodelling of marginal settlements which provided for the recognition of those already in existence, for the confirmation of tenure, for loans for house building and for the installation of urban services in the *barriadas* or *pueblos jovenes* ('young towns') as they became known thereafter.

From this and similar case histories, Turner (esp. 1968*b*) has drawn a sharp distinction between what he calls the 'bridgeheader' and the 'consolidator' in spontaneous settlements. He identifies three basic functions of the dwelling environment – location, tenure and amenity – and he points out that the relative weight given to each by a household will vary from time to time in accordance with the household's socio-economic condition and expectations. Poor and insecure households, perhaps dependent upon casual jobs in an uncertain labour market, will probably wish to maximize employment opportunities and therefore place a high premium upon the location of their dwelling in close proximity to sources of employment, which will usually be in the inner parts of the cities (Fig. 6.4). On the other hand, the less poor, more regularly employed will have a wider radius of housing choice and will the more easily be able to seize a building plot on the urban periphery. Their priorities for freedom of movement (in search of jobs) will be correspondingly lower, while the importance they attach to the attainment of an improved dwelling environment may well be higher.

In polar terms, therefore, within the low incomes group of the Third World city, the 'bridgeheader', who is often a recent migrant from the countryside seeking entry to the urban system, may be contrasted in Turner's typology with the 'consolidator', who has already obtained a fairly firm foothold and whose expectations are rising, particularly with regard to socio-economic status and his dwelling environment, and to a degree this distinction can be correlated with the earlier work of Stokes (1962) who formulated a general typology of slums the major element in which was a sharp contrast between 'slums of hope' and 'slums of despair'. The latter, Stokes asserted, are stagnant or decaying areas in both the physical and the social senses which are not contributing in any way to the progress of the city. 'Slums of hope', in contrast, are inhabited by rela-

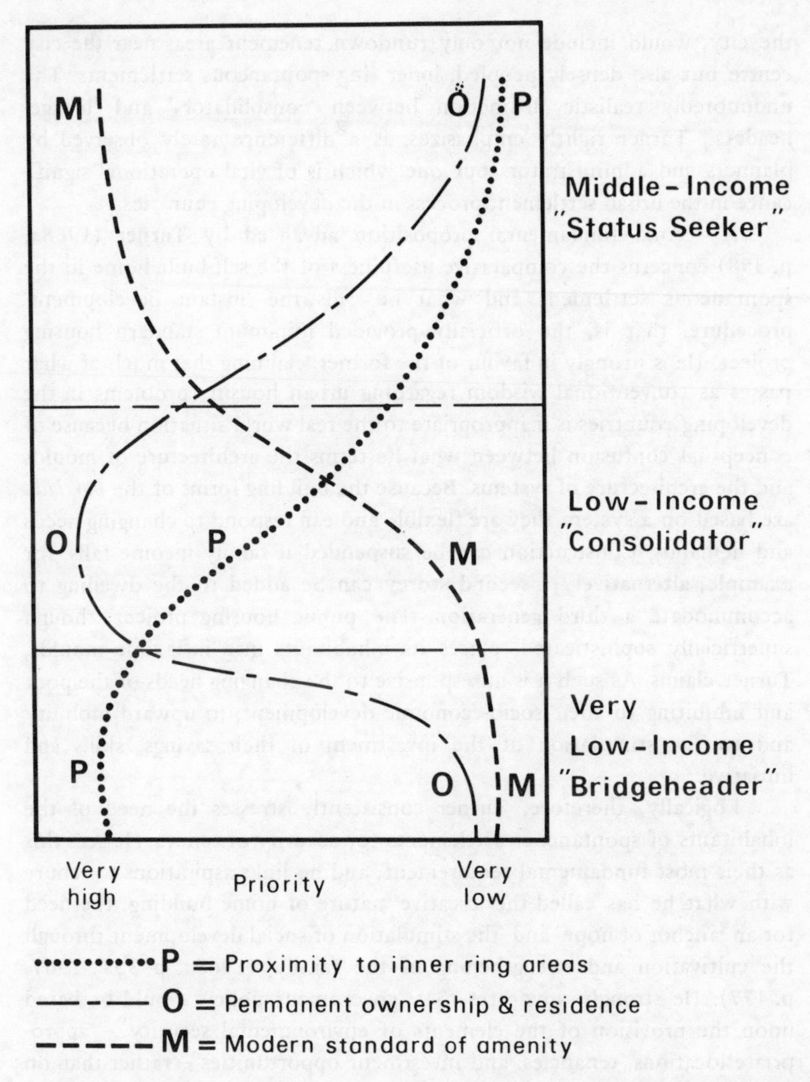

Fig. 6.4 Housing desires of low income populations in Third World cities (after Turner)

tively dynamic groups capable of improving their area. In the *barriada* context, the inhabitants of 'slums of hope' would be Turner's 'consolidators', whilst the 'slums of despair', occupied both by the permanent urban poor trapped in a culture of poverty and by the newest migrants to the city, would include not only rundown tenement areas near the city centre but also densely peopled, inner ring spontaneous settlements. The undoubtedly realistic distinction between 'consolidators' and 'bridge-headers', Turner rightly emphasizes, is a difference rarely observed by planners and administrators but one which is of vital operational significance in the urban settlement process in the developing countries.

A second fundamental proposition advanced by Turner (1968*a*, p. 358) concerns the comparative usefulness of the self-built home in the spontaneous settlement and what he calls the 'instant development' procedure, that is, the officially provided minimum standard housing project. He is strongly in favour of the former, claiming that much of what passes as conventional wisdom regarding urban housing problems in the developing countries is inappropriate to the real world situation because of conceptual confusion between what he terms the architecture of moulds and the architecture of systems. Because the building forms of the *barriada* are based on a system they are flexible and can respond to changing needs and demands. Construction can be suspended if family income falls, for example; alternatively a second storey can be added to the dwelling to accommodate a third generation. The public housing project, though superficially sophisticated, places its inhabitants into inflexible moulds, Turner claims. As such it is unresponsive to the changing needs of the poor and inhibiting to their socio-economic development, to upward mobility and to the stimulation of the investment of their savings, skills and initiative.

Logically, therefore, Turner consistently stresses the need of the inhabitants of spontaneous settlements for security of tenure. He sees this as their most fundamental requirement; and he links aspirations to tenure with what he has called the 'creative' nature of home building, the need for an 'anchor of hope' and 'the stimulation of social development through the cultivation and strengthening of the family' (1968*a*, p. 357; 1967, p. 177). He strongly advocates that 'government policy should be based upon the provision of the elements of environmental security – appropriate locations, tenancies, and investment opportunities – rather than on the direct construction of new buildings' (Turner and Goetz, 1967, p. 123). His general conclusion, which is supported by Mangin (1967*a*, pp. 85–9), is that spontaneous settlements represent a solution rather than a problem: they represent a solution to the housing problem of the low income group of the cities of the developing countries as conceptualized by the urban poor themselves. All too often, official efforts to solve the same problem succeed only in frustrating the spontaneous problem-solving efforts of the urban poor; consequently what has to be learned more widely is that 'successful urban planning and low-income housing policies in transitional contexts depend upon the alignment of government action with the priorities and forces of popular settlement' (Turner, 1968*b*, p. 362).

In situ provision in perspective

There can be no doubt that, due in good measure to the work of Turner and Mangin, planning attitudes towards spontaneous settlements have undergone a large measure of revision during the last decade. Whereas formerly spontaneous settlements were almost universally condemned as chaotic and disorganized misery belts, populated by poverty-stricken migrants fresh from the countryside who were ripe for revolution, today considerable discrepancies in their evaluation are evident. Housing policies in consequence are in a state of considerable transition.

At one end of the scale, reflecting a still common attitude but one which is coming under increasing attack, stands perhaps Prebisch (1963, p. 23) who has written of Latin American cities generally that:

> An appreciable proportion of the increase in the active population is not properly absorbed in the production process: economic development passes it by. This is mainly true of the population that moves from the country areas to the towns. . . . This must invariably happen in the process of economic development, but what is not inevitable is the fate of such people. Far from achieving integration in city life, and sharing in better patterns of living, they put up their wretched shantytowns and else eke out a hand to mouth existence in a whole wide range of ill-paid personal services with periods of out-and-out unemployment. Thus, poverty, frustration and resentment surge in from the country to the towns where symptoms of concentration of income are already so conspicuous.

There is also Lerner (1967, p. 24), who has written in scathing terms of '"tin can cities" that infest metropolitan centres of every developing country from Cairo to Manila', and has seen their inhabitants as '"displaced persons", the DPs of the developmental process as it now typically occurs in most of the world, a human flotsam and jetsam that has been displaced from agricultural life without being incorporated into modern industrial life'. Likewise, there is Juppenlatz (1970), who has cast his book on the urban squatter problem in the developing world in terms of 'ever mounting numbers . . . defying law and authority' and 'erecting shelters in defiance of all urban standards and regulations', and has characterized the problem of spontaneous settlements as a major part of what he calls the 'urban sickness' of Third World cities (pp. 12–13). The outward appearance of the spontaneous settlements, asserts Juppenlatz, '. . . is that of a fungus attached to and growing out from the carapace of the city . . . whether hidden inside the fungin is a more deadly virus, waiting to take its toll like the plague, is something which is not yet known, only feared' (p. 5).

At the opposite pole is a growing number of those who emphasize the positive aspects of spontaneous settlements in contributing towards the solution of the immense problem of urban shelter in the Third World. Though some high status occupations may be noted among the inhabitants of the spontaneous settlements of almost every Third World city – Abrams (1966*a*, p. 17) quotes the following house signs in the squatter areas of Davao, Philippines, for example: 'Dental Clinic', 'Physicians and Surgeons', 'Notary Public', 'Master Plumber: Licensed' and 'Wanted: House-maid' – as Mangin (1967*a*; p. 71) has forcefully pointed out, squatter settlements are overwhelmingly composed of poor families who work hard and aspire to get ahead legitimately. It is now becoming more widely recognized that in general they are not centres of political subversion, nor of organized crime, though petty crime does exist in them of course. Moreover, family and kinship in many cases have been reported to be strong. Within this welcome reassessment, however, it is necessary to clarify the extent to which Turner's picture of the 'ideal' squatter settlement, populated by 'consolidators' and rapidly improving *in situ* in its physical facilities, may be considered representative of a general Third World situation.

As has already been indicated, Turner's major prescription for the solution of the housing problems of Third World cities is the assisted development of spontaneous settlements linked essentially with security of tenure for their inhabitants. Security of tenure, he argues, is essential to the progressive improvement both of the individual dwelling and physical facilities for the community as a whole, especially if communal labour is to be involved in the provision of community facilities. On the other hand, there are certain significant difficulties in such possible programmes, some of which Turner himself acknowledges (see Dwyer, 1972*b*). Perhaps most important of all is the magnitude of the change in attitudes – and especially attitudes of the landowning elites who are so heavily involved in politics throughout the Third World – towards property rights that would necessarily be involved in any widespread adoption of prescriptions along the lines advocated by Turner.

As Mangin (1970*b*, p. xxxvi) has pointed out, the kind of community action represented by the Cuevas type of squatter invasion may be possible only in a state where there is a degree of laxity in government control both national and local: one in which some degree of tolerance towards deviant behaviour may be expected, but only provided that such behaviour does not directly threaten the major economic interests and power of the ruling groups. Apart from this level of permissiveness, no modern state either in the industrially advanced or in the developing countries has yet gone so far as to allow large groups of poor people to work out their own solutions to their major problems in defiance of previously established and generally recognized rights. Most of the Lima invasions legitimized to date have, it seems, been on public land. It remains to be seen whether the transfer of urban land from private ownership to the inhabitants of spontaneous settlements can be successfully arranged on a large scale within the Third World.

At the more local level, while there are undoubtedly instances, like those quoted by Turner, of spontaneous settlements which have either begun with, or quickly assumed, regular layouts, there are also many more in which the densities of population are far too high and the building patterns too chaotic to permit of their easy rationalization. In Lima itself a considerable difference is apparent in this respect between the older, inner area spontaneous settlements, for example that of El Augustino, and the outer *barriadas* such as Cuevas, and even in the case of Cuevas after the major part of the settlement had been laid out in regular fashion chaotic accretive growth later appeared on the lower parts of the hillslopes surrounding the valley (Fig. 6.5). In general, the seizure of land on an organized basis which extends to the allocation of individual plots according to a rational layout plan does not seem to be at all representative of the circumstances of growth of spontaneous settlements in either Africa or Asia. And in eastern Asia in particular the excessive density of population in such settlements is a major problem almost everywhere. The Manila squatters of the North Harbour area, for example, show an almost total disregard for the provision of any community space whatsoever between their shacks and the settlement crowds to within 2 or 3 inches of trains passing along the railway tracks. Broadly similar situations exist in Djakarta, Kuala Lumpur, Singapore, Hong Kong, Bangkok and Calcutta, while in Karachi, in the single-storeyed hut and mud house area along the River Lyari, 'every available foot of land has been built upon so that

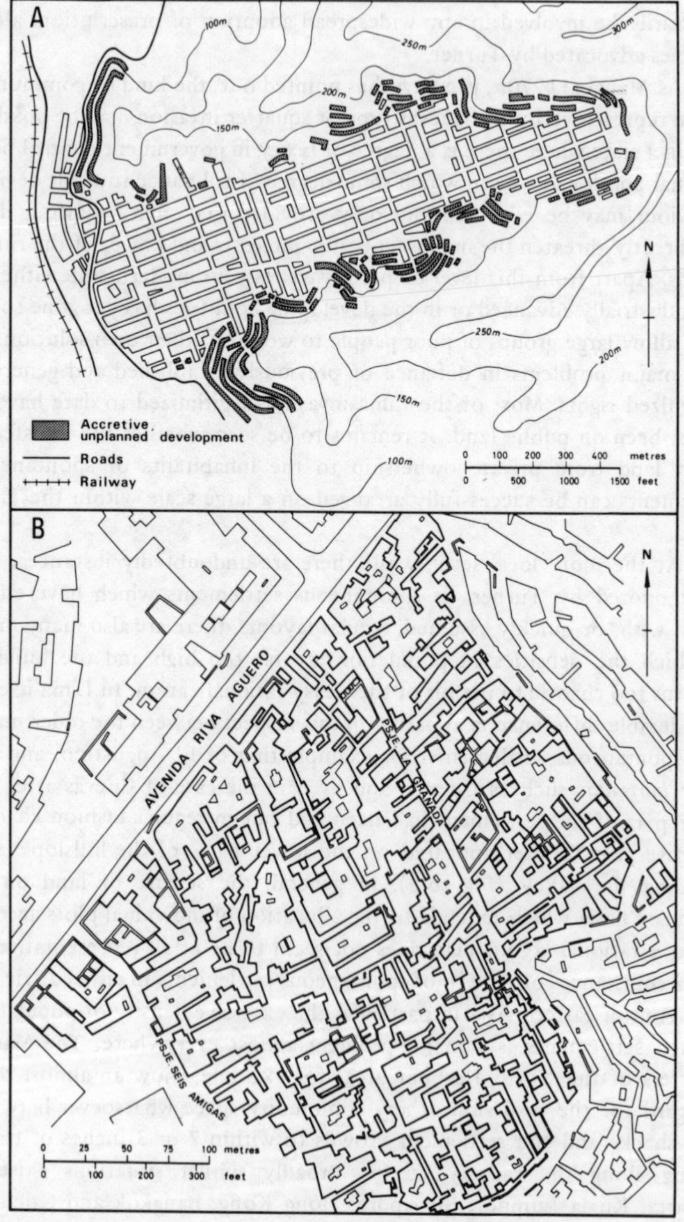

Fig. 6.5 Layout of the Cuevas and part of the El Augustino *barriadas*. Note the much more irregular form of El Augustino (Caminos, 1969)

instead of streets and roads there are narrow and winding lanes which provide the only approach to the houses', and in some parts of the area the population density exceeds 2 400 persons to the hectare (1 000 persons to the acre) (Khan, 1971, p. 128).

Moreover, whilst there are problems of high density associated with spontaneous settlement in many areas, the relatively low density character of much spontaneous settlement elsewhere presents formidable difficulties of other kinds within the Third World setting of general poverty. Densities in regularly laid out settlements in Lima such as Comas and Cuevas are generally well below 250 persons to the hectare (100 persons to the acre) (Cotler and Laquian, 1971, p. 121). In the Cuevas settlement in 1965, for example, the gross density was 133 persons per hectare (Turner, in Caminos *et al.*, 1969, p. 132). Turner (1967, pp. 169–72) writes of the typical *barriada* family of Lima building houses 110 sq. m (1 200 sq. ft) in area and that when the squatter invasion of the Cuevas area took place the majority of the individual building plots marked out were 8 by 16.5 m. He recounts (1968*b*, p. 356) a case history in which the subject complains of his newly allocated government house with its 3.7 by 5.5 m (12 by 18 ft) floor area because in his old squatter shack 'twenty people could sit inside and be comfortable', and he quotes (1967, p. 167) with approval Patrick Geddes' early prescription for the happiness of the Indian poor: 'I have to remind all concerned that the essential need of a house and family is room and that the essential improvement of a house and family is more room.' 'Observations of what ordinary families in urbanizing countries do, when they are free to act as they will', writes Turner (*ibid.*), 'show that they prefer to live in large unfinished houses – or even large shacks – rather than in small finished ones'. This is, of course, true as far as it goes. It is entirely reasonable on an individual level if only the individual family and not the community as a whole is to be considered, but it does immediately raise the major issues of the ultimate form of the city and what can be afforded by basically poor societies in terms of urban land and the extension of services.

Turner (1967, p. 178) tends to minimize these important aspects of the problem. He omits the cost and alternative use aspects of land throughout his writings; he contends that: 'Initially sewers and even water mains are unessential' (a statement which may have some validity for a desert city such as Lima, given efficient pit disposal of wastes, but can have little for a city built in a swamp such as Calcutta); and as for transport he writes merely that, 'an efficient bus service requires very little capital and, in any case, is usually a commercial proposition'. Perhaps of most vital importance, however, is the overall view he holds of the form of the city. This is never clear. The fostering of spontaneous settlement will, it seems inevitably imply in a majority of cases a widely spread city of relatively low density with such settlements on the periphery, and while this may have merit as a possible solution to the housing problem in certain circumstances, inherent difficulties of transport services, of the extension of roads, water supply, lighting and sewerage, of industrial location and of the journey to work must also be recognized. Turner (1966, p. 524) himself quotes the case of Arequipa, Peru, which in 1960 had a regularly built-up area of 900 hectares (2 220 acres) and an additional built-up area of *barriadas* covering 1 100 hectares (2 720 acres) the average gross density in the *barriadas* being only 22 per hectare (9 per acre).

At the micro level, one of the most critical difficulties lies in the poor design and layout both of the individual dwelling and of the community as a whole when constructed almost wholly by unskilled and often ignorant workers who, if not direct migrants, may be only a few years removed from rural hinterlands. At the level of the individual dwelling there is usually a marked tendency to produce already known but basically unsatisfactory forms, either those of the houses of the poor in the countryside or those of the urban slum near the city centre.

Further, Turner's strongest argument, the self-improving nature of Lima's peripheral *barriadas*, also requires considerable qualification when considered within a wider Third World context. Though there can be no doubt that spontaneous improvement is a marked feature of certain Latin American squatter situations and that it has rightly attracted a good deal of international attention recently as one of the most significant examples of the creative forces latent in the poor of the Third World, it must also be recognized that such improvement is not characteristic of a large number of other squatter cases.

There are, in fact, good grounds for claiming that on a general Third World scale spontaneous settlements are characterized by the very poor and not Turner's 'consolidators', who are the upper strata of the urban poor; and that, moreover, such very poor people are probably destined to remain in their present economic plight for a considerable period yet to come, given the overall circumstances of population growth, development and income distribution in the Third World. Juppenlatz (1970, p. 104), for example, has claimed that only 15 per cent of Manila's squatter families can be considered to be clearly above subsistence level, whereas 4 per cent are destitute and dependent upon Social Welfare and the remaining 81 per cent living 'below the minimum line of subsistence, but above destitution'.

Again, Solow (1968, pp. 88–9) reported in 1968 that a case study of the El Manguito spontaneous settlement in San Salvador showed that 95 per cent of the families had incomes of less than US$50 a month and 71 per cent had less than US$25 a month. This was at a time when over five central American countries as a group 56 per cent of all urban families earned less than US$90 a month. Another case study, of a spontaneous settlement in Guatamala City, at about the same time showed that 70 per cent of the families had incomes of less than US$60 a month and 92 per cent less than US$90 a month (*ibid.*). In the Asima squatter area of Baghdad, 94 per cent of the families were living in huts built of reeds and mud when the site was investigated by Phillips. On average there were 1.1 rooms per family and 4.7 persons to a room. The possessions of the families indicated extreme poverty (Table 6.2) and caused Phillips (1958, p. 417) to comment that: 'Even these semi-urban people remain too poor to own furniture, and therefore they continue to sleep, sit, and eat on the ground, unrolling a rug or mat for the purpose if they have one.' Similarly, Laquian (1968, p. 191) demonstrated in his study of Barrio Magsaysay in Manila both the very limited extent of the savings of the inhabitants and that the most common aspirations in the expenditure of savings (and hoped-for future savings of the poorest of the settlers) were first for

Table 6.2 Household possessions of Asima sample families

Item	*Families having one or more*	
	Number	*Percentage*
Bedding (mats and comforters)	251	96.9
Kerosene cooking stove (one burner)	228	88.0
Rug (unrolled for sitting)	213	82.2
Storage chest	206	79.5
Radio (battery)	33	12.7
Table (to hold radio)	29	11.2
Bicycle	11	4.2
Chair or bench	6	2.3
Charcoal heating stove	2	0.8
Sewing machine	1	0.4

Families interviewed: 259.

Source: Phillips, 1958, p. 417.

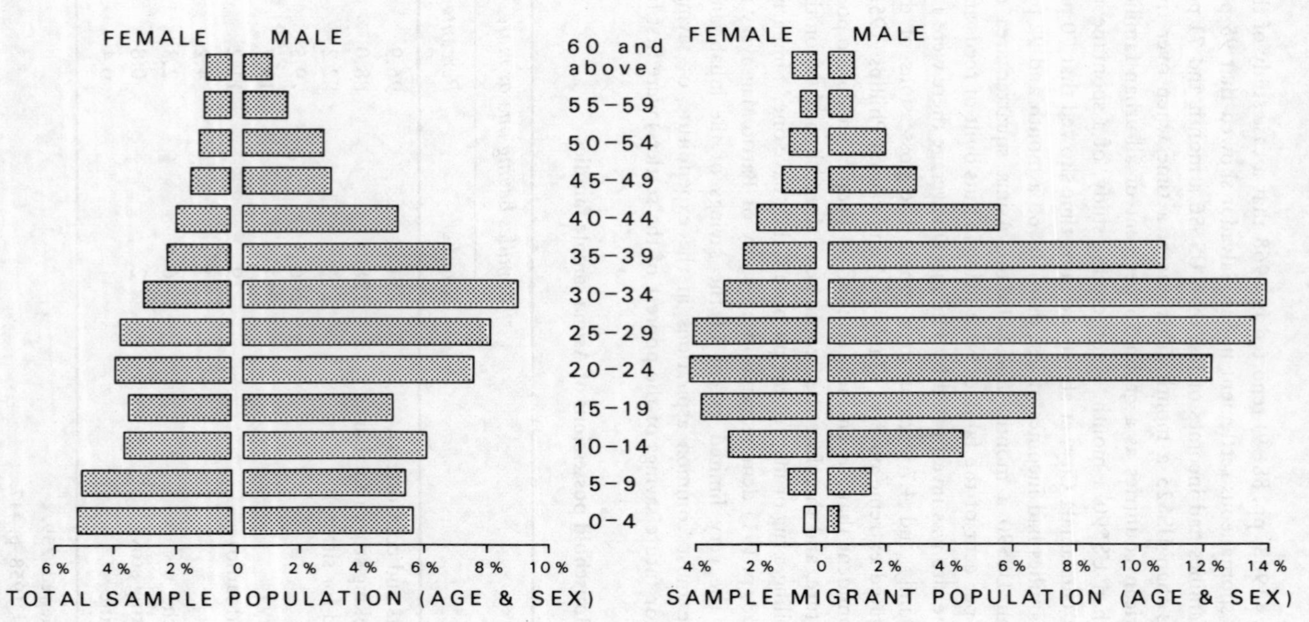

Fig. 6.6 Demographic characteristics of in-migration to Calcutta

furniture and basic household appliances and secondly for the furtherance of the education of the children. Savings expenditure for the repair or improvement of the house took up only 17 per cent of the total.

In these circumstances, it is possible to set against the improving parts of the Lima *barriadas* the generally static experience of the *bustees* of Calcutta, for example, and most east Asian squatter areas seem to conform more to the Calcutta pattern in this respect than to that of the improving parts of the Lima *barriadas*. Only to a degree can improving activities be related to family income, however, for the reality of the Third World situation is much more complex. The selective in-migration of working-age males who leave their families behind in the countryside (Fig. 6.6) is obviously a highly important factor in the formation and evolution of physical characteristics of the *bustees* of Calcutta, as is the form of tenure, for most of the *bustees* are rooming-houses run by a principal tenant. Selectivity of a different kind, involving the sometimes considerable proportions of female household heads, deserted by common law husbands, which are well known in Latin America (for example in the *ranchos* of Caracas: see Marchand, 1966) and Caribbean squatter settlements, will also be important in prospects for the spontaneous improvement of squatter settlements, as it will in the case of the large numbers of temporary target migrants in East African towns referred to in chapter 2. The form of tenure is also significant in the case of many of the squatter 'yards' of Kingston, Jamaica. Although family occupation is more normal in the Kingston case, there too the relationship is often that of subtenants to principal tenant or landlord rather than a pattern of owner occupation. Again, prospects for eventual tenure may also play a role of importance. Where squatter control is firm – as for example in Hong Kong, where extensions to structures may be demolished and the building materials confiscated – it is usually not worth trying to improve an owner–occupied structure, whatever the family income.

Finally, the relocation of certain spontaneous settlements may become necessary for reasons of social engineering, an approach to the planned urban development of Third World cities referred to as a possible future development in the later part of chapter 2. Some fragmentary evidence relating to a possible negative relationship between the function of cities as centres of economic and social change in the Third World and the volume of migration from the countryside was cited there, and particular reference was made to the fairly rapid development in recent years of ecological zones within the cities distinguished by markedly rural demographic, socio-economic and psychological characteristics. Often, it seems, such zones are areas of spontaneous settlement. To this kind of observation, tentative though it may be, must be added an additional set of considerations of an ecological nature which also has important bearing on the question of possible planned residential mixing. This is the segregation of communities by ethnic grouping or colour which is characteristic of many Third World cities and so often has significant political implications. As Bonilla (1970, p. 73) has pointed out, for example, though Negroes are slightly in a numerical majority in the *favelas* of Rio de Janeiro, there are almost equivalent proportions of mixed-bloods and whites. Brazilians often point to this heterogeneity as evidence of the country's racial democracy but this misses the essential point for, while Rio's Negroes may not be alone in the *favelas*, as an urban group they are almost all located in such areas.

Ethnic grouping on these or similar lines is usually associated with historical situations of international migration in which the migrant group has become predominantly urban-oriented within the host country. The migration of Asians to East Africa is a classic case in point, as is the very similar situation of the Chinese and Indian communities in South-east Asia. In Malaysia, for example, the Chinese comprise less than two-fifths of the total population but they outnumber Malays by more than three to one in towns and cities of 20 000 and above. In Kuala Lumpur, the capital city, as in all other Malayan towns and, indeed, in South-east Asia generally, the result has been extreme residential segregation along ethnic lines. From its foundation as a mining camp in the late nineteenth century, Kuala Lumpur was a Chinese city, and occupationally and residentially the Malays remained peripheral to it. Ecologically, the basic pattern of the community was set during the colonial period when an urban core of Chinese shophouses developed and the Malays became largely concentrated in the official Malay reserve of Kampong Bahru and a series of semirural *kampongs* fringing the city. In more recent years the position has begun to change fundamentally, for with the achievement of Malaysia's independence political power in the state has become concentrated in the hands of the Malays and at the same time a swelling tide of Malay in-migration from the countryside has begun to engulf the capital city. Squatter settlements have proliferated, but as relatively small communities very distinctively either Malay or Chinese. The general parallels with the East African urban situation are very clear as are the similarities in the political and social tensions arising in the cities along ethnic lines, tensions which tend to be both crystallized and magnified by the extent of residential segregation.

Improving the worst city in the world

From the Lima situation, which was the starting point for the above discussion, attention will now be turned to Calcutta because in Calcutta perhaps the most coherent and comprehensive attempt to date has been made to plan for the future of a major city in accordance with the harsh economic realities of the Third World situation, and in the planning housing improvement has been given a good deal of attention. Calcutta has been called the worst city in the world, and with good reason. It represents possibly the extreme of urban decay yet known in the contemporary world: and, sadly, all the signs are that its nadir has not yet been reached. Calcutta is a frightening example to the authorities of other major Third World cities such as Bombay, Djakarta, Manila and Lagos which, inexorably, seem to be headed along the same path to comprehensive physical decadence.

To a degree, Calcutta's contemporary housing and other major environmental problems may be said to stem from the very site of the city. Its development is a classic case of locational economic advantages outweighing site difficulties, for probably 'nowhere in India are the adverse physiographic, climatic and topographic conditions so much at variance with the economic opportunities' (Kar, 1968, p. 330). The city lies in the Ganges delta, 130 km (80 miles) upstream from the Bay of Bengal, amid bogs, marshes and salt lakes, with the water table frequently at the surface and nowhere more than a few feet below it. Contemporary Calcutta is literally a city in a swamp, but the original British foundation was located on the banks of the winding Hoogly distributary along a narrow belt of comparatively high levee ground (Fig. 6.7). From the Hoogly's levees, the land slopes away from the river, drained by a maze of streams, channels and creeks in a manner typical of a deltaic lowland. These physiographic characteristics, coupled with the subtropical monsoonal climatic regime of the delta, with its humid, enervating summers, provide one of the least attractive settings for urban settlement in the world.

Calcutta was founded in 1690 by a group of British traders as a defensible trading post; indeed the major objective of the early settlers in otherwise illogically developing a site on the left bank of the Hoogly was to keep the river between themselves and the most powerful of the Indian rulers of the day. The city grew as the riches of Bengal attracted increasing numbers of merchants to the protection of its fort and other defensive works, and by the middle of the following century half of India's seaborne trade was passing through Calcutta (Murphey, 1964, p. 242). Bengali

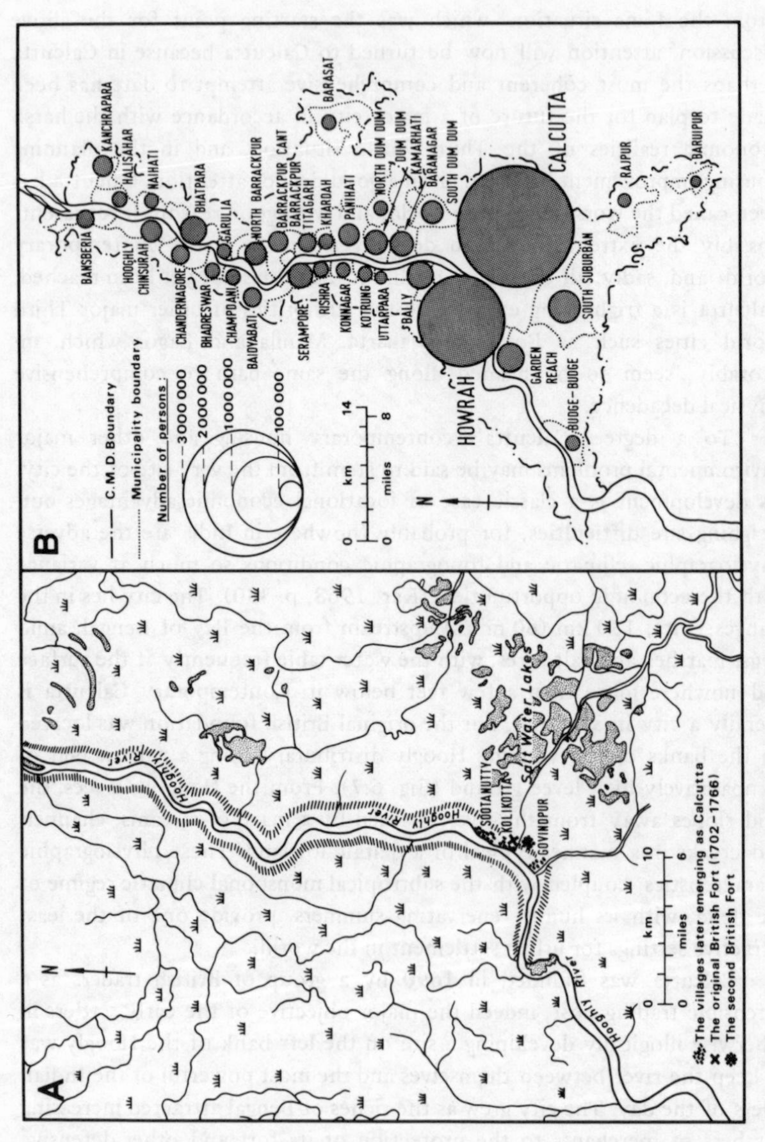

Fig. 6.7 (A) The site of Calcutta: (B) The Calcutta conurbation, 1961

cotton textiles, especially the light muslins, were acknowledged to be the finest in the world and were in great demand in eighteenth-century Europe; other important exports were sugar, silk, shellac, saltpetre and hides. Shipping activity along the Hoogly grew by leaps and bounds, and with it population.

An estimate of population for 1822 gave Calcutta 200 000 persons with a further 100 000 across the river in the more recent twin city of Howrah (Kar, 1968, p. 336). A new fort, on the site of the present Fort William, had been built in 1722: downstream, warehouses stretched along the Garden Reach, which was the principal anchorage. Facing the open glacis around the fort and extending to the north of it, a spacious European settlement of garden houses grew up, but surrounding this well-regulated urban core on all sides, and occupying virtually the whole of Howrah, were the native quarters of poor hutments, narrow ill-cared-for lanes, decaying water courses, stagnant pools, ricefields and fragments of jungle. As Moorhouse (1971, p. 258) has remarked, by the time Kipling came to Calcutta in the late 1890s, it had become widely known as the City of Stinks as well as the City of Palaces. As a contemporary English writer put it about the same time:

> Most of us have had no occasion to go about anywhere except in the Dalhousie Square, Old Court House Street, Chowringhee and Park Street area, which make a mere fringe along only half of the West side of the built-up mass of Calcutta. . . . One can walk day after day for hours in the lanes of North Calcutta without meeting a single European . . . we have all heard Calcutta described glowingly and quite sincerely as the fairest city in the East . . . but the speakers are plainly unaware of the real conditions. . . . It should be made thoroughly known that the city is in a most serious condition, and only prompt, big and concerted action will maintain our commercial supremacy and save Calcutta and Howrah from becoming the largest slum in the world (Richards, 1914, quoted in Moorhouse, 1971, p. 262).

Modern industry came to Calcutta in 1854 with the erection of the first power-driven mill for processing the jute grown in the delta, and during the next fifty years a string of such mills grew up along the banks of the Hoogly, each giving rise to a settlement and shaping the narrow, elongated form of what was to become the Calcutta conurbation. At about the same time the Bengal–Bihar coalfields, only 160 km (85 miles) west of the city, started to be brought into production, and a little later rich iron ore reserves began to be exploited in South Bihar. With the erection of the first iron and steel mills near these deposits, Calcutta became the communication nerve-centre for a growing industrial region, with the result that between 1884 and 1912 the volume of its import and export trade expanded by 100 and 280 per cent respectively (Kar, 1968, p. 337). To its port and jute industries was added a significant general engineering component as well as most of the consumer goods industries characteristic of a large metropolis, and through the extension of railways and roads the conurbation grew into a continuous built-up ribbon stretching 65 km (40 miles) along the Hoogly from Banasbaria–Kalyani in the north to Ulubaria–Budge Budge in the south, but with a width of only 5 to 7 km (3 to 4 miles).

These industrial developments resulted in little, if any, improvement in general living conditions during the present century, even though, as its capital (until superseded by New Delhi in 1912) Calcutta was supposed to be one of the showpieces of Britain's Indian Empire. The reasons were many and interlinked. Some were to be found in the greed and lack of concern of the merchants and industrialists, both expatriate and Indian; others in prevailing official attitudes, both in the government of the Raj and in that of the Calcutta Corporation, which had been created in 1876 largely on an elected basis. 'In Bengal', wrote the penultimate British Governor of Bengal, R. G. Casey, in a memorandum to the Viceroy, Lord Wavell, in 1944,

> the administration for generations has traditionally been concerned with law and order and revenue. It is only recently, and relatively suddenly, that they have been called upon to adjust themselves to coping with the full range of matters that concern a modern government, for which their previous training and tradition have ill-fitted them. In consequence, they are making a rather poor fist of things . . . the risk is that if things go on as they are going on at present, we may well see the situation degenerate into something quite unpleasant, which we shall all regret . . . as near a breakdown as no matter (Casey, 1962, quoted in Moorhouse, 1971, p. 268).

Another major set of reasons lay in the sheer speed of population growth and rapidly rising densities of population, especially within the inner areas of Calcutta and Howrah. The Census Superintendent wrote as early as 1911 that Calcutta was 'ceasing to be a Bengali city', for even at that date less than half of its inhabitants spoke Bengali and more than half originated from Bihar, Orissa and the United Provinces (Kar, 1968, (p. 340). The other industrial towns of the Hoogly valley presented a similar picture: in Bhatpara for instance four-fifths of the inhabitants spoke Hindi. In large part the in-migration was a response not only to the attractions of Calcutta but also to constant poverty, frequent epidemics and recurrent famine in its hinterland.

> Along with the rapid stride of industrialisation and consequent growth of population along the Hoogly valley during 1901–31 there was a remarkable depopulation in the rural districts of Midnapur, Bardwan, Nadia, Murshidabad, all within about 250 km orbit of Calcutta, due to the hazards of recurrent floods (in 1902, 1913), ravages of malaria, cholera and influenza epidemic (1901–11, 1918) and famine (in 1915–16). This rural depopulation within the economic orbit of Calcutta went hand in hand with the growth and concentration of labour in the Hoogly valley (*ibid.*).

Though it is perhaps somewhat misleading in the circumstances of the overcrowded Indian countryside to write of rural depopulation, a rural–urban migration of considerable magnitude had certainly begun, one which was not slowed even by the world trade depression of late 1920s and early 1930s and has continued apace ever since.

Between 1931 and 1941 the population of the conurbation recorded a 70 per cent increase, from 2.5 to 4.3 million, and by the early 1970s the 8 million mark had been well passed. A very substantial proportion of recent population growth – one estimate (Calcutta Metropolitan Planning Organization, 1966, p. 11) puts it at 30 per cent – has been due to the continual inflow of migrants from the hinterland, and to this stream a significant new component has been added since the late 1940s, one of refugees moving out of East Pakistan as a consequence of the political partition of Bengal. Of the 4 million refugees who came into West Bengal between 1946 and 1956, at least 1 million settled within the Calcutta urban area. More recently the upheaval in East Pakistan which culminated in the formation of the new state of Bangladesh resulted in a renewed refugee influx of major proportions. Calcutta's future population prospects obviously depend very much on political and economic prospects in Bangladesh, as well as on anticipated trends in natural increase within the conurbation and conditions in the countryside which forms its immediate hinterland. The hinterland is at present very little urbanized (in the four-state area of West Bengal, Orissa, Bihar and Assam, excluding the Calcutta area only 7 per cent of the total population lives in urban places as defined by the 1961 census of India), and forms a reservoir of some 100 million rural dwellers (*ibid.*, p. 8). If by the mid-1980s the overall level of urbanization in this area (13 per cent in 1961, including Greater Calcutta) increases only slightly, to 16 per cent, together with natural increase within the conurbation this would imply a population of about 12.5 million for Calcutta. Alternatively, should even the comparatively modest level of urbanization of India as a whole in 1961, which was 18 per cent, be reached in the four-state area by the mid-1980s, then probably up to 2 additional millions of population would have to be anticipated for the conurbation (*ibid*., pp. 9–10).

Calcutta has been said to be a city of 8 million with proper urban facilities for perhaps 0.25 million, and the basic statistics relating to contemporary living conditions in the city are frightening. The Ganges delta is the home of endemic cholera and for long Calcutta has been known as the cholera capital of the world. Within the most crowded areas of the city cholera multiplies during each hot, rainy season; then travellers carry the disease all over India, and to nearby countries as well. It was these circumstances which in 1959 attracted the World Health Organization to Calcutta in order to carry out a comprehensive review of the city's sanitation facilities. The conclusion was entirely predictable: urgent and energetic measures to overcome chronic deficiencies in water supply and drainage and the disposal of sewage and garbage were long overdue, but the deterioration of the urban fabric had assumed such dimensions that the situation could be corrected only as part of a comprehensive rehabilitation plan on a metropolitan scale. The forceful nature of the WHO Report (Wolman *et al.*, 1960) led directly to the creation of the first physical planning agency in West Bengal. This was the Calcutta Metropolitan Planning Organization, which came into being in 1961 as an *ad hoc* agency created by executive order on the initiative of the Chief Minister.

Housing in the Calcutta Metropolitan Plan

After five years of preparatory work, the Calcutta Metropolitan Planning Organization published its Basic Development Plan for the conurbation in 1966. The Plan is an important document both because of its approach to the housing problem and, in a wider context, because it marks a radical departure from the static land use master plans which are so frequently produced, and almost as regularly shelved, in the developing countries. The deficiencies of the conurbation's physical facilities, as well as the constraints imposed by India's national and regional economies of scarcity, are clearly set out in the Plan; indeed one of its principal features is that it considers Calcutta in its regional and national setting, unlike most master plans which all too often examine and prescribe for urban problems on only a local level. The Plan as a whole is an indicative, policy-oriented document rather than a definitive land use plan based on a statutory map governing land use allocations in terms of zoning regulations and other controls. As one of its authors (Rosser, 1970*a*, p. 4) has stated, it is 'essentially concerned with political decision-making, with planning and implementation, seen as a single, permanent, continuous process which, ideally, must be fully integrated with the normal structure of Government'; the notion of any dichotomy between urban planning, as an expert technical exercise quite unrelated to the politics of resource allocation, and its implementation by 'the Government', is comprehensively rejected.

In respect of daily living conditions in Calcutta, the major physical deficiencies identified in the Plan are the most elemental: drainage and sewerage, water supply and the shortage of shelter itself. The maximum elevation within the metropolitan district is only about 10 m (35 ft) above mean sea level and the area has little natural drainage. Most of the numerous small streams which form an intricate network throughout the area are in an advanced stage of deterioration through silting, with the result that during periods of heavy rainfall knee-deep flooding is frequent. Only half of the Calcutta Corporation's part of the conurbation is adequately sewered; there is no sewerage system at all in Howrah or most of the remainder of the conurbation (Fig. 6.8). The vast majority of the people depend on service privies for the disposal of excreta, small sheds containing a seating platform with an earthenware bowl underneath. The contents of the bowls are periodically emptied into trailers by municipal sweepers for transport to disposal pits on the edge of the city. But the bowls are usually filled to overflowing and when flooding takes place faecal materials are spread throughout houses, roads and lanes; they also drain into the numerous shallow ponds, or tanks, which are easily cut out of the waterlogged soil and in which many hundreds of thousands of people bathe and wash their clothes and utensils.

Calcutta's piped water supply has always been inadequate. Until 1820 the upper classes received water from the Great Tank in what is now Dalhousie Square: in the native quarters, however, people had to fend for themselves (Moorhouse, 1971, p. 269). In 1820 the first pumping of water from the Hoogly was introduced. Filtered water was supplied to a limited part of the Calcutta Corporation area from 1870; but though the supply has since been periodically augmented, because of the rapid growth of population, the *per capita* supply of filtered water in the conurbation declined by almost half between 1931 and 1965, to 28 gallons a day. There

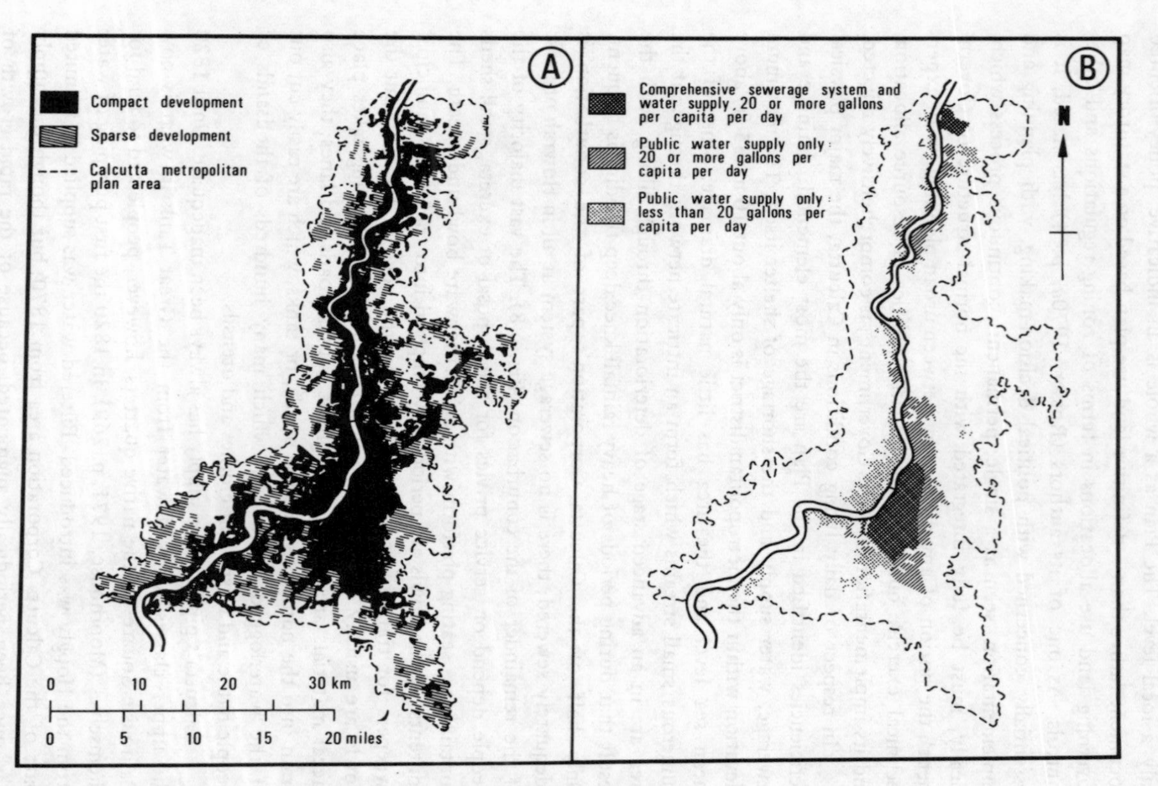

Fig. 6.8 Urban land use and sewered areas in the Calcutta conurbation

was also a simultaneous decline in the supply of unfiltered water from the Hoogly. The unfiltered supply is, of course, intended for non-drinking purposes such as street cleaning, fire fighting and sewer maintenance, but in practice, because of the shortage of supply of filtered water, considerable use is made of it for human consumption. Even so, an estimated 1.7 million people within the conurbation had no public water supply system whatsoever in 1966 (CMPO, 1966, p. 27). Hence the insanitary hand-dug tanks which throughout Calcutta serve for drinking, washing and sometimes even excretion as well.

The Plan outlined an equally desperate position in respect of urban shelter (*ibid.*, pp. 85–94). There are at least 100 000 pavement dwellers within the conurbation who have no shelter at all. There are also very substantial refugee encampments abutting Calcutta on the east and south-east and large tenement areas in the inner parts of the city of Calcutta itself. But the greatest problem is the *bustee*. *Bustees* are found throughout the conurbation, fragmented into more than 3 000 pockets which exhibit some of the worst urban living conditions in the world (Fig. 6.9). They are collections of huts built of non-permanent materials, usually without any urban services whatsoever apart from a minimal number of service privies. The tenure characteristics of the *bustees* are distinctive. The land is owned by a landlord who rents it to a person or persons called *thika* tenants. The *thika* tenants usually build the huts and rent them out to families and individuals room by room. In all, about 912 000 persons (a relatively high proportion of whom were single males) were living in the central *bustees* of Calcutta, Howrah and Bally in 1966, and the total *bustee* population of the conurbation as a whole was well over 1.75 million. Not surprisingly, the *bustees* are the primary focus of Calcutta's chronic cholera, smallpox, tuberculosis and other public health problems.

In many senses the sheer inadequacy and constant deterioration of shelter in the fullest environmental and social senses is central to a very broad range of Calcutta's current problems, and the Plan fully acknowledges this in the prominence it gives to the improvement of housing conditions in both the short- and the long-term perspective.

> The improvement of both the quality and the quantity of housing is regarded as critical to the future of the Calcutta Metropolitan District. Public responsibilities will not be met until, at some time, each family in the area has the opportunity to meet its housing needs in full. Housing, therefore, must be an explicit and integral part of governmental objectives and programmes for the renewal and development of the metropolis,

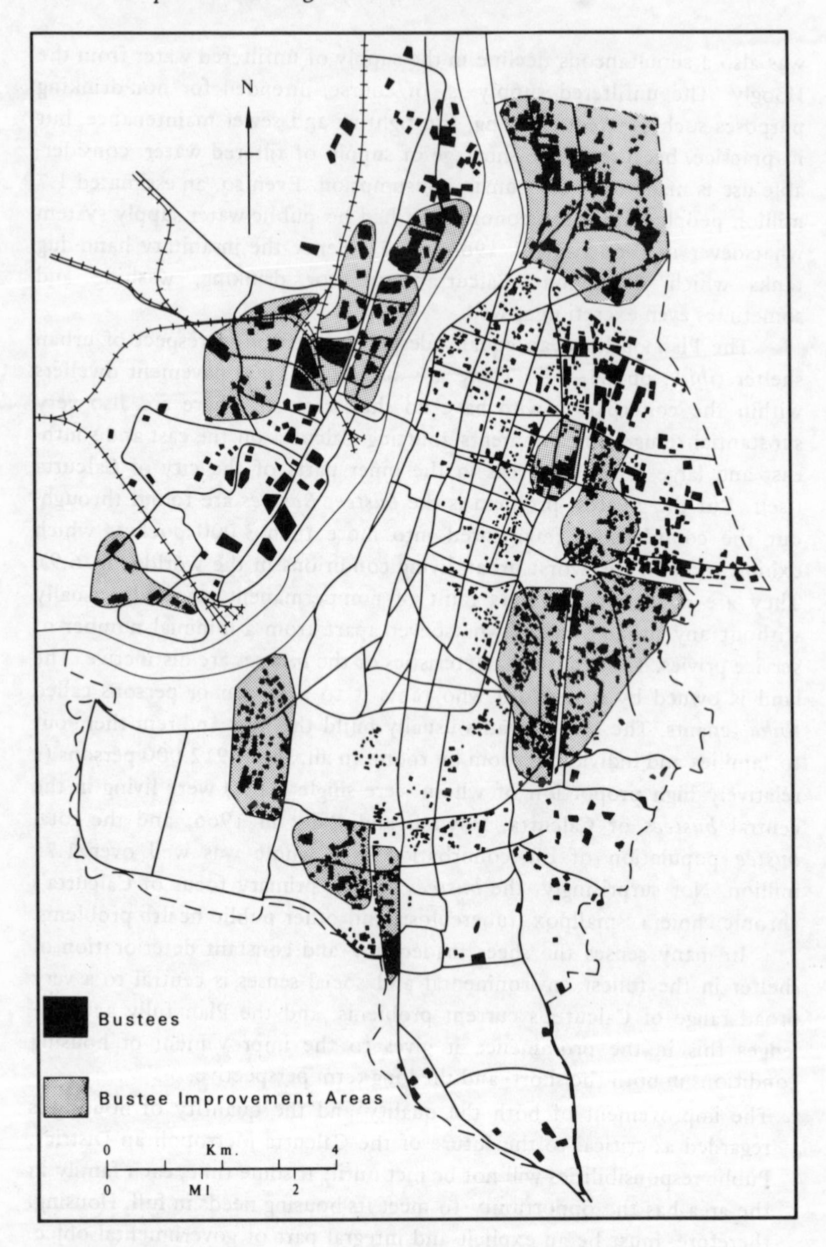

Fig. 6.9 Distribution of *bustees* in Calcutta

the Plan asserts unequivocally (CMPO, 1966, p. 88). Yet it also recognizes that in terms of conventional housing an average of 65 000 new units a year would be required for the metropolis over the twenty-year period from 1966 to 1985 in order to eliminate existing overcrowding and provide for those without any shelter at all. Further, the burden of this provision would almost certainly fall on the public sector; yet to carry out such a programme, annual construction costs alone would amount to more than the central government devoted annually to low-cost housing schemes throughout India during the Third Plan. Therefore any such programme is clearly out of the question. The financial resources are simply not available in India, quite apart from the inability of the construction industry, and of the administrative system, to cope with such a major effort in public housing. During the first three Indian five-year plans (that is over the fifteen-year period to 1966) the total number of *bustee* rehousing units constructed in Calcutta under the slum clearance programme in fact amounted to only 9 000 (Rosser, 1972*a*, p. 181).

The immediate alternative proposed was much more realistic for it recognized that the vast majority of *bustee* dwellers will spend the remainder of their lives in the *bustees*. It implicitly recognized also that, as Rosser (1972*a*, p. 186) has put it, despite their appalling living conditions, far from being cancerous growths upon the city (the middle class and formerly the official view) the *bustees* perform several major positive functions within the urbanization process as a whole. Through their scattered location throughout the inner areas of the conurbation, the *bustees* provide the means of very considerable physical mobility to some of the poorest of the urban population in their search for employment and, once employment is found, for accommodation in close proximity to the work place. The *bustees* themselves also provide a variety of employment in small-scale industries (such as miscellaneous light engineering, blacksmithing, the manufacture of metal boxes and, lower down the scale, rag picking and used paper collection) to the extent that it has been reported that 8.6 per cent of all rooms in the *bustees* are wholly or partly places of work (Bose, 1967, p. 70). Above all, however, the *bustees* represent a spontaneous, indigenous solution to the problem of housing Calcutta's urban poor at rents that can be afforded and they provide a narrow but important range of housing choices in relation to income levels and household composition through variations in hut and room size. They also encourage and reward small-scale private enterprise in the field of housing in that their existence is fundamentally based upon investment in hut construction by a multitude of *thika* tenants. In Calcutta city alone, for example, the 30 000 huts in the *bustees* are owned by 20 000 individuals and let out to a population of over 700 000. As Rosser (1972*a*, p. 187) states,

> All these functions are vitally related to the operation of Calcutta's urban system; a positive housing policy would recognise their importance and seek methods of encouraging and developing them more efficiently, an approach made all the more necessary by the recognition that no feasible alternative to the *bustee* exists, or is likely to within the city's relevant urban future.

What was proposed was a massive *bustee* improvement scheme, together with planned physical reception arrangements properly located for future population increases, though it was also recognized that, ultimately, the only lasting solution to the problems posed by most of the existing *bustees* would be clearance and rehousing, and indeed that some immediate clearances would be necessary for public works. Recognition was thus given to the fact that the real problem of uncontrolled urban settlement in the Third World is often not the individual housing unit, poor though it may be, but rather two undesirable attributes which are all too frequently associated with it: first, the deteriorated environment in which this type of housing characteristically occurs, and secondly its haphazard location in unplanned manner in relation to the rational development of the city as a whole.

The *bustee* improvement programme was to be focused initially on Calcutta, Howrah and Bally, and during the initial five-year period, 1966–71, was to cover 537 000 inhabitants, or just over half of the *bustee* populations of Calcutta and Howrah and almost all that of Bally (Fig. 6.9). It was proposed that approximately 2 000 acres of *bustee* lands should be publicly acquired, the owners being paid in long-term bonds together with a small initial cash payment. Such basic community facilities as schools, hospitals, parks, play spaces and community centres would be installed but the larger part of the programme would be based upon environmental improvement *in situ*. In particular, the provision of an adequate supply of clean and safe water through the sinking of tube wells would be given high priority with the objective of providing one water tap and two baths for every 100 persons. A sanitary sewer system, with appropriate latrines on the basis of four per 100 persons, would also be set up; existing tanks would be made sanitary or filled in; and storm water drainage would be greatly improved. Street lighting would be introduced and the major lanes would be paved. In addition, major emphasis would be placed upon transforming the attitudes of the *bustee* dweller and modernizing habits of domestic hygiene and refuse disposal through the development of vigorous community organizations and supporting management programmes in the *bustees*.

As an essential adjunct to the *bustee* improvement programme, the Plan recommended the provision of incentives to encourage appropriate settlement in key new development areas. It stressed that the overall programme of official investment in shelter must be oriented towards providing a sound locational and environmental base for housing rather than an attempt to provide large quantities of conventional housing, which would be an exercise in futility in India's circumstances. It therefore advocated that large areas of land should be publicly acquired for development and that in the first instance such land should mainly be given over to the orderly extension of non-permanent hut construction arranged in a proper layout in such a manner as to facilitate its replacement by more permanent, conventional housing, should this ever become possible. Such areas would, of course, be provided with basic utilities from the start.

After the Plan

The housing policies briefly outlined above were only part of the comprehensive strategy towards the Calcutta conurbation and its region proposed in the Plan. Immediate action on a five-year development programme was recommended which included in addition to the shelter projects the development of three new towns, two urban renewal projects, the provision of more primary and secondary school places, the development of urban community services, major improvements in the transport system, including new bridges across the Hoogly, the building of new port facilities, and the institution of significant administrative and fiscal changes. The latter included the consolidation of the numerous municipal authorities into nine only; the establishment of a state planning agency for West Bengal; the transformation of the CMPO into a statutory body; and the creation of overall administrative authorities in such vital areas as industrial development, transport and housing.

In the event, implementation of the Plan was far from encouraging at first, due in large part to an almost continual state of crisis in the city. Massive dislocation of orderly development was caused by the influx of refugees from Bangladesh at a time when politically the city was in a state of near chaos. In 1967 the Communists gained control of the West Bengal state government but their rule lasted only for a chaotic eleven months before President's rule was imposed from New Delhi. New elections were held in 1969 and again a Left-wing coalition was successful. However this administration managed to continue for only nine months before President's rule was again deemed necessary by the central government. A further election was held in March 1971 and resulted in a coalition between the Congress Party and the Communist Party of India, but in face of ever-mounting disorder President's rule had to be imposed once again, in July of the same year. Finally, in March 1972, the Congress Party succeeded in gaining a clear majority of seats in the state assembly. This sequence of events precipitated a near breakdown in state and local government as well as a serious deterioration in law and order throughout both the province and the conurbation.

Against this background, the fate of the Plan will not surprise anyone who knows a little of Calcutta's political and social history. One comment (Ashraf and Green, 1972, p. 329) has claimed that,

> One can but contemplate the history of government in Calcutta for the lasty fifty years, review the more immediate reasons for the premature fall of the United Front Government of West Bengal towards the end of 1967, and wonder if the planners have not singularly failed to assess political realities. . . . There could hardly be a climate more adverse to the implementation of a Plan of such breadth and depth than that prevailing in Calcutta, and especially since 1965.

But this kind of criticism is all too easy to make, and if the planners concerned had not believed change in the existing political realities to be possible, then probably the Plan would never even have been attempted in the form it assumed. Yet even active planning advocacy, which the Plan espoused, has its limits. The sad fact is that, like the merchants and industrialists of old, successive municipal administrations within Greater Calcutta have shown themselves during the last two decades or so to be largely insensible to the real problems and to be far more concerned with political advantage, and often personal aggrandisement, than with meeting the legitimate urban needs of the mass of the people. The continuing ineffectiveness of Calcutta's urban government is undoubtedly in part due to constitutional machinery which is ill-designed to produce concerted action among the various authorities, national, regional and local, but this is by no means the sole reason for lack of progress. A much more basic reason is that for far too long the city has been ruled by elements concerned primarily with achieving their own narrow and selfish ends.

Some progress has been made, nevertheless. A powerful Metropolitan

Development Authority was established in 1970 and a substantial development programme for the conurbation was adopted with a budget of 1 500 million rupees, in part from a new tax levied to finance urban improvement (Row, 1972, p. 13). Significantly, after provision for the development of better traffic facilities, housing improvement received the largest financial allocation, a sum of 309 million rupees being set aside for *bustee* improvement, low-cost housing and the development of new areas. The *bustee* improvement programme has started to be implemented. It has also been announced that in addition to the work scheduled under the 1970 development programme, construction of a new bridge across the Hoogly and of the first component of a rapid transit system is to be started. The Hoogly Bridge Commissioners and the Water and Sanitation Authority recommended for the conurbation in the Plan are now in existence and legislation has been drawn up for a Metropolitan Traffic and Transport Authority. In addition, the new state government has abolished the Calcutta Corporation, a move which may, in the long run, prove to be the most important single event of the first five years or so after the Plan.

Conclusion

In the paragraphs above new approaches to Third World housing problems which have grown out of the detailed consideration of the case of Lima's *barriadas* were outlined and evaluated in some detail, and attention was also paid to the Calcutta situation, where an important attempt has been made to fit similar approaches into the context of a regional and local development plan for a major city. Several qualifications were made to the approach adopted by Turner to the Lima situation, but even allowing these considerable merit remains: the criticisms serve rather to reveal the complexity of the problem of spontaneous settlement on a Third World scale and to indicate something of the high degree diversity both in physical form and in socio-economic characteristics which exists among spontaneous settlements, diversity which, as Delgado's work (1969) has demonstrated, future action-oriented research will have to probe more deeply through detailed fieldwork in order to establish realistic typologies with operational relevance.

The basic underlying fact, which is emphasized both by Turner and by the tenor of this present book (and which must be faced more squarely both in academic research and in ongoing administration and planning) is that urban housing problems in the Third World have now reached such formidable dimensions, and within the foreseeable future are likely to become so much more serious, that they are not capable of solution by the mere transference of Western-style attitudes and methods, even allowing for the doubtful possibility of improved capital inputs into housing and the development of conventional construction capacities markedly larger than those at present in existence in most Third World countries. The economic and social forces at work in shaping urban residential patterns in the contemporary Third World setting must in these circumstances be further evaluated as a high priority in future urban research. Physical planning, in turn, must seek to turn such findings to advantage in the improvement of the living conditions of the vast majority of the urban inhabitants of the Third World, who are the very poor, for attempts to create wholly Western-style cities have in the past largely failed to meet housing needs and are certain to be doomed to failure in the future. In particular, as a short- to medium-term measure the Calcutta approach – that every possible housing unit should be conserved, including those in illegal occupation of the land, and priority given to environmental improvement – will have to be much more widely adopted as a fundamental basis for planning; and decisive action on the major issue of ownership of urban land, which is central to the kind of programme advocated by Turner, will have to be sought.

Yet it is also relevant at this point to look back at the examples of Caracas and Hong Kong which were examined in chapters 4 and 5. In Hong Kong, the government has housed over 1 million squatters in multi-storey dwellings and has sought to eliminate spontaneous settlements from the urban landscape through the construction of massive resettlement estates and the strict control of new squatting. Some further comments bearing on the previous discussion in chapter 5 may now be made. The first is that Hong Kong's achievement of rates of economic growth which have probably been unparalleled in any other part of the developing world during the last two decades (Dwyer, 1965) has made it easier to achieve relatively high capital inputs in urban housing. It is also worth noting that as Hong Kong is virtually a city state there is an important element of uniqueness about it compared with most other Third World urban situations, not so much in respect of in-migration (for between 1 and 2 million refugees have been received from mainland China since the late 1940s) but more because of the degree of attention within the total planning effort that can be paid to the urban areas in the absence of sizeable rural hinterlands. The political situation of Hong Kong must also be mentioned. Political activity is minimal – the only real choices are between remaining under British control or reverting to China – and the colony is run in a competent manner by career civil servants rather than by politicians with half an eye on the next election.

Despite these elements of uniqueness, there are, nevertheless, important lessons to be learned from Hong Kong (see Dwyer, 1971*d*). It has been the Hong Kong experience, especially in the early 1950s before the resettlement schemes were begun, that uncontrolled spontaneous settlement can quickly paralyse a city in terms of overall planned physical development for higher rates of economic growth, for example in the pre-empting of sites that may eventually be required for non-residential purposes such as the extension of infrastructure facilities, and in the blocking of access to sites on the urban periphery immediately beyond the squatter settlements. The faster the planned physical development proceeds in such situations, the more necessary it becomes to relocate larger and larger numbers of squatters, and this must inevitably become the experience of most Third World cities, if only because of the degree of importance spontaneous settlements have already assumed in the urban fabric. The best means to persuade settlers to move from areas that must be cleared will need to be thought out carefully in each case. Such strategic clearances may prove politically difficult but it will be vital that they be accomplished.

Equally vital will be the exercise of control over the location of future spontaneous settlement. At present such control is virtually non-existent in many cities and in such circumstances no overall city planning can be effective. If the award of tenure to squatters is to form a major part of policy, as Turner advocates, then at best it can only be selective, that is, applicable only in areas approved as part of a coherent, overall urban plan and coupled with realistic measures to discourage the growth of squatter areas elsewhere. So far, the major example of this kind of approach has been Hong Kong, though within the context of massive resettlement in multistoreyed permanent accommodation outlined in chapter 5. Strict squatter control has formed a major part of urban policies in Hong Kong in recent years and the methods employed would possibly repay study by planning agencies elsewhere. Despite such policies, the relationship of the Resettlement Department to the squatters remained generally good. This has possibly been due to the considerable care which is devoted to explaining the necessity for clearances to the people concerned, to the general climate of firmness which is now well established and widely recognized within Hong Kong, to the relative absence of politicians, and also, of course, to the fact that the government is in a position to offer to all those moved alternative permanent accommodation which, though built to minimum space standards, is available at a rent the poor can afford.

With regard to space standards in government resettlement projects in Hong Kong – until recently 2.2 sq. m (24 sq. ft) per person and now 3.2 sq. m (35 sq. ft) – the fact that there is as yet no evidence that the high densities involved have led to the kinds of breakdown that sociological theory would postulate is of great potential significance since some Third World housing agencies are currently working on the formulation of minimum tolerable housing standards for their own particular cultural contexts. This is an extremely important field of research because the general tendency so far has been for permitted residential building standards to be too high in the context of the realities of the economic situation of the vast majority of the urban inhabitants of developing countries. Current 'low-cost' construction in Caracas falls into this category as chapter 4 indicated. Several hundreds of thousands of people in Hong Kong have already proved the need to revise widely accepted previous conclusions in this field. This aspect of Hong Kong's housing achievement, among others of potential significance (Dwyer, 1968*b*, 1970), has as yet, however, neither been very widely recognized nor subjected to detailed research investigation.

A further major point of relevance in the Hong Kong situation lies in the form of the city that has been produced. A basic difficulty with massive solutions to housing problems along Turner's lines and those advocated for new settlements in Calcutta is that it is exceedingly difficult to reconcile them to anything but cities that are relatively low in population density by Third World standards. There is an inherent contradiction between such city forms and the economic status of the vast majority of the urban inhabitants of the Third World in the sense that such inhabitants cannot afford to pay for much transport. In contrast, largely because of official housing policies, an extremely compact, high density urban area has been created in Hong Kong. This has greatly simplified problems of the journey to work and the extension of services; and it will probably also mean success for the mass transport rail system which is planned.

To point to this contrast, and to make the other allusions to the Hong Kong situation above, is not necessarily to advocate the transferability of Hong Kong urban policies elsewhere. The above paragraphs merely serve to emphasize further the difficulty of the housing problems in the Third World, especially in the complex relationship with other vital aspects of city development, to say nothing of the interconnection with problems of regional planning and of rural development as such. In the future, it seems, an increasing proportion of planning agencies in Third

World cities will be forced to recognize the inevitable and to begin actively to consider the necessity for planned spontaneous settlements. Resistance to such policies is, nevertheless, likely to occur, for example from interests intent on preserving a Western city image for political and nationalistic reasons. Therefore high density but, it is to be hoped, true minimum standard housing projects along Hong Kong lines are likely to grow in importance also. There may be cases in which a mixture of the two approaches may be thought most appropriate. For example, while endorsing *bustee* improvement *in situ*, it has recently also been suggested by Ford Foundation consultants in Calcutta (Kingsley and Kristof, 1971, pp. iii–3) that where there are *bustees* of low gross density in attractive locations it should be possible to relocate *bustee* dwellers into high-rise housing on site, leaving land over for sale at prices sufficient to cover a substantial proportion of the total costs of the scheme.

We are as yet only at the beginning of vast processes of urban growth which will undoubtedly transform the Third World during the next three or four decades and both in research and in the application of the present body of planning knowledge we are woefully equipped to meet this challenge. The importance of the thinking of those who now advocate housing solutions based on spontaneous settlement lies not in the fact that in the present state of knowledge they provide complete answers, but rather in the new channels for further research inquiry and policy innovation such thinking has opened up. At the same time, given the fact that certain important housing agencies (for example in Hong Kong, Singapore, Rio de Janeiro and Caracas) still accept, and will probably continue to accept, the possibility of at least limited solutions through high density, multistoreyed housing, the evaluation of existing experience in this respect, particularly in Hong Kong, which is the foremost example, must also be given more attention than it has received so far in planning research.

Photo: United Nations

Plate 17 Self-help in Lima: Possession of the land, with minimal shelter

Photo: D. J. Dwyer

Plate 18 Self-help in Lima: Improvement of the initial dwelling

Photo: D. J. Dwyer

Plate 19 Self-help in Lima: Achievement of satisfactory shelter

Photo: D. J. Dwyer

Plate 20 Self-help in Lima: A new suburb takes shape

Photo: D. J. Dwyer

Plate 21 Self-help in Lima: Installation of basic services through community participation

Photo: D. J. Dwyer

Plate 22 Self-help in Lima: Development of community facilities, here a school

7

Spontaneous settlement in perspective

If your blanket is short, learn to double up if you want to cover yourself.

Filipino *barrio* saying

The image of the Third World's urban future is clear, given the likely continuation of present major trends. By the end of the century urbanization will have continued at such a pace that many Third World countries of moderate population size – Zambia and Ghana in Africa, South Vietnam and Malaysia in Asia, Venezuela and Peru in Latin America, for example – will probably have undergone such fundamental change that for them the general image of the Third World which now prevails, in which a high proportion of national populations lives in the countryside and the predominant problems are those associated with rural poverty, will have become quite unreal. By the end of the century, the present high rates of natural increase within the Third World's urban areas will have continued unchecked in most cases, and all Third World countries, regardless of size, will have experienced further massive movements of people towards the cities. It is likely that the largest cities will have proved the most powerful magnets and will be overwhelmed. Living conditions will be at their worst in the great metropolitan areas, for by that time they may consist only of a grossly congested and deteriorated inner ring surrounded by vast grey areas of spontaneous settlement, without roads or any services, and crisscrossed by super highways linking enclaves of business with the residential areas of the elite. Population may lap in huge waves between the city and the countryside, according to whether living conditions are marginally better in the one or the other. Life in spontaneous settlements will have become the norm for the majority of urban populations. Then there may be not one but many Calcuttas.

Ways forward: technological development

How can such a future be avoided, or, at least, its worst aspects, mitigated so far as urban housing is concerned? In the present state both of knowledge and practice, as it is hoped this book has demonstrated, there is no clear consensus. Yet a vast urban crisis is emerging in the Third World – that surely is indisputable – the urbanization process is accelerating, and the time to find solutions steadily grows shorter. For Kenya, for example, the most optimistic expectation is that by the year 2000 there will be eight times as many people living in the urban areas as in 1970 and therefore, if current low environmental standards are not to deteriorate still further, the elements of Kenya's urban infrastructure, including housing provision, will need to be multiplied by at least the same proportion (Rosser, 1972*c*, p. 40).

In these desperate circumstances, within the last decade, and especi-

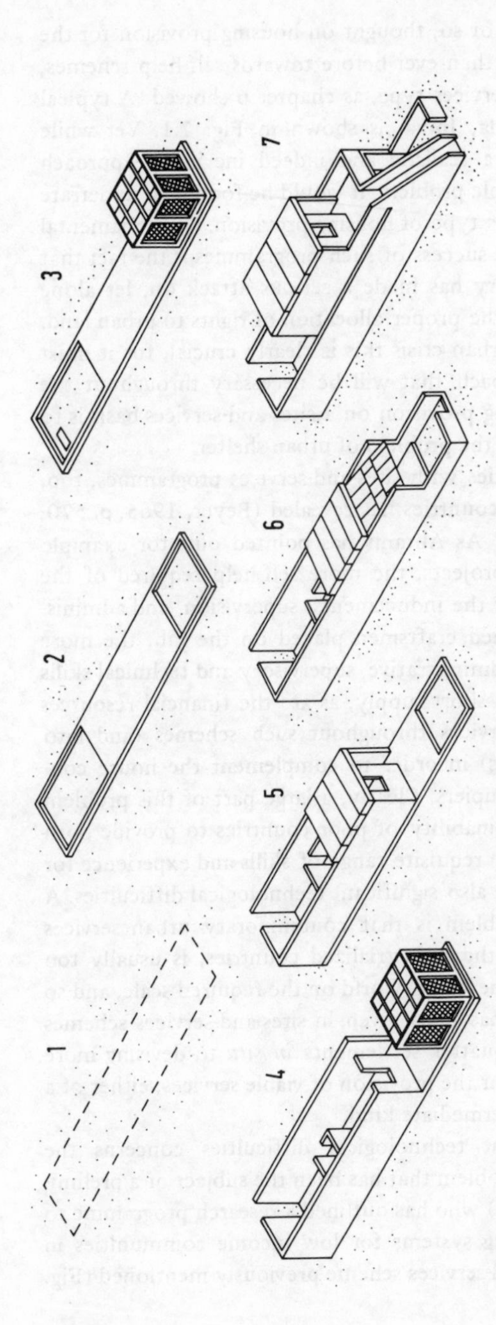

1
2
3
4
5
6
7
1 Stage One 10 by 50 foot lots are laid out by the association
2 Stage Two Foundation walls and plinth are constructed to assure urban control and structural security
3 Stage Three The hutment association distributes the land and the dwellers move onto their lots
4 Stage Four Working together with technical assistance, the community builds common walls
5 Stage Five Individually or in groups, one section is covered over. Ownership officially goes to the dweller
6 Stage Six Porch is covered and front yard enclosed
7 Stage Seven: According to the needs and means of the inhabitants, more sections are added and additional floors are constructed

Fig. 7.1 A housing scheme for Baroda, India (after Benninger)

ally within the last five years or so, thought on housing provision for the urban poor has moved more than ever before towards self-help schemes, particularly of the sites-and-services type, as chapter 6 showed. A typical example, proposed for Baroda, India, is shown in Fig. 7.1. Yet while welcoming such schemes as a realistic and indeed inevitable approach towards an otherwise intractable problem, it would be foolish to underrate the difficulties involved in this type of housing provision. Of fundamental relevance to the prospects for success of such programmes is the fact that as yet no Third World country has made a serious attack on, let alone solved, the basic problem of the proper allocation of rights to urban land. Yet in view of the coming urban crisis this is clearly crucial, for it must underpin much of the approach that will be necessary throughout the developing countries if housing provision on a sites-and-services basis is to have an appreciable impact on the problem of urban shelter.

There are other difficulties with sites-and-services programmes, too, as recent experience in some countries has revealed (Beyer, 1965, p. 570; Abrams, 1966*a*, pp. 170–4). As Abrams has pointed out, for example (p. 170): 'In urban housing projects, the more self-help required of the occupant, the greater must be the inducements, supervision, and administrative costs. The more trained craftsmen placed on the job, the more efficient the operation.' But administrative, supervisory and technical skills are almost always in critically short supply, as are the financial resources for extending basic urban services throughout such schemes (and into already existing squatter areas) in order to complement the house construction activities of the occupiers. Clearly, a large part of this problem relates back to the all-round inability of poor countries to provide both the financial resources and the requisite range of skills and experience for problem solving, but there are also significant technological difficulties. A highly important current problem is that contemporary urban services technology, as developed in the industrialized countries, is usually too expensive to transplant into the Third World on the required scale, and so far relatively little attention has been given in sites-and-services schemes and projects for improving squatter settlements *in situ* to devising more suitable technological forms for the provision of viable services, either of a wholly indigenous or of an intermediate kind.

One example of current technological difficulties concerns the disposal of human wastes, a problem that has been the subject of a preliminary report by Winblad (1972) who has outlined a research programme to develop alternatives to existing systems for low income communities in Africa. In the Baroda sites-and-services scheme previously mentioned (Fig.

7.1), an incremental programme of services provision was incorporated, starting with public water taps and communal latrines, and going on in sequence to drainage, water supply, electricity and finally to individual prefabricated water closet units of simple design. But the planner of the scheme, Benninger (1972, p. 164), was obviously doubtful about such provision being accomplished, for the provision of municipal facilities was isolated in his physical design so that other aspects of the system could continue to grow independently. Back lanes between the lots were provided to carry services as and when they became available, a realistic design solution because the prospects of providing even minimal urban services on a mass scale in the Third World, given the present state of technology, are remote. In India generally, as in many other parts of Asia and also in tropical Africa, poor water supply, together with inadequate waste collection and virtually no facilities for the disposal of excreta, are almost universal in the cities outside the elite areas. For Africa, it has been estimated that only about 8 per cent of urban families has access to a sanitary sewage system (Winblad, 1972, pp. 1–2); and the pollution of water with human wastes is the chief reason for the widespread incidence of the enteric diseases in African towns.

The conventional response to such urban environmental problems, Winblad aptly observes, is to apply standard solutions from the industrialized countries: the answer to problems of human waste disposal is invariably seen (as in Benninger's Baroda scheme) as waterborne sewage systems, for example. Yet such systems are expensive to install and operate even under the most favourable conditions:

> In a typical African urban area with an irregular settlement pattern, water shortage, and in the case of inland locations a lack of recipients, waterborne sewer systems will be prohibitively costly. . . . Even if the total net savings of a developing country in Africa were used to provide the urban population with utilities of such standards, the funds would be insufficient (Winblad, 1972, p. 3).

The inescapable conclusion, which applies equally to most other parts of the Third World, is therefore that 'the great majority of people in Africa are not likely in this century to be able to afford any other sanitary installations than those they can build themselves' (*ibid.*, pp. 3–4).

The essential technological problem in these circumstances is to widen the choice of satisfactory urban services systems for spontaneous settlements to embrace systems which are appropriate for the financial and technical resources of developing countries. As Winblad (*ibid.*, p. 5) observes, in pre-industrial and rural societies dwellings are usually built by the householders themselves, often with the help of neighbours. Groups of dwellings exhibit a high degree of self-containment and form part of a balanced ecological system. Building materials are obtained from the local environment free of charge, and no infrastructure provision is required from external sources. Each local community maintains its own paths as well as its sources of water supply, and in a rural setting of relatively low population density the disposal of excreta and refuse need not present any serious problem. In an urban environment this balanced pattern of shelter soon breaks down, for while it may still be possible to build a dwelling in a spontaneous settlement, and to improve it over the years so that what starts as a minimal shelter eventually becomes a very acceptable if simple house, at urban densities the natural ecological balance is seriously upset in so far as infrastructure requirements are concerned. It is no longer possible to rely on primitive methods of movement, by foot along paths, nor is it usually possible to find and maintain sufficient local sources of water supply.

Additionally, the disposal of human wastes and household refuse can no longer be accomplished with safety by traditional methods because of the danger of soil and watercourse pollution. A situation thus arises (as it has arisen in so many of the Third World's urban areas) in which a large number of urban shelters may be built, spontaneously or through sites-and-services schemes, at a cost individual families can afford, but this type of development proceeds out of phase with progress towards solutions of the problems of infrastructure provision which concurrently arise on a community scale. In these circumstances, urban development, within the limits set by prevailing official attitudes, the state of technology and the availability of financial and other resources, markedly fails to satisfy the total environmental requirements of the city's inhabitants.

In respect of the technological variable, Winblad (1972, p. 9) points out that so far the main thrust of research on housing in the developing countries has been very much directed towards the superstructure, that is, the building itself, its layout and overall layout of towns and cities. Very little work has been done on devising appropriate utility systems. There is, as yet, no corresponding choice of materials, components and technical solutions as for the dwelling itself; for human waste disposal, for example, the choice is limited either to archaic traditional systems, such as pits, which are clearly unsatisfactory at urban population densities, or to fully modern systems such as waterborne sewage collection and treatment plants, which are too expensive. This lack of innovative work is all the more surprising when the basic facts of capital availability for infrastructure provision are considered.

In British New Towns, for example, the average investment in urban utilities was running at about US$500 per person at the end of the 1960s, and in Swedish municipalities at US$600, whereas in a country like Tanzania it was being argued for the purposes of national development planning that no more than US$8 per urban inhabitant could be spent (*ibid.*). There is therefore a clear need for intermediate utility systems to fill the gap between traditional and modern systems which affects the low income urban dweller. With such intermediate systems, not only would total capital requirements be kept well below the level for modern systems but the population density allowed by the system with safety would be well above that of traditional systems, and thus also lower the overall costs of urban development.

In respect of latrine design, any such intermediate system would have to be both simple and inexpensive in construction and operation and would have to ensure that there was no contamination of surface water, surface soil or ground water entering springs or wells. Excreta would have to be screened from flies and animals and if possible the handling of fresh excreta would have to be eliminated or at least reduced to a minimum (Winblad, 1972, p. 13). In addition, the system would need to be compatible with local habits and religious practices; it could not employ for its day-to-day functioning any skill not normally found among the users; and if it was to be used in existing spontaneous settlements it would have to be capable being fitted into them with the minimum of disturbance.

This is a formidable list of requirements and no method widely used at present fills all of them. Urban planning in most developing countries envisages the extension of pipe networks as the ultimate solution to the problem of disposing of human wastes but, it seems, there is little or nothing in the design or engineering of such networks that is capable if being substantially modified further to suit Third World conditions. Such pipe systems are already built at minimum standards even in the industrialized countries, yet even so the capital required for them would clearly exceed the financial capacity of most developing countries if they were to be used on a mass scale. The implication must be that they can only be installed for a minority of fortunate households without in any way solving the problem for the majority.

An alternative to the normal water closet is the more recent vacuum system, in which wastes are drawn from the privy to a nearby collecting point by a vacuum pump using only a relatively small amount of flushing water. Collecting trucks may be substituted for extensive pipe networks in this system and there is therefore a considerable saving in capital costs. But operational costs are likely to be high, the equipment has to be imported from the industrialized countries, and it is relatively sophisticated. According to Winblad (1972, pp. 28–9), African experience so far indicates a high rate of system failures. In Dar es Salaam in mid-1972, for instance, only three of the city's ten vacuum trucks were in operation due to lack of spare parts.

All in all, it does not seem likely that water closet, vacuum or similarly sophisticated systems of waste disposal will ever reach the mass of the population of the Third World's spontaneous settlements. Modifications to ensure the more satisfactory application of traditional methods will probably have to be at least the short- to medium-term answer. This could involve the discouragement of soil infiltration methods of disposal, which at urban population densities give rise to severe problems of pollution, and also the abandonment of ideas of ultimately providing individual household facilities in favour of communal facilities in which the excreta falls into a simple concrete box set into the ground and is removed periodically by means of hand-operated cesspit emptiers (yet to be developed) and carried away perhaps even by animal-powered carts (*ibid*., p. 29). This is very far from the image of the urban future most Third World planners hold for their cities. It is a relatively sad alternative to the present impasse in this vital aspect of services provision for existing spontaneous settlements and future sites-and-services schemes, but perhaps, for the present at least, it is the only practical one.

Other technological aspects

The thrust of the foregoing paragraphs is that if technological development for cities in the developing countries is to become effective on the scale required to reach the mass of the people it will have to be adaptable to available financial resources, to religion, culture and skills, and to local materials, rather than, as so often in the past, being transferred from external patterns with only token regard for indigenous circumstances. This is true not only in the matter of urban services, which clearly cannot be wholly provided by the urban poor through individual effort, but also in new developments in house construction, given that the official provision of standardized housing to replace spontaneous settlements is likely to remain a significant element in urban policies in many developing countries for the foreseeable future.

All too often variations on the approach to house-building technology in Ghana in 1952, described by Abrams (1966*a*, p. 166), are in process of being repeated in other developing countries even today:

> In Ghana, a firm of consultants, who charged $210 000 for their guidance, told the government in 1952 that their own prefabricated product would help resolve Ghana's housing enigma. Soon precast concrete walls poured in Europe were hauled across the seas to Accra's promontory, lowered to rocking canoes and paddled precariously by intrepid natives past pitching breakers to the distant shore; then they were laboriously transported and set up, miles away, to compose a few lonely exhibits. The company contracted to build 168 model houses at Accra, Kumasi and Takoradi, and set up three factories in Ghana to manufacture its product. But when the cost of sixty-four completed houses ran up to $448 000 and had been translated into the number of cocoa beans needed for payment, the government, on the advice of a United Nations mission, quietly gave up the venture.

Malaysia, with the industrialized housing system imported from Denmark that was referred to in chapter 3, is a more recent case in point. Another, strangely enough in view of the radical evolution of official policies towards its *pueblos jovenes*, is Peru, in some respects.

In Lima, the government of Peru, with assistance from the United Nations Development Programme Special Fund, started the Proyecto Experimental de Vivienda (or PREVI, as it is called) in July 1968, using a mixed team of local and United Nations personnel. The overall objective was to develop new methods and techniques for application on a significant scale as part of Peru's housing policy, and so far these new approaches have been sought through three pilot projects: in low-cost housing design, the improvement of inner urban areas and planning the rational establishment and growth of new spontaneous settlements (Anon, 1970). Activities in the field of low-cost housing design have proved controversial, especially in so far as they centred round an international competition held by PREVI in 1969 for the design of 1 500 dwellings, which was opened to all Peruvian architects and to thirteen invited foreign architects.

This expensive competition was clearly not aimed at solving the problem of mass housing which concerns the urban poor, for the specifications contained in the brief for the competitors indicated dwellings suitable rather for lower white-collar workers seeking regular housing than for the inhabitants of Lima's *pueblos jovenes* (Peru, Government of, and UNO, 1968, pp. 22–4). Some of the schemes submitted were quite elaborate, and one at least required the use of heavy machinery for lifting substantial structural elements. It has since been decided to build pilot groups of houses in various parts of the project area, using a large number of the designs submitted, not merely those of the competition winners. Meanwhile criticism of these activities has grown considerably in Lima, especially at the lack of practical results that can be applied on a significant scale to current projects. Doubts that the improved design and advanced technology stimulated by the project can make possible reductions in building costs of such an order as to effect the present housing situation markedly have been expressed locally. Finally, as Robin and Terzo (1972, p. 53) have stated,

> . . . there is a body of opinion which holds that the very idea of bringing foreign international consultants to provide 'ideas' for the development of low income housing was itself a bad idea; that foreign consultants cannot quickly achieve a full understanding of local conditions such as settlement patterns, construction systems and the use of materials; and that therefore their proposals introduce only superficial observations of the local scene. As a result, it is said, a technology is being produced at PREVI which is not adapted to the local capabilities or economy, and which does not sufficiently consider the need for labour intensive processes in construction.

The resources for the rational development of Third World cities are so few and the needs so many that PREVI's activities in the field of low-cost housing design seem to violate what should be a basic premise for action-oriented research in the field of technological development for Third World housing: that it is almost never possible to justify expensive investigations that are not directly oriented towards building cities for the poor, cities planned round the basic housing and other environmental needs of the mass of the people. Seen in this light, international competitions to design prefabricated lower middle income housing are an expensive irrelevance as, on a greater scale, are the supposedly 'low-cost' housing schemes, in reality too expensive for the poor to live in, which characterize the housing effort of many developing countries, as chapter 3 showed. What is needed in housing design, construction methods and services provision for Third World cities are means of reducing costs which can be applied at the widest level, to benefit the lowest socio-economic ranks of the urban population, without the need for much mechanisation and with labour-intensive techniques. Here some work in India, carried out by Zielinski

(1969) for the Calcutta Metropolitan Planning Organization, is of interest and relevance (see also Banerji, 1972).

Investigations in and around Calcutta have shown that in official low-cost housing schemes the cost of materials is about 45 per cent of total costs. Thus, given continuing official involvement in the construction of urban dwellings, any system which lowers the cost of materials may substantially reduce total costs and thus both allow more homes to be built and provide housing opportunities to families lower down the economic scale. As is well known internationally, the principal elements of the shell of a house lend themselves to mass fabrication.

It does not necessarily follow from this, however, that sophisticated, large-scale prefabrication industries should be the objective of developing countries such as India. This is far from being the case, since the obvious need of the day is for labour intensive techniques wherever possible. A simple style of prefabrication, without the use of expensive equipment or large-scale mechanization, is what is required if traditional building techniques are to be supplemented. The standardized components should be easily made by relatively unsophisticated labour, readily transportable and capable of manual assembly, and of as few varieties as possible.

In the construction system pioneered by Zielinski, standardized reinforced concrete panels 1.5 inches thick are used. There are only two standard panels, a roof panel 10 by 3 ft and a wall panel 9 by 3 ft, specialized door, window and ventilator panels all being cast from the basic mould for the wall panel (Fig. 7.2). The panels have ribs about 8 inches in depth which provide the required rigidity; they are reinforced with steel bars tied with wire, the amount both of steel and concrete being less than half that required in traditional casting operations. The panels can be cast either in wood or in steel moulds by relatively unskilled labour and after curing in water they are easily movable to the construction site.

The process of housebuilding is thereafter reduced to assembling the panels by simple methods. To make the lifting and assembling of the elements easier, a three-part simple hoist with a wheeled base has been designed (Fig. 7.2). This could quite easily be constructed locally from timber. The wall panels are placed side by side in a cement concrete foundation and are attached to each other by filling the gap between them with cement and mortar. The roof panels, in turn, fit on to the wall panels, forming a boxlike structure which is strong and rigid in spite of the thin walls. No interior wall finishes are necessary, though the space between the inward-projecting ribs of the panels could be filled in with mud plastering or some other insulating material.

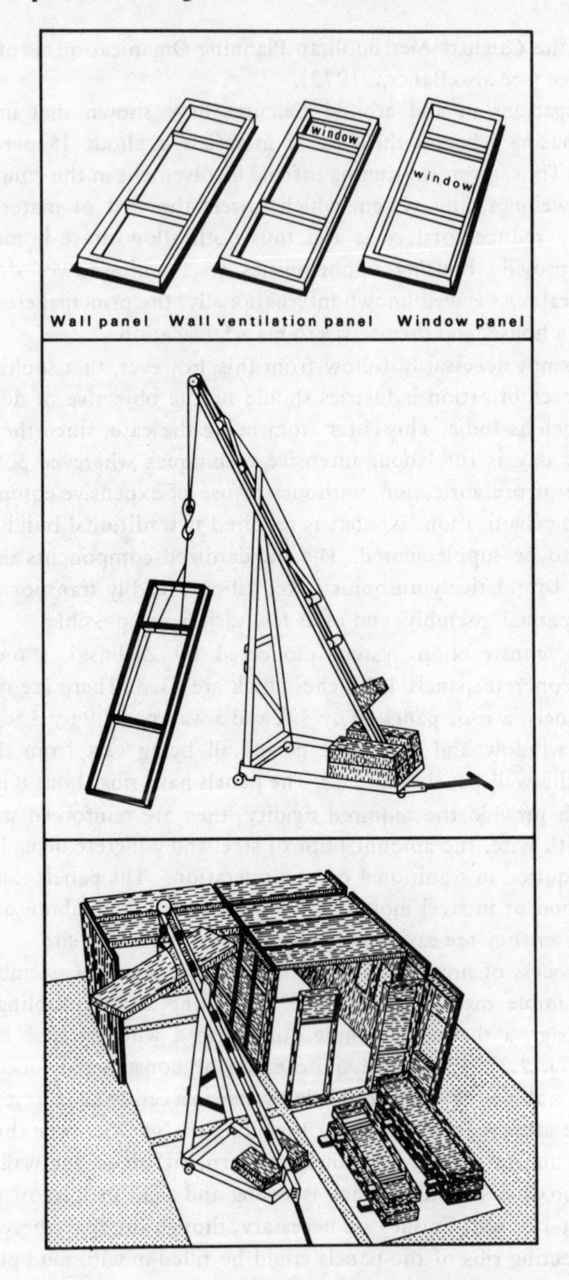

Fig. 7.2 The Universal Concrete Panel System

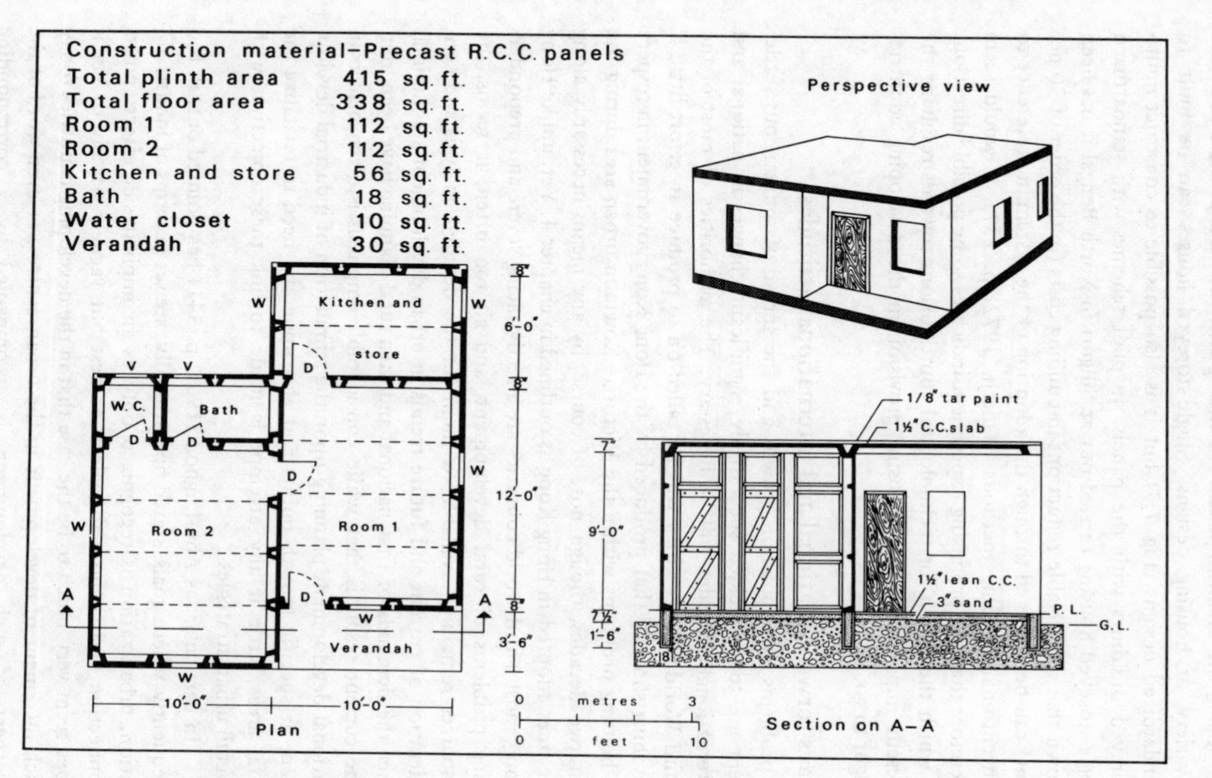

Fig. 7.3 Design of a UCOPAN house

Using the Zielinski panels as building elements, it is possible to evolve a variety of housing designs. Single-storeyed houses can be built to standardized designs (Fig. 7.3) but it is also possible to construct multi-storeyed buildings with the panels. In pilot schemes with standardized single-storeyed housing carried out at Siliguri in North Bengal it has been shown that appreciable reductions in building costs (in the order of 30 per cent) can be expected through the adoption of the system in preference to conventional building methods (Banerji, 1972, p. 237). It would seem therefore that this promising experiment indicates some possible directions in which the search for technological contributions towards resolving the present impasse in urban housing provision in the developing countries ought to go.

Ways forward: national and international attitudes

If problems of population growth and the spread of spontaneous settlement are to be tackled successfully, significant changes in national and international attitudes will be necessary. The authorities of most of the Third World's larger cities will be called on to produce an effort little if anything short of that produced by the Hong Kong government in respect of housing problems within the Victoria–Kowloon urban area during the last two decades, though not, of course, by any means necessarily along the lines adopted in Hong Kong as outlined in chapter 4. Yet, unlike Hong Kong, most Third World countries are already facing severe and preponderating problems of rural development, and all too often, it seems, the resources remaining available to them for the detailed analysis and consideration of current and future trends in urban development are minimal once the demands of first national and then rural planning have been met. The current result is that while considerable emphasis is often placed in national development planning upon the stimulation of industrial development at specific growth points and also upon the need to revitalize the rural areas, little if any attempt is made to link these objectives with overall urban strategies.

In particular, as Abu-Lughod (1965, p. 341) has pointed out, all too frequently where goals, stated operationally, are set in terms of industrialization, urbanization is recognized only as an implicit side effect and its connection with industrial goals is at best but vaguely perceived. Yet it does seem very much to be the case that in the developing countries today each increment of development in the urban centres, or even word of the prospect of such development, is accompanied by a corresponding response in the influx of people from the countryside. There is some evidence from small towns in which the effect of establishing one factory or other modern enterprise is observable, for example, that because the new source of wealth attracts large numbers from the countryside, the increase in employment resulting specifically from such a project may well be accompanied by an overall increase in unemployment and in casual and irregular employment within the town (UN Bureau of Social Affairs, 1957*a*, p. 126). Even if the developing countries manage to attain greater rates of economic growth in the future, therefore, in the absence of coherent urban strategies their problems of urbanization far from becoming more amenable to solution may well be compounded, the more so since in the development process sizeable reductions in rural work forces are to be expected through the modernization of agriculture.

At present, so far as the cities are concerned, most national development planning in the Third World proceeds, as Catherine Bauer Wurster (1956, p. 68) put it, 'from the cradle in economic and resource policy to the grave in urban slums'. The present urban crises in some cities, and the certainty, given present official attitudes, of the coming crises in many more, is being virtually ignored; indeed in many countries strong rural and anti-urban attitudes still persist, despite the obvious demographic facts of rural–urban migration and massive urban population growth. In tropical Africa[1], for example, as Rosser (1972*c*, p. 33) points out, 1.6 million people lived in urban areas and 98.4 million people in rural areas in 1920, an urban proportion of only 1.6 per cent. However, by the end of the present century 105.6 million people will be living in urban areas and 419 million in rural areas. This implies an urban proportion of 20 per cent; it will mean the growth of towns and cities at rates probably greater than anywhere else in the world and will produce astonishing changes in the urban populations of many African countries even within the present decade, as Table 7.1 indicates.

Yet official responses to this situation have essentially been short-term and political rather than based on systematic planning which includes a good measure of consideration of the consequences, and certainty, of massive urban population growth. As Rosser (1972*c*, p. 64) has bluntly stated, the anti-urban (or more precisely, anti-migration) attitudes of politicians in tropical Africa are unmistakable and 'back to the land' exhortations are even now the prevailing theme of political speeches. The futility of this approach is apparent to virtually all students of the urbanization process, yet it continues to be echoed by prominent political

[1] Thirty-five countries of Middle Africa, excluding the Sudan in the north and South Africa in the south (for precise definition see C. Rosser, 1972*c*, p. 15).

leaders not only in Africa but in many other parts of the Third World also. As the Minister for Regional Administration in pre-Amin Uganda put it in a typical Third World statement:

> The common man could justifiably criticize his government if all investment was concentrated into one particular area of the country. . . . Developing countries are desperately short of capital, and you must realize that such countries cannot afford to spend huge sums of money in urban areas on extravagent infrastructure (*ibid.*).

As a result, in all too many countries not only do rural development programmes have highest priority in national development plans but true urban development programmes are strikingly lacking.

Table 7.1 Projected growth of the total and urban population 1970–80: selected countries in tropical Africa

Country	*Total population in millions*			*Urban population in millions*		
	1970	*1980*	*% inc.*	*1970*	*1980*	*% inc.*
Nigeria	66.1	87.6	32.5	10.1	17.7	75.3
Ghana	9.0	12.5	38.9	1.5	2.8	86.7
Zaire	17.4	22.4	28.7	2.2	3.6	63.6
Kenya	10.8	15.1	39.8	0.9	1.7	88.9
Uganda	8.5	11.3	32.9	0.2	0.4	100.0
Tanzania	13.2	17.4	31.8	0.7	1.4	100.0
Ethiopia	25.0	31.5	26.0	1.2	1.9	58.3
Zambia	4.2	5.9	40.5	1.0	1.7	70.0
Senegal	3.9	5.0	28.2	1.0	1.5	50.0
Totals	158.1	208.7	32.0	18.8	32.7	73.9

Note: These figures are based on estimates prepared by the Economic Commission for Africa Demography and Social Statistics Section. They include for individual countries estimates of population growth through migration across national borders, an important factor in many African countries.

Source: Rosser, 1972*c*, p. 35.

In part, the thinking behind statements such as this does concern the urban areas, for there is a somewhat desperate but nevertheless widespread official hope that rural development will somehow have the effect at least of slowing down current rates of rural–urban migration and perhaps even of reversing the trend. Again quoting Rosser (1972*c*, p. 67):

The theme everywhere is: develop the rural areas and thereby arrest urban growth; send the migrants back to the rural areas and thus solve the problem of urban unemployment and the attendant evils of rising urban crime rates, proliferating slums and squatter settlements and the increasing congestion and deterioration of the urban environment.

In its extreme form this can result operationally in the kind of situation described by Laquian (1972, p. 8) in the Philippines:

> Rural land reform is the popular slogan in the Philippines but urban land reform is rarely mentioned or thought about. In fact there is a danger that success with the former may be achieved at the price of the latter as there has been a proposal to sell government land in Greater Manila to get capital for a Land Bank. At a time when governments in most parts of the world are buying urban land to make room for planned expansion, the Philippine Government is thinking of doing the opposite.

A further example that may be quoted is that of Zambia. There, 'repeated exhortations of "back to the land" have not been supported by sufficient economic encouragement either to return to the land or to remain on it in the first place' (Simmance, 1972, p. 9); in fact, the overall result of official development policies has probably been precisely the opposite inasmuch as real income in the rural areas has fallen drastically relative to that in the urban areas during the last decade (*ibid*., pp. 6–7). The current national development plan, the Second National Development Plan (1972–76), suggests that the gap between urban and rural incomes has now ceased to widen and that it is unlikely that urbanization will continue at its previous rates. It predicts an expected growth rate of the urban population of 6.8 per cent a year as compared with the 8.7 per cent between 1963 and 1969 and also that rural–urban migration will slacken, the latter on the grounds that recent years have seen a major inrush of wives to join husbands already in the towns which is now at an end. It is also expected in the Plan that lack of urban employment opportunities and rising costs of housing will act as disincentives to in-migration and that more efficient rural development will enable the countryside to absorb higher proportions of the labour force.

All this is familiar Third World thinking: the vital question for Zambia must be to what extent it may prove to be wishful thinking. According to Simmance (1972, pp. 39, 51), 'the rural development approach . . . is still somewhat nebulous and differs little – apart from the selection of "intensive development zones" – from the unsuccessful strategy in the First National Development Plan'; and even if the rural development programmes are in the end largely successful, 'none of this need mean, of course, that the rural share of the population can be stabilised, let alone increased'. The inescapable fact is that in Zambia, as in certain other Third World countries of moderate population size, phrases such as 'the 80 per cent of our population who live in the rural areas' are either already well out of date or very soon will be: overall, Simmance estimates, probably 45 per cent of Zambia's population is now urban or peri-urban, if those living both in the cities and towns are within 40 km (25 miles) of the line-of-rail are taken into account (*ibid.*, p. 34). Yet this kind of realization is dawning only painfully slowly on Third World development planners. Smaller-scale Calcuttas are already in the making almost unperceived, notably in the cases of Djakarta and Lagos.

At the national level there is a great deal of rethinking to be done within the developing countries in respect of the formulation of coherent and comprehensive urban strategies within frameworks of national planning. During the last three or four decades urbanization and migration have rapidly assumed the status of key elements within the development process; and their present importance in turn calls attention to the huge gap which exists in the development policies of so many countries in respect of the spatial aspects of planning, especially in terms of urban and regional planning. All too often no coherent view of the spatial nature of the economy is held by the central planners, and the spatial consequences of economic inputs, particularly in respect of the national hierarchy of urban places and effects upon migration patterns, is largely ignored.

Yet such spatial monitoring at national and regional levels is vital for the formulation of comprehensive action programmes to alleviate the problems of individual towns and cities. National programmes need to be broken down into coherent regional strategies and the latter, in turn, need to be linked not only to problems of rural development but also both to solving the problems of the present towns and cities and to the possible creation of new urban growth points. Briefly, national and regional policies on urban and regional development are needed, yet the necessary administrative machinery for the formulation and implementation of such policies is lacking almost everywhere. As Green and Milone (1972, pp. 20, 23) have put it for Nigeria:

> There has, in fact, been no planning specifically for urban and regional development in Nigeria. At best, there has been a local, *ad hoc* response to uncontrolled city growth, as in the commissioning of metropolitan plans for Kano and Kaduna; or, as in Western Nigeria, where a number

of town planning authorities have been set up (whose activities in all but three cases, however, have in practice been confined to little more than the approval of new building plans). . . . Sub-national planning at the level of the twelve constituent States or four former Regions has been as devoid of policy on urbanization and regional development as planning at the Federal level.

There would be no problem if the end results of administrative arrangements of this kind were satisfactory. But, as this book has shown in respect of many aspects of the growth of spontaneous settlement, as well as in a growing number of other aspects of the evolution of urban environments in the Third World which have not been touched on here, clearly the end results are far from satisfactory; indeed, as Rodwin (1971, p. 3) has observed, 'increasingly vociferous criticisms of the quality and costs of urbanization and the absence of significant choice in living patterns make it essential today to re-examine and possibly change traditional ways of influencing urban and regional development'.

As the foregoing paragraphs have indicated, one major step forward would be the development of capability to define development goals not only nationally and sectorally but also spatially in terms of regions and urban systems. Equally important would be the development of evaluative and administrative capacities capable of devising and carrying out urban strategies (both national and regional and also in terms of individual cities and towns) at levels which imply official recognition that such strategies are at least equal in importance to other major sectors of development planning. As things stand at present, severe shortages not only of professional urban planners but also of high-level administrative staff, lack of policy at the highest level about the ownership, use and development of urban land, lack of coordination between ministries and other administrative bodies concerned with aspects of urban affairs, adverse attitudes of economic planners towards regional and urban development planning and generally low priorities for the towns and cities in schemes of national planning, are only too common. There is, in sum, little perception of urbanization, properly guided, as a positive force in national social and economic development.

Way forward: action planning in the urban areas

In a sense, as the foregoing paragraphs have shown, a good part of solutions to the problems of individual towns and cities, including those of spontaneous settlement, can come only from above: that is, as part of national strategies which recognize the current importance of urbanization and in-migration, which consider in detail the spatial consequences of national developmental decisions, and which include regional planning as an important component of the overall planning approach.

Yet within each town and city the precise nature of the remedies to be applied must be determined by local circumstances. As far as urban housing provision is concerned, it is worth repeating once more that there is no conceivable solution to current housing problems along conventional Western lines: that much is surely clear from the tenor of this book, especially from chapter 6. Third World urban populations are everywhere overwhelmingly poor, and their poverty is of a totally different order from that of the poor in industrialized countries; this is a fundamental fact which should condition both urban planning and housing provision. Planning should be directed not towards 'development' but rather to what is the much more realistic prospect, 'underdevelopment' as a constant state, at least for the foreseeable future. All too often both visiting 'experts' and local planners persist in considering situations in 'we' and 'they', terms. 'We' are the privileged minority of the West and the local elites of the developing countries; 'they' are the vast mass of the urban population of the Third World. The planning objective, in terms of housing and of urban development generally, always seems to be to try somehow to make 'them' somewhat closer to the model of 'us', despite the fact that in the prevailing demographic, social and economic situation of the Third World this is a highly unlikely prospect.

In one sense, what is needed is a much more extensive investigation into the Third World city in such disciplines as geography, sociology, social anthropology and psychology in order to evaluate further the economic, social, cultural and other forces at work in shaping patterns of urban development. Yet it is also true, as this book has shown, that existing knowledge of the urbanization process in the Third World in general and of the nature of housing problems in particular, is all too often either ignored or badly applied. Much the same mistakes are being made all round the Third World; the lessons from urban areas where some measure of success has been achieved in housing provision or in the evolution of shelter policies for the urban poor, such as Lima, Calcutta, Singapore and the Victoria–Kowloon urban area of Hong Kong, are but little known internationally and have not so far been the object of detailed comparative study. In searching for realistic housing policies, it seems, each Third World country is striving to reinvent the wheel independently (Rosser, personal communication).

Very often the most that is done in housing adds up to a pale imitation of Western procedures in low-cost housing provision which benefits, not the poor, but a small and privileged section of the middle class. Nowhere have the essential legislative, administrative and organizational reforms which must underpin housing programmes directed towards the masses been fully accomplished, though considerable progress has been made in one or more of these directions in each of the four cities mentioned above. Almost everywhere, both administrative resources for the urban areas and legislators dedicated to the concept of cities for the poor are in extremely scarce supply.

All this indicates the necessity for a revolution in attitudes, not only nationally but also locally in terms of individual towns and cities. What is needed is not the further elaboration and refinement of techniques of master planning for individual urban areas, which usually result only in paper schemes overtaken by events, which lie gathering dust in planning offices, nor the application of elaborate mathematical models to data of questionable quality and relevance, but the formulation of realistic and flexible action programmes broadly based on the needs of the mass of the people (Koenigsberger, 1964). As Alonso (1971, p. 205–6) has put it:

> Detailed long-range urban plans that are an inventory of specific future investments and programmes are . . . inappropriate in nations undergoing profound and often sudden changes. In many countries the national leadership is often changed by coup or revolution, and diverse crises are frequent, such as sudden deterioration in terms of trade, fiscal crises, or even war. Since the national government is *de facto* the metropolitan government in most of these countries, in part because of the disproportionate importance of the capital in national economies, these sudden changes belie the picture implicit in long-range comprehensive plans of a smooth and steady development. Underneath these short-range crises, there are the deeper tides of social transformation, affecting customs and life-styles, redistributing power and privilege among social groups. Since few can lay claim to a clear vision of the future structure of the society, not too much stock can be put on detailed plans for the physical city that will be the container for that society. Where the society is in the process of change, urban plans must themselves be processes, not static pictures.

Rosser (1972*b*, p. 83) has pointed out that: 'Calcutta is a jungle of special authorities, each with inadequate finance, indifferent management, competing and often conflicting powers, and often very low levels of technical efficiency among their inflated staffs.' So too are most other large Third World cities, and this is a basic fact which cannot be ignored in terms of physical planning. The preparation of a physical plan for a city therefore cannot be a self-contained exercise in its own right; recommendation cannot be divorced from implementation; and current needs demand ongoing action planning, perhaps in many cases only at the level of reaction to existing or anticipated urban crises, at least at the beginning of the action planning process. Because of their population explosion and inadequate economic base, Third World cities are encountering a range of government and managerial problems that are quite outside both the historical and the current experience of today's industrialized countries. Their solution is not to be found in yesterday's books, in the conventional master planning approach of former years, or in current Western planning practice. This is the basic reason why local planning attitudes must be reformed and why, as Rosser has repeatedly stressed, emphasis must move to managerial and operational coordination and away from 'urban planning' in the conventional sense of the latter term (*ibid.*, p. 89).

As regards the provision of urban housing, the revolution in planning approaches which is necessary is likely to be severely limited in its success in the absence of recognition of the necessity for fundamental changes in attitudes towards urban land rights (such as has already begun to become apparent in the case of Lima and, in theory at least, also in Calcutta), since it is simply not realistic to argue that the millions of people currently occupying spontaneous settlements in Third World cities are in illegal possession of land and should be expelled from it. By and large, most existing spontaneous settlements will have to be legalized (except, that is, where they constitute insurmountable obstacles to rational urban expansion) and the most that can now be hoped for is the implementation of local strategies designed to channel the inevitable development of further spontaneous settlements into acceptable spatial patterns.

As has been amply demonstrated in this book, however, a feature of every spontaneous settlement is initiative; and many settlements also demonstrate the ability of substantial segments of the urban poor to mobilize resources of incremental capital for the piecemeal purchase of building materials, impressive resources of constructional skills and, at the most elemental level, impressive resources of simple human energy for building purposes. Action planning for individual towns and cities must seek to turn these resources to advantage in a coordinated manner because they are very large in total. Their harnessing must form an important part of action planning concerned with Third World housing problems and

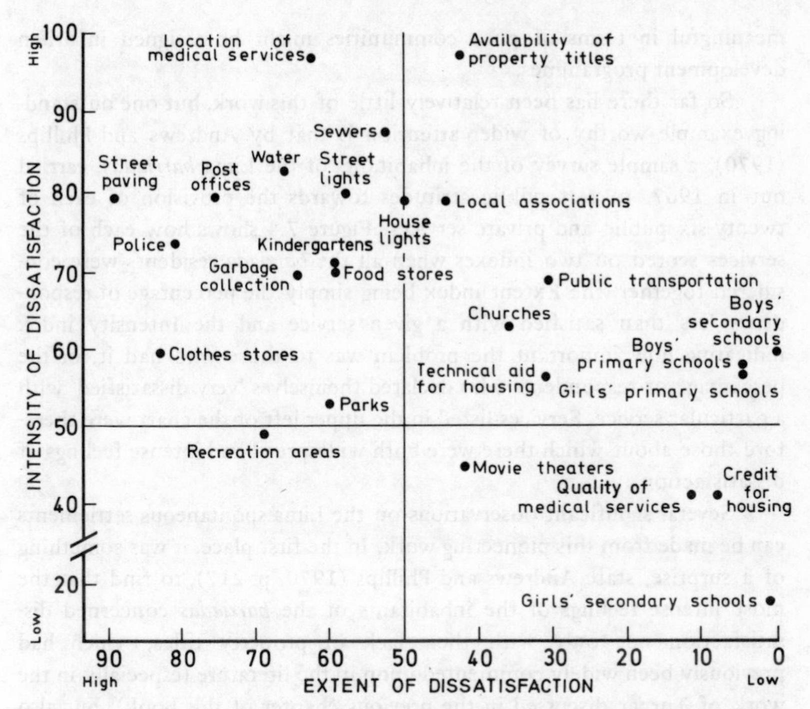

Fig. 7.4 Attitudes to public and private services in the Lima *barriadas* (Andrews, 1970)

official provision 'from above' must complement rather than replace them.

In the first instance, an important place in action planning programmes conceived on this basis must be given to identifying needs, harnessing energies and organizing responses among the urban poor. This, in turn, implies much greater investment in carefully conceived and oriented field work within the spontaneous settlements of Third World cities than has been the case so far, though not by means necessarily field work based upon a purely academic approach of the kind that is highly theoretical in concept and often concludes only that still further research needs to be undertaken. What is needed rather is research which provides accurate and up-to-date scientific descriptions of the spontaneous settlements and their inhabitants, which would be useful both as raw data for current planning and eventually as bench marks against which subsequent change could be evaluated, and also research aimed at evaluating problems and aspirations as perceived by squatters themselves, so that priorities meaningful in terms of poor communities might be assigned in urban development programmes.

So far there has been relatively little of this work, but one outstanding example worthy of wider attention is that by Andrews and Phillips (1970), a sample survey of the inhabitants of the Lima *barriadas*, carried out in 1967, to test public attitudes towards the provision of each of twenty-six public and private services. Figure 7.4 shows how each of the services scored on two indexes when all the *barriada* residents were considered together, the Extent index being simply the percentage of respondents less than satisfied with a given service and the Intensity index indicating how important the problem was to those who had it, or the percentage of respondents who declared themselves 'very dissatisfied' with a particular service. Services listed in the upper left of the chart were therefore those about which there were both widespread and intense feelings of dissatisfaction.

Several significant observations on the Lima spontaneous settlements can be made from this pioneering work. In the first place, it was something of a surprise, state Andrews and Phillips (1970, p. 217), to find that the most intense feelings of the inhabitants of the *barriadas* concerned dissatisfaction not only with their lack of property titles, which had previously been widely commented upon in the literature (especially in the work of Turner discussed in the previous chapter of this book), but also with the location of medical services. Although only a small minority of respondents were dissatisfied with the quality of medical care, 97 per cent felt very strongly that medical services should be closer and ranked this aspect of lack of service provision higher than the need for improvements in such physical facilities as water supply, lighting and street paving. This indicated an urgent need for the formulation of action programmes on local medical posts, mobile clinics and perhaps even the provision of paramedical personnel.

Among the physical facilities, the unpaved condition of *barriada* streets was shown to be the most widespread source of dissatisfaction, presumably because of the dust problem caused by Lima's dry climate, but priorities for water and sewage installation were also high. Of those families not having piped water, two-thirds purchased it from privately operated tanker trucks at costs which suggested that the extension of community distribution systems might produce savings which would substantially help to finance a full installation later. With regard to low priority needs, it is significant that education facilities were generally thought to be satisfactory (though this does not, of course, mean that the schools were good by objective educational standards); that the provision of technical aid for house construction ranked rather low on the list of priorities; and that there was little interest in obtaining credit for house building through institutional channels. In respect of credit availability, which has received some attention in the literature as a component of the solution to Third World urban housing problems (Elliot, 1968), it seemed rare for failure to find credit to cause much difficulty; further, the vast majority of house builders in the *barriadas* neither expected nor requested it. In the Third World's spontaneous settlements generally, it seems, there is a reluctance to assume any continuing financial burden and most families prefer to add to their houses piecemeal as and when money and time became available.

A large part of the problem of developing further research of this nature in the developing countries, as also with the extension of realistic action planning, lies not only in the necessity for rethinking basic attitudes towards current urban problems, which has been emphasized above, but also in the availability of correctly trained local personnel. In both research and planning, suitable techniques need to be derived from first principles based on observation of activity patterns and problems of the people living in the spontaneous settlements; in addition, flexibility needs to be an essential attribute of such techniques in order to deal with the rapid changes both in politics and in the location and scale of the various urban problems that are characteristic of the contemporary Third World. But there is a considerable problem of the availability of local people sufficiently well trained both to pioneer new techniques and to engage in their continuous execution and reassessment; and there is currently a great need for the establishment of further centres for urban planning research and training within the developing countries themselves.

Meanwhile, the 'expert' imported on a short-term contract from the West, who should be playing an important role in the planning process but essentially a subsidiary one (probably most fruitfully in introducing advanced methods of analysis and in certain aspects of the training of local personnel) fills a gap which is far too large and often, perforce, must use problem-solving approaches developed in his own country in meeting very different conditions in the Third World. And rarely, of course, can the 'expert' be expected to build local institutions capable of carrying the plan forward after he has gone. At the same time, a very high proportion of urban planners and administrators from the developing countries continues to receive basic professional training in the industrialized countries, within a socio-economic context that is largely irrelevant to the problems of the

Third World city and using philosophies and techniques of planning that have only minimal relevance to their home countries.

Given a measure of change in this situation, and the eventual development of sufficient cadres of local personnel, it is worth emphasizing again that the essential problems of the Third World's urban spontaneous settlements lie equally in the field of organization, and the harnessing of the energies of the poor, as in 'administration' and 'planning' *per se*. Because of the financial constraints which characterize all developing countries, the emphasis in development must be on organized self-help to the greatest possible extent, and in many cases stress will have to be placed on environmental improvement rather than on house building as such, for many of the houses built in spontaneous settlements are minimally acceptable as shelters. The human resources involved and the energies latent in the Third World's urban poor are potentially very great, but they require mobilization of a degree that as yet has hardly been begun anywhere. This implies conscious efforts to reduce the gap between the planner and those whose futures are being planned and the gap between the administrator and the public.

Equally important, it implies the implementation of policies of mass community organization and development on metropolitan scales to complement the hesitant start that is currently being made in community social work in individual problem areas of some Third World cities (Clinard, 1966, 1971). These cities are cities of clubs and other voluntary organizations (Little, 1965) but as yet this fact has been very little recognized or utilized at the metropolitan level in planning schemes. In the Tollygunge area of Calcutta, for example, a Calcutta Metropolitan Planning Organization (Rosser, 1970*b*, p. 131) survey recorded 128 voluntary organizations in five of the city's wards and indicated that in aggregate their activities were very important to the functioning of that part of the city:

> For example, the 78 sports clubs provide from their own funds and efforts the only public recreational facilities and playgrounds that currently exist in an area containing close on a quarter of a million people. Every single one of the 39 small public libraries and reading rooms in this area has been provided by voluntary effort. There are 20 clinics presently being run by voluntary agencies, as also four small hospitals, seven primary schools and three secondary schools.

The same kinds of organization exist in embryonic form in many spontaneous settlements throughout the Third World and could be turned to immense advantage by planning which included active programmes of community development as an important component.

All in all, there is a pressing need to get down to the grassroots of the problems currently being posed by the growth of spontaneous settlements in the towns and cities of the developing countries. This calls for continuous field monitoring and careful evaluation of existing situations. It calls for the identification of the most pressing problems in each local situation and the evolution of vigorous action programmes aimed at containing, if not solving, them. It calls for recognition of the permanency of spontaneous settlement as a major urban form in the overall planning of towns and cities. Above all, it calls both for understanding of the problems and the aspirations of the inhabitants of such settlements and for the mobilization of their energies in soundly conceived self-help schemes. At a higher level, there is an equal need in many countries for a rethinking of national strategies development to include recognition of the causes and consequences of the swift and massive urban changes that are currently in process in the Third World. And, as the earlier part of this chapter indicated, the need for new urban technology for the developing countries to complement new thought on urban development is also pressing.

Conclusion

The list of needs is daunting and even if many are met the most hopeful prospect for the immediate future probably will be only that the worst aspects of local situations will be ameliorated rather than that permanent solutions to the problems posed by spontaneous settlements will appear. But what is the alternative to the massive acceleration in problem solving, in research, in action planning and in implementation, that is so vitally necessary at the present time? Undoubtedly it is a life for many more hundreds of thousands of future urban dwellers in the Third World of the kind already being lived on the streets of Calcutta.

Kishan Babu and his wife live on the sidewalk outside of a respectable address in Central Avenue in Calcutta:

> Every night at about ten o'clock he and his family spread some matting on the same patch of sidewalk under the same portico. About forty persons are there – the same forty every night. They all say they are from Gujarat, a thousand miles away. But most of them like Kishan Babu and his young wife, Lila, were born in Calcutta and grew up on its streets. They have never lived indoors.

> The people under the next portico down the avenue are all from Bihar. And so it goes. On closer examination the clusters of sidewalk dwellers almost seem to be reproductions of Indian villages. The most striking difference is that the men greatly outnumber the women, and many of them send money home to their families.
>
> Kishan Babu's cluster is more settled. Everyone in it pursues the same trade – one of the oldest and most marginal occupations known to this city in which productive work is even harder to find than a home. It is a three-stage operation, requiring plenty of enterprise. First they buy stainless steel pots from a wholesaler on credit. Then they go from door to door in middle-class neighbourhoods and exchange the pots for old clothes. Finally, they sell the old clothes and pay the wholesaler. In this way Kishan Babu and his wife clear 4 or 5 rupees a day (about 60 cents). They are always able to select their clothes from what they collect along the way and their earnings are enough, barely, for their food.
>
> Their only other major expense is the rent they pay for a locker, or stall, in a shanty on the other side of the avenue. It is five feet square, with a low metal roof that leaks and a damp dirt floor. It is here they cook their evening meal over a wood fire. It was also here that Lila Babu gave birth to her two children, Dillip and Maya. To understand why the Babus choose to sleep on the sidewalk instead of indoors it is only necessary to visit the stall. The visitor regains the street with a deep sense of relief (Lelyveld, 1967).

Is this how it *must* be? Must increasing numbers of urban families in the Third World be condemned to such levels of existence? In an age when man has reached the moon, surely not.

Bibliography

ABRAMS, CHARLES (1965) 'The uses of land in cities', *Scientific American*, 213, 151–60.

ABRAMS, CHARLES (1966*a*) *Housing in the Modern World*, Faber.

ABRAMS, CHARLES (1966*b*) *Squatter Settlements: the problem and the opportunity*, Washington: Department of Housing and Urban Development, 1966.

ABU-LUGHOD, JANET (1961) 'Migrant adjustment to city life: the Egyptian case', *American Journal of Sociology*, 67, 22–32.

ABU-LUGHOD, JANET (1965) 'Urbanization in Egypt: present state and future prospects', *Economic Development and Cultural Change*, 13 (1964–65), 313–43.

ABU-LUGHOD, JANET (1969) 'Varieties of urban experience: contrast, coexistence and coalescence in Cairo', in I. M. Lapidus, ed., *Middle Eastern Cities*, California University Press, pp. 159–87.

ADAMS, D. W. (1969) 'Rural migration and agricultural development in Colombia', *Economic Development and Cultural Change*, 17 (1968–69), 527–38.

ADEDEJI, ADEBAYO (1971) 'Ibadan', in Laquian (1971), pp. 55–69.

AGENCIA PARA EL DESARROLLO INTERNACIONAL (1970) *Mesa Redonda Sobre el Problema de la Vivienda en las Urbanizaciones, Marginales*, Washington.

ALI BIN ESA (1971) 'Kuala Lumpur', in Laquian (1971), pp. 93–110.

ALONSO, WILLIAM (1971) contribution to Sixth Rehovoth Conference, Israel, 1971, summarized in Raanan Weitz, ed., *Urbanization and the Developing Countries: Report of the Sixth Rehovoth Conference*, Praeger, 1973, pp. 205–6.

AMATO, P. W. (1969) 'Population densities, land values, and socioeconomic class in Bogotá, Colombia', *Land Economics*, 45, 66–73.

AMATO, P. W. (1970) 'Elitism and settlement patterns in the Latin

American city', *Journal of the American Institute of Planners*, **36**, 96–105.

AMES, M. M. (1968) 'Modernization and social structure in Jamshedpur', *Development Digest*, **6**, 55–61.

ANDREWS, F. M. and PHILLIPS, G. W. (1970) 'The squatters of Lima: who they are and what they want', *Journal of Developing Areas*, **4**, 211–24.

ANDREWS, PAUL, CHRISTIE, MALCOLM, and MARTIN, RICHARD (1972) 'Squatter manifesto', *Ekistics*, **34**, 108–13.

ANDREWS, PAUL, CHRISTIE, MALCOLM, and MARTIN, RICHARD (1973) 'Squatters: the evolution of a lifestyle', *Architectural Design*, **18**, 16–25.

ANON (1970) 'PREVI, Lima, low-cost housing project', *Architectural Design*, **40**, 187–205.

ARCINAS, FE RODRIGUEZ (1955) 'A socio-economic study of Manila squatters', *Philippine Sociological Review*, **3**, 35–41.

ASHRAF, A. (1967) *The City Government of Calcutta: a study of inertia*, Calcutta Research Studies, Asia Publishing House.

ASHRAF, A., and GREEN, LESLIE (1972) 'Calcutta', in W. A. Robson and D. E. Regan, eds., *Great Cities of the World: their government politics and planning*, Allen & Unwin, pp. 297–330.

ASHTON, G. T. (1972) 'The differential adaptation of two slum subcultures to a Colombian housing project', *Urban Anthropology*, **1**, 176–94.

ATKINSON, G. A. (1961) 'Mass housing in rapidly developing tropical areas', *Town Planning Review*, **31** (1960–61), 86–101.

AWAD, HASSAN (1964) 'Morocco's expanding towns', *Geographical Journal*, **130**, 49–64.

BACK, K. W. (1962) *Slums, Projects and People: some psychological problems of relocation in Puerto Rico*, Duke University Press.

BALAN, JORGE (1970) 'Migrant–native socioeconomic differences in Latin American cities: a structural analysis', *Ekistics*, **30**, 398–406.

BANCO OBRERO (1959; 2nd edn., 1961) *Proyecto de Evaluación de los Superbloques*, Caracas.

BANCO OBRERO (1967) *Plan Nacional de Vivienda 1965–8*, Caracas.

BANCO OBRERO (1968) *40 Años Del Banco Obrero, 1928–68*, Caracas.

BANCO OBRERO (n.d.) *Viviendas en Pendiente*, Caracas.

BANERJI, SUJIT (1972) 'Innovative techniques in low-cost housing, the North Bengal experience', in Dwyer (1972*c*), pp. 321–9.

BARAKBAH, S. M. (1971) 'The problem of illegal squatters in urban areas of Kedah State, Malaysia', *Journal of Administration Overseas*, **10**, 201–9.

BEALS, R. (1951) 'Urbanism, urbanization and acculturation', *American Anthropologist*, **53**, 1–10.

BEAUJEU-GARNIER, JACQUELINE (1962) 'Les migrations vers Salvador', *Les Cahiers D'Outre Mer*, **15**, 292–300.

BEAUJEU-GARNIER, JACQUELINE, and SANTOS, MILTON (1967) 'Le "Centre" de la ville de Salvador', *Les Cahiers D'Outre-Mer*, **20**, 322–44.

BENNINGER, C. C. (1972) 'Design criteria for developing contexts: housing for Baroda, India', *Ekistics*, **33**, 162–5.

BERCKHOLTZ-SALINAS, PABLO (1963) *Barrios Marginales, Abberación Social*, Lima.

BERRY, B. J. L., SIMMONS, J. W., and TENNANT, R. J. (1963) 'Urban population densities', *Geographical Review*, **53**, 389–405.

BETTISON, D. G., and APTHORPE, R. J. (1961) 'Authority and residence in a peri-urban social structure – Ndirande, Nyasaland', *Nyasaland Journal*, **14**, 7–39.

BEYER, G. H. (1965) *Housing and Society*, Collier-Macmillan.

BEYER, G. H., ed. (1967) *The Urban Explosion in Latin America*, Cornell University Press.

BLAIR, T. L. V. (1966) 'Man's quest for shelter in urbanising Africa', in Town Planning Institute, *Proceedings of the Town and Country Planning Summer School*, London, pp. 160–71.

BOGUE, D. J., and ZACHARIAH, K. C. (1962) 'Urbanization and migration in India', in Roy Turner (1962), pp. 27–54.

BONILLA, FRANK (1970) 'Rio's Favelas: the rural slum within the city', in W. Mangin (1970*b*), pp. 72–84.

BOR, WALTER, and SMULIAN, J. (1970) 'Planning in Venezuela with special reference to the recent development of three new cities', unpublished paper, Regional Studies Association, Conference on Urbanization and Regional Change, Oxford.

BOSE, NIRMAL KUMAR (1967) 'Calcutta: a premature metropolis', in *Cities: a 'Scientific American' Book*, Penguin, pp. 67–85.

BOSE, NIRMAL KUMAR (1968) *Calcutta: a social survey*, Bombay.

BREESE, GERALD (1963) 'Urban development problems in India', *Annals of the Association of American Geographers*, **53**, 253–65.

BREESE, GERALD (1966) *Urbanization in Newly Developing Countries*, Prentice-Hall.

BREESE, GERALD (1968) 'Some dilemmas in poverty, power and public policies in cities of underdeveloped areas', in W. Bloomberg and S. Schmandt, eds., *Power, Poverty and Urban Policy*, Beverly Hills, Sage Publications, pp. 465–89.

BREESE, GERALD, ed. (1969) *The City in Newly Developing Countries: Readings on Urbanism and Urbanization*, Prentice-Hall.

BRISSEAU, JANINE (1963) 'Les Barrios de Petare: faubourgs populaires d'une banlieue de Caracas', *Les Cahiers d'Outre-Mer*, **16**, 7–42.

BRUNER, E. M. (1959) 'Kinship organization among the urban Batak of Sumatra', *Transactions of the New York Academy of Sciences*, **22**, 118–25.

BRUNER, E. M. (1961) 'Urbanization and ethnic identity in North Sumatra', *American Anthropologist*, **63**, 508–21.

BRUNER, E. M. (1963) 'Medan: The role of kinship in an Indonesian city', in A. Spoehr, ed., *Pacific Port Towns*, Honolulu, pp. 2–12.

BRUSH, J. E. (1968) 'Spatial patterns of population in Indian cities', *Geographical Review*, **58**, 362–91.

BRUSSELS, FREE UNIVERSITY OF: INTERNATIONAL INSTITUTE OF DIFFERING CIVILIZATIONS (1971) *Urban Agglomerations in the States of the Third World: their political social and economic role*, Brussels.

BRYCE-LAPORTE, R. S. (1968) 'Family adaptation of relocated slum dwellers in Puerto Rico: implications for urban research and development', *Journal of Developing Areas*, **2**, 533–40.

BUCHANAN, IAIN (1971) 'Resettlement and the slum-dweller's search for security: a Singapore case-study', *Journal of the Singapore Planning and Urban Research Group*, pp. 13–23.

BUCHANAN, IAIN (1972) *Singapore in South East Asia*, G. Bell.

BURNS, LELAND (1966) 'Cost-Benefit Analysis of Improved Housing: A Case Study', *Ekistics*, **21**, 304–12.

BURNS, LELAND, and TJIOE, B. KHING (1968) 'Housing and human resource development', *Journal of the American Institute of Planners*, **34**, 396–401.

BUTTERWORTH, D. S. (1962) 'A study of the urbanization process among Mixtec migrants from Tilaltongo in Mexico City', *America Indigena*, **22**, 257–74.

CABELLO, OCTAVIO (1966) 'Housing, population-growth and economic development', in J. Mayone Stycos and Jorge Arias, eds., *Population Dilemma in Latin America*, Washington (Pan-American Assembly on Population), Columbia Books, pp. 101–22.

CALCUTTA METROPOLITAN PLANNING ORGANISATION [CMPO]

(1966) *Basic Development Plan for the Calcutta Metropolitan District 1966–86*, Calcutta.

CALCUTTA METROPOLITAN PLANNING ORGANISATION [CMPO] (1967) *Howrah Area Development Plan 1966–86*, Calcutta.

CALDWELL, J. C. (1968) *African Rural–Urban Migration: the movement to Ghana's towns*, New York, C. Hurst.

CAMINOS, HORACIO, GOETHARD, R., PATEL, PRAFUL, AND GATTONI, G. (1973) 'A progressive development proposal: Dandora, Nairobi, Kenya', *Ekistics*, 36, 205–13.

CAMINOS, HORACIO, TURNER, J. F. C., and STEFFAN, J. A. (1969) *Urban Dwelling Environments*, MIT Press.

CAPLOW, THEODORE (1952) 'The modern Latin American city', in Sol Tax, ed., *Acculturation in the Americas*, New York, Cooper Square, pp. 255–60.

CARLSON, ERIC (1961) 'Evaluation of housing projects and programmes: a case report from Venezuela', *Town Planning Review*, 31 (1960–61), 187–209.

CARLSON, ERIC (1968) 'Community integration and community development in high rise housing', in National Swedish Institute for Building Research, *The Social Environment and Its Effect on the Design of the Dwelling and Its Immediate Surroundings*, Stockholm, pp. 171–93.

CARROL, JOHN J. (1966) 'Philippine social organisation and national development', *Philippine Studies*, 14, 573–90.

CASASCO, J. A. (1969) 'The social function of the slum in Latin America: some positive aspects', *America Latina*, 12, 87–112.

CATAPUSAN, B. T., and DIAZ-CATAPUSAN, F. E. (1954) 'Social adjustment of migrant families', *Philippine Sociological Review*, 2, 11–16.

CHANA, T. and MORRISON, H. (1973) 'Housing systems in the low income sector of Nairobi, Kenya', *Ekistics*, 36, 214–21.

CHANG SHUB ROH (1970) 'Looc, Dumaguete City: a study of an urban slum community', *Silliman Journal*, 17, 248–85.

CHAPMAN, E. C. and ALLEN, A. C. B. (1965) 'Internal migration in Thailand', unpublished paper, Australia and New Zealand Association for the Advancement of Science, Hobart Meeting.

CHUNG HYUN RO *see* RO.

CLARKE, C. G. (1966) 'Population pressure in Kingston, Jamaica: a study of unemployment and overcrowding', *Transactions of the Institute of British Geographers*, No. 38, 165–82.

CLINARD, M. B. (1966) *Slums and Community Development: experiments in self-help*, Collier-Macmillan.

CLINARD, M. B. (1971) 'The absorption problems of in-migrants', unpublished paper presented at the Sixth Rehovoth Conference, Israel.

COCKBURN, CHARLES (1970) *Construction in Overseas Development*, London, Overseas Development Institute.

COLE, J. P. (1956) 'Some town planning problems of Greater Lima', *Town Planning Review*, **26** (1955–56), 242–57.

COMHAIRE, J. L. (1956) 'Economic change and the extended family', *Annals of the American Academy of Political and Social Science*, **305**, 45–52.

CONCANNON, T. A. L. (1955) 'A new town in Malaya: Petaling Jaya, Kuala Lumpur', *Malayan Journal of Tropical Geography*, **5**, 39–43.

CONVERSE, JAMES (1965) 'Some aspects of the adjustment of rural to urban migrants in Bogotá, Colombia', unpublished manuscript, Ohio State University, Department of Agricultural Economics.

COTLER, JULIO, and LAQUIAN, A. A. (1971) 'Lima', in Laquian (1971), pp. 111–33.

CORRADA, RAFAEL (1969) 'The housing program', in Rodwin *et al.* (1969), pp. 236–51.

DALAND, R. T. (1969) 'Urbanization policy and political development in Latin America', *American Behavioral Scientist*, **12**.

DANBY, MILES (1971) 'Design for change', *Planning Outlook*, **11**, 9–30.

DAVIS, KINGSLEY (1969) *World Urbanization 1950–70*, Vol. 1: *Basic Data for Cities, Countries and Regions*, Population Monograph Series No. 4, University of California.

DAVIS, KINGSLEY (1971) 'The role of urbanization in the development process', unpublished mimeographed paper presented at the Sixth Rehovoth Conference, Israel.

DAVIS, KINGSLEY (1972) *World Urbanization 1950–70*, Vol. 2: *Analysis of Trends, Relationships and Development*, Population Monograph Series No. 9, University of California.

DELER, JEAN-PAUL (1970) 'Croissance accélérée et formes de sous développement urbaine à Lima', *Les Cahiers D'Outre-Mer*, **23**, 73–94.

DELGADO, CARLOS (1969) 'Three proposals regarding accelerated urbanization problems in metropolitan areas: the Lima case', *American Behavioural Scientist*, **12** (1968–69), 34–45.

DESCLOITRES, ROBERT, REVERDY, JEAN-CLAUDE and DESCLOITRES, CLAUDINE (1961) *L'Algérie des bidonvilles*, Paris.

DESHMUKH, M. B. (1956) 'Delhi: a study of floating migration', in UNESCO (1956), pp. 144–225.

DIAMOND, STANLEY, and BURKE, FRED G. eds. (1969) *The Transformation of East Africa*, Basic Books.

DIETZ, A. G. H. (1969) 'Urban-squatter settlements in Peru: a case history and analysis', *Journal of Inter-American Studies*, **11**, 353–70.

DIETZ, A. G. H., KOTH, M. N. and SILVO, J. A. (1965) *Housing in Latin America*, MIT Press.

DIOP, A. (1960) 'Enquete sur le migration toucouleur à Dakar', *Bulletin de l'Institut Française d'Afrique Noire*, **22**, 393–418.

DOLFUS, OLIVIER (1958) 'Lima, quelques aspects de la capitale de Pérou en 1958', *Les Cahiers d'Outre-Mer*, **11**, 258–71.

DWYER, D. J. (1964) 'The problem of in-migration and squatter settlement in Asian Cities: two case studies, Manila and Victoria–Kowloon', *Asian Studies*, **2**, 145–69.

DWYER, D. J. (1965) 'Size as a factor in economic growth: some reflections on the case of Hong Kong', *Tijdscrift Voor Economische en Sociale Geografie*, **56**, 186–92.

DWYER, D. J. (1968*a*) 'The city in the developing world and the example of South East Asia', University of Hong Kong, *Supplement to the Gazette*, **15**, No. 6, reprinted in *Geography*, **53**, 353–64.

DWYER, D. J. (1968*b*) 'Problems of urbanization: the example of Hong Kong', in Institute of British Geographers, *Land Use and Resources; studies in applied Geography*, London, pp. 169–85.

DWYER, D. J. (1969) 'A policy for small industrial units', in J. England, ed., *The Hong Kong Economic Scene*, Hong Kong University: Department of Extra-Mural Studies, pp. 9–15.

DWYER, D. J. (1970) 'Urban squatters: The relevance of the Hong Kong experience', *Asian Survey*, **10**, 607–13.

DWYER, D. J. (1971*a*) 'Housing Provision in Hong Kong', in Dwyer (1971*d*), pp. 33–47.

DWYER, D. J. (1971*b*) 'Problems of the small industrial unit', in Dwyer (1971*d*), pp. 123–36.

DWYER, D. J. (1971*c*) 'The urbanization of the new territories', in D. J. Dwyer, ed., *The Changing Face of Hong Kong*, Royal Asiatic Society: Hong Kong Branch, pp. 75–90.

DWYER, D. J. ed. (1971*d*) *Asian Urbanization: a Hong Kong casebook*, University of Hong Kong Press.

DWYER, D. J. (1972*a*) 'Absorption problems of in-migrants in metropolitan cities of developing countries', *International Technical Cooperation Centre Review,* 1, 1–7.

DWYER, D. J. (1972*b*) 'Attitudes towards spontaneous settlement in Third World countries', in Dwyer (1972*d*), pp. 168–78.

DWYER, D. J. (1972*c*) 'Urbanization as a factor in the political development of South East Asia', *Journal of Oriental Studies,* 10, 23–32.

DWYER, D. J., ed. (1972*d*) *The City as a Centre of Change in Asia*, University of Hong Kong Press.

DWYER, D. J., ed. (1974) *The City In the Third World*, Macmillan.

DWYER, D. J. and LAI, CHUEN-YAN (1967) *The Small Industrial Unit in Hong Kong: Patterns and Policies*, University of Hull, Occasional Papers in Geography No. 6.

DOUGHTY, P. L. (1972) 'Peruvian migrant identity in the urban milieu', in T. Weaver and D. White, eds., *The Anthropology of Urban Environments*, Society for Applied Anthropology, Monograph No. 11, Washington, pp. 39–59.

EAMES, E. (1967) 'Urban migration and the joint family in a North Indian village', *Journal of Developing Areas,* 1, 163–77.

ELDREDGE, H. W., ed. (1967) *Taming Megalopolis*, Doubleday Anchor, 2 vols.

ELIZAGA, J. C. (1969) 'A study on Immigrations to Greater Santiago (Chile)', in G. Breese (1969), pp. 332–59.

ELKAN, WALTER (1968) 'Circular Migration and the growth of towns in East Africa', *Ekistics,* 25, 238–41.

ELKAN, WALTER (1970) 'Urban unemployment in East Africa', *International Affairs,* 46, 517–28.

ELLIOTT, S. M. (1968) *Financing Latin American Housing*, Praeger.

EMERY, P. A. (1963) 'Creative aspects of shanty towns', *Ekistics,* 15, 268–71.

EPSTEIN, D. G. (1972) 'The genesis and function of squatter settlements in Brasilia', in T. Weaver and D. White, eds., *The Anthropology of Urban Environments*, Society for Applied Anthropology, Monograph No. 11, Washington, pp. 51–8.

ETHERTON, DAVID, ed. (1971) *Mathare Valley: a case study of uncontrolled settlement in Nairobi*, Housing Research and Development Unit, University of Nairobi.

EWING, J. R. (1969) 'Town planning in Delhi: a critique', *Economic and Political Weekly,* 4, No. 40, 1591–600.

EYRE, L. A. (1972) 'The shanty towns of Montego Bay, Jamaica', *Geographical Review*, 62, 394–413.

EYRE, L. A. (n.d.) *The Shanty Town: a reappraisal*, University of the West Indies, Department of Geography, Research Notes No. 3.

EZE, J. O. N. (1970) 'The urban concept in relation to inter-tropical Africa: a re-appraisal', in R. H. Osborne, ed., *Geographical Essays in Honour of K. C. Edwards*, University of Nottingham, Department of Geography, pp. 161–9.

FIELD, A. J., ed. (1970) *City and Country in the Third World: issues in the modernization of Latin America*, Harper & Row.

FLINN, W. L. (1968) 'The process of migration to a shantytown in Bogatá, Colombia', *Inter-American Economic Affairs*, 21, 77–89.

FLINN, W. L. and CAMACHO, A. (1969) 'The correlates of voter participation in a shantytown barrio in Bogotá Colombia', *Inter-American Economic Affairs,* 22, 47–58.

FLINN, W. L. and CARTANO, D. G. (1970) 'A comparison of the migration process to an Urban Barrio and to a Rural Community: Two Case Studies', *Inter-American Economic Affairs,* 24, 37–49.

FLINN, W. L. and CONVERSE, J. W. (1970) 'Eight assumptions concerning rural–urban migration in Colombia: a three-shantytowns test', *Land Economics,* 46, 456–66.

FONSECA, RORY (1969) 'The walled city of Old Delhi: urban renewal and an indigenous community', *Landscape,* 18, 13–25.

FRANCO, P. S. (1971) 'Caracas', in Laquian (1971), pp. 135–50.

FRANKENHOFF, C. A. (1967) 'Elements of an economic model for slums in a developing economy', *Economic Development and Cultural Change,* 16, 27–36.

FRIEDEN, B. J. (1966) 'The search for housing policy in Mexico City', *Town Planning Review,* 36 (1965–66), 75–94.

FRIEDMANN, JOHN (1966) *Regional Development Policy: a case study of Venezuela*, MIT Press.

FRIEDMANN, JOHN (1968) 'The strategy of deliberate urbanization', *Journal of the American Institute of Planners,* 34, 364–73.

FROOMKIN, JOSEPH (1955) 'Fiscal Management of municipalities and economic development', *Economic Development and Cultural Change*, 3, 309–20.

FUNG, BOSCO (1969) 'Diamond Hill area: a geographical study of a squatter settlement', unpublished BA dissertation, Department of Geography and Geology, University of Hong Kong.

GALLIN, B. (1966) *Hsin Hsing, Taiwan, a Chinese village in change*, California University Press.

GAMER, R. E. (1972) *The Politics of Urban Development in Singapore*, Cornell University Press.

GOLDRICH, D., PRATT, R. B. and SCHULLER, C. R. (1968) 'The political integration of lower-class urban settlements in Chile and Peru', Social Science Institute, Washington University, St Louis, *Studies in Comparative International Development*, 3 (1967–68), No. 1, 3–22.

GOLGER, OTTO J. (1968) 'An environmental study of squatter and resettlement housing in Hong Kong', unpublished PhD thesis, University of Hong Kong, Department of Architecture.

GOODSTADT, L. F. (1969) 'Urban housing in Hong Kong 1945–63', in I. C. Jarvie, ed., *Hong Kong: a society in transition*, Routledge, pp. 257–98.

GORYNSKI, JULIUS (1971) 'Modern and traditional design and techniques in construction and housing', *Ekistics*, 31, 353–9.

GREEN, LESLIE and MILONE, VINCENT (1972) *Urbanization in Nigeria: A Planning Commentary*, New York, Ford Foundation: International Urbanization Survey.

GULICK, JOHN (1967) 'Baghdad: a portrait of a city in physical and cultural change', *Journal of the American Institute of Planners*, 33, 246–55.

GUTKIND, P. C. W. (1961) 'Urban conditions in Africa', *Town Planning Review*, 32, 20–31.

HAMBRO, E. (1955) *The Problem of Chinese Refugees in Hong Kong*, Leyden.

HAMDAN, G. (1960) 'The growth and functional structure of Khartoum', *Geographical Review*, 50, 21–40.

HAMMEL, E. A. (1964) 'Some characteristics of rural village and urban slum populations on the coast of Peru', *Southwestern Journal of Anthropology*, 20, 346–58.

HANCE, W. A. (1970) *Population, Migration and Urbanization in Africa*, Columbia University Press.

HARRIS, W. D. (1971) *The Growth of Latin American Cities*, Ohio University Press.

HARRIS, W. D., HOSSE, HANS A. *et al.* (1963) *Housing in Peru*, Washington, Pan-American Union.

HARRIS, W. D. and GILLIES, J. (1963) *Capital Formation for Housing in Latin America*, Washington, Pan-American Union.

HARRISON, R. S. (1967) 'Migrants in the city of Tripoli, Libya', *Geographical Review*, 57, 397–423.

HARVEY, M. (1968) 'Implications of migration to Freetown: a study of relationship between migrants, housing and occupation', *Civilisations*, 18, 247–69.

HAUSER, P. M., ed. (1957) *Urbanization in Asia and the Far East*, Unesco, Calcutta.

HAUSER, P. M., ed. (1961) *Urbanization in Latin America*, Columbia University Press.

HAUSER, P. M. and SCHNORE, L. F., eds. (1965) *The Study of Urbanization*, Wiley.

HAZELHURST, PETER (1971) 'Calcutta struggles to stem inrush of Bengalis seeking to escape starvation', *The Times*, 31 May.

HEEREN, H. J. (1955) 'The Urbanization of Djakarta', *Economi dan Keunangan Indonesia*, 8, 696–736.

HERBERT, J. D. and VAN HUYCK, A. P., eds. (1968) *Urban Planning in the Developing Countries*, Praeger.

HERRICK, B. H. (1965) *Urban Migration and Economic Development in Chile*, MIT Press.

HILL, G. W. (1963) 'The adjustment of rural migrants in an urban Venezuelan community', *Migration News*, 12, No. 2, 1–6, and No. 3, 7–14.

HOLLINGSHEAD, A. B. and ROGLER, L. H. (1963) 'Attitudes Towards Slums and Public Housing in Puerto Rico', in L. J. Duhl ed., *The Urban Condition*, New York, Basic Books, pp. 229–45.

HONG KONG GOVERNMENT (1956) *Hong Kong: Review for the year 1955*, Hong Kong.

HONG KONG GOVERNMENT, CENSUS AND STATISTICS DEPARTMENT (1962) *Report on the 1961 Census*, Hong Kong, 3 vols.

HONG KONG GOVERNMENT, CENSUS AND STATISTICS DEPARTMENT (1972) *Hong Kong Population and Housing Census 1971, Main Report*, Hong Kong.

HONG KONG GOVERNMENT, COMMISSIONER FOR RATING AND VALUATION (1971) *Annual Departmental Report 1970–1*, Hong Kong.

HONG KONG GOVERNMENT, COMMISSIONER FOR RESETTLEMENT (1955) *Annual Departmental Report 1954–5*, Hong Kong.

HONG KONG GOVERNMENT, COMMISSIONER FOR RESETTLEMENT (1972) *Annual Departmental Report 1971–2*, Hong Kong.

HONG KONG GOVERNMENT, DISTRICT COMMISSIONER, NEW TERRITORIES (1956) *Annual Departmental Report 1955–6*, Hong Kong.

HONG KONG GOVERNMENT, HOUSING AUTHORITY (1972) *Annual Report 1971–2*, Hong Kong.

HONG KONG GOVERNMENT, HOUSING BOARD (1969) *Report of the Housing Board 1967–8*, Hong Kong.

HONG KONG GOVERNMENT, HOUSING BOARD (1972) *Report of the Housing Board 1972*, Hong Kong.

HONG KONG HOUSING SOCIETY (1971) *Annual Report 1969–70*, Hong Kong.

HOPKINS, KEITH (1969) 'Public Housing Policy in Hong Kong', University of Hong Kong, *Supplement to the Gazette,* **16**.

HOPKINS, KEITH (1971*a*) 'Housing the poor' in *idem* 1971*b*.

HOPKINS, KEITH, ed. (1971*b*) *Hong Kong the Industrial Colony*, Hong Kong.

HOSELITZ, B. F. (1955*a*) 'Generative and parasitic cities', *Economic Development and Cultural Change,* **3** (1954–55), 278–94.

HOSELITZ, B. F. (1955*b*) 'The city, the factory and economic growth', *American Economic Review,* **45**, 166–84.

HOSELITZ, B. F. (1958) 'Urbanization and economic growth in Asia', *Economic Development and Cultural Change,* **6** (1957–58), 42–54.

HOSELITZ, B. F. (1962) 'The role of urbanization in economic development: some international comparisons', in Roy Turner (1962), pp. 157–81.

HOSELITZ, B. F. (1963) 'The social, economic and technological problems of rapid urbanization', in Hoselitz and W. E. Moore, eds., *Industrialization and Society*, New York, Humanities Press.

HOUGHTON, D. H. (1960) 'Men of two worlds: some aspects of migratory labour in South Africa', *South African Journal of Economics*, **28**, 180–1.

HOUSTON, J. M. (1968) 'The foundation of colonial towns in Hispanic America', in R. P. Beckinsale and J. M. Houston, eds., *Urbanization and its Problems*, Blackwell, pp. 352–90.

HOWTON, F. W. (1969) 'Cities, slums and acculturative process in the developing countries', in Meadows and Mizruchi, pp. 431–47.

HUGHES, R. H. (1951) 'Hong Kong: an urban study', *Geographical Journal,* **117**, 1–23.

INDIA: INSTITUTE OF TOWN PLANNERS (1955) *Quarterly Journal*, No. 3, p. 1, quoted by Rosser (1972*a*; in Dwyer, 1972*d*), 184.

INTER-AMERICAN DEVELOPMENT BANK (1969) *Eighth Annual Report: Socio-economic Progress in Latin America*, Washington.

INTERNATIONAL UNION OF LOCAL AUTHORITIES (1968) *Urbanization in Developing Countries: report of a symposium*, The Hague.

ISAACS, H. R. (1968) 'India's ex-untouchables', in S. F. Fava, ed.,

Urbanism in World Perspective, New York, Crowell, pp. 350–2.

JAKOBSON, LEO (1971) *Urbanization and National Development*, Beverly Hills, Sage Publications.

JAKOBSON, LEO, and PRAKASH, V., eds. (1970) *The Urbanization Process in South-East Asia*, Beverly Hills, Sage Publications.

JOHNSON, E. A. J. (1970) *The Organization of Space in Developing Countries*, Harvard University Press.

JONES, EMRYS (1964) 'Aspects of urbanisation in Venezuela', *Ekistics*, **18**, 420–5.

JUPPENLATZ, MORRIS (1970) *Cities in Transformation: the urban squatter problem of the developing world*, University of Queensland Press.

KAR, N. R. (1968) 'Calcutta Conurbation', in R. L. Singh, ed., *India: regional studies*, Calcutta, pp. 330–53.

KAYE, BARRINGTON (1960) *Upper Nankin Street, Singapore: a sociological study of households living in a densely populated area, Singapore*, University of Malaya Press.

KHAN, ZAFAR AHMAD (1969) 'Population growth of Karachi: the example of a large city in developing countries', *Pakistan Geographical Review*, **24**, 111–29.

KINDLEBERGER, C. P. (1952) 'A review of the economy of Turkey; the economic development of Guatamala; Report on Cuba', *Review of Economics and Statistics*, **34**, 391–4.

KINGSLEY, T. G. and KRISTOF, F. S. (1971) 'A housing policy for metropolitan Calcutta', Ford Foundation Advisory Planning Group, Calcutta Metropolitan Planning Organisation, unpublished report, Calcutta.

KLASSEN, L. H. and Burns, L. S. (1963) 'The position of housing in national social and economic policy', in Pan-American Union, *Capital Formation for Housing in Latin America*, Washington, pp. 108–19.

KNOOP, HENRI (1966) 'Some demographic characteristics of a suburban squatting community of Leopoldville: a preliminary analysis', *Cahiers Economiques et Sociaux*, **4**, 119–46.

KOENIGSBERGER, OTTO (1964) 'Action planning', *Architectural Association Journal*, **79**, 306–12.

KOENIGSBERGER, OTTO (1970) 'Housing in the national development plan: an example from Nigeria', *Ekistics*, **30**, 393–7.

KUPER, HILDA, ed. (1965) *Urbanization and Migration in West Africa*, California University Press.

LAI, D. C. Y. and DWYER, D. J. (1964) 'Tsuen Wan: A New Industrial Town in Hong Kong', *Geographical Review*, **54**, 151–69.

LAI, D. C. Y. and DWYER, D. J. (1965) 'Kwun Tong, Hong Kong: a study of industrial planning', *Town Planning Review*, **35**, 299–310.

LAPORTE, R. S. B. (1968) 'Family adaptation of relocated slum dwellers in Puerto Rico', *Journal of Developing Areas*, **2**, 56–9.

LAPWORTH, CHARLES, with ZIMMERN, HELEN (1912) *Tripoli and Young Italy* (quoted by R. S. Harrison, 'Migrants in the city of Tripoli, Libya', *Geographical Review*, **57**, ref. p. 415).

LAQUIAN, A. A. (1964) 'Isla de Kokomo: politics among urban slum dwellers', *Philippine Journal of Public Administration*, **8**, 112–22.

LAQUIAN, A. A. (1968) *Slums are for People*, University of the Philippines, College of Public Administration, Manila.

LAQUIAN, A. A., ed. (1971) *Rural–Urban Migrants and Metropolitan Development*, Intermet, Toronto.

LAQUIAN, A. A. (1972) 'The need for national urban strategy in the Philippines', unpublished paper, South East Asia Development Advisory Group Seminar on Planning for Urbanisation within National Development Planning in South East Asia, Manila.

LEA, J. P. (1973) 'Underlying determinants of housing location: a case study from Swaziland', *Journal of Modern African Studies*, **11**, 211–25.

LEEDS, ANTHONY (1969) 'The significant variables determining the character of squatter settlements', *America Latina*, **12**, 44–86.

LEEDS, ANTHONY and LEEDS, ELIZABETH (1970) 'Brazil and the myth of urban rurality: urban experience, work and values in "Squatments" of Rio de Janeiro and Lima', in A. J. Field (1970), pp. 229–85.

LELYVELD, JOSEPH (1967) 'Kishan Babu', *New York Times*, 8 September.

LERNER, DANIEL (1967) 'Comparative analysis of processes of modernisation', in H. Miner (1967), pp. 21–38.

LEWIS, OSCAR (1952) 'Urbanization without breakdown: a case study', *Scientific Monthly*, **45**, 31–41.

LEWIS, OSCAR (1966) 'The culture of poverty', *Scientific American*, **214**, 19–25.

LEWIS, OSCAR (1969) *A Death in the Sanchez Family*, Random House.

LEUNG WAI TUNG (1972) 'Tsuen Wan Town: a study of a new town in Hong Kong', unpublished MPhil thesis, University of Hong Kong, Department of Geography and Geology.

LITTLE, KENNETH (1960) 'West African urbanization as a social process', *Cahier d'Etudes Africaines*, **1**, 90–102.

LITTLE, KENNETH (1965) *West African Urbanization: a study of voluntary associations in social change*, Cambridge University Press.

LITWACK, EUGENE (1960) 'Geographical mobility and extended family cohesion', *American Sociological Review*, **25**, 385–94.

LLEWELLYN-DAVIES, WEEKS, FORESTIER-WALKER and BOR (1969) *El Tablazo New City*, Caracas, Ministerio de Obras Publicas, Direccion de Planeamento, i, Report; ii, Appendices.

MABOGUNJE, A. L. (1962) 'The growth of residential districts in Ibadan', *Geographical Review*, **52**, 56–77.

MABOGUNJE, A. L. (1968) *Urbanization in Nigeria*, University of London Press.

McEWEN, A. M. (1972) 'Stability and change in a shanty town: a summary of some research findings', *Sociology*, **6**, 41–57.

McGEE, T. G. (1967) *The Southeast Asian City*, G. Bell.

McGEE, T. G. (1971) *The Urbanization Process in the Third World*, E. Bell.

McGEE, T. G. and McTAGGART, W. D. (1967) *Petaling Jaya: A Socio-Economic Survey of a New Town in Selangor, Malaysia*, Pacific Viewpoint Monograph No. 2, Wellington.

McNICOLL, GEOFFREY (1968) 'Internal migration in Indonesia: descriptive notes', *Indonesia*, No. 5, 29–92.

MANALAD-SANTIAGO, ASTEYA (1969) 'Reorganizing for housing and urban development', *Philippine Journal of Public Administration*, **13**, 214–32.

MANASTER, K. A. (1968) 'The problem of urban squatters in developing countries: Peru', *Wisconsin Law Review*, **23**, 23–61.

MANGIN, WILLIAM (1967*a*) 'Latin American squatter settlements: a problem and a solution', *Latin American Research Review*, **2**, 65–98.

MANGIN, WILLIAM (1967*b*) 'Squatter settlements', *Scientific American*, **217**, 21–9.

MANGIN, WILLIAM (1970*a*) 'Urbanization case history in Peru, in Mangin (1970*b*), pp. 47–54.

MANGIN, WILLIAM, ed. (1970*b*) *Peasants in Cities: readings in the anthropology of urbanization*, Houghton Mifflin.

MANGIN, WILLIAM (1971) 'Autobiographical notes on a rural migrant to Lima, Peru', *Sociologus*, **21**, 58–76.

MANGIN, WILLIAM (1973) 'Sociological, cultural and political characteristics of some urban migrants in Peru', in Southall (1973), pp. 315–50.

MANGIN, WILLIAM and TURNER, J. F. C. (1969) 'Benavides and the Barriada movement', in Oliver (1969), pp. 127–36.

MANN, WILLIAM (1972) 'Citizen participation Chilean style', *Ekistics*, 34, 101–3.

MARCHAND, BERNARD (1966) 'Les Ranchos de Caracas: contribution a l'étude des Bidonvilles', *Les Cahiers d'Outre-Mer*, 19, 106–43.

MARCHAND, BERNARD (1969) 'La structure urbaine de Caracas', *Annales de Geographie*, 78, 286–309.

MARRIS, PETER (1960) 'Slum clearance and family life in Lagos', *Human Organization*, 19, 123–8.

MARSMAN, J. J. M. (1969) 'Ciudad Guayana', *Tijdschrift Voor Economische en Sociale Geografie*, 60, 168–79.

MARTIN, R. J. (1969) 'The ecology of a squatter settlement', *Architectural Review*, 145, 213–14.

MAUNDER, W. F. (1969) *Hong Kong Urban Rents and Housing*, Hong Kong.

MAYER, P. (1962) *Townsmen or Tribesmen*, Oxford University Press, Cape Town.

MEADOWS, PAUL and MIZRUCHI, E. H., eds. (1969) *Urbanism, Urbanization and Change: comparative perspectives*, Addison-Wesley.

MENDOZA, C. A. (1969) *La Vivienda en el Area Metropolitana de Caracas*, Caracas.

MEUNCH, L. H. and MUENCH, C. Z. (1968) 'Planning and antiplanning in Nigeria: Lagos and Ibadan', *Journal of the American Institute of Planners*, 34, 374–81.

MINER, HORACE, ed. (1967) *The City in Modern Africa*, Pall Mall Press.

MITCHELL, J. C. (1961) 'Wage labour and African population movements in Central Africa', in K. M. Barbour and R. M. Prothero, eds., *Essays on African Population*, Routledge, pp. 193–248.

MITCHELL, J. C. (1969) 'Urbanization, detribalization, stabilization and urban commitment in Southern Africa: a problem of definition and measurement: 1968', in Meadows and Mizruchi (1969), pp. 470–93.

MITRA, ASOK (1968) 'Delhi – capital city', CFPI Reprography Unit, New Delhi.

MOORHOUSE, GEOFFREY (1971) *Calcutta*, Weidenfeld & Nicolson.

MORSE, R. M. (1965) 'Recent research on Latin American urbanization: a selective survey with commentary', *Latin American Research Review*, 1, 35–74.

MORSE, R. M. (1971*a*) 'Trends and issues in Latin American urban research, 1965–1970, Part I', *Latin American Research Review*, 6, No. 1, 3–52.

MORSE, R. M. (1971*b*) 'Trends and issues in Latin American urban research, 1965–1970, Part II', *Latin American Research Review*, **6**, No. 2, 19–75.

MURPHEY, RHOADS (1964) 'The city in the swamp: aspects of the site and early growth of Calcutta', *Geographical Journal*, **130**, 241–56.

NAIROBI, UNIVERSITY OF: HOUSING RESEARCH AND DEVELOPMENT UNIT (1971) *Mathare Valley: a case study of uncontrolled settlement in Nairobi*, Nairobi.

NELSON, JOAN (1970) 'The urban poor, disruption or political integration in Third World cities?', *World Politics*, **22**, 393–414.

NERFIN, MARC (1965) 'Towards a housing policy', *Journal of Modern African Studies*, **3**, 543–65.

NEVITT, A. A. ed. (1967) *The Economic Problems of Housing*, Macmillan.

NEWLING, B. E. (1956) 'Urban growth and spatial structure: mathematical models and empirical evidence', *Geographical Review*, **56**, 213–25.

NG, RONALD (1970) 'A study of recent internal migration in Thailand', *Journal of Tropical Geography*, **31**, 65–78.

NORWOOD, H. C. (1972) 'Ndirande, a squatter colony in Malawi', *Town Planning Review*, **43**, 135–50.

OKEDIJI, F. O. and ABOYADE, O. (1967) 'Social and economic aspects of environmental sanitation in Nigeria: a tentative report', *Journal of the Society of Health*, **2**, 10 (quoted in Hance, 1970, p. 282).

OLIVER, PAUL, ed. (1969) *Shelter and Society: new studies in vernacular architecture*, Barrie & Jenkins.

OLIVER, PAUL (1971) *Shelter in Africa*, Barrie & Jenkins.

PATCH, R. W. (1961) 'Life in a callejon', *American Universities Field Staff Reports Service*, **8**, No. 6.

PATEL, S. B. (1973) 'A research programme for urban housing', *Economic and Political Weekly*, **8**, No. 14, 671–6.

PEATTIE, LISA R. (1968) *The View from the Barrio*, University of Michigan Press.

PENDRELL, NAN (1968) 'Squatting in Salvador: an exploratory study', unpublished PhD thesis, Columbia University.

PENFOLD, A. H. (1966) 'Cuidad Guayana, planning a new city in Venezuela', *Town Planning Review*, **36** (1965–66), 225–48.

PENFOLD, A. H. (1969) 'Cuidad Guayana', *Architectural Design*, **39**, 435–44.

PENFOLD, A. H. (1970) 'Caracas: urban growth and transportation', *Town Planning Review*, **41**, 103–20.

PERU, GOVERNMENT OF, AND THE UNITED NATIONS ORGANIZATION (1968) *An International Competition for the Design of a Low-Cost Housing Project in Lima, Peru*, Lima (mimeograph).

PHILIPPINES: NATIONAL HOUSING COUNCIL, SPECIAL COMMITTEE (1969) 'Squatting and slum-dwelling in metropolitan Manila', *Ekistics*, 27, 29–36.

PHILIPPINES, UNIVERSITY OF THE: INSTITUTE OF PLANNING (1969) 'A planning strategy for metropolitan Manila, A.D. 2000', *Ekistics*, 28, 140–8.

PHILLIPS, D. G. (1958) 'Rural-to-urban migration in Iraq', *Economic Development and Cultural Change*, 7 (1957–58), 405–21.

PIDGEON, MONICA (1972) 'Campamento', *Architectural Design*, 42, 739–45.

PLOTNICOV, L. (1967) *Strangers to the City: urban man in Jos, Nigeria*, University of Pittsburgh Press.

PLOTNICOV, L. (1970) 'Rural–urban communications in contemporary Nigeria: the persistence of traditional social institutions', *Journal of Asian and African Studies*, 5, 66–82.

POETHIG, R. P. (1971) 'The squatters of Southeast Asia', *Ekistics*, 31, 121–5.

PONCET, EDMOND (1970) 'Notes sur l'Evolution Recente de l'Agglomeration du Caire', *Annales de Geographie*, No. 431, 78–111.

PORTES, ALEJANDRO (1971) 'The urban slum in Chile: types and correlates', *Land Economics*, 47, 235–48.

PORTES, ALEJANDRO (1972) 'Rationality in the slum: an essay on interpretive sociology', *Comparative Studies in Society and History*, 14, 268–86.

PREBISCH, RAUL, ed. (1963) *Towards a Dynamic Policy for Latin America*, New York, United Nations.

PRESCOTT, JON A. (1971) 'Hong Kong: the form and significance of a high density urban development', in Dwyer (1971*d*), pp. 11–19.

PROTHERO, R. MANSELL (1964) 'Continuity and change in African population mobility', in Steel and Prothero (1964), pp. 189–214.

PRYOR, E. G. (1971) 'An assessment of the Need and Scope for Urban Renewal in Hong Kong', unpublished PhD thesis, Department of Geography and Geology, University of Hong Kong.

PULLEN, GRENVILLE (1966) 'Some problems of rapid urbanization in Lagos, Nigeria', *Journal of Tropical Geography*, 23, 55–61.

RABUSHKA, A. (1971) 'Integration in urban Malaya: ethnic attitudes among Malays and Chinese', *Journal of Asian and African Studies*, 6, 91–107.

RAMOS, C. P. (1961) 'Manila's metropolitan problem', *Philippine Journal of Public Administration*, **5**, 89–117.

RAYMAEKERS, PAUL (1961) 'Le squatting à Leopoldville', Inter-African Labour Institute, *Quarterly Review of Labour Problems in Africa*, **8**, 22–44.

REDFIELD, ROBERT and SINGER, M. B. (1955) 'The Cultural Role of Cities', *Economic Development and Cultural Change*, **3** (1954–55), 53–73.

RICHARDS, E. P. (1914) *Report to the Calcutta Improvement Trust*, Calcutta.

RIDDELL, J. (1965) 'The housing needs of developing countries: some recent trade union initiatives', *Civilizations*, **15**, 31–40.

RO, CHUNG HYUN (1971) 'Seoul', in Laquian (1971), 151–65.

ROBIN, JOHN P. and TERZO, F. C. (1972) *Urbanization in Peru*, Ford Foundation, International Urbanization Survey.

RODWIN, LLOYD (1967) 'Measuring housing needs in developing countries', in Eldredge, 2, 1011–17.

RODWIN, LLOYD (1970) *Nations and Cities: a comparison of Strategies for Urban Growth*, Houghton Mifflin.

RODWIN, LLOYD (1971) 'Strategies for regional growth: a research agenda', unpublished paper, Sixth Rehovoth Conference, Israel.

RODWIN, LLOYD and ASSOCIATES (1969) *Planning Urban Growth and Regional Development: the experience of the Guyana program of Venezuela*, MIT Press.

ROGLER, L. H. (1967) 'Slum neighbourhoods in Latin America', *Journal of Inter-American Studies*, **9**, 507–28.

ROMANI, J. H. and Thomas, M. L. (1954) *A Survey of Local Government in the Philippines*, University of the Philippines, Institute of Public Administration.

ROMANOS, ARISTIDIS (1969) 'Illegal settlements in Athens', in Oliver (1969), pp. 137–55.

ROMANOS, ARISTIDIS (1970) 'Kipoupolis: the significance of unauthorised housing', *Architectural Association Quarterly*, **2**, 14–26.

ROSE, A. J. (1967) *Patterns of Cities*, Melbourne.

ROSS, M. H. (1972) *The Political Integration of Urban Squatters*, Illinois, Northwestern University Press.

ROSSER, COLIN (1970*a*) 'Urbanization in eastern India: the planning response', unpublished paper, Regional Studies Association Conference on Urbanization and Regional Change, Oxford.

ROSSER, COLIN (1970*b*) 'Action planning in Calcutta: the problem of community participation', *Journal of Development Studies*, 6 (1969–70), 121–40.

ROSSER, COLIN (1972*a*) 'Housing and urban change in Calcutta', in Dwyer (1972*d*), pp. 179–90.

ROSSER, COLIN (1972*b*) *Urbanization in India*, New York, Ford Foundation, International Urbanization Survey, New York.

ROSSER, COLIN (1972*c*) *Urbanization in tropical Africa: a demographic introduction*, New York, Ford Foundation, International Urbanization Survey.

ROUCH, JEAN (1954) *Migration in the Gold Coast*, Accra.

ROW, A. T. (1972) 'Calcutta, the leading edge', unpublished manuscript, Calcutta.

SADOVE, ROBERT (1973) 'Urban needs of developing countries', *Finance and Development*, 10, 26–31.

SAFA, H. I. (1964) 'From shanty town to public housing: a comparison of family structure in two urban neighbourhoods in Puerto Rico', *Caribbean Studies*, 4, 3–12.

SALMEN, L. F. (1969) 'A perspective on the resettlement of squatters in Brazil', *America Latina*, 12, 73–95.

SANTIAGO, A. M. (1969) 'Reorganizing for Housing and Urban Development in the Philippines', *Ekistics*, 28, 440–6.

SCHMITT, R. C. (1966) 'Density, Health, and Social Disorganization', *Journal of the American Institute of Planners*, 32, 38–40.

SCHNORE, LEO F. (1968) 'On the spatial structure of cities in the two Americas', in Hauser and Schnore (1965), pp. 347–98.

SCHOLZ, FRED. (1972) 'Karachi – Beispiel für die Bewältigung des Flüchtlingsproblem in Pakistan', *Geographische Rundschau*, 24, 309–20.

SCHORR, A. L. (1970) 'Housing policy and poverty', in Peter Townsend, ed., *The Concept of Poverty*, Heinemann.

SCHULMAN, SAM (1966) 'Latin American shantytown', *New York Times Magazine*, 16 January; reprinted in Eldredge (1967), 2, 1004–11.

SEN, S. N. (1960) *The city of Calcutta: a socio-economic survey*, Calcutta.

SEWELL, G. H. (1964) 'Squatter settlements in Turkey: analysis of a social, political and economic problem', unpublished PhD dissertation, Massachussetts Institute of Technology.

SILBERSTEIN, PAUL (1969) 'Favela living: personal solution to larger problems', *America Latina*, 12, 183–201.

SIMMANCE, A. J. F. (1972) *Urbanization in Zambia*, New York, Ford Foundation: International Urbanization Survey.

SINGAPORE: GOVERNMENT OF, HOUSING AND DEVELOPMENT BOARD (1973) *Annual Report 1972*, Singapore.

SMITH, C. T. and BLAKEMORE, HAROLD (1971) *Latin America: Geographical Perspectives*, Methuen.

SMITH, WALLACE F. (1971) *Housing: the social and economic elements*, University of California Press.

SMYLY, W. Y. (1961) 'Tsuen Wan township', *Far Eastern Economic Review*, 33, 395–421.

SOLOW, ANATOLE A. (1968) 'Housing in Latin America', *Town Planning Review*, 38 (1967–68), 83–102.

SOUTHALL, A. W. (1973) *Urban Anthropology*, New York, Oxford University Press.

SOUTHALL, A. W. and GUTKIND, P. C. W. (1957) *Townsmen in the Making – Kampala and its Suburbs*, Kampala, East African Institute of Social Research, East African Studies No. 9.

SOUTHALL, A. W., ed. (1961) *Social Change in Modern Africa*, Oxford University Press for International African Institute.

SOUTHALL, A. W. (1969) 'The growth of urban society', in Diamond and Burke (1969), pp. 463–93.

SOVANI, N. V. (1966) *Urbanization and Urban India*, Asia Publishing House.

STEEL, R. W. and PROTHERO, R. MANSELL (1964) *Geographers and the Tropics: Liverpool Essays*, Longmans.

STERNSTEIN, LARRY (1971) *Planning the Developing Primate City: Bangkok 2000*, Canberra, Australian National University, School of General Studies, Department of Geography, Occasional Paper No. 9.

STOKES, C. J. (1962) 'A theory of slums', *Land Economics*, 38, 187–97.

STONE, R. L. and MARSELLA, JOY (1968) 'Mahirap: a squatter community in a Manila suburb', in W. F. Bello and Alfonso de Guzman II, eds., *Modernization: its impact on the Philippines III*, Ateneo de Manila University, Institute of Philippine Culture, IPC Papers No. 6, pp. 65–91.

SUZUKI, PETER (1960) 'Village solidarity among Turkish peasants undergoing urbanization', *Science*, 132, 891–2.

SUZUKI, PETER (1964) 'Encounters with Istanbul: urban peasants and village peasants', *International Journal of Comparative Sociology*, 5, 208–16.

TAN SOO HAI (1972) 'Summary of trends in housing conditions and housing needs as well as actual provision for public low-cost housing in Malaysia', unpublished paper, South East Asian Low-Cost Housing Conference, Singapore.

TANGRI, S. S. (1968) 'Urban growth, housing and economic development: the case of India', *Asian Survey*, **8**, 519–38.

TEULIERES, ROGER (1955) 'Bidonvilles du Brésil: les favelles de Belo-Horizonte', *Les Cahiers D'Outre Mer*, **8**, 30–55.

TEXTOR, R. B. (1956) 'The northeastern Samlor driver in Bangkok', in Unesco, *The Social Implications of Industrialization and Urbanization: five studies in Asia*, Calcutta, pp. 1–47.

THAMMASAT UNIVERSITY; DEPARTMENT OF SOCIAL WORK (1970) *Social Work Survey of the Squatter Slum at Klong Toey, Bangkok* (mimeograph) Bangkok.

THOMAS, P. K., ed. (1973) *National Conference on Tall Buildings*, New Delhi, Indian National Group of the International Association for Bridge and Structural Engineering.

TORREALBA, RAFAEL M. (1968) *La Politica Nacional de Vivienda y los Organismos Officiales que se Encargan de Llevarla a Cabo*, Caracas, Banco Obrero.

TREWARTHA, G. T. (1969) *A Geography of Population: world patterns*, Wiley.

TRUJILLO, A. S. (1968) *El Gobernio Metropolitano y Limatropoli*, Lima.

TURIN, D. A. (1967) 'Housing in Africa: some problems and major policy issues', in Nevitt (1967), pp. 200–14.

TURNER, ALAN and SMULIAN, JONATHAN (1971) 'New cities in Venezuela', *Town Planning Review*, **42**, 3–27.

TURNER, J. F. C. (1963) 'Dwelling resources in South America', *Architectural Design*, **33**, 360–93.

TURNER, J. F. C. (1966) 'Uncontrolled urban settlement: problems and policies', University of Pittsburg, Inter-Regional Seminar on Development Policies and Planning in relation to Urbanization, Working Paper No. 11; reprinted in Breese (1969), pp. 507–34.

TURNER, J F. C. (1967) 'Barriers and channels for housing development in modernizing countries', *Journal of the American Institute of Planners*, **23**, 167–81.

TURNER, J. F. C. (1968*a*) 'The squatter settlement: architecture that works', *Architectural Design*, **38**, 355–60.

TURNER, J. F. C. (1968*b*) 'Housing priorities, settlement patterns and urban development in modernizing countries', *Journal of the American Institute of Planners*, **34**, 354–63.

TURNER, J. F. C. (1971) 'Housing issues and the standards question', unpublished mimeographed paper, Rehovoth Conference on Urbanization and Development in Developing Countries, Israel.

TURNER, J. F. C. and GOETZE, ROLF (1967) 'Environmental Security and Housing Input', *Ekistics*, **23**, 123–8.

TURNER, J. F. C. *see also* Caminos *et al.*

TURNER, ROY, ed. (1962) *India's Urban Future*, University of California Press.

UMEH, J. A. (1972) 'Economics and politics of African slums and shanty towns', *Journal of the Royal Town Planning Institute*, **58**, 215–18.

UNITED NATIONS (1965) *Housing in Africa*, New York.

UNITED NATIONS: BUREAU OF SOCIAL AFFAIRS (1957*a*) *Report on the World Social Situation*, New York.

UNITED NATIONS: BUREAU OF SOCIAL AFFAIRS (1957*b*) 'Demographic Aspects of Urbanization in the ECAFE Region', in Hauser (1957), pp. 96–127.

UNITED NATIONS: DEPARTMENT OF ECONOMIC AND SOCIAL AFFAIRS (1951) *Low Cost Housing in South and South East Asia: Report of a Mission of Experts*, New York.

UNITED NATIONS: DEPARTMENT OF ECONOMIC AND SOCIAL AFFAIRS (1960) *Population Growth and Manpower in the Philippines*, New York.

UNITED NATIONS: DEPARTMENT OF ECONOMIC AND SOCIAL AFFAIRS (1962*a*) *Public Administration Problems of New and Rapidly Growing Towns in Asia*, New York.

UNITED NATIONS: DEPARTMENT OF ECONOMIC AND SOCIAL AFFAIRS (1962*b*) *Statistical Indicators of Housing Conditions*, New York.

UNITED NATIONS: DEPARTMENT OF ECONOMIC AND SOCIAL AFFAIRS (1962*c*) *Report of the Ad Hoc Group of Experts on Housing and Urban Development*, New York.

UNITED NATIONS: DEPARTMENT OF ECONOMIC AND SOCIAL AFFAIRS (1965) *World Housing Conditions and Estimated Housing Requirements*, New York.

UNITED NATIONS: DEPARTMENT OF ECONOMIC AND SOCIAL AFFAIRS (1967) *Planning of Metropolitan Areas and New Towns*, New York.

UNITED NATIONS: DEPARTMENT OF ECONOMIC AND SOCIAL AFFAIRS (1968*a*) 'Urbanization Development Policies and Planning', *International Social Development Review*, No. 1, New York.

UNITED NATIONS: DEPARTMENT OF ECONOMIC AND SOCIAL AFFAIRS (1968*b*) *Methods for Establishing Targets and Standards for Housing and Environmental Development*, New York.

UNITED NATIONS: DEPARTMENT OF ECONOMIC AND SOCIAL AFFAIRS (1970) 'Growth of the world's urban and rural population 1920–2000', *Ekistics*, 29, 467–76.

UNITED NATIONS: DEPARTMENT OF ECONOMIC AND SOCIAL AFFAIRS (1971*a*) *Improvement of Slums and Uncontrolled Settlements*, New York.

UNITED NATIONS: DEPARTMENT OF ECONOMIC AND SOCIAL AFFAIRS (1971*b*) *The World Population Situation in 1970*, New York.

UNITED NATIONS: DEPARTMENT OF ECONOMIC AND SOCIAL AFFAIRS, CENTRE FOR HOUSING BUILDING AND PLANNING (1971) *Human Settlements,* 1, No. 1 (and subsequent issues).

UNITED NATIONS: ECONOMIC COMMISSION FOR ASIA AND THE FAR EAST (1965) *Review of the Housing Situation in ECAFE Countries*, Bangkok.

UNITED NATIONS: ECONOMIC COMMISSION FOR LATIN AMERICA (1963) *Urbanization in Latin America: Results of a Field Survey of Living Conditions in an Urban Sector*, mimeograph, New York.

UNESCO (United Nations Educational, Scientific and Cultural Organization) (1956*a*) *The Social Implications of Industrialization and Urbanization: five studies in Asia*, Calcutta.

UNESCO (1956*b*) *The Social Implications of Industrialization and Urbanization in Africa South of the Sahara*.

VAN HUYCK, A. P. (1967) 'An approach to mass housing in India with special reference to Calcutta', in Eldredge (1967), 2, 1018–30.

VAN HUYCK, A. P. (1968) 'The housing threshold for lowest-income groups: the case of India', in Herbert and Van Huyck, pp. 64–109.

VAN HUYCK, A. P. and ROSSER, K. C. (1966) 'An environmental approach to low-income housing', *International Development Review*, 8, 15–18.

VAN VELSEN, J. (1960) 'Labor migration as a positive factor in the continuity of Tonga tribal society', *Economic Development and Cultural Change*, 8, 265–78.

VAUGHAN, T. D. and DWYER, D. J. (1966) 'Some aspects of postwar population growth in Hong Kong', *Economic Geography*, 42, 37–51.

VERSLUYS, J. D. N. (1964) 'Urbanization in Southeast Asia', in Nels Anderson, ed., *Urbanism and Urbanization*, Leiden.

VILORIA, L. A. (1971) 'Manila', in Laquian (1971), pp. 135–50.

WELLS, ALFRED (1969) 'Low-cost housing in Casablanca', *Architectural Association Quarterly*, 1 (1968–69), 44–53.

WHEATON, W. L. C. and WHEATON, M. F. (1972) 'Urban housing and economic development', in Dwyer (1972*d*), pp. 141–51.

WIGGLESWORTH, J. M. (1971) 'The development of new towns in Hong Kong', in Dwyer (1971*d*).

WINBLAD, UNO (1972) *Evaluation of Waste Disposal Systems for Urban* Consulting Group for Planning, Architecture and Building Ltd. Copenhagen, 1972.

WIRTH, LOUIS (1938) 'Urbanism as a way of life', *American Journal of Sociology*, **44**, 1–24.

WOLFE, M. (1968) 'Recent changes in urban and rural settlement patterns in Latin America', *International Social Development Review*, No. 1, 55–62.

WOLMAN, A., CRONIN, H. F., GULLICK, L. and POLLITZER, R. (1960) *Assignment Report on Water Supply and Sewage Disposal, Greater Calcutta*, New Delhi, World Health Organization.

WONG, LUKE SUI KONG (1969) 'A geographical study of squatter areas in the Victoria–Kowloon urban areas', unpublished MA thesis, University of Hong Kong, Department of Geography and Geology.

WURSTER, C. B. (1956) 'The pattern of urban and economic development: social implications', *Annals of the American Academy of Political Science*, **305**, 60–9.

WERTHEIM, W. F. (1964) *East–West Parallels: sociological approaches to modern Asia*, The Hague.

YEH, S. H. K. and LEE YOKE SAN (1968) 'Housing conditions in Singapore', *Malayan Economic Review*, **13**, 11–38.

ZACHARIAH, K. C. (1966) 'Bombay migration study: a pilot analysis of migration to an Asian metropolis', *Demography*, **3**, 378–92; reprinted in Breese (1969), pp. 360–75.

ZIELINSKI, Z. A. (1969) 'The role of prefabrication in low-cost housing', in Calcutta Metropolitan Planning Organization, *Papers on Housing*, Calcutta, pp. 20–9.

Index